# Jesus *the* Purifier

# Jesus *the* Purifier

John's Gospel and the Fourth Quest for the Historical Jesus

## Craig L. Blomberg

Baker Academic
a division of Baker Publishing Group
Grand Rapids, Michigan

© 2023 by Craig L. Blomberg

Published by Baker Academic
a division of Baker Publishing Group
Grand Rapids, Michigan
www.bakeracademic.com

Paperback edition published 2024
ISBN 978-1-5409-6901-9

Printed in the United States of America

All rights reserved. No part of this publication may be reproduced, stored in a retrieval system, or transmitted in any form or by any means—for example, electronic, photocopy, recording—without the prior written permission of the publisher. The only exception is brief quotations in printed reviews.

The Library of Congress has cataloged the hardcover edition as follows:
Names: Blomberg, Craig L., 1955– author.
Title: Jesus the purifier : John's gospel and the fourth quest for the historical Jesus / Craig L. Blomberg.
Description: Grand Rapids, Michigan : Baker Academic, a division of Baker Publishing Group, [2023] | Includes bibliographical references and index.
Identifiers: LCCN 2022026502 | ISBN 9781540962959 (cloth) | ISBN 9781493439966 (ebook) | ISBN 9781493439973 (pdf)
Subjects: LCSH: Jesus Christ—Historicity. | Bible. John—Criticism, interpretation, etc.
Classification: LCC BT303.2 .B528 2023 | DDC 232.9/08—dc23/eng/20220803
LC record available at https://lccn.loc.gov/2022026502

Unless otherwise noted, Scripture quotations are from THE HOLY BIBLE, NEW INTERNATIONAL VERSION®, NIV® Copyright © 1973, 1978, 1984, 2011 by Biblica, Inc.® Used by permission. All rights reserved worldwide.

Baker Publishing Group publications use paper produced from sustainable forestry practices and post-consumer waste whenever possible.

24   25   26   27   28   29   30      7   6   5   4   3   2   1

*For Paul N. Anderson*
whose persistent pursuit of a fourth quest
convinced me and inspired me to contribute to it
and whose encouragement and support
over the years have meant more than he realizes

# Contents

Preface    ix
Abbreviations    xiii
Introduction    xvii

1. The Original Quest for the Historical Jesus    1
2. No Quest and New Quest?    33
3. Launching the Third Quest with a Jewish Jesus    69
4. The Jesus Seminar and Its Kin: A Step Back in Time    105
5. Has the Third Quest Played Itself Out?    135
6. Foreshadowing the Fourth Quest: Rehabilitating the Gospel of John    179
7. Purification, Baptism, and Transformation in John 1–4    223
8. Purification Starting to Change in John 5–11    259
9. Ritual Purity Fades Away in John 12–21    291
10. Purity and the Historical Jesus of the Synoptics    333

    Conclusion    373

    Index of Authors    383
    Index of Scripture and Other Ancient Writings    391

# Preface

In January 2011, I was privileged to teach a combined master's- and doctoral-level seminar on the quests for the historical Jesus at Golden Gate Baptist Seminary in San Francisco. I confidently announced that they were receiving the results of my initial research for a book on that topic that I was going to write "over the next few years." If any of my students even remember that statement, they probably have decided quite a while ago that I was a false prophet! One project after another intervened, usually at others' requests, so the pace of my work on this book slowed to almost a standstill.

In 2016, nevertheless, Denver Seminary launched a ThM program, with one of the tracks for specialization being New Testament studies. We determined that one of the required seminars would be a class on the historical Jesus, so my research was given fresh impetus. I am now teaching that seminar every other fall; even as a professor emeritus and teaching only one course at the seminary each semester, it will be the course I teach one semester every other year as long as the people in charge want me to do so. My notes, outlines, and course materials have grown, and a sabbatical term in the fall of 2019 for research at Tyndale House, Cambridge, proved invaluable along the way. I am grateful to the faculty, administration, and board of trustees of Denver Seminary for granting me that—my last paid sabbatical prior to retirement.

As always in recent years, I am deeply indebted to a succession of research assistants who have helped me considerably, and particularly to Hannah Pachal, who is now my colleague as an adjunct professor of New Testament at the seminary. Darlene Seal also proved helpful on several fronts, even as she was completing her PhD at McMaster Divinity College in Hamilton, Ontario. I am thrilled that she will be joining our faculty in a full-time capacity beginning in the fall of 2022, even as I take a large step away from many of my teaching responsibilities there.

The Carey S. Thomas Library on our campus has continued to be immensely helpful, not least in purchasing many electronic versions of important books and in participating in the ever-growing Digital Theological Library. Our interlibrary loan service is remarkably efficient as well, for which I have Omee Thao particularly to thank. As many of us have discovered during the COVID pandemic, the technological bonanza of digitizing theological library resources came at just the right time to prevent our research and writing efforts from grinding to almost a complete halt. I am also grateful to Peter Williams and the whole staff of Tyndale House, Cambridge, for continuing to make their facilities such a congenial atmosphere for advanced research.

I do not remember which conference on which continent it was when I first met Paul Anderson of George Fox University in Oregon. Over the years we have had wonderful chats, especially at meetings of the Society of Biblical Literature and of the Studiorum Novi Testamenti Societas. Paul was kind enough to send me complimentary copies of various writings of his in the 1990s and 2000s, and it was he who introduced me to the "John, Jesus, and History" seminar of the Society of Biblical Literature. Indeed, he has doubtless been the single biggest "mover and shaker" behind what is now being recognized even in some circles outside the seminar as the "fourth quest for the historical Jesus." I learned several years ago that he was working on a significant book on Jesus from this perspective, and I was hoping it would appear in time for me to carefully read and digest it, and then interact with it and build on it for this book. That has not happened, although Paul tells me there is still a good chance it will come out (with Eerdmans) before mine does. I sincerely hope now that it does, because I have written consciously building on his work to date, though clearly there will be many details in his new book that I won't have known about in time to interact with here. Still, if anyone deserved to write a book to *introduce* readers to the fourth quest, it is Paul. Mine is offered in hopes merely of furthering it.

For all this pioneering influence and for his professional and personal encouragement, I dedicate this volume to Paul Anderson, in hopes that God may grant him many more years of scholarship and service. It is at this juncture that Christian academic books increasingly add, in English or Latin, "but to God be all the glory." I don't disagree with this sentiment in the least. But I am reminded of how one of my colleagues typically finishes his public prayers with the words "We pray all this in Jesus's name but for our sakes." I also recall the two versions of the simple Lutheran mealtime prayer with which I grew up. One version said, "Come, Lord Jesus, be our guest; may this food by thee be blest." The other version substituted "to us" for "by thee." I always thought both were profoundly true. If God gets all the glory from a particular book, I think that readers should derive all the benefit. At least that is my prayer for this book.

# Abbreviations

## General

| | | | |
|---|---|---|---|
| cf. | *confer*, compare | n(n). | note(s) |
| chap(s). | chapter(s) | orig. | original |
| e.g. | *exempli gratia*, for example | par(s). | and parallel(s) |
| Eng. | English | p(p). | page(s) |
| esp. | especially | repr. | reprinted |
| Fr. | French | rev. | revised |
| Ger. | German | sec. | section |
| Gk. | Greek | Span. | Spanish |
| Heb. | Hebrew | s.v. | *sub verbo*, under the word |
| i.e. | *id est*, that is | Swed. | Swedish |
| lit. | literally | v(v). | verse(s) |
| mg. | margin | | |

## Bible Versions

| | | | |
|---|---|---|---|
| ASV | American Standard Version | NET | New English Translation |
| CEB | Common English Bible | NIV | New International Version |
| CJB | Complete Jewish Bible | NJB | New Jerusalem Bible |
| CSB | Christian Standard Bible | NKJV | New King James Version |
| ESV | English Standard Version | NLT | New Living Translation |
| KJV | King James Version | NRSV | New Revised Standard Version |
| NAB | New American Bible | REB | Revised English Bible |
| NASB | New American Standard Bible | RSV | Revised Standard Version |

## Other Ancient Sources

| | | | |
|---|---|---|---|
| *Ant.* | Josephus, *Jewish Antiquities* | *Did.* | Didache |
| b. | Babylonian Talmud | *Flaccus* | Philo, *Against Flaccus* |

| | | | |
|---|---|---|---|
| Gos. Thom. | Gospel of Thomas | Nid. | Tractate Niddah |
| J.W. | Josephus, *Jewish War* | Ohal. | Tractate Ohalot |
| m. | Mishnah | P.Oxy. | Papyrus Oxyrhynchus |
| Mart. Pol. | Martyrdom of Polycarp | Ps.-Clem., *Rec.* | Pseudo-Clement, *Recognitions* |
| Nat. Hist. | Pliny, *Natural History* | | |
| Naz. | Tractate Nazir | | |

## Secondary Sources: Journals, Major Reference Works, and Series

| | | | |
|---|---|---|---|
| AB | Anchor Bible | ExpTim | Expository Times |
| AJT | Asia Journal of Theology | HTR | Harvard Theological Review |
| ATR | Anglican Theological Review | HTS | Hervormde teologiese studies |
| BBR | Bulletin for Biblical Research | IBS | Irish Biblical Studies |
| BDAG | Walter Bauer, Frederick W. Danker, William F. Arndt, and F. Wilbur Gingrich. *Greek-English Lexicon of the New Testament and Other Early Christian Literature.* 3rd ed. Chicago: University of Chicago Press, 2000 | ICC | International Critical Commentary |
| | | IVPNTC | IVP New Testament Commentaries |
| | | JAAR | Journal of the American Academy of Religion |
| | | JBL | Journal of Biblical Literature |
| Bib | Biblica | JECH | Journal of Early Christian History |
| BibInt | Biblical Interpretation | | |
| BNTC | Black's New Testament Commentaries | JETS | Journal of the Evangelical Theological Society |
| BR | Biblical Research | JGAR | Journal of Gospels and Acts Research |
| BSac | Bibliotheca Sacra | | |
| BTB | Biblical Theology Bulletin | JGRChJ | Journal of Greco-Roman Christianity and Judaism |
| BZ | Biblische Zeitschrift | | |
| CBQ | Catholic Biblical Quarterly | JJMJS | Journal of the Jesus Movement in Its Jewish Setting |
| ChrRJ | Christian Research Journal | | |
| CT | Christianity Today | JJS | Journal of Jewish Studies |
| CTR | Criswell Theological Review | JSHJ | Journal for the Study of the Historical Jesus |
| CurBR | Currents in Biblical Research | | |
| CurBS | Currents in Research: Biblical Studies | JSJ | Journal for the Study of Judaism |
| DRCH | Dutch Review of Church History | JSNT | Journal for the Study of the New Testament |
| DSD | Dead Sea Discoveries | JSP | Journal for the Study of the Pseudepigrapha |
| EC | Early Christianity | | |
| ECC | Eerdmans Critical Commentary | JSQ | Jewish Studies Quarterly |
| EGGNT | Exegetical Guide to the Greek New Testament | JTS | Journal of Theological Studies |
| | | LS | Louvain Studies |
| EstBíb | Estudios bíblicos | NAC | New American Commentary |
| EstTeo | Estudios teológicos | NBf | New Blackfriars |
| ETL | Ephemerides Theologicae Lovanienses | NCB | New Century Bible |
| | | NCBC | New Cambridge Bible Commentary |
| EvQ | Evangelical Quarterly | | |

# Abbreviations

| | | | |
|---|---|---|---|
| NCCS | New Covenant Commentary Series | *SNTSU* | *Studien zum Neuen Testament und seiner Umwelt* |
| *Neot* | *Neotestamentica* | SP | Sacra Pagina |
| NICNT | New International Commentary on the New Testament | *SVTQ* | *St. Vladimir's Theological Quarterly* |
| NIGTC | New International Greek Testament Commentary | *TBei* | *Theologische Beiträge* |
| | | *Them* | *Themelios* |
| NIVAC | NIV Application Commentary | *TJ* | *Trinity Journal* |
| *NovT* | *Novum Testamentum* | *TLZ* | *Theologische Literaturzeitung* |
| NTL | New Testament Library | TNTC | Tyndale New Testament Commentaries |
| *NTS* | *New Testament Studies* | | |
| PNTC | Pillar New Testament Commentary | *TU* | *Texte und Untersuchungen* |
| | | *TynBul* | *Tyndale Bulletin* |
| *Presb* | *Presbyterion* | *TZ* | *Theologische Zeitschrift* |
| PRS | *Perspectives in Religious Studies* | WBC | Word Biblical Commentary |
| | | WestBC | Westminster Biblical Companion |
| *RB* | *Revue biblique* | | |
| *RevExp* | *Review and Expositor* | *WTJ* | *Westminster Theological Journal* |
| *RHPR* | *Revue d'histoire et de philosophique religieuses* | | |
| | | *WW* | *Word and World* |
| RNT | Reading the New Testament | ZECNT | Zondervan Exegetical Commentary on the New Testament |
| *RSR* | *Revue de sciences religieuses* | | |
| *SCJ* | *Stone-Campbell Journal* | | |
| *ScrTh* | *Scripta Theologica* | ZKT | *Zeitschrift für katholische Theologie* |
| *SEÅ* | *Svensk exegetisk årsbok* | | |
| SGBC | Story of God Bible Commentary | ZNW | *Zeitschrift für die neutestamentliche Wissenschaft* |
| *SIDA* | *Scripta Instituti Donneriani Aboensis* | ZTK | *Zeitschrift für Theologie und Kirche* |
| *SJT* | *Scottish Journal of Theology* | | |

# Introduction

Forty years ago, in my first full draft of my doctoral dissertation, I began my introduction with the words "The quest for the historical Jesus continues unabated." When I showed the draft to my wife, she laughed out loud. She remembered, as I hadn't, that I had begun my MA thesis with the identical sentence. So I substituted something a little different. From the early 1950s to the late 2000s, one could have begun just about any piece of Jesus research with that same opening line. In fact, the historical Jesus has interested a huge number of scholars for nearly 250 years now. Studies, nevertheless, ebb and flow. From the early 2010s to the present, there have not been as many historical Jesus books as in each of the previous six decades, and even fewer of great merit or influence. For the first time in a long time, a significant number of people are asking if scholarship has done all it can in the quest, apart from perhaps very focused studies in just one or two areas of Jesus's life or on very specific passages from the Gospels.

There has also seldom been as much compartmentalization of New Testament scholarship as we see today, along with what I have heard called the "clumpification" of researchers along the lines of their preferred method or methods. It is possible to carry on happily and productively as a specialist in one narrow field and be largely unaware of the vast majority of New Testament scholarship outside that field or methodology. The amount that continues to appear in print and online seems to grow exponentially from one year to the next. Who can possibly keep up? Some continue to try; others stop trying but publish their thoughts anyway! A major example of these tendencies involves historical Jesus research and Johannine scholarship. To read the Jesus books and articles from the 1960s to the present, one would hardly guess that during that identical period an entire subdiscipline of analysis of the Gospel of John was rehabilitating the historical reliability of key parts of that Gospel.

This book has two primary goals. The first is to tell important parts of the story of what are generally considered to be three quests for the historical Jesus (or three phases of the one quest) from the late eighteenth century to the present. A very large, two-volume work of more than 1,400 pages is slated to appear from Zondervan in August of 2022, too late to be consulted for this book. Initially researched and nearly finished by Colin Brown, it has been completed, edited, and further updated by Craig Evans. *A History of the Quests for the Historical Jesus* will thus no doubt be a definitive reference work for the foreseeable future, though the number of people who read straight through it probably will be limited. I am hopeful that the much shorter five-chapter survey I provide here will be more accessible to a wider audience. How have people told the story so far? How does that story need to be corrected or supplemented? Who are the major players to date, and what is the heart of their contributions? What has largely been missing throughout the enterprise? Key answers to these questions appear here.

The last five chapters address my second goal: determining how we make further progress in the quest. What was dubbed the "new look on John" in the late 1950s has grown into a fledgling fourth quest—one that gives the Fourth Gospel parity with the Synoptic Gospels in searches for the Jesus of history. That does not mean that an equal percentage of one's portrait of Jesus must come from each corpus. Instead, it means that once someone has decided on their methods, including their use or nonuse of various criteria of authenticity, they should apply them equally to all four Gospels across the board. It may turn out that more will come from one Gospel than from another, but one should not prejudge the answer to that question, as has been done by almost everyone from the 1840s on. After sketching these developments in Johannine studies in chapter 6, I spend three chapters applying one specific method of excavating the Fourth Gospel to see what studies based solely on the Synoptics may have missed, even though a good case can be mounted for the authenticity of what was missed. I focus on one major result of that endeavor: the role of Jesus and purity, including ritual purity.

Ritual purity and impurity are not well known or understood, especially in the Western world, where we have few close analogies to them today. So before we turn to the analysis of key texts, we need a certain amount of background information, which will come in the first part of chapter 7. The rest of chapters 7, 8, and 9 will work their way through the relevant passages in John to see what emerges. The final main chapter of the book compares our findings with the Synoptic presentation of Jesus and purity, at least in those passages and those portions of passages that stand the best chance of coming from the oldest and most authentic parts of the Jesus tradition. The Synoptics disclose a fairly radical Jesus, several steps removed from keen observance of purity laws, or so it would seem on first inspection. More careful scrutiny paints a somewhat more nuanced portrait, but it is only in John's Gospel where we see that there is a trajectory of development in Jesus's approach to the issue. And it is only when the relevant passages are shorn of their most probably redactional parts that the trajectory appears most clearly. At the outset of his public career, Jesus is firmly embedded in the ritually purifying ministry of John the Baptist, complete with water baptism. Gradually, however, he moves away from this emphasis, stressing moral or ethical purity—a spiritual baptism, as it were. This topic remains reasonably prominent until his last trip to Jerusalem and his passion and resurrection there, when it recedes into a very small corner of the overall picture. Still, resurrection itself, narrated in detail in John, is a hugely purifying activity.

In an earlier work on Jesus's meals with sinners, I observed how the theme of "contagious holiness" characterized Jesus's behavior. Instead of the common Old Testament model, mostly intensified in Second

Temple Judaism, of assuming that influence can run in only one direction, from the ritual and moral impurity of the unholy to the righteous in order to corrupt them, Jesus taught and demonstrated that the pure could help make the impure pure. Cleansing can flow from the righteous to the unrighteous. The upshot of this book is to extend that observation to all the major areas of purity on which Jesus's teaching and lifestyle impinged, not just to the topic of those with whom one eats. This book also offers a model of one approach to mining John's Gospel for historical information, which holds the potential to be used to add other themes to our "database" of the authentic Jesus.

Studying the Jesus of history takes place in a discipline that intentionally does not presuppose Christian faith. There have been many throughout the quests who have assumed that whatever does not pass their historical criteria simply didn't happen, which is a major non sequitur and historical faux pas. So much of the remains of ancient history, which might have enabled us to confirm details in the Gospels, are simply lost forever. For the same reason, some of what we have reason to believe to be historical might be discovered not to be, had we more evidence available to us. History, by its very nature, assesses probabilities and should never claim certainties, although some things attain a sufficiently high probability to become virtual certainties. Plenty of other items, however, do not. Historical Jesus scholars need not limit what they believe about Jesus to that for which a historical case can be mounted, nor does this book claim that only those sections in the Fourth Gospel that pass our criteria actually happened. But to have certain parts of that Gospel authenticated by historical criteria can give a person even greater confidence in the trustworthiness of those sections. If they form a large enough portion of a book, then belief in other sections less testable may still turn out to be the more rational choice.

To the vexed question that Albert Schweitzer raised about remaking one's Jesus in one's own image, I must reply that Jesus as a purifier would not have been one of my top ten categories for him during the first fifty years of my life. In addition, while I have always made some effort to try to model Christian living in a winsome way, I am enough of an introvert that I doubt any of my close friends would describe me as someone who goes around trying to find as many people as possible whose lives are a mess in hopes that the areas of my life in which I am less broken will rub off on them. I have been greatly challenged by my findings and hope to do better with however many years I have left. But the main point of this book most certainly does not enshrine a concept that I was raised with, or consciously taught in some school or church, and I have observed that that branch of evangelical Christianity in which I have more often than not found myself tends to be more concerned with avoiding what its members perceive to be "the corruption of the world" than with venturing into unknown areas and becoming "risk-takers for God." But I have also known plenty of exceptions to this generalization and have had glimpses of Christian friends and acquaintances being the most loving, outgoing, forgiving, and sacrificing people I have known anywhere. I have participated in churches and parachurch ministries with significant numbers of such people, and the results of their ministries have usually been counterculturally productive. In a day in which Christians in many parts of the world, including where I live, are respected considerably less than they used to be, and with at least some of that disrespect fairly deserved, the potential for positive impact through genuine and sincere Christian models of living with others becomes enormous and enormously important.

My conclusion will pull together more of these threads. Meanwhile, step into your time machine, be ready for a whirlwind tour of the past two and a half centuries, and be intrigued by the multifaceted approaches scholars have taken with Jesus of Nazareth. Put your analytical thinking caps on; be ready to be stretched by new ideas, whether on the ideological left, right, or even center; reject every hackneyed caricature or criticism of those you might naturally disagree with; and see what there is to learn from each of the four quests for the historical Jesus. And if the proposal for a way forward that the second half of the volume offers doesn't satisfy, please don't just carp, but propose "a still more excellent way"!

# 1

# The Original Quest for the Historical Jesus

A significant amount of the last roughly 250 years of New Testament scholarship has devoted itself to the investigation of the life of Jesus of Nazareth. In 1910, the English title given to the translation of Albert Schweitzer's magisterial survey of late-eighteenth- and nineteenth-century studies on the topic, published in German four years earlier, bequeathed to the world *The Quest of the Historical Jesus*.[1] Historians ever since have often sensed that Schweitzer's survey also brought an era or stage of the quest to a close. This chapter will first present a composite of common ways that the story of this original quest is recounted. It will then highlight key additions and corrections that need to be made to that story, both in terms of individual scholars and with respect to overall trends. Finally, it will suggest what "the historical Jesus" should mean. All three of these tasks will disclose that the original quest relied heavily and sometimes exclusively on the Synoptic Gospels—Matthew, Mark, and Luke. Less well known are

---

1. Albert Schweitzer, *The Quest of the Historical Jesus: A Critical Study of Its Progress from Reimarus to Wrede* (London: A. & C. Black, 1910). The German volume was *Von Reimarus zu Wrede: Eine Geschichte der Leben-Jesu-Forschung* (Tübingen: J. C. B. Mohr, 1906)—i.e., "From Reimarus to Wrede: A History of the Life-of-Jesus Investigation."

the diverse approaches taken to the Gospel of John in these investigations, so the fourth task of the chapter will be to survey that diversity and the rationale for the various positions it discloses.

## The Common Narrative

A representative way of telling the story of the original quest for the historical Jesus could well proceed as follows.[2] The first scholar to undertake a critically rigorous investigation of the Jesus of history was a German professor in Hamburg, *Hermann Samuel Reimarus* (1694–1768). Disavowing the supernatural, Reimarus embraced deism and rationalism. He believed that Jesus never intended to break from Judaism, preached the imminent coming of the kingdom of God in this world to be established through political methods, died without achieving his goals, and was alleged by his disciples to be resurrected because they stole and hid his body.[3] Reimarus attacked traditional Christianity, but knowing how controversial his work would be, he declined to publish it during his lifetime. At the same time, he wanted to promote natural theology and tolerance in the public square.[4] So he left his manuscript with a friend, the librarian at Wolfenbüttel, *Gotthold Ephraim Lessing* (1729–81). Lessing would publish seven excerpts from this manuscript between 1774 and 1778 anonymously, but Reimarus's son later acknowledged that his father had written them.[5]

---

2. How many key scholars to choose is, of course, a key variable, as is the length of their treatment. For excellent balance and succinctness, see Ralph P. Martin and Carl N. Toney, *New Testament Foundations: An Introduction for Students* (Eugene, OR: Cascade Books, 2018), 196–202, and the literature there cited.

3. Hermann Samuel Reimarus, *Fragments*, ed. Charles H. Talbert, trans. Ralph S. Fraser (Philadelphia: Fortress, 1970 [Ger. orig. 1768]). Per Bilde argues that progress has been made, but only among those scholars who have "deepened and extended" Reimarus's insights, seeing Jesus specifically as an apocalyptic prophet ("Can It Be Justified to Talk about Scholarly Progress in the History of Modern Jesus Research since Reimarus?," in *The Mission of Jesus: Second Nordic Symposium on the Historical Jesus, Lund, 7–10 October 2012*, ed. Samuel Byrskog and Tobias Hägerland [Tübingen: Mohr Siebeck, 2015], 5–24). In other words, Reimarus brought all the right issues and approaches into being at the very beginning of the quest.

4. Jonathan C. P. Birch, "Reimarus and the Religious Enlightenment: His Apologetic Project," *ExpTim* 129 (2018): 245–53.

5. Andrew Arterbury, "Hermann Samuel Reimarus," in *Encyclopedia of the Historical Jesus*, ed. Craig A. Evans (New York: Routledge, 2008), 496.

Lessing himself became particularly famous in the history of religion and philosophy for his assertion that "accidental truths of history can never become the proof of necessary truths of reason."[6] For Lessing, because religion had to be based on reason, what could be recovered historically about Jesus had no necessary bearing on faith. There was an "ugly, broad ditch" between the two.[7]

One of Reimarus's formidable opponents was also a key player in the development of a historically rigorous approach to the New Testament: *Johann Salomo Semler* (1725–91). While rejecting Reimarus's radical conclusions about Jesus's life, he did insist on "freeing" the Bible from traditional dogma, including divine inspiration, and treating it like any other collection of humanly authored books.[8] Most of Semler's interests focused on the rethinking of the canon of Scripture. *Johann David Michaelis* (1717–91), Semler's contemporary, became the first to write a New Testament introduction, which included addressing questions about the historical setting and circumstances of the various sections, books, or authors of the New Testament.[9] By today's standards, neither writer would appear that radical, but in their day they were posing unprecedented challenges to a Christian world not used to questioning church tradition in this fashion.

The rationalist school of thought reached its zenith, at least in terms of its application to the life of Jesus, with the writings of *Heinrich Eberhard Gottlob Paulus* (1761–1851). Paulus gave all Jesus's miracles rational explanations. Jesus fed the five thousand by inspiring a spirit of sharing of the food that the people had in fact brought. He appeared to walk on the water but was actually on the shore or very shallow parts of the lake. He never entirely died on the cross, so he was able to revive

---

6. Gotthold Ephraim Lessing, "On the Proof of the Spirit and the Power," in *Lessing's Theological Writings: Selections in Translation*, ed. Henry Chadwick (Stanford, CA: Stanford University Press, 1957 [Ger. orig. 1777]), 56.

7. For a brief exposition and critique, see Geoffrey Bromiley, "History and Truth: A Study of the Axiom of Lessing," *EvQ* 18 (1946): 191–98.

8. Werner Georg Kümmel, *The New Testament: The History of the Investigation of Its Problems*, trans. S. MacLean Gilmour and Howard C. Kee (Nashville: Abingdon, 1972; London: SCM, 1973), 62–69.

9. Johann David Michaelis, *Introduction to the New Testament*, trans. Herbert Marsh (Cambridge: Rivington, 1793 [Ger. orig. 1750]).

and later be rescued from the tomb by his followers.[10] Paulus believed he was helping to salvage the Gospel accounts for a post-Enlightenment world, so that his real emphasis was on the moral teaching and inner motives and intentions of Jesus that humanity should emulate.[11]

A scholar better known in the world of philosophy than in the guild of theologians actually spanned both disciplines. *Friedrich Schleiermacher* (1768–1834) combined rationalism with a form of psychologizing that prioritized a person's inner consciousness. His best-known work became his *On Religion: Speeches to Its Cultured Despisers*.[12] Even those who rejected his approach, if they came to know him personally, recognized his heart for presenting the faith in a way that would capture the minds of those who couldn't accept its traditional forms. But he also wrote a lengthy life of Jesus and was the last really well-known German intellectual to do so while believing in the general reliability of the Gospel of John.[13]

*Ferdinand Christian Baur* (1792–1860) was a New Testament scholar who never wrote a life of Jesus but still reflected deeply on Jesus's role in founding Christianity. Baur appropriated the dialectical and evolutionary philosophy of G. W. F. Hegel, with his famous "thesis-antithesis-synthesis" approach to history, in order to place Jesus, along with Peter, James, and Matthew, in the initial, Jewish articulation of Christianity. Paul, in particular, adapted the gospel for the Gentiles, creating an antithesis to Jewish Christianity. Luke and John became second-century synthesizers, patching over the huge division in earliest Christianity that had existed between Peter and Paul.[14] Although Baur's

---

10. Warren S. Kissinger, *The Lives of Jesus: A History and Bibliography* (New York: Garland, 1985), 18–19.

11. Russell Morton, "Quest of the Historical Jesus," in Evans, *Encyclopedia of the Historical Jesus*, 473. See also William Baird, *History of New Testament Research*, vol. 1, *From Deism to Tübingen* (Minneapolis: Fortress, 1992), 208.

12. Friedrich Schleiermacher, *On Religion: Speeches to Its Cultured Despisers*, trans. and ed. Richard Crouter (Cambridge: Cambridge University Press, 1988 [Ger. orig. 1799]).

13. Friedrich Schleiermacher, *The Life of Jesus*, ed. Jack C. Verheyden, trans. S. MacLean Gilmour (Philadelphia: Fortress, 1975 [Ger. orig. 1864, ed. K. A. Rutenik, from notes on Schleiermacher's lectures primarily in 1832]). He did, however, influence his followers Wilhelm M. L. de Wette and Friedrich Lücke to take a similar tack. See Baird, *History of New Testament Research*, 1:221–35.

14. The major work available in English impinging on this theory is Ferdinand Christian Baur, *Paul the Apostle of Jesus Christ: His Life and Work, His Epistles and His Doctrine* (London: Williams & Norgate, 1876 [Ger. orig. 1845]). The work that most lays out his views on the Gospels

writings focused more on Paul than on Jesus, his dialectical thought supplied much of the inspiration for the next writer to be mentioned.

The conflict between rationalists and traditional Christian believers led *David Friedrich Strauss* (1808–74) to argue for a third way. Jesus's miracles appeared to be supernatural events but were not; neither, however, should they be rationalized. Strauss understood the wondrous events in the Gospels as pious legends, intended neither to provide literal, historical narratives nor to deceive, but as theological truth in mythological garb. While others had highlighted what they believed were key contradictions among the Gospel parallels, Strauss was the first to discuss them at length. The sheer number that he "discovered" formed a key reason he adopted his mythological approach. As with Reimarus, Strauss believed that Jesus expected an immediate, political kingdom on earth, and his followers after his death had to shift gears in order that the movement he began could continue.[15] The first edition of Strauss's life of Jesus proved so controversial that he lost his teaching positions in Tübingen and Zurich. In his second and third editions he successively backtracked some, but he remained alienated from the church and most of the academy. So in his fourth and final edition he returned to essentially the positions of his first edition but with more polemical force.[16]

Quite different was the situation with *Ernest Renan* (1823–92), the one Frenchman (and Roman Catholic) in this otherwise monolithic parade of German scholars. Unlike the others, Renan also had the opportunity to travel to Israel on multiple occasions and became especially familiar with the topography of Galilee in detail.[17] Representing the romantic school of philosophy, Renan had the ability to retell the story of Jesus with an attractive sentimentality. He divided the life of Jesus into two major sections, beginning with his Galilean "springtime."

---

is Baur, *Kritische Untersuchungen über die kanonischen Evangelien: Ihr Verhältniss zu einander, ihren Charakter und Ursprung* (Tübingen: Fues, 1847). I will use the conventional names for the authors of the four Gospels without necessarily implying traditional views of authorship.

15. David Friedrich Strauss, *The Life of Jesus Critically Examined*, ed. Peter C. Hodgson, trans. George Eliot (Philadelphia: Fortress, 1972 [Ger. orig. 1835]).

16. Peter C. Hodgson, introduction to Strauss, *Life of Jesus*, xxxviii–xlvii.

17. Eben Scheffler, "Ernest Renan's Jesus: An Appraisal," *Neot* 33 (1999): 195–96.

This was his period of great popularity and great moral teachings. A very different and darker period ensued as he first predicted and then experienced suffering and death in Jerusalem.[18] Renan's life of Jesus sold more copies both on the continent and (in English translation) in the British Isles and the United States than any other nineteenth-century "life of Christ."[19]

If the first third of the 1800s belonged primarily to the rationalists, and the middle of the century to the dialecticians and the romantics, classic liberal theology (now often referred to as "old" or "nineteenth-century" liberalism) held sway in the final third. Here the evolutionary spirit of Darwin clearly shone through. Humanity could expect *moral* progress just as it was clearly enjoying technological progress. The themes of the fatherhood of God, the brotherhood of man, and the love-centered ethic of Jesus dominated this form of liberal theology. And no one was a more articulate and winsome exponent of this perspective than *Adolf Karl Gustav von Harnack* (1851–1930).[20] For Harnack and his supporters, debates about the miraculous were beside the point. The heart of the gospel, and of the Gospels, was the moral teaching of Jesus. Natural theology endorsed it, the Sermon on the Mount encapsulated it, and people of many religious and ideological backgrounds could embrace it.[21]

Harnack would be rebutted in 1902 by a French Catholic, *Alfred Loisy* (1857–1940), one year after the original German edition of Schweitzer's survey of the quest had appeared. Loisy is best known for his affirmation that "Jesus foretold the kingdom" but "it was the church that came" instead.[22] But what he meant by that was that one could know Jesus only through the institution—the church—that developed

---

18. Ernest Renan, *The History of the Origins of Christianity*, vol. 1, *The Life of Jesus*, trans. William M. Thomson (London: Mathieson, 1890 [Fr. orig. 1863]).

19. Kissinger, *Lives of Jesus*, 24–28.

20. Adolf von Harnack, *What Is Christianity?*, trans. Thomas Bailey Saunders (New York: G. P. Putnam's Sons; London: Williams & Norgate, 1901). See also Harnack, *The Sayings of Jesus: The Second Source of St. Matthew and St. Luke*, trans. J. R. Wilkinson (New York: G. P. Putnam's Sons; London: Williams & Norgate, 1908).

21. See J. C. O'Neill, *The Bible's Authority: A Portrait Gallery of Thinkers from Lessing to Bultmann* (Edinburgh: T&T Clark, 1991), 226–29.

22. Alfred Loisy, *The Gospel and the Church*, ed. Bernard B. Scott (Philadelphia: Fortress, 1976), 166.

# The Original Quest for the Historical Jesus

out of his movement.[23] By this time, liberal theology had gained a foothold, nevertheless, in numerous European countries, along with North America. The original quest for the historical Jesus might come to an end with Schweitzer, but the philosophical underpinnings that spawned its numerous nontraditional portraits of Jesus were here to stay.

The scholar who most anticipated and prepared the way for Schweitzer's own perspectives was *Johannes Weiss* (1863–1914). A prolific writer during a comparatively short career, Weiss became best known for a slim volume, *Jesus' Proclamation of the Kingdom of God*.[24] Anticipating developments in form criticism (see below, 34–35), he focused on Jesus's sayings and stressed that Jesus believed the kingdom was coming so soon that in some respects he could speak of it as already present, especially with respect to Satan's defeat. Directly contrary to the tenets of liberal theology, the kingdom would arrive entirely through God's activity rather than human effort, but disciples should prepare for its arrival by practicing a greater righteousness.[25]

*Albert Schweitzer* (1875–1965) extended to Jesus's entire ministry what Weiss had applied to his teachings. A true polymath, Schweitzer earned doctorates in theology, philosophy, and medicine, as well as becoming a concert organist. He decided when he was eighteen that he would study only until he was thirty to prepare for his life's work, after which he would give himself fully to the service of God and humanity.[26] He became best known to the world for his decades of ministry as a missionary doctor in the jungles of West Africa, establishing and working at a hospital in Lambaréné, in what eventually became the country of Gabon. His life choices mirrored his conclusions about the abiding significance of Jesus. Although Jesus first expected God to supernaturally usher in the kingdom during his lifetime (Matt. 10:23), he came to realize that it would be only through his own suffering and death that this would occur. Because Schweitzer, like Reimarus,

---

23. Bernard B. Scott, introduction to Loisy, *Gospel and the Church*, xxxviii.
24. Johannes Weiss, *Jesus' Proclamation of the Kingdom of God*, trans. and ed. Richard H. Hiers and David L. Holland (Philadelphia: Fortress; London: SCM, 1971 [Ger. orig. 1892]).
25. Eckhard J. Schnabel, "Johannes Weiss," in Evans, *Encyclopedia of the Historical Jesus*, 676.
26. O'Neill, *Bible's Authority*, 250–51.

Strauss, and Weiss, believed in a fully "this-worldly" kingdom that did not appear even after Jesus's death, he had to acknowledge that this part of Jesus's life was a failure. But Jesus's significance lay elsewhere, as Paul came so clearly to understand with his language of being one with God "in Christ."[27] A mystical union of believers with the spirit of Jesus could enable them to live a life of love for God and humanity. Unlike his predecessors, Schweitzer developed a "reverence for life" that led him to avoid, as much as possible, the taking of the lives of any living creatures. In 1952, he received the Nobel Peace Prize for his work.

Intriguingly, on the same day in 1901 that a short work by Schweitzer on a sketch of the life of Jesus was released, *William Wrede* (1859–1906) published his major treatment of the messianic secret in Mark.[28] Wrede argued that Jesus never understood himself to be the Messiah; that was a development in the thinking of the early church. In order to claim that Jesus himself actually did hold this position, Christians, even before Mark wrote his Gospel, attributed to Jesus his self-revelation to various people whom he then commanded not to tell anyone about it. Mark, more than any other Gospel writer, seized on this ploy and utilized it in his narrative. Wrede was reacting to the dominant conviction of the scholarship of the second half of the nineteenth century that Mark's was the first Gospel written (a view not widely held throughout church history before this era) and therefore the most reliable.[29] Wrede's explanation of the motif of the messianic secret in Mark threw open the doors to the conviction that not even the earliest Gospel could be trusted, especially in its Christology.

Schweitzer believed that Wrede's option was potentially as viable as his approach. But these two approaches were the only genuine options: either accept Wrede's "literary-critical" solution or follow Schweitzer's "thoroughgoing eschatological" one. Schweitzer was passionately per-

---

27. Albert Schweitzer, *The Mysticism of Paul the Apostle*, trans. William Montgomery (London: A. & C. Black, 1931; repr., with new foreword, Baltimore: Johns Hopkins University Press, 1998).

28. William Wrede, *The Messianic Secret*, trans. J. C. G. Greig (London: James Clarke, 1971 [Ger. orig. 1901]).

29. See esp. Heinrich Julius Holtzmann, *Die synoptischen Evangelien: Ihr Ursprung und geschichtlicher Charakter* (Leipzig: Engelmann, 1863).

suaded that "late Jewish apocalyptic" was the key to understanding Jesus. Like many in his day, Jesus was convinced of God's imminent coming into this world to establish his kingdom. Eventually he came to see that he was the Messiah, whose death would bring about that breakthrough. For Schweitzer, the only other viable option was that it was all a literary fiction. So he arranged his account of the investigations of the life of Jesus so that Wrede's and his views would be the last two he presented, in that order, with everything building to his own perspectives.[30]

Perhaps even more significant than Schweitzer's own views about Jesus was his conviction that "each successive epoch of theology found its own thoughts in Jesus" and that "each individual created Jesus in accordance with his own character."[31] The rationalists created a rational, nonsupernatural Jesus; the romantics found a sentimental, pathos-filled Jesus; the liberals, a Jesus who taught progress through moral effort. Many following Schweitzer would accuse him of falling victim to the same malaise. Enamored with Jewish eschatology and apocalyptic, he created as one-sided a picture of the eschatological Jesus as his predecessors had done with their theologies or philosophies. And thus Schweitzer could be viewed not only as brilliantly summarizing the history of Jesus research before him but also as ending the first quest, or the first phase of the quest, for the historical Jesus.[32] Or so goes the common narrative.

### Additions and Corrections

It is impossible to recount the history of any even moderately complex set of events without oversimplifying and sometimes even distorting them. Some historians intentionally try to limit the detrimental effects of this process; others deliberately manipulate what they choose to narrate and how they decide to narrate it to their own ends. On a spectrum

---

30. Simon J. Gathercole, "The Critical and Dogmatic Agenda of Albert Schweitzer's *The Quest of the Historical Jesus*," *TynBul* 51 (2000): 261–83.
31. Schweitzer, *Quest of the Historical Jesus*, 6.
32. O'Neill (*Bible's Authority*, 250–65) thinks that Schweitzer was essentially Stoic, trying to fit Jesus into a Stoic mold.

from one of these ends to the other, Schweitzer winds up much closer the second. Because his remained the only fairly comprehensive overview of the period he surveyed for many years after it was written, and because he was both so insightful at many points and so elegant in his writing, *The Quest of the Historical Jesus* exercised a hugely disproportionate amount of influence over scholarly understanding of eighteenth- and nineteenth-century lives of Jesus. Today, of course, other surveys exist.[33] Of many possible items that could be listed, the following "additions and corrections" are most relevant to this study. They are divided into two sections: first comments on specific scholars or schools of thought and then more general trends.

### *Specific Scholars or Schools of Thought*

The first comment is perhaps the most obvious one: *Schweitzer selected and arranged his material, along with his critiques of each scholar or school of thought, so that those who even in part saw Jesus against the background of Jewish eschatology or apocalyptic are the most praised.* Even though Reimarus and Strauss each generated huge controversies by their writings for completely different reasons, which Schweitzer acknowledged, he still commended them more than most in the nineteenth century would have.[34] As for liberal theology, and different from other critics, what Schweitzer insisted was really wrong was its lack of understanding of eschatology. Even more than most in German scholarship, he had little hesitation in concluding that everyone else was essentially wrong to the extent that they differed from him! An either-or mentality pervaded his writing, and he seldom looked for middle ground.[35]

Second, *the quest for the historical Jesus didn't start with Reimarus.* From the time of the Protestant Reformation onward, people became

---

33. See esp. Gregory W. Dawes, ed., *The Historical Jesus Quest: Landmarks in the Search for the Jesus of History* (Leiderdorp: Deo, 1999; Louisville: Westminster John Knox, 2000), 1–238.

34. Robert Morgan, "Reimarus, Schweitzer, and Modern Theology," *ExpTim* 129 (2018): 154–64.

35. See the excellent analysis in Michael J. Thate, *Remembrance of Things Past? Albert Schweitzer, the Anxiety of Influence, and the Untidy Jesus of Markan Memory* (Tübingen: Mohr Siebeck, 2013).

more and more interested in a life of Jesus. Tucker Ferda summarizes the trends between the Reformation and Reimarus as deeper reflection on Jesus's mental states and motivations, numerous Gospel harmonies with criteria to aid in organizing material, the popularization of the idea of Jesus's early success followed by growing opposition, the conviction that Jesus tried to persuade people that they could accept or reject his instruction of their own volition, an emphasis on tensions between Jesus's ethics and his atonement, and paraphrases of the Gospels that began to periodize Jesus's life with numerous subdivisions and tables of contents.[36] James Charlesworth observes that the English deist Thomas Chubb, already in 1738, published *The True Gospel of Jesus Christ Asserted*, in which, Charlesworth says, "he affirmed that Jesus' true message was the imminent coming of God's Rule (the Kingdom of God) and the true gospel was to be found in Jesus' preaching of good news to the poor."[37] While the deists redefined the miracles, they did not necessarily reject the rest of the Gospels. A flurry of scholarship at the end of the eighteenth and beginning of the nineteenth centuries, nevertheless, involved attempts to refute Reimarus and the deists. But the deists, including Paulus early in the nineteenth century, believed they were salvaging Christianity for modern people who could not believe in the supernatural. Many disagreed, though, and scholarship at the beginning of the nineteenth century was at least as concerned with rebutting the rationalists as with defending them.[38]

Third, Schleiermacher saw Jesus's teachings, including his teachings for the disciples in community, as reflective of Jesus's inner consciousness. So his life of Jesus was more than just an attempt to psychologically analyze him in a way that scholars would come increasingly to realize simply couldn't be done—for lack of evidence.[39] *To accuse*

---

36. Tucker S. Ferda, *Jesus, the Gospels, and the Galilean Crisis* (London: Bloomsbury T&T Clark, 2019), 60.

37. James H. Charlesworth, *The Historical Jesus: An Essential Guide* (Nashville: Abingdon, 2008), 2.

38. Marijke H. de Lang, "Literary and Historical Criticism as Apologetics: Biblical Scholarship at the End of the Eighteenth Century," *DRCH* 72 (1992): 149–65.

39. See Roy A. Harrisville, *The Bible in Modern Culture: Baruch Spinoza to Brevard Childs*, 2nd ed. (Grand Rapids: Eerdmans, 2002), 62–82.

*Schleiermacher of merely reading his philosophical and theological commitments into his historical Jesus work seems very one-sided.* Equally important is the extent to which his philosophy and theology derived from the data he discovered in the Gospels. Years later, Charles Hodge, the stalwart American Reformed theologian, who had been a guest of the Schleiermachers in Germany when he was a young man, would report that, as much as he disagreed with Schleiermacher's perspectives, his experience with their family worship convinced him they would be singing the same hyms of praise together in heaven![40] Both were sincerely working with the same sacred text.

Fourth, *neither can Strauss fairly be charged with just finding a Jesus amenable to his own philosophy.* While the rationalists reflected a widespread school of thought in their day, there was no such thing as a school of mythologizing that led to Strauss's approach. Of course, Hegel's dialectic led him to look for a synthesis or a mediating alternative between supernaturalism and naturalism in the interpretation of the Gospels. But Strauss's proposals about the role of myth or legend were largely his own; he was not simply reading into the texts some abstract philosophical approach that he had already imbibed. It would only be a generation later, with the development of the history-of-religions school of biblical scholarship, when appeal to mythology would become a distinct approach practiced by a discrete group of scholars (see below, 44–45).[41]

Fifth, *Renan was far more complex a thinker than simply a romantic, and his romanticism featured prominently only in his narration of the "Galilean springtime" up to the "Galilean crisis" of Jesus's life.* Balancing that, however, was Renan's firsthand knowledge, unparalleled among life-of-Jesus scholars at that time, of Galilee, so that even his imaginative sketches filling in the gaps in the Gospel accounts had an aura of plausibility to them, at least in their day.[42] Renan's life of

---

40. Charles Hodge, *Systematic Theology*, 3 vols. (Grand Rapids: Eerdmans, 1989 [orig. 1875]), 2:440.
41. Thanks particularly to the work of Wilhelm Bousset, esp. in *Kyrios Christos: A History of the Belief in Christ from the Beginnings of Christianity to Irenaeus*, trans. John E. Steely, rev. ed. (Waco: Baylor University Press, 2013 [Ger. orig. 1913]).
42. Scheffler, "Ernest Renan's Jesus," 195.

Jesus was quickly translated into English and arguably had the greatest impact in the United States of all the early quests. David Burns suggests that Renan created "an imaginative brand of biblical criticism that struck a balance between the demands of reason and the doctrines of religion." This balance enabled otherwise fairly secular American thinkers who "sought to purge Christianity of its supernatural dimensions" to still find something wonderful in the religious imagination and "make common cause with an ancient peasant from Galilee."[43]

Sixth, *despite Schweitzer's broad generalization about everyone remaking Jesus in their own image, it was only with the liberal theology of moral progress and the approach of someone like Harnack where he saw this principle at work in detail.*[44] In Europe, this was an era of the discovery and discussion of "great men," those who by the clarity of their vision and force of their will could catapult themselves into positions of power and profoundly influence their societies.[45] Liberal theology, if it could not accept the supernatural, could at least portray Jesus as one such great man and, at times, as the greatest man who ever lived. J. C. O'Neill observes that Harnack's view of the gospel was based firmly "on an iron determinism." History therefore seems meaningless until one trusts fully "in the fatherly goodness of God." Yet "through faith in him anyone can come to the same acceptance, and discover the same freedom and peace."[46] Ironically, even in strongly opposing this perspective, Schweitzer, too, depicted Jesus as a great man, yet as a consistent apocalypticist who believed he could usher in the fullness of God's kingdom, first in his own life and, later, at least by his atoning death.[47] Ward Blanton argues that the real possibility

---

43. David Burns, *The Life and Death of the Radical Historical Jesus* (Oxford: Oxford University Press, 2013), 5.
44. Schweitzer, *Quest of the Historical Jesus*, 168–89.
45. Halvor Moxnes, *Jesus and the Rise of Nationalism: A New Quest for the Nineteenth-Century Historical Jesus* (London: I. B. Tauris, 2012), 17–38.
46. O'Neill, *Bible's Authority*, 226.
47. Carl R. Holladay stresses that one must judge Schweitzer finally by his second, 1913, edition, not translated into English until Bowman's edition of 2001, where Schweitzer removed a key passage that had contributed to the original perception of his Jesus as a failure ("Schweitzer's Jesus: Crushed on the Wheel of the World?," *EC* 3 [2012]: 435–67). The kingdom still did not appear right after Jesus's death as Jesus had imagined, but he had understood his death after the image of Isaiah's Suffering Servant. See esp. Schweitzer, *Quest of the Historical Jesus*, 348–49.

of change for the better in the future, symbolized by eschatology, was the central linchpin to Schweitzer's views. Relinquishing it could come "only at the cost of the loss of the freedom of culture itself."[48]

Seventh, *Wrede hardly remade Jesus in his own image with the development of the theory of the messianic secret any more than Strauss did with his mythologizing.* It was clear by the close of the nineteenth century that an emphasis on Markan priority played into a distinctively Protestant agenda. The elaborate expansion of Peter's confession on the road to Caesarea Philippi in Matthew 16:16–19 was the central Roman Catholic text for the establishment of the papacy; with Markan priority, Matthew's distinctives could more easily be dismissed as editorial additions. Matthew's was also the most Jewish of the four Gospels, rejecting at many points Mark's more "law-free" or Pauline message. Those who wanted to distance themselves from Jesus's Jewish roots could do so much more readily if Mark rather than Matthew were the earliest of the Gospels.[49] With Wrede, if even Mark's historicity could be questioned at numerous points, then the other three Gospels had even less a chance of being historical. But none of Wrede's distinctives came from an established philosophical perspective; he was pioneering a new theory.

Eighth, Matthew 10:23 could retain such significance for Schweitzer because he accepted Matthean priority here.[50] Thus, Jesus could shift gears from thinking he would live to see the kingdom arrive to believing that he had to die in order for that to happen. But most of Mark was paralleled in Matthew as well, so Schweitzer could rely on either Gospel. *It is difficult, therefore, to see how Schweitzer fell victim to the trend he claimed to discern in others. He was scarcely promoting believers becoming fiery, apocalyptic preachers, nor did he represent any school of thought that sought to create such individuals.* A major point of Schweitzer's work was that he was defending a portrait of

---

48. Ward Blanton, *Displacing Christian Origins: Philosophy, Secularity, and the New Testament* (Chicago: University of Chicago Press, 2007), 164.
49. For the anti-Catholic and anti-Jewish implications for many who supported Markan priority, see David L. Dungan, *A History of the Synoptic Problem: The Canon, the Text, the Composition, and the Interpretation of the Gospels* (New York: Doubleday, 1999), 329, 339.
50. Schweitzer, *Quest of the Historical Jesus*, 328–31.

Jesus that was *not* congenial to anyone's worldview, even his own.[51] Of course, he sought his life's work based on Jesus's abiding significance as he understood it. But, according to his understanding, that was the meaning of the *spirit* of Jesus with which believers may unite, not the earthly or human Jesus who, despite his grand, sweeping vision of the imminent kingdom, died without it being implemented either then or later.

## General Trends

*Rejecting the supernatural, to one degree or another, has clearly undergirded every scholarly contribution discussed so far.* The eighteenth-century Scottish philosopher David Hume had thrown down the gauntlet with his arguments that it would always be less likely that a supernatural explanation accounts for a wondrous event than a natural one.[52] Despite opposition almost from the outset and despite having been largely debunked today,[53] Hume was believed then, and is still sometimes believed, to have carried the day. At the end of the nineteenth century, Ernst Troeltsch could articulate the three abiding principles of Hume's legacy as defining "the historical-critical method."[54] First is "the principle of criticism or methodological doubt, which implies that history only achieves probability." Second, the principle of analogy makes "present experience and occurrence . . . the criteria of probability in the past." Third, "the principle of correlation (or mutual interdependence) implies that all historical phenomena are so interrelated that a change in one phenomenon necessitates a change in the causes leading to it and in the effects it has."[55] All three principles

---

51. See esp. Schweitzer, *Quest of the Historical Jesus*, 478–87.
52. David Hume, "Of Miracles," in *An Enquiry Concerning Human Understanding*, sec. 10 (orig. 1748).
53. Of many good refutations, see esp. Craig S. Keener, *Miracles: The Credibility of the New Testament Accounts*, 2 vols. (Grand Rapids: Baker Academic, 2011), 1:107–208.
54. Edgar Krentz, *The Historical-Critical Method* (Philadelphia: Fortress, 1975), 55.
55. Ernst Troeltsch, "On the Historical and Dogmatic Methods in Theology," accessed July 17, 2021, http://thestairview.com/wp-content/uploads/2018/06/Troeltsch-On-the-Historical-and-Dogmatic-Methods.pdf (Ger. orig. 1898), 2–3. For a good rebuttal, see Stewart E. Kelly, "Miracle, Method, and Metaphysics: Philosophy and the Quest for the Historical Jesus," *TJ* 29 (2008): 45–63.

disturbed many traditional believers, though only the second and the third are actually objectionable. The first principle, that determining what happened in history, including religious history, involves degrees of probability, is true enough, but some degrees are high enough (and sufficiently higher than the probabilities attaching to each of the other options) that they merit acceptance. The principles of analogy and correlation, on the other hand, claim too much. They exclude not only a monotheistic understanding of God—as is embraced in Judaism, Christianity, and Islam—but also genuinely free human agency. Nothing, also, can ever be truly new.[56] Moreover, miracles of the kind found in the life of Jesus have been experienced and documented throughout church history, and especially in today's world, so even if one accepts the principle of analogy, it does not entail what the antisupernaturalists claimed it did.[57] To further complicate matters, today many scholars use "historical-critical" basically as a synonym for research that is grounded in ancient history, thoroughly analytical and scholarly rigorous, which ought to command consent from all sides.[58] As with so many aspects of scholarship, until one understands a given author's use of terms, attempts at assessment can prove at best futile and at worst based on misinterpretations.

*The period of scholarship surveyed by Schweitzer was also the period that saw an intense scrutiny of the Synoptic problem*—the question of the literary relationships among the first three Gospels and the sources on which they relied. This was no coincidence. Not only did the conclusion of Markan priority free Protestants, or so they thought, from the shackles of Catholicism and Judaism (see above, 14), but also it gave them as the earliest foundational Gospel the one with the

---

56. See further Paul Wells, "The Lasting Significance of Ernst Troeltsch's Critical Moment," *WTJ* 72 (2010): 199–217. Despite the title, which reflects only one component of the article, Wells also gives a very compelling critique of Troeltsch's work.

57. See esp. Keener, *Miracles*, 1:209–599, 2:712–59, 769–856, 870–84; also Craig S. Keener, *Miracles Today: The Supernatural Work of God in the Modern World* (Grand Rapids: Baker Academic, 2021).

58. See Roy A. Harrisville, *Pandora's Box Opened: An Examination and Defense of Historical-Critical Method and Its Master Practitioners* (Grand Rapids: Eerdmans, 2014). The Troeltschian kind of "historical-critical" methodology appears on one solitary page in this thorough overview.

lowest Christology. In other words, Mark, so the claim went, had the least amount of material of any of the Gospels supporting the deity of Christ. One could then easily envisage a development of Christian understanding of Jesus as increasingly stressing the exalted nature of Jesus, first in Matthew and Luke and then even more so in John. The desire for a Jesus who was nothing more than a human being, however great, was easier to fulfill with Mark. One simply had to follow the trajectory backward from John to Mark and keep going in order to envision the portrait of a merely human Messiah at the beginning of the tradition, which became increasingly augmented even during the years leading up to the composition of the first Gospel.[59]

*It is astonishing to see the extent of the ethnocentrism of the largely German quest.* Schweitzer epitomizes this braggadocio when he writes in the first two sentences of his very first chapter, "When, at some future day, our period of civilization lies closed and completed before the eyes of later generations, German theology will stand out as a great, a unique phenomenon in the mental and spiritual life of our time. For only in the German temperament can there be found in the same perfection the living complex of conditions and factors—of philosophical thought, critical acumen, historical insight, and religious feeling—without which no deep theology is possible."[60] Later, in treating Renan, he speaks of the "standing enigma" of the greatness of French art compared to its poetry, "which scarcely ever goes beyond the lyrical and sentimental, the artificial, the subjective, in the worst sense of the word. Renan is no exception to this rule."[61]

Little wonder that one can show links between historical Jesus research and various forms of politics, all in the service of German nationalism.[62] This is not yet the spirit of the Third Reich, nor are the Germans yet inventing an Aryan Jesus (on which, see below, 36, 54); after all, Schweitzer himself sees Jesus as entwined with late-Jewish apocalyptic. But the seeds have all been sown for more disturbing and

---

59. See the explanations in Peter M. Head, *Christology and the Synoptic Problem: An Argument for Markan Priority* (Cambridge: Cambridge University Press, 1997).
60. Schweitzer, *Quest of the Historical Jesus*, 3.
61. Schweitzer, *Quest of the Historical Jesus*, 159.
62. Moxnes, *Jesus and the Rise of Nationalism*, 39–60, 95–120.

dangerous early-to-mid-twentieth-century developments in German theology and Jesus research.

*Closely related is Schweitzer's complete lack of treatment of British scholarship.* Scholars in Victorian Britain wrote numerous lives of Jesus that increasingly utilized the best insights of historical criticism without the inappropriate limitations of the historical-critical method. Arguably, the three most influential were Frederic Farrar, Cunningham Geikie, and Alfred Edersheim.[63] All three were at one time Anglican clergymen. Edersheim came from Jewish lineage and had, among nineteenth-century historical Jesus scholars, an unparalleled grasp of the ancient rabbinic literature. His *Life and Times of Jesus the Messiah* from 1883 continues to be reprinted and utilized in conservative circles, even though scholars now recognize that one must sift carefully through rabbinic traditions, some of which predate Jesus but many of which emerged only hundreds of years later.[64]

Of course, Schweitzer cannot be held responsible for not including lives of Jesus that would appear just after the publication of his *Quest*. And he added a detailed, final chapter in the 1913 edition, updating his survey through 1912. There he did acknowledge a few British and a few other French writers. He did the same in two even longer chapters just preceding that one, on the increasingly international debate about the historicity of Jesus.[65] Yet he had plenty of opportunity to update his survey further, as it continued to be reprinted throughout his lifetime, but he turned his scholarly attention largely to Paul instead. In addition, it is important to observe that during the periods he did survey there were other, more conservative Jesus scholars, even in Germany, who did not receive the recognition they deserved.[66]

---

63. Daniel L. Pals, *The Victorian "Lives" of Jesus* (San Antonio: Trinity University Press, 1982). Intriguingly, these were the three scholars used most by Latter-day Saints scholar and writer James E. Talmage in his widely touted *Jesus the Christ: A Study of the Messiah and His Mission according to Holy Scriptures both Ancient and Modern* (Salt Lake City: The Deseret News, 1915).

64. For representative dating, see H. L. Strack and Günter Stemberger, *Introduction to the Talmud and Midrash*, trans. Markus Bockmuehl (Minneapolis: Fortress, 1992).

65. Schweitzer, *Quest of the Historical Jesus*, 355–477.

66. One thinks particularly of E. W. Hengstenberg and Theodor Zahn (on whom, see below, 25–26).

Dale Allison has suggested that it might be better to categorize the perspectives of the quest topically rather than chronologically.[67] It becomes too easy to think that scholarship is always progressing, when sometimes it largely just recycles perspectives, even if in slightly new form, after they have been largely forgotten. The third quest lends itself to this approach (see below, 70–71), but *too many cause-and-effect relationships have been discerned throughout the original quest to make it optimal to create a thematic taxonomy.*

A very different reaction to the original quest raises far more important questions. Wasn't the uniform result of the quest the increase of skepticism and disbelief in once-Christian circles, even if some of the contributors genuinely believed they were trying to save the faith for modernity? In fact, going all the way back to Lessing, if true religion can't be based on the vicissitudes of historical study, isn't all this historical Jesus research irrelevant for Christian belief? Or maybe the situation is even worse, so that it is inevitably detrimental to faith? Shouldn't the right approach for the Christian be to simply accept the full inspiration and truthfulness of Scripture, as the church has historically believed, and not engage in anything that resembles the historical-critical method? And what exactly do we mean by "historical Jesus research" in the first place? By now it has become clear that not everyone was using the expression in the same way. The questions are actually complex ones, and the answers are not straightforward.

## Defining the Historical Jesus

*Martin Kähler* (1835–1912) published a small but very influential book in 1892 called *The So-Called Historical Jesus and the Historic, Biblical Christ*.[68] Kähler forcefully made the point that what historical Jesus studies reconstructed of Jesus's life should never be confused with the divine Messiah (or Christ) of the New Testament. Whether or not every

---

67. Dale C. Allison Jr., "The Secularizing of the Historical Jesus," *PRS* 27 (2000): 135–51. Cf. Bernard B. Scott, "From Reimarus to Crossan: Stages in a Quest," *CurBS* 2 (1994): 253–80.

68. Martin Kähler, *The So-Called Historical Jesus and the Historic, Biblical Christ*, trans. and ed. Carl E. Braaten (Philadelphia: Fortress, 1988 [Ger. orig. 1892]).

part of the Gospels' portrait of Jesus was historical (Ger. *historisch*), overall it was certainly historic (Ger. *geschichtlich*)—that is, of monumental significance—and an authority by which the believer should live. Many Christians and even a few scholars have subsequently looked back at the historical Jesus quest, finding it at best unnecessary and inappropriate and at worst downright deleterious.[69] If Jesus research does not yield the Christ of the New Testament, then its portrait is inferior or even dangerous, they assert. Recalling Lessing's views and recognizing how the results of historical research regularly change, they see no point in engaging in that which by definition cannot produce definitive results and has often led people away from Christian faith. One believes by an act of the will, one pledges to remain faithful to one's commitment, and one does not let today's supposed scholarly consensus about Jesus's influence or undermine that promise, because tomorrow they may change anyway.

There are commendable features of this approach. If all a given field of study ever accomplished were simply to weaken Christian faith, believers should never want to participate. Still, we must define our terms carefully. John Meier stresses the distinction between the real Jesus, the canonical Jesus, and the historical Jesus.[70] The real Jesus is everything that he was in his earthly life, which encompasses far more than any records of his life contained or ever could have contained—as with every other figure in history (cf. John 21:25, despite the hyperbole). The canonical Jesus is what can be learned about Jesus from the books of the biblical canon.[71] It resembles but is not identical to the composite picture that results from *all* ancient evidence, because later Christian

---

69. Finding the quest inappropriate: Luke T. Johnson, *The Real Jesus: The Misguided Quest for the Historical Jesus and the Truth of the Traditional Gospels* (San Francisco: HarperSanFrancisco, 1997); Frank Thielman, "The Secularizing of the Historical Jesus," *PRS* 27 (2000): 135–51; finding it dangerous: Robert L. Thomas and F. David Farnell, eds., *The Jesus Crisis: The Inroads of Historical Criticism into Evangelical Scholarship* (Grand Rapids: Kregel, 1998).

70. John P. Meier, *A Marginal Jew: Rethinking the Historical Jesus*, vol. 1, *The Roots of the Problem and the Person* (New York: Doubleday, 1991), 21–40. See also Per Bilde, *The Originality of Jesus: A Critical Discussion and a Comparative Attempt* (Göttingen: Vandenhoeck & Ruprecht, 2013), 27.

71. For information in the New Testament not found in the four Gospels, see esp. David M. Allen, *The Historical Character of Jesus: Canonical Insights from Outside the Gospels* (London: SPCK, 2013; Minneapolis: Fortress, 2014).

writings, both orthodox and heterodox, as well as a small number of non-Christian Jewish, Greek, and Roman texts, give us additional information about Jesus, though not that much compared to the rich testimony of the four Gospels. The canonical Jesus is what traditional, historic Christianity has always deemed authoritative, even though many people engaged in historical Jesus study have preferred to make their own reconstructions of Jesus the most authoritative, or else they reject everyone's pictures as authoritative for their lives, professing merely historical or antiquarian interest in Jesus. The historical Jesus, thus, for any given scholar is what they believe can be reconstructed about the man, Jesus of Nazareth, using historical tools alone.

It is true that many historical Jesus scholars have made the historical-critical method, as defined by Troeltsch, the foundation of their work.[72] While some Christians choose to bracket their faith in the supernatural or redefine what has historically been deemed to be supernatural, the very conservative critiques of Jesus research do have a point here. It is hard to see much value in pursuing the quest for the historical Jesus along Troeltschian lines. To be sure, there could be some value in demonstrating, if it were possible, that even the Jesus of the historical-critical method was worth studying, valuing, and even emulating. But major portions of the Gospel record would always remain off limits this way. It is better to argue that historical Jesus research need not require purely naturalistic assumptions and to be open to wherever the evidence genuinely leads.[73]

Nevertheless, historical study of Jesus by either method is crucial for believers for at least two major reasons. First, in dialogue with non-Christians, it allows Christians to insist that there really was an early first-century Jew who lived in Israel by the name of Jesus. From non-Christian sources alone, they can confirm that his ministry intersected with that of a man named John famous for baptizing his fellow Jews

---

72. A modern programmatic, book-length restatement was made by Van A. Harvey, *The Historian and the Believer: The Morality of Historical Knowledge and Christian Belief*, rev. ed. (Urbana: University of Illinois Press, 1996).

73. See esp. Peter Stuhlmacher, *Historical Criticism and Theological Interpretation of Scripture: Toward a Hermeneutics of Consent*, trans. Roy A. Harrisville (Philadelphia: Fortress, 1977; repr., Eugene, OR: Wipf & Stock, 2003).

as a sign of repentance, and that he was born out of wedlock, had a brother named James, gathered disciples (five of whom are named), frequently took controversial positions on interpretations of Jewish law, was believed by his followers to be the Messiah, and ran sufficiently afoul of the authorities that he was crucified during the time Pontius Pilate was prefect of Judea. Nevertheless, his followers believed that they saw him risen from the dead and within a short period of time were meeting regularly, singing songs, and worshiping him as if he were a god.[74]

This may not seem like a lot compared to the rich amount of detail in the canonical Gospels, but in a world that wrote almost exclusively about the exploits of kings, queens, other nobility, military rulers and their battles, or people in official or institutional positions of power in philosophy or religion, this is actually quite a bit. Plus, apart from Josephus, we simply don't have any other writings of first-century historians who may have discussed people and events in Israel; the available sources treat Greek and Roman events almost exclusively. At any rate, we do have plenty to refute those who claim Jesus never existed.[75] And historical Jesus research enables the believer to say a whole lot more about Jesus than just what the non-Christian sources allow us to compile, as we will see by the end of this survey (below, 174–75). This kind of information has actually led a number of people over the years to turn from unbelief to Christian faith.[76]

The second reason for historical study of the life and times of Jesus is to better understand the information that we do have within the New Testament canon. Not only are all contemporary readers separated by two thousand years of history, but also most are separated by significant geographical and cultural barriers as well. Even visits to Israel do not enable anyone to see everything (or even most things) as

---

74. See esp. Robert E. van Voorst, *Jesus outside the New Testament: An Introduction to the Ancient Evidence* (Grand Rapids: Eerdmans, 2000).

75. So also Bart D. Ehrman, *Did Jesus Exist? The Historical Argument for Jesus of Nazareth* (New York: HarperOne, 2013); Maurice Casey, *Jesus: Evidence and Argument or Mythicist Myths?* (London: Bloomsbury T&T Clark, 2014).

76. One thinks of individuals such as Sir William Ramsay, C. S. Lewis, Josh McDowell, Eta Linnemann, and Lee Strobel, to name some of the most high-profile examples.

they originally looked, though we can get glimpses and hints here and there. Without historical research, people usually default to what they know best as they envision the appearance, culture, dynamics, and meaning of events in ancient narratives. And what people know best are contemporary customs and practices that are often quite different from ancient ones. Historical research also helps one better understand what would have stood out as important, unusual, countercultural, controversial or attention-getting in first-century settings, which is not always what one would first imagine today. A scrutiny of even just the four canonical Gospels uncovers emphases that Christians have not always highlighted, as well as subsidiary elements that have too often been elevated to major ones.[77] The last four chapters of this book will highlight one key area that receives very little attention in the Christian world today.

Meier's explanation of what we are seeking in historical Jesus research proves helpful: "The historical Jesus is not the real Jesus, but a fragmentary hypothetical reconstruction of him by modern means of research."[78] *The historical Jesus is the sum total of those aspects of Jesus's life, whether they appear inside or outside the Bible, that probably can be authenticated through ordinary historical research, without presupposing Christian faith.* The historical Jesus quest is not an enterprise for every Christian, nor should it ever become the most important part of any Christian's life. But it need not be constrained by the historical-critical method as defined by Troeltsch, and we should be thankful for those gifted and called to participate in the quest, rather than condemning them. Questers may well pick up on themes in Jesus's life that were more important than the church has regularly made them, or they may understand the significance of aspects of his life much more accurately.

There is one issue, however, that is almost entirely missing from our discussion thus far. Even Schweitzer does not let on how crucial a topic it was, how much debate it engendered, and how many different

---

77. At a popular level, an outstanding demonstration of this appears in Philip Yancey, *The Jesus I Never Knew* (Grand Rapids: Zondervan, 1995).

78. Meier, *Marginal Jew*, 1:31.

positions emerged on it, even in just the nineteenth century. That topic is the question of how to treat the Gospel of John in a Jesus quest.

## The Gospel of John

To read Schweitzer, one could conclude that, with rare exceptions, only the very unenlightened participants in the original quest ever allowed the Gospel of John to figure in their historical research. The dramatic differences between John and the Synoptics are obvious to anyone who carefully reads them. The fact that we have three Gospels that are as similar as they are makes John's distinctives stand out all the more. Surely here Schweitzer's either-or mentality makes sense. Either we may follow the Synoptics or we may accept John, but we can't have it both ways. In reality, however, things are more complicated. *Late eighteenth- and nineteenth-century lives of Jesus demonstrated at least eight discrete approaches to the Fourth Gospel.*

Probably the oldest approach and one that continued to flourish in the English-speaking church world even throughout the twentieth century was to *harmonize John with Matthew, Mark, and Luke*, so that his material was worked into chronologically plausible places in a synopsis or life of Christ. In nineteenth-century Germany, Paulus inserted the Synoptic material into a larger Johannine framework.[79] In France, Edmund de Pressensé wrote a book that appeared simultaneously in French and in English translation, *Jesus Christ: His Times, Life, and Work*,[80] and "offered a militant defense of the Gospel of John as a source for the life of Jesus, though he by no means rejected the methods of historical criticism."[81] In Great Britain, this approach was even more common throughout this period.[82]

A second position was actually to *prioritize John and Matthew*, because of the nearly unanimous early church tradition that they were

---

79. Kissinger, *Lives of Jesus*, 18.
80. Edmund de Pressensé, *Jesus Christ: His Times, Life, and Work* (New York: Scribner, Welford, 1868).
81. Pals, *Victorian "Lives" of Jesus*, 62.
82. Pals, *Victorian "Lives" of Jesus*, 91.

written by two of Jesus's twelve apostles, whereas Mark and Luke were written by much more obscure figures. Michaelis, in his introduction, forthrightly articulates this perspective, not because of a prior belief in the inspiration or inerrancy of Scripture, but because he was aware of the many discrepancies that he believed were actual contradictions among the four Gospels. It only made sense to him to assume that Mark and Luke were responsible for the inferior historical record when one had to choose among the various canonical texts.[83] By the mid-1800s, this approach became less common because increasing numbers of scholars were convinced that none of the four Gospels was written by the individuals to whom eighteen centuries of church tradition had attributed them.

A third perspective began with a different, recurring early church conviction that a Hebrew source of some kind underlay Matthew's Gospel.[84] Perceiving some of the same stylistic and potentially Semitic features in the Greek of the Fourth Gospel, it postulated that John had relied on the same source that Matthew did. But whereas Matthew was believed to have been written to a primarily Jewish Christian church or collection of Christian communities, John was said from the second century onward to have been written to predominantly Gentile Christian congregations in and around Ephesus in western Asia Minor. If Christianity were to succeed in the Gentile world, certain aspects of the life of Jesus would have to be selected in order to *contextualize the gospel in ways that would best relate to the issues that the Ephesian church was facing there*. This explains many of the differences in John. Gotthold Lessing was the most famous exponent of this perspective.[85]

Fourth, Theodor Zahn, while not writing a life of Jesus, penned a very detailed and influential conservative introduction to the New Testament in three large volumes, which first appeared in 1904. Reflecting a long-standing alternative to the critical skepticism that had emerged during the 1800s, Zahn argued that John set out consciously to *supplement the Synoptics*, deliberately not repeating most of what

83. Michaelis, *Introduction to the New Testament*, 95.
84. Beginning already with Papias in the first quarter of the second century.
85. Lessing, *Lessing's Theological Writings*, 80–81.

they covered well. Zahn pressed the matter even further, arguing that numerous parts of John's Gospel simply aren't understandable, or at least are not very clear, unless one already knows the information of the Synoptics. John was therefore presupposing this knowledge on the part of the Christians he was addressing, thirty years or so after the composition of Matthew, Mark, and Luke. Unlike the advocates of most of the other positions, Zahn went into great detail to defend his case, with examples from throughout the Fourth Gospel.[86] Arguably most helpful of all is his thorough treatment of the apparent contradiction between John and Synoptics on the date of the Passover (see further below, 315–20). His work bears careful study by those today, including various evangelicals, who have not spent the same amount of time on this issue and yet glibly dismiss the solution Zahn defended, when they see it presented by others, as hopefully obscurantist.[87] Moreover, Zahn's overall approach to John remarkably resembles the highly touted "discoveries" by more recent scholars about John presupposing knowledge of the Synoptics on the part of his readers even without having a literary relationship with them (see also below, 189–92).[88] In England, Cambridge scholar B. F. Westcott wrote a very learned commentary on John, defending its historical reliability, and his colleague J. B. Lightfoot had completed quite a bit of his own before his death. Both had extensive treatments, apart from the commentary proper, defending historicity.[89]

Fifth, Friedrich Schleiermacher strove to *make John alone "basic" or foundational for his understanding of Jesus*.[90] He rejected the idea that John was supplementing the Synoptics in favor of the view that he was supplementing "the oral tradition that was ultimately incorporated

---

86. Theodor Zahn, *Introduction to the New Testament*, trans. John Moore Trout et al. (Edinburgh: T&T Clark, 1909 [Ger. orig. 1904]), 3:254–98.

87. E.g., Kenton Sparks, *God's Word in Human Words: An Evangelical Appropriation of Biblical Scholarship* (Grand Rapids: Baker Academic, 2008), 162–64.

88. See esp. Richard Bauckham, ed., *The Gospels for All Christians: Rethinking the Gospel Audiences* (Grand Rapids: Eerdmans, 1998).

89. B. F. Westcott, *The Gospel according to St. John* (London: John Murray, 1881). Lightfoot's extensive notes and handwritten manuscript pages were finally published as J. B. Lightfoot, *The Gospel of St. John: A Newly Discovered Commentary*, ed. Ben Witherington III and Todd D. Still, assisted by Jeanette M. Hagen (Downers Grove, IL: IVP Academic, 2015).

90. Schleiermacher, *Life of Jesus*, 170, 188.

into the other Gospels."[91] Schleiermacher also rejected the notion that John had learned Hellenistic philosophy like that of Philo of Alexandria, despite some superficial similarities (most notably about Jesus as the *logos* or "Word"), because he could not see where John would have had any exposure to these ideas. Moreover, he pointed out, if the prologue of John's Gospel (1:1–18) reflected the clearest exposition of these views, why did they not recur in the same way throughout the body of the Gospel? Instead, Schleiermacher thought that the oral tradition behind the Synoptics omitted the long discourses of John's Gospel because they were harder to transmit that way. In what remains a major challenge to consensus thinking even today, he was not at all fazed by the early temple cleansing in John (2:13–22) that appeared to contradict the Synoptic location during the last week of Jesus's life (Mark 11:15–18 pars.). Unlike other lives of Jesus, his insisted that it was "highly probable that a purification of the temple took place often. Selling and buying in the temple grounds was a malpractice that anyone had a right to prevent." As a result, "Christ can often have found it necessary to do so."[92] Stephen and Martin Westerholm label the distinction that Schleiermacher made between John and the Synoptics as "dramatic," in which only "John presents an internally coherent text informed by 'one and the same tendency from beginning to end' (*LJ*, 159). The narrative is not 'full of gaps.' John 'specifies' the periods that he skips, 'and he skips them because they contain nothing of interest to his special tendency' (*LJ*, 159)."[93]

Yet this is no fundamentalist acceptance of what the church historically deemed reliable, since Schleiermacher is more than ready to assign all kinds of problems to the historicity of the Synoptics. The other major rationalists did not go this far but did often prefer John's Gospel because it contained fewer miracles than the Synoptics.[94] Schleiermacher declared that critical study shows the Synoptics are edited compilations

---

91. Schleiermacher, *Life of Jesus*, 261.
92. Schleiermacher, *Life of Jesus*, 364.
93. Stephen Westerholm and Martin Westerholm, *Reading Sacred Scripture: Voices from the History of Biblical Interpretation* (Grand Rapids: Eerdmans, 2016), 323. In-text references are to Schleiermacher, *Life of Jesus*.
94. Schweitzer, *Quest of the Historical Jesus*, 81.

or "aggregations" of stories that were circulating among the early Christians. No consistent point of view appears here, the stories are not always arranged in any discernible order, and contexts differ from one Gospel to the next. "No account of the life of Christ as a unity could be discovered from them."[95] John wanted to rectify all this and to be sure that the divinity of Christ clearly shone through his writing. While hardly anyone today would follow Schleiermacher in detail, he certainly anticipated several of the tenets of form criticism (see below, 34–35) and is worth reconsidering, even if just to be sure that one can articulate why he is wrong in those places he is alleged to be.

Sixth, Renan took a quite different tack. He decided to *accept the chronology and sequence of material in John as correct*, especially where the Synoptics have none or seem to be grouping accounts together topically or thematically. He believed that someone who came to the Fourth Gospel without already preconceived predilections would prefer its narration and that its author was the better biographer. But its lengthy discourses were largely fictitious insertions that John added to the rest of the Gospel that was, for the most part, reliable.[96]

Harnack added a seventh viewpoint. For him, the Fourth Gospel could not be considered a historical authority in the normal sense of the expression. The author of John "acted with sovereign freedom, transposed events and put them in a strange light, drew up the discourses himself and illustrated great thoughts by imaginary situations." Still, even if one cannot for the most part retrieve reliable history from this Gospel, it can be an authority to *answer questions like, "What vivid views of Jesus' person, what kind of light and warmth, did the Gospel disengage?"*[97] Other "liberal" lives of Jesus held similar views, though often allowing a little bit of influence of some details from the Fourth Gospel in their narratives, which otherwise closely followed the Synoptics.[98] Wrede found John better than either Matthew or Luke in preserving Mark's messianic secret, along with the fact that his fol-

---

95. Schleiermacher, *Life of Jesus*, 159.
96. Renan, *Life of Jesus*, xv. See his lengthy appendix for specific details (267–316).
97. Kissinger, *Lives of Jesus*, 55, 56; italics added.
98. Schweitzer, *Quest of the Historical Jesus*, 174.

lowers misunderstood him until after the resurrection.[99] Otherwise, he adopted the growing consensus of favoring the Synoptics over John.

Eighth, perhaps the largest group of Jesus researchers came to *marginalize John's Jesus entirely or almost entirely*. Baur argued that as John's historical value sinks, the Synoptics' rises.[100] Still, as Horton Harris notes, Baur held that John "possessed outstanding literary merit and moral insight even though the events narrated were not historically true."[101] Some just ignored John; Schweitzer opines that Reimarus, for example, "brought the Synoptic and Johannine narratives into harmony by in practice leaving the latter out of account."[102] Strauss, on the other hand, argued in detail why John should be rejected. He actually took the time to point out what he believed were the major contradictions between John and the Synoptics, what some of the attempts to harmonize them claimed, and how he found the harmonizations wanting. Unfortunately, in few instances did the solutions Strauss rejected match the approaches conservative scholars in the twentieth and twenty-first centuries would take; in many instances the strained harmonizations Strauss considered *did* merit rejection.[103] But as creative as Strauss was on so many topics, envisioning and interacting with possible solutions that hadn't already been articulated wasn't something he undertook. Strauss also found the discourses too hard to remember for him to think that they would be preserved intact. But where there are short parallels within Jesus's discourses in John to Synoptic teachings, Strauss acknowledges that there may be authentic kernels of what Jesus actually said.[104] Weiss considered John dispensable simply because he taught so little about the kingdom.[105] Subsequent scholarship, however, would suggest that more was present than is indicated just by the three occurrences of the term "kingdom"

---

99. Wrede, *Messianic Secret*, 182–83, 210.
100. See Kümmel, *New Testament*, 128.
101. Horton Harris, *The Tübingen School: A Historical and Theological Investigation of the School of F. C. Baur* (Oxford: Clarendon, 1975; repr., Grand Rapids: Baker; Leicester: Apollos, 1990), 193.
102. Schweitzer, *Quest of the Historical Jesus*, 24.
103. E.g., Strauss, *Life of Jesus*, 367–71.
104. Strauss, *Life of Jesus*, 381–86.
105. Weiss, *Jesus' Proclamation of the Kingdom of God*, 60.

in John, especially when one looks for conceptual as well as verbal parallels (see below, 209–11). Loisy rejected even John's more plausible chronology, thinking that it made no sense for the Synoptics to be more reliable in other features but not in this one. Indeed, he speculated that a three-and-a-half-year ministry had allegorical significance, showing the period to be one of the last half-weeks of Daniel's seventy weeks of years in Daniel 9:24–27.[106]

William Baird seems correct, then, when he summarizes the situation at the end of the 1800s as one in which "the Gospel of John remained a point of contention." One could still find defenders of its historical reliability, but the loudest voices were perhaps those who valued it solely for its "theological intent" and/or "mystical character."[107] Because louder voices can drown out quieter ones, the rejection of the historical value of John would continue to dominate twentieth-century Johannine research as well, but as we will see (below, 180–208), there were many thoughtful minority voices also.

## Conclusion

Albert Schweitzer's survey of life-of-Jesus research up through the end of the nineteenth century remains invaluable, but it must be supplemented by firsthand reading of the sources where possible, along with a variety of other scholars' takes from varying perspectives. His agenda made it clear that he would commend anyone who hinted at his thoroughgoing eschatology as the key to understanding Jesus and that he would criticize those who didn't. Not everyone remade Jesus in their own image, at least not nearly to the same extent, and it is hard to see how that criticism applies to Schweitzer himself. Of course, many who considered themselves Christians fashioned their lives along the lines of the Jesuses they reconstructed, but that is hardly the same as creating Jesus in one's own mold. And virtually everyone who writes a life of Jesus has studied him for a long time, so that even preliminary conclusions can affect life choices. It can appear by the time one writes

---

106. Loisy, *Gospel and the Church*, 30–34.
107. Harris, *Tübingen School*, 136.

their major works that they are simply following the philosophical or theological perspectives to which they were previously committed, but that can be because earlier study of Jesus had already led them to those perspectives. The process is much more dialectic than one-directional.

In any event, Schweitzer's survey of German and a few French works must be supplemented by overviews of the scholarship of other countries, especially Great Britain. There, lives of Jesus proved noticeably more conservative, and not for lack of scholarly rigor. The historical-critical method, as articulated by Troeltsch, must be distinguished from historical criticism, pure and simple, which seeks to understand the biblical accounts considering all the relevant historical, cultural, literary, linguistic, and rhetorical contexts in which they appeared. For the most part, those Schweitzer surveyed did adopt something like what Troeltsch would codify, but not everyone did (or else they varied the extent to which they did), and many Schweitzer did not survey did not adopt Troeltsch's criteria at all. Historical Jesus research can be viewed simply as that which can be demonstrated as probable from the study of history, apart from presupposing Christian faith or an inspired Scripture. A portrait of the historical Jesus must not be confused with either the real Jesus or the canonical Jesus, but the historical Jesus still has great value both in the public square, where people have widely divergent religious presuppositions and convictions, and in the church, where believers have widely divergent grasps of the content, meaning, and emphases of the canonical Gospels.

Conspicuously lacking in most "original quest" Jesus research was significant input from the Fourth Gospel. That was true despite a greater diversity of approaches to John than Schweitzer lets on. The reasons varied, but the major differences between John and the Synoptics played a large part in the perspectives adopted. There is little evidence, however, that many of the "questers" examined in detail the nature of these differences and the possibilities of harmonizing them plausibly, especially since some of the solutions suggested in their day were quite fanciful. Usually, when the Gospel of John was rejected, it was just written off from the outset. When one contrasts this with the meticulous and repetitive weighing of the arguments for all the different permutations of the Synoptic problem, the difference becomes striking. It is hard to resist the conclusion that many of the questers simply did not want John's distinctive take on Jesus to feature in their writings, because they would have to grapple with his seemingly higher Christology and more direct claims on their lives.

# 2

# No Quest and New Quest?

Few ideas in biblical scholarship stay dormant for very long. What goes around comes around. Did Albert Schweitzer's book on the quest for the historical Jesus actually end that quest for a while? What really happened to the quest in the years and decades after his blockbuster publication? Again, there is a common narrative that picks up key elements of the answers to these questions.[1] But as with the nineteenth-century quest, more detailed scrutiny makes significant additions and corrections to that narrative necessary. As I did in chapter 1, in this chapter I will lay out the simplified version of the story and then retrace its steps, focusing in more detail on four aspects or phases of the sequel to Schweitzer: the immediate aftermath, the rise of form criticism, the period of Nazi Germany, and the new quest.

## The Common Narrative

A composite of many brief accounts of Jesus research during the first seventy or eighty years of the twentieth century might read as follows: Schweitzer's devastating critique put *an end to the quest, at least in*

---

1. See esp. Walter P. Weaver, *The Historical Jesus in the Twentieth Century: 1900–1950* (Harrisburg, PA: Trinity Press International, 1995). See also W. Barnes Tatum, *In Quest of Jesus: A Guidebook* (Atlanta: John Knox, 1982), 71–79; N. T. Wright, *Jesus and the Victory of God*, Christian Origins and the Question of God 2 (London: SPCK; Minneapolis: Fortress, 1996), 21–25.

*its nineteenth-century forms*. If even Schweitzer could not avoid recreating Jesus in his own image, after showing how everyone else had done so before him, what hope could there be for others to avoid the vicious circle of concluding where they started? Besides, this was the era of the history-of-religions school of thought in New Testament studies, which highlighted parallels between the New Testament's conceptions of Jesus and thinking in other ancient religions, especially Greco-Roman ones. The highest Christology in the Gospels is best attributed to the creative invention of early Christian writers or traditions that treated Jesus as if he were a pagan god of some kind.[2]

This was also the era in which *the discipline of form criticism*, which originally emerged in Old Testament scholarship, was increasingly being applied to New Testament study as well. Form criticism analyzed and labeled the distinct literary forms of which the Gospels were comprised, based on the conviction that they originally circulated in small units or groupings relatively independently of one another. Thus, their selection, arrangement, and wording, especially in the Synoptic Gospels, was the product of the combined influence of the transmission of the oral tradition and the decisions of the Gospel writers themselves. Based on putative analogies with other ancient Middle Eastern, Eastern European, and North African cultures, the typical history or evolution of each literary form could then be traced, making it possible to project backward and envision what the original form of a given saying or episode of Jesus's life was. Definable "tendencies of the tradition" could enable one to see how a given portion of the Gospels most likely developed over time before it was written down. In so doing, one could begin to sift the more authentic portions of a given passage from later accretions. The results of the process attributed far more to the "post-Easter" period of Gospel formation than to the "pre-Easter" period that contained what Jesus actually said and did.[3] *Rudolf Bultmann* (1884–1976), one of the pioneers and certainly the

---

2. See esp. Wilhelm Bousset, *Kyrios Christos: A History of the Belief in Christ from the Beginnings of Christianity to Irenaeus*, trans. John E. Steely, rev. ed. (Waco: Baylor University Press, 2013 [Ger. orig. 1913]).

3. See the introduction to Edgar V. McKnight, *What Is Form Criticism?* (Philadelphia: Fortress, 1969).

most influential exponent of Gospel form criticism, once commented that he thought we could know almost nothing of Jesus beyond the mere fact *that* he lived.[4]

Bultmann, as a Lutheran, was also convinced that if justification was truly by faith and not works, then Christianity could not be based on historical evidence. Here he was influenced more by Martin Kähler than by Albert Schweitzer. Christian faith must be directed toward the biblical Christ rather than the historical Jesus. The Christ as the early church preached him, just like the proclaimed word of his apostles as they continued to promote him, was what brought men and women to himself, irrespective of what the human Jesus of Nazareth was like. Anything else was akin to attempted salvation by works rather than pure faith.[5] The worldview of the first century, moreover, meant that Strauss had been right in one very important way: much of the Gospel accounts was made up of unhistorical myths and legends. That did not diminish their spiritual value, however; one simply had to look for the theological message encased in the mythological forms or, as Bultmann termed it, to demythologize the accounts.[6] A final, central thrust of Bultmann's theology was existentialism. The gospel message is not about securing one's eternal destiny but about living the most "authentic" human existence possible in the present. The *kerygma* (Gk. for "proclamation") confronted sinful people with a better, more loving, more other-centered way to live that had the potential to transform the world.[7]

---

4. This would come to be known as "the mere thatness" (*das bloße Daß*) of Jesus. See Gerhard Ebeling, "Das bloße 'Daß' und die Lehre von der Anhypostasie," in *Theologie und Verkündigung: Ein Gespräch mit Rudolf Bultmann* (Tübingen: J. C. B. Mohr, 1962), 115–16.

5. See, e.g., Rudolf Bultmann, "The Primitive Christian Kerygma and the Historical Jesus," in *The Historical Jesus and the Kerygmatic Christ: Essays on the New Quest of the Historical Jesus*, ed. Carl E. Braaten (New York: Abingdon, 1964 [Ger. orig. 1962]), 15–42. Cf. Heinz Zahrnt, *The Historical Jesus*, trans. J. S. Bowden (London: Collins; New York: Harper & Row, 1963), 88–89. Paul Althaus points out that Luther's soteriology was always predicated on the credibility of Scripture and the work of the Holy Spirit, so that appealing to *sola fide* as requiring the rejection of all historical evidence is a non sequitur (*The So-Called Kerygma and the Historical Jesus*, trans. David Cairns [Edinburgh: Oliver & Boyd, 1959 (Ger. orig. 1958)], 53–54).

6. Rudolf Bultmann, *Jesus Christ and Mythology* (New York: Scribner, 1958; London: SCM, 1960 [Ger. orig. 1951]), 11–44.

7. Bultmann, *Jesus Christ and Mythology*, 45–85.

The devastation wreaked by two world wars in Europe proved profoundly troubling for Christianity, whether in its more traditional, orthodox form or in its more modern, existentialist garb. It also prevented biblical studies from proceeding at anything close to the pace it had previously taken. When people did write lives of Jesus, moreover, they may have avoided the trap of re-creating him in their own philosophical or religious images, but they didn't avoid the trap of trying to make him as non-Jewish as possible. With the amount of anti-Semitism in the world, many scholars wanted to make Jesus look as little like a typical first-century Jew as they could. In extreme cases, they created the Aryan Jesus, someone who was not Jewish at all, but descended from white, European ancestry.[8] In other instances, the wars, along with the rise of both fascism and communism, simply took considerable time away from scholarship, including New Testament study, slowing considerably the growth of academic study of Jesus.

One task that scholars poked away on, however, goes right back to where Schweitzer ended his survey of previous research. While some jumped on Schweitzer's bandwagon of consistently futurist eschatology, C. H. Dodd swung the pendulum to the other end of the spectrum, believing that Jesus taught consistently realized eschatology (i.e., the arrival of the kingdom of God) in Jesus's very own ministry.[9] After World War II, Joachim Jeremias synthesized the two approaches and spoke of a *sich realisierende Eschatologie* (an eschatology in the process of realizing itself).[10] This last approach caught on and, with a few notable exceptions, has largely become the standard explanation for the combination of present and future statements about the arrival of the kingdom in the Gospels.[11] Still, these discussions did not in and of themselves lead to new, full-blown lives of Christ.

---

8. Susannah Heschel, *The Aryan Jesus: Christian Theologians and the Bible in Nazi Germany* (Princeton: Princeton University Press, 2008). Cf. Peter M. Head, "The Nazi Quest for an Aryan Jesus," *JSHJ* 2 (2004): 55–89.

9. Esp. in C. H. Dodd, *The Parables of the Kingdom* (London: Nesbit, 1935; New York: Scribner, 1937).

10. Joachim Jeremias, *The Parables of Jesus*, trans. S. H. Hooke, 3rd ed. (London: SCM; Philadelphia: Westminster, 1972 [Ger. orig. 1947]).

11. For an overview, see Wendell Willis, ed., *The Kingdom of God in 20th-Century Interpretation* (Peabody, MA: Hendrickson, 1987). John Dominic Crossan introduced the category

Like everything else in society, biblical scholarship did not resume full-tilt immediately after World War II and Hitler's demise. But by the early 1950s, in Marburg, Germany, at a reunion of a number of Bultmann's former students, one of them, *Ernst Käsemann* (1906–98), delivered an address on the problem of the historical Jesus[12] and set in motion a chain of events that would lead to the beginning of what called itself *the "new quest of the historical Jesus,"* which was also the title of a book at the end of the 1950s by one of those students, James M. Robinson.[13] A key problem with the nineteenth-century quest had been the reliance on positivistic historiography—the belief that with the right tools and sources one could arrive at an objective account of events as they actually happened.[14] That was what had made Schweitzer's critique so devastating; he showed that no one was nearly as unbiased as they thought they were. The new quest, on the other hand, acknowledged what Bultmann had himself taught, that "presuppositionless exegesis" was impossible.[15] Nor did one have to return to a relatively nontheological core of the Gospels, stripped of its theological shell. The kerygma could, in places, be theological and historical at the same time.[16]

The new quest did not necessarily authenticate more teachings or deeds of Jesus, or other events in the canonical Gospels, than the original

---

of an entirely this-worldly "permanent eschatology," esp. in his *In Parables: The Challenge of the Historical Jesus* (New York: Harper & Row, 1973), which garnered some followers for the next two or three decades, but it has now largely receded from sight.

12. Ernst Käsemann, "Das Problem des historischen Jesus," *ZTK* 51 (1954): 125–53.

13. James M. Robinson, *A New Quest of the Historical Jesus* (London: SCM; Naperville, IL: Allenson, 1959).

14. Most English-language summaries at this point cite the famous statement from nineteenth-century historiographer Leopold von Ranke about recovering history "as it actually was," and they often reproduce the German they find secondhand in some other English-language source (*wie es eigentlich gewesen*), without realizing that this four-word expression is incomplete, nonsensical German and that they should have added von Ranke's next word, to produce *wie es eigentlich gewesen ist*.

15. Rudolf Bultmann, "Is Exegesis without Presuppositions Possible?," in *Existence and Faith: Shorter Writings of Rudolf Bultmann*, trans. and ed. Schubert M. Ogden (New York: Meridian, 1960; London: SCM, 1961 [Ger. orig. 1957]), 289–96.

16. A perspective that would await more detailed defense in the more conservative work by I. Howard Marshall, *Luke: Historian and Theologian* (Exeter: Paternoster; Grand Rapids: Zondervan, 1970). Cf. Craig L. Blomberg, "Luke: I. H. Marshall and Historical Redaction," *EvQ* 93 (2022): 1–16.

quest had; indeed, at times it seemed it did not advance that far beyond Bultmann. But it recognized the need to develop "criteria of authenticity" for the task in order to regularize the process.[17] Drawing on some precedents from earlier eras, the four most common criteria that scholars agreed on were double dissimilarity (often abbreviated simply to "dissimilarity"), multiple attestation, Palestinian environment, and coherence. "(Double) dissimilarity" looked for what the Gospels alleged Jesus said or did that was significantly different from both conventional first-century Palestinian Judaism and conventional fledgling Christianity after Jesus's lifetime, so that it was unlikely that anyone from either of those movements or backgrounds would have invented it. "Multiple attestation" referred to the appearance of the item in more than one Gospel source (where literary independence was likely) or literary form within the various Gospels or elsewhere in the New Testament (sometimes thus separated off and called the criterion of "multiple forms"). "Palestinian environment" insisted that some element of the Gospels fit the social or cultural setting of the time and place in which Jesus lived. "Coherence," finally, authenticated Gospel data that didn't in and of themselves meet one of the other three criteria, but which were fully consistent with or logical corollaries of others that did meet those criteria.[18]

*Günther Bornkamm* (1905–90) wrote the first major study of the life of Jesus from an avowed new-quest perspective, and it arguably remains the best example from this period.[19] Bornkamm did seem much more optimistic about what he could recover of the historical Jesus from the Synoptics—information from most every phase of his ministry, including examples of most forms of his teachings and deeds—and he regularly stressed the remarkable authority and immediacy of Jesus's presence that the sources disclose. As for so many in the original quest, the announcement of the arrival, at least in part, of the kingdom of God proved central for Jesus. Healings and exorcisms had some roots

17. I. Howard Marshall, *I Believe in the Historical Jesus* (Grand Rapids: Eerdmans; London: Hodder & Stoughton, 1977; repr., Vancouver: Regent College Publishing, 2001), 128–34.
18. Nicely summarized in R. S. Barbour, *Traditio-Historical Criticism of the Gospels: Some Comments on Current Methods* (London: SPCK, 1974).
19. Günther Bornkamm, *Jesus of Nazareth*, trans. Irene McLuskey and Fraser McLuskey (New York: Harper; London: Hodder & Stoughton, 1960 [Ger. orig. 1956]).

in history, whether they were supernatural, strictly speaking. But when it came to nature miracles, including the resurrection, Bornkamm had to demur. Similarly, when it came to ascribing atoning significance to the crucifixion, Bornkamm stopped short of doing so. Similar Jesus studies, with some variations, appeared from other German scholars, such as Ernst Fuchs and Hans Conzelmann.[20]

Fuchs also joined forces with Hans-Georg Gadamer and Gerhard Ebeling in helping to develop what became known as the "new hermeneutic."[21] This was not a method for historical Jesus research per se, but rather an emphasis on the ability of the biblical text in general to create what was dubbed a *Sprachereignis* ("language event"). Put differently, readers did not merely interpret the text; the text could interpret them. For one engaged in a close study of the text, a hermeneutical circle developed where each successive reading brought the potential of more closely approximating its meaning, even if one could never interpret it comprehensively. The ability of readers to change their minds about the meaning or significance of the text, through a close encounter with it, demonstrated the power of language events. The power of the word was at least reified, if not at times almost deified, in order to account for how the historical Jesus could address modern people as the kerygmatic Christ. Like the new quest itself, scholars were looking for what seemed to them as intellectually viable ways for God still to act in history, both through Jesus and in Christians' lives today, without resorting to a full-blown supernaturalism that they believed modern science and technology had disproved.[22]

To conservative scholars, however, the new questers often seemed just about as antisupernaturalist as many in the original quest had been,

---

20. Ernst Fuchs, *Studies of the Historical Jesus*, trans. Andrew Scobie (London: SCM; Naperville, IL: Allenson, 1964 [Ger. orig. 1960]); Hans Conzelmann, *Jesus: The Classic Article from RGG Expanded and Updated*, trans. J. Raymond Lord, ed. John Reumann (Philadelphia: Fortress, 1973 [Ger. orig. 1959]).

21. Hans-Georg Gadamer, *Truth and Method*, ed. Garrett Barden and John Cumming (New York: Seabury; London: Sheed & Ward, 1975 [Ger. orig. 1960]); Gerhard Ebeling, *Word and Faith* (London: SCM; Philadelphia: Fortress, 1963), esp. 305–32.

22. For a detailed, incisive, but not unsympathetic overview and critique, see Anthony C. Thiselton, *The Two Horizons: New Testament Hermeneutics and Philosophical Description* (Exeter: Paternoster; Grand Rapids: Eerdmans, 1980), 293–356.

and as Bultmann himself had been as well. Miracles, including Jesus's resurrection, were thus rarely, if ever, taken literally. Neither the new questers nor the new hermeneuticians saw the Jesus of history as truly God any more than the nineteenth-century questers had viewed him as such. The most explicit christological titles in the Gospels usually were deemed inauthentic or unhistorical. Still, the new quest was prepared to grant Jesus a small amount of implicit Christology.[23] The authority with which Jesus spoke and acted, combined with his ability to directly mediate God's presence, justified the Gospel writers' using the exalted language for Christ that they employed. Instead of deriving Jesus's understanding of his own ontology from his explicit statements about himself, which were still judged to be secondary, the new quest derived it from his more implicit language, such as using "Abba" for "Father" or prefacing his solemn pronouncements with "Amen." Sayings were thus treated fairly atomistically, and broader questions about Jesus's aims and purposes were still largely off limits.[24] On the other hand, faith did need at least a modicum of historical evidence on which to be grounded, and the new quest believed that it had found enough.[25] As the new quest was consolidating its findings in the mid-1970s, Norman Perrin wrote about Jesus,

> He was baptized by John the Baptist, and the beginning of his ministry was in some way linked with that of the Baptist. In his own ministry Jesus was above all the one who proclaimed the Kingdom of God and who challenged his hearers to respond to the reality he was proclaiming. The authority and effectiveness of Jesus as proclaimer of the Kingdom of God was reinforced by an apparently deserved reputation as an exorcist. In a world that believed in gods, in powers of good and evil, and in demons, he was able, in the name of God

23. Ernst Käsemann, "The Problem of the Historical Jesus," in *Essays on New Testament Themes*, trans. W. J. Montague (London: SCM; Naperville, IL: Allenson, 1964 [Ger. orig. 1954]), 15–47. Randy L. Maddox describes the shift as "the willingness to engage in restrained inferences about the claims and self-understanding of Jesus from his message and actions" ("The New Quest and Christology," *PRS* 11 [1984]: 49).

24. For several of these and related observations, see Donald L. Bell, "New Quest of the Historical Jesus—A Critique," *ATR* 44 (1962): 414–20.

25. Robinson, *New Quest of the Historical Jesus*, 104.

and his Kingdom, to help those who believed themselves to be possessed by demons.

A fundamental concern of Jesus was to bring together into a unified group those who responded to his proclamation of the Kingdom of God irrespective of their sex, previous background or history. A central feature of the life of this group was eating together, sharing a common meal that celebrated their unity in the new relationship with God, which they enjoyed on the basis of their response to Jesus' proclamation of the Kingdom. In this concern for the unity of the group of those who responded to the proclamation, Jesus challenged the tendency of the Jewish community of his day to fragment itself and in the name of God to reject certain of its own members. This aroused a deep-rooted opposition to him, which reached a climax during a Passover celebration in Jerusalem when he was arrested, tried by the Jewish authorities on a charge of blasphemy and by the Romans on a charge of sedition, and crucified. During his lifetime he had chosen from among his followers a small group of disciples who had exhibited in their work in his name something of his power and authority.

That, or something very like it, is all that we can know; it is enough.[26]

Many of the same individuals who pioneered the new quest also participated in a new critical methodology called redaction criticism (Ger. *Redaktionsgeschichte*).[27] "Redaction" is a synonym for "editing." It had become clear that form criticism could take one only so far in studying the development of the Gospel tradition. The Gospel writers were more than cut-and-paste compilers of the traditions they inherited. They chose what to preserve, what to reword, and what to excise from their sources, both oral and written. They organized that material into an intentional structure or outline. There were patterns in the ways in which they added, reworded, or omitted details from

---

26. Norman Perrin, *The New Testament, an Introduction: Proclamation and Parenesis, Myth and History* (New York: Harcourt Brace Jovanovich, 1974), 287. Intriguingly, Dennis C. Duling, in his editing of the second edition of this book (1985, after Perrin's death), almost doubles the amount of information he includes in this passage as authentic (see pp. 411–12). That may represent Duling's views, but it most certainly was not Perrin's!

27. Norman Perrin, *What Is Redaction Criticism?* (Philadelphia: Fortress, 1969). The three pioneers are usually held to be Willi Marxsen on Mark, Bornkamm on Matthew, and Conzelmann on Luke.

passages they took from their sources. There were recurring themes that were more important in one Gospel than in the others. All these features figured to one degree or another into the redaction critic's attempt to determine the contribution of each individual evangelist.[28] But it was also regularly assumed that what was redactional could not also be historical; the otherwise anonymous authors of the Gospels, in other words, could never have learned of information they chose to include or highlight that was (1) unique to their Gospel, (2) theologically meaningful, and (3) reasonably historically accurate all at the same time.[29] Redaction criticism thus put additional limits on what could be retrieved from the Gospels and attributed to the historical Jesus.

The new quest, like most of the lives of Jesus produced after Schweitzer's tome, had *little time for the Gospel of John*. John might be inspirational, and it certainly represented part of the church's distinguished kerygmatic tradition, with its very exalted Christology, but it could hardly be used in service of historical Jesus research. There were a handful of separate studies that defended the trustworthiness of larger or smaller portions of the Fourth Gospel, but they seldom influenced lives of Christ.[30] Increasingly, scholars would not even discuss the similarities and differences between the Synoptics and John and the various explanations proposed for them, but simply assumed that it was an unalterable datum of scholarship that John was of little historical value for reconstructing a life of Jesus.[31]

Thus ends the whirlwind survey of no quest through new quest. What additions and corrections are the most important ones to make to this common narrative? The rest of this chapter will retrace the four

---

28. Initially, diachronic observations were separated off from synchronic ones and treated as "composition criticism" or "tradition criticism," but eventually only "redaction criticism" survived, referring to all parts of the process.

29. Grant R. Osborne, "Redaction Criticism," in *Interpreting the New Testament: Essays on Methods and Issues*, ed. David A. Black and David S. Dockery (Nashville: Broadman & Holman, 2001), 128–49. Cf. Mark Goodacre, "Redaction Criticism," in *Dictionary of Jesus and the Gospels*, ed. Joel B. Green, Jeannine K. Brown, and Nicholas Perrin, 2nd ed. (Downers Grove, IL: IVP Academic, 2013), 767–71.

30. See esp. Franz Mussner, *The Historical Jesus in the Gospel of St. John*, trans. W. O'Hara (New York: Herder & Herder, 1967).

31. E.g., Bornkamm, *Jesus of Nazareth*, 14.

main stages sketched out here to provide some of the most important answers to this question.

## Was There Really a Period of No Quest?

The part of the common narrative most in need of correction is that which dubs the period between the first and second quests the period of "no quest." It is true that pure rationalism did not make a comeback, but it had largely been limited to the late eighteenth and early nineteenth centuries anyway. Seeing widespread use of myth in the Gospels would recur some in the history-of-religions school and certainly in Bultmann and form criticism, but neither of those movements produced many full-fledged lives of Jesus. A romantic like Renan had no real successors.[32] But the (old) liberal lives of Jesus against which Schweitzer had been most scathing in his critiques continued to appear in a number of circles.[33] Admittedly, there was no one as influential as Harnack, but *Shirley Jackson Case* (1872–1947) and his "Chicago School" of colleagues made a significant dent in the American landscape with their emphasis on social backgrounds.[34] Whereas most scholars in all the different camps had previously written lives of Jesus in which his message was seen as first of all addressed to the individual, Case stressed understanding the sociological contexts of Jesus's teaching and ministry. For Case, Jesus was merely a powerful prophet, but his teachings are still some of the best the world has ever seen. Case also recognized that one couldn't limit authentic material to Mark and Q (material common to Matthew and Luke not found in Mark) as so many before him had wanted to do. "Every statement in the records is

---

32. On the failure of Renan's constructs of Jesus's "Galilean springtime" followed by his "Galilean crisis" and his self-removal to Jerusalem feeling like a failure, so central to Renan's portrait, see Tucker S. Ferda, *Jesus, the Gospels, and the Galilean Crisis* (London: Bloomsbury T&T Clark, 2019).

33. Pride of place, among those not otherwise cited in this chapter, goes to James Mackinnon, *The Historic Jesus* (London: Longmans, Green, 1931). See Warren S. Kissinger, *The Lives of Jesus: A History and Bibliography* (New York: Garland, 1985), 67–72.

34. Shirley Jackson Case, *Jesus: A New Biography* (Chicago: University of Chicago Press, 1927). Cf. already Shailer Matthews, *The Social Teaching of Jesus: An Essay in Christian Sociology* (New York: Macmillan, 1897).

to be judged by the degree of its suitableness to the distinctive environment of Jesus, on the one hand," he wrote, "and to that of the framers of gospel tradition at one or another stage in the history of Christianity, on the other."[35]

Attempts to psychologize or determine the inner life of Jesus did noticeably shrink after Schweitzer. This meant that all but the most conservative scholars were reluctant to speak of Jesus's messianic consciousness. And it made little sense to most to envision Jesus as the Messiah unless he was aware of that fact. In the mid-twentieth century, Ethelbert Stauffer would explain that "the nineteenth-century ideal was a *biography* of Jesus—that is to say, a representation of the psychological development of Jesus, of his mind and his activities, rendered with narrative vividness, analytic insight, and plausibility."[36] That is what scholars realized was unattainable. But that did not stop writers from producing what Stauffer called histories of Jesus—much more modest and selective arrangements of reliable data, perhaps with some cause-and-effect relationships creating a limited chronology, but without psychologizing.

*The history-of-religions* (Ger. *religionsgeschichtliche*) *school of thought* spanned the late nineteenth and early twentieth centuries. By far its most successful and influential proponent, *Wilhelm Bousset* (1865–1920), wrote his classic work, *Kyrios Christos,* just one year too late for Schweitzer to interact with it, even in his second edition.[37] While originally scholars who relied heavily on Jewish backgrounds, like Schweitzer himself, were identified as participating in the *religionsgeschichtliche* approach, it increasingly became associated solely with those who found Greco-Roman parallels and backgrounds to the major contours of Jesus's life and activity. The christological titles came under particular scrutiny. Three different stages of the early church tradition were postulated in fairly lockstep sequence: first, Palestinian Jewish Christianity, then Hellenistic Jewish Christianity, and finally Hellenistic

---

35. Case, *Jesus*, 115.
36. Ethelbert Stauffer, *Jesus and His Story*, trans. Dorothea M. Barton (London: SCM; New York: Knopf, 1960), xiii.
37. Bousset, *Kyrios Christos*, appeared in 1913; Schweitzer's update considered works published through 1912.

Gentile Christianity.[38] Scholars worked backward through the sequence to see how close to Jesus they should attribute a given detail from the Gospels. Most "high Christology" was attributed to one of the two Hellenistic stages. Even if something showed all the signs of being both Jewish and from the land of Israel, that still did not guarantee its origin with Jesus, since it could have been the Palestinian Jewish Christian community that invented it. Years later, Martin Hengel would demonstrate in massive detail how all these cultural influences could be detected within Israel, especially in and around Jerusalem, in the earliest days of the Jesus movement, so that such classifications were heuristic at best and misleading at worst.[39] But two to three generations of students were taught differently before the corrective emerged and began to convince most scholars.

In any event, lives of Jesus continued to appear in the opening decades of the twentieth century, Schweitzer notwithstanding. A few even appeared in Germany, most notably Adolf Schlatter's *Die Geschichte des Christus* in 1923.[40] *Adolf Schlatter* (1852–1938) was grudgingly acknowledged by his contemporaries as a master of the background literature, especially in Judaism, against which we must read all four Gospels.[41] He did not utilize the Fourth Gospel for his life of Jesus for strategic reasons: the general disdain that it held in the scholarly guild for historical Jesus research and the complications it added if it were to be properly synthesized with Synoptic study. Yet he wrote a major

---

38. Clearly discussed and codified later in Reginald H. Fuller, *The Foundations of New Testament Christology* (New York: Scribner; London: Lutterworth, 1965).

39. Martin Hengel, *Judaism and Hellenism: Studies in Their Encounter in Palestine during the Early Hellenistic Period*, trans. John Bowden, 2 vols. (London: SCM; Philadelphia: Fortress, 1974). Earlier on, Zahrnt (*Historical Jesus*, 62) perceptively observed that the question the history-of-religions school could never answer was why Christianity alone survived among all the Greco-Roman options. Zahrnt's answer was, "Here, then, we have not the eternal event of myth but unique, unrepeatable history; not an idea, but a happening; not a cultic drama, but history in earnest; not metaphysics, but eschatology; not symbol, but Word; not an outlook, but faith" (63).

40. Adolf Schlatter, *Die Geschichte des Christus* (Stuttgart: Calwer, 1923); translated as *The History of the Christ: The Foundation for New Testament Theology*, trans. Andreas J. Köstenberger (Grand Rapids: Baker, 1997).

41. See Robert Yarbrough, "Adolf Schlatter's Contribution to Interpretation of the Fourth Gospel," in *The Gospel of John in Modern Interpretation*, ed. Stanley E. Porter and Ron C. Fay (Grand Rapids: Kregel Academic, 2018), 81–99.

commentary on John in which his approval of its historicity became clear.[42] Conservatives, however, at times also distrusted Schlatter because he did not hold to the authenticity of every detail in the Gospel accounts but was honest enough to admit when he felt other explanations better accounted for a problematic text's presence.

*Joseph Klausner* (1874–1958) may have been the most significant of a handful of Jewish scholars who began studying and writing about Jesus in the early twentieth century.[43] Klausner was clear that he felt responsible to write primarily for fellow Jews and that he did not accept Jesus as anything more than a prophet, but in the vein of Old Testament prophecy, as one who could have imagined himself as the coming (this-worldly) Messiah. Interestingly, he identified Schweitzer as the inaugurator of a *new* period of historical Jesus research, one that he hoped would continue to take Jewish backgrounds very seriously. It was not to be, however; indeed, it would not come consistently until the third quest (see below, 69–103). Nevertheless, Stanley Porter's selective discussion of lives of Jesus written during this period,[44] along with Warren Kissinger's fuller bibliography,[45] make it clear that *"no quest" is a very misleading term for this period*. The quest diminished considerably only among the Germans, and then in part due to Kähler's broadside against the historical Jesus in favor of the biblical Christ (on Kähler, see above, 19–20),[46] but even then only after form criticism came into its heyday with the massively influential work of Rudolf Bultmann.

## Bultmann and the Rise and Fall of Form Criticism

Chronologically, Rudolf Bultmann was the third in a trio of German scholars who began appropriating for New Testament study the method

---

42. Adolf Schlatter, *Der Evangelist Johannes: Wie er spricht, denkt und glaubt; Ein Kommentar zum vierten Evangelium* (Stuttgart: Calwer, 1930).
43. Joseph Klausner, *Jesus of Nazareth: His Life, Times, and Teaching*, trans. Herbert Danby (New York: Macmillan, 1925 [Heb. orig. 1922]).
44. Stanley E. Porter, *The Criteria for Authenticity in Historical-Jesus Research: Previous Discussion and New Proposals* (Sheffield: Sheffield Academic, 2000), 36–47.
45. Kissinger, *Lives of Jesus*, 115–212. Kissinger's bibliography is not divided up by periods of time, but just glancing through it for any decade since the rise of modern biblical scholarship shows how many entries appear without fail.
46. William E. Hull, "New Quest of the Historical Jesus," *RevExp* 64 (1967): 329.

known as *Formgeschichte* (lit., "form history"), which had started life as an Old Testament procedure. The other two scholars were K. L. Schmidt, who focused on the frameworks, outlines, and literary seams of the Synoptic Gospels, and Martin Dibelius, who was prepared to grant somewhat more historical value to a variety of literary forms in the Synoptics.[47] But neither man would leave his mark the way Bultmann did. At his peak, many people considered Bultmann to be the most important and influential New Testament scholar in the world. British scholarship never came under his sway to the degree that American scholarship did. But especially among Lutherans worldwide, his influence was enormous.

Had *Formgeschichte* remained merely an analytical tool, it would scarcely have made the waves that it did. The Gospels are not monolithic documents but are made up of accounts of Jesus's teaching in parables of various kinds and sizes, short proverbs, and lengthier discourses (some or all of which might be composite documents stitched together from shorter original pieces). Jesus also engages in conflicts or controversies with various religious leaders, most commonly groups of Pharisees, and ends those conversations with a short, dramatic pronouncement (e.g., "The Son of Man is Lord of the Sabbath" [Matt. 12:8 pars.]; or "Give back to Caesar what is Caesar's and to God what is God's" [Mark 12:17 pars.]). He performs healings, exorcises demons, and demonstrates miraculous powers over nature. The list could be considerably expanded, but the observation here that different interpretive principles at times attach themselves to the different literary forms should scarcely cause controversy. Form critics, however, went on to envision a possible *Sitz im Leben* ("situation in life") in which early Christians would reuse each form. Most important of all, they would postulate tendencies of the tradition that would expand, embellish, reword, relocate, and in other ways modify and even distort the discrete

---

47. Rudolf Bultmann, *The History of the Synoptic Tradition*, trans. John Marsh (Oxford: Blackwell; New York: Harper & Row, 1963 [Ger. orig. 1921]); K. L. Schmidt, *Der Rahmen der Geschichte Jesu: Literarkritische Untersuchungen zur ältesten Jesusüberlieferung* (Darmstadt: Wissenschaftliche Buchgesellschaft, 1969 [orig. 1919]); Martin Dibelius, *From Tradition to Gospel*, trans. Bertram Lee Woolf (New York: Scribner, 1965; repr., London: James Clarke, 2000 [Ger. orig. 1919]).

units of Jesus material it inherited. The critic's task then, like peeling layers off certain kinds of fruit, was to keep stripping these later accretions away until one got to the solid pit or core of what Jesus actually said or did, if in fact there was such a core in any given instance at all.[48]

Bultmann's famous exclamation that he thought we could know almost nothing about the historical Jesus actually came in the context of discussing the knowledge of Jesus's inner thoughts or consciousness.[49] If one combs through his magisterial *History of the Synoptic Tradition*, which assesses the tradition history of every example of every literary form he extracts from the Synoptics, one finds at least sixty-seven sayings of Jesus that Bultmann finds authentic, including fifteen aphoristic sayings, sixteen prophetic-apocalyptic sayings, six law/church-order sayings, ten "I" sayings, and twenty similes or parables.[50] It is also important to realize that Bultmann began his career quite skeptical of the authenticity of the Gospel tradition, became more open to acknowledging an authentic core in the middle of his career, but ended it quite skeptical again. Unfortunately, the middle period of his scholarship is less well known even though much better supported.[51]

Still, the tendencies of the tradition that form critics proposed relied on analogies from oral folklore, as Axel Olrik had studied it at the beginning of the twentieth century, from places as far away from ancient Israel as contemporary Europe.[52] One very general pattern that Bultmann perceived in many places, the "law" of increasing distinctness, was later demonstrated in more sophisticated studies to apply less than 50 percent of the time.[53] On a larger scale, the ancient Medi-

---

48. See further Craig L. Blomberg, "Form Criticism," in *Dictionary of Jesus and the Gospels*, ed. Joel B. Green, Scot McKnight, and I. Howard Marshall (Downers Grove, IL: InterVarsity, 1992), 243–50. See also Nicholas Perrin, "Form Criticism," in *Dictionary of Jesus and the Gospels*, ed. Joel B. Green, Jeannine K. Brown, and Nicholas Perrin, 2nd ed. (Downers Grove, IL: IVP Academic, 2013), 288–94.

49. See Althaus, *So-Called Kerygma*, 72–73.

50. Ernst Baasland, "Consistent Jesus Research? Bultmann's Die Geschichte der synoptischen Tradition (1921) and Jesus (1926) Revisited," *ETL* 91 (2015): 415–60, esp. 427.

51. Baasland, "Consistent Jesus Research?," esp. 417–35.

52. Axel Olrik, "Epic Laws of Folk Narrative," in *The Study of Folklore*, ed. Alan Dundes (Englewood Cliffs, NJ: Prentice-Hall, 1965 [Ger. orig. 1909]), 129–41.

53. Leslie R. Keylock, "Bultmann's Law of Increasing Distinctness," in *Current Issues in Biblical and Patristic Interpretation: Studies in Honor of Merrill C. Tenney Presented by His Former Students*, ed. Gerald F. Hawthorne (Grand Rapids: Eerdmans, 1975), 193–210. See also

terranean worlds were far more likely to abridge detailed narratives than to expand on them. It is true that Matthew and Luke are both about half again as long as Mark, but when one compares paralleled passages, more than half the time Matthew's versions are shorter and about two-thirds of the time Luke's versions are shorter. The reason Matthew and Luke are longer overall is that they include a greater number of episodes from the life of Christ overall, not because they consistently expand on the episodes from Mark that they reproduce.[54]

British Gospels scholars appreciated the interpretive potential of form criticism but were much more cautious about the supposed history of the forms. T. W. Manson and Vincent Taylor were perhaps the best known of those who embraced this pair of perspectives.[55] Cautions that they and other early critics of form criticism marshaled included (1) the remarkably short oral period that the Synoptic tradition underwent before the first written accounts appeared, compared to the majority of analogies in other settings that were being utilized; (2) the occasional use of a kind of shorthand for taking brief notes of a rabbi's teaching by his disciples;[56] (3) the presence of hostile eyewitnesses to Jesus's life at the earliest stages of the tradition, forming a check on unbridled modification and distortion; (4) the existence of a center of leadership of the early Christian community that checked up on new developments in the progress of the gospel to ensure faithfulness to the tradition; (5) the so-called difficult sayings of Jesus that would not likely have been preserved, or at least not in the form they were, unless they were authentic and important; (6) the lack of teachings ascribed to Jesus anywhere on important topics of early church controversy, if people had felt free to invent them, especially when an authoritative word from the Lord would have solved matters much

---

E. P. Sanders, *The Tendencies of the Synoptic Tradition* (Cambridge: Cambridge University Press, 1969).

54. Craig L. Blomberg, "The Tradition History of the Parables Peculiar to Luke's Central Section" (PhD diss., University of Aberdeen, 1982), 25–27.

55. T. W. Manson, *The Teaching of Jesus: Studies of Its Form and Content* (Cambridge: Cambridge University Press, 1935); Vincent Taylor, *The Formation of the Gospel Tradition* (London: Macmillan, 1933).

56. This would be expanded later by Alan Millard, *Reading and Writing in the Time of Jesus* (Sheffield: Sheffield Academic, 2000), 175–76, 202–4, 227–29.

more easily; (7) distinctions like those found in 1 Corinthians 7:10–12 between what the historical Jesus spoke, which Paul can quote, and what he never addressed, so that Paul has to rely on what he believes the Lord is telling him more directly;[57] and (8) the recognition that sometimes the nature of a theological position, such as God acting in history, requires people to recount accurate information in order to maintain credibility.[58]

It is easy for people who have only a superficial familiarity with Bultmann to think that all his major views rise or fall together. In fact, the kind of form criticism he adopted significantly predated his appropriation of existential philosophy. His demythologizing goes back, in part at least, to Strauss, and it is independent of both form criticism and existentialism. Dibelius, for example, utilized very similar form-critical categories and procedures without reframing the kerygma for the modern world in terms of existentialism. Taylor used form criticism without either existentialism or demythologizing. Plenty of existential philosophers knew nothing of form criticism, and the history-of-religions school also believed in the presence of myth in the Gospels, and the need to work with and around it, well before form criticism in the New Testament became at all common. These distinctions will become important later when we look at some of the current scholarly landscape (see below, 156–58).

*With the rise of redaction criticism, form criticism began to recede into the background.* As noted already, all the pioneering redaction critics insisted that they were not questioning form criticism, just building on it. But already in the late 1950s, the firstfruits of a very different kind of understanding of the oral transmission of Jesus's deeds and teachings emerged. Harald Riesenfeld, in a short article that drew far more attention than might have been expected, and Birger Gerhards-

---

57. For a detailed defense of this understanding of these verses, which has increasingly carried the day in the last twenty-five years, see Anthony C. Thiselton, *The First Epistle to the Corinthians: A Commentary on the Greek Text*, NIGTC (Exeter: Paternoster; Grand Rapids: Eerdmans, 2000), 519–27.

58. On all these points, see further Craig L. Blomberg, *Jesus and the Gospels: An Introduction and Survey*, 3rd ed. (Nashville: B&H Academic; London: Inter-Varsity, 2022), 63, 132–35, 148, 580, and the literature there cited.

son, in a detailed book-length work, began what some would later call *the guarded-tradition hypothesis*.[59] Examining ancient Jewish models of education through memorization and observing the care of ancient scribal copying, these two Swedish scholars argued that it would have been much more likely that the first Christians, revering Jesus as they did, would have exercised great care in the transmission of accounts of his words and deeds. Although their work came to be associated with the suggestion that a lot could have been memorized word for word, both scholars, particularly Gerhardsson in later works,[60] repeatedly stressed that they were not making such ambitious claims. They recognized the differences among Gospel parallels and the different potential explanations for their existence. They simply recognized that what was almost entirely absent from the form and redaction critics' work and from both quests for the historical Jesus thus far was an appreciation of how carefully most ancient Mediterranean cultures passed on by word of mouth the epic stories of their communities, along with the teachings and deeds of their religious leaders. Concurrently, other researchers, not directly involved in New Testament research, were redoing Olrik's studies. Preeminent among these was Harvard professor A. B. Lord in his 1960 publication, *The Singer of Tales*.[61] Later researchers would use the expression *informal, controlled oral tradition* for the models of the transmission of highly valued oral folklore in preliterate or semiliterate traditional communities. This became an intermediate alternative between the more formally controlled oral tradition proposed by the Scandinavians and the largely informal and uncontrolled tradition envisaged by the major form critics.[62] The amount of variation and similarity among the Synoptic parallels was strikingly parallel to the freedom and limits that oral storytellers in traditional communities in

59. Harald Riesenfeld, "The Gospel Tradition and Its Beginnings," *TU* 73 (1959): 43–65; Birger Gerhardsson, *Memory and Manuscript: Oral Tradition and Written Transmission in Rabbinic Judaism and Early Christianity*, trans. Eric J. Sharpe (Lund: Gleerup; Copenhagen: Munksgaard, 1961).

60. See esp. Birger Gerhardsson, *The Origins of the Gospel Tradition* (London: SCM; Philadelphia: Fortress, 1979).

61. A. B. Lord, *The Singer of Tales* (Cambridge, MA: Harvard University Press, 1960).

62. Kenneth E. Bailey, "Informal Controlled Oral Tradition and the Synoptic Gospels," *AJT* 5 (1991): 34–54 (repr., *Them* 20 [1995]: 4–11).

the "old world" exhibited when "performing" their most valued sagas.[63] Things were not nearly as free and loose as they were in the models Bultmann and the original form critics had worked with, even if not quite as fixed and rigid as in the guarded tradition.

While redaction critics continued to give lip service to building on form criticism, they increasingly focused just on their own discipline. Many of their findings about the individual distinctives of a given Gospel remained valid regardless of what model of oral tradition one used to account for the earliest period in the life of the church. In a perceptive study during the "cusp" years in which the new quest was giving way to the third quest, Klaus Haacker showed how empirical studies of oral tradition coalesced around the fact that changes to literary forms were most likely to occur in the earliest stages of transmission, after which further modifications became very rare.[64] This was the exact opposite of what Bultmann and Dibelius had claimed—namely, that alterations grew exponentially the further removed one was from the originating tradition. From the 1980s onward, one observed a precipitous decline in form-critical study. The handbooks on critical methods continued for the most part to treat it, though sometimes in combination with other methods, but actual books and journal articles suggesting new dimensions or applications of Gospel form criticism all but vanished. Catalogues of literary forms still appear, and they prove useful for hermeneutics, but studies advancing the analysis of the tendencies of the transmission of the tradition have largely disappeared. Study of oral tradition continues, but in new directions, as we will see below (166–71), not particularly bound up with the identification of distinct literary forms.

## The War Years and Their Aftermath

Anti-Semitism did not appear out of the blue when Hitler came to power in Germany in 1933. The emergence of Zionism in the nine-

---

63. A. B. Lord, "The Gospels as Oral Traditional Literature," in *The Relationships among the Gospels: An Interdisciplinary Dialogue*, ed. William O. Walker Jr. (San Antonio: Trinity University Press, 1978), 33–91.

64. Klaus Haacker, "Leistung und Grenzen der Formkritik," *TBei* 12 (1981): 67.

teenth century, with its sporadic political efforts to re-create a Jewish homeland in Israel, was due to a variety of factors, but one of them certainly was the sense among various Jews that they were never entirely safe or welcome in Europe or Russia.[65] But the amount of the hatred and the willingness of many Germans to act on it took a dramatic turn for the worse during the Third Reich. Perhaps no one could have imagined the Holocaust and its extent, but neither was it "random" that the Nazis selected the Jewish people for persecution. Waves of discontent, much of it built on misinformation, stereotyping, and prejudice, had been building for some time. Christianity's very mixed history of relationships with Jewish people certainly made the potential for atrocities easier.

What does any of this have to do with the historical Jesus? Simply this: while most New Testament scholars around the world (which realistically in this era meant Europe, North America, and just a small handful of other places) would almost always acknowledge Jesus as a Jew, he was always a Jew "with a difference." The Gospels showed him regularly at odds with "the Jews." Scholars in the last fifty years have studied at length the use of this general label in the New Testament and now recognize that it seldom if ever actually denotes all Jewish people alive at a certain time or even in one given location; rather, it can refer to Judeans, Jewish leaders, one group of Jewish people present on a certain occasion, those Jews who rejected Jesus, and so on.[66] Still, the damage had already been done; the generalized language of the Jewish (!) New Testament writers had led to centuries of some Christians labeling all Jewish people as "Christ-killers."

The historical Jesuses of the original quest and of the twentieth century through the end of World War II, so many of them birthed in Germany, to one degree or another were significantly removed from conventional Judaism. Bultmann, Käsemann, and several other leading Jesus scholars actually were part of the "Confessing Church," which

---

65. William I. Brustein, *The Roots of Hate: Anti-Semitism in Europe before the Holocaust* (Cambridge: Cambridge University Press, 2003).

66. Among many good studies, see esp. Stephen Motyer, *Your Father the Devil? A New Approach to John and the "Jews"* (Carlisle: Paternoster, 1997); Lars Kierspel, *The Jews and the World in the Fourth Gospel: Parallelism, Function, and Context* (Tübingen: Mohr Siebeck, 2006).

opposed the persecution of Jews,[67] but several were part of the mainline German Christian movement that at best ignored the problem and at worst conspired to help it. Gerhard Kittel, best known for his years of work on the *Theological Dictionary of the New Testament*, was one of the more forthcoming in his anti-Semitism,[68] while Walter Grundmann, well known later for his commentaries in German on the Gospels, helped establish and teach at an institute in eastern Germany that lasted from 1939 to 1945 and actually promoted an Aryan Jesus.[69] We have noted where occasionally Jesus scholars tried to emphasize Jesus's Jewishness, especially if they were Jews themselves, but these were the exceptions and not the rule. *It should come as no surprise, then, that one important generalization about the new quest, given that many of its initiators were Germans who had lived through the Third Reich, is that their depictions of Jesus still tended to focus too much on the distinctives between Jesus and conventional Judaism.*[70]

### The Postwar Period and the New Quest

The scholarship of *Joachim Jeremias* (1900–1979) poses a challenge for anyone trying to write history with neatly defined phases and categories. He employed form criticism but wrote extensively about the historical Jesus. He preceded a conscious "new quest" but anticipated and even went beyond many of its conclusions. Jeremias was a comparatively conservative German Lutheran who wrote a whole book on what we can know about the proclamation of Jesus as the first of an intended two-volume New Testament theology that he did not live to complete.[71]

---

67. Todd Brewer, "Preaching Politically in Turbulent Times," *Mockingbird*, September 30, 2019, accessed July 28, 2021, https://mbird.com/religion/preaching-politically-in-turbulent-times/; Fergus Kerr, "The Theology of Ernst Käsemann," *NBf* 62 (1981): 100.

68. Heschel, *Aryan Jesus*, 184–89.

69. Heschel, *Aryan Jesus*, 67–105.

70. Earlier, Klausner (*Jesus of Nazareth*, 97) had remarked, "The most liberal of Aryans can never come to terms with Jesus the Semite, Jesus the Jew, nor make any compromise with Christianity's rejection of the things of daily life, which (so such critics erroneously suppose) is a Jewish characteristic."

71. Joachim Jeremias, *New Testament Theology*, vol. 1, *The Proclamation of Jesus* (London: SCM; New York: Scribner, 1971). Cf. Jeremias, *Jesus and the Message of the New*

His book on Jesus's parables, some would argue, was the most influential work on that topic of the twentieth century.[72] Its first German edition appeared in 1947, a scant two years after the end of the war. He knew Aramaic well and believed that where one could easily translate the Greek of Jesus's teaching in the Synoptics fairly literally back into fluent Aramaic, there was a strong likelihood of finding authentic Jesus material. In fact, his hermeneutic placed greater authority on those texts than on the rest of Jesus's teaching even in their canonical forms.[73] At the same time, his work on the parables identified no fewer than ten different tendencies of the developing tradition, so that with almost every parable in the Gospels, one had to separate off an authentic core from secondary accretions that had attached themselves to it.[74] The Jesus he recovered was multifaceted and inspiring, proclaiming the arriving kingdom and teaching that now heralded the dawn of salvation. A crisis had emerged in Israel; time was short; repentance was urgent because judgment was at hand. The very hostility toward Jesus that many of the Jewish people eventually displayed simply confirmed how different Jesus was from the majority of the populace. Israel had come to ruin and would be replaced by the Gentile church (Matt. 21:43).[75]

Similar sentiments about Jesus's differences from Judaism can be found scattered about the writings of Bornkamm, Käsemann, Fuchs, Conzelmann, and other German new questers. In fact, the development of *the criteria of authenticity* reflects this trend. The *double-dissimilarity* criterion held priority of place for most new questers, and in practice, dissimilarity from conventional Judaism was more important than dissimilarity from the early church. Several scholars highlighted significant problems with both the criteria themselves and the way they were used.[76] The dissimilarity criterion could highlight

---

*Testament*, ed. K. C. Hanson (Minneapolis: Fortress, 2002), a compilation of four previously published booklets spanning 1963–65.

72. Jeremias, *Parables of Jesus*. See also Jeremias, *Rediscovering the Parables* (London: SCM; New York: Scribner, 1966).

73. Michael Labahn, "Joachim Jeremias," in *Encyclopedia of the Historical Jesus*, ed. Craig A. Evans (New York: Routledge, 2008), 319.

74. Jeremias, *Parables of Jesus*, 23–114.

75. Jeremias, *Parables of Jesus*, 70, 77.

76. See esp. Morna D. Hooker, "Christology and Methodology," *NTS* 17 (1971): 480–87; Hooker, "On Using the Wrong Tool," *Theology* 75 (1972): 570–81. Less one-sided but still aware

only what was distinctive about Jesus, not what was characteristic, should the two ever differ. *Multiple attestation* worked only when one was confident that the multiple sources in which a teaching or event appeared were truly independent. It certainly did not mean that Matthew, Mark, and Luke were to be treated as three witnesses, although Mark, Q, and L (a source of material unique to Luke) could be. One of the few historical uses of John could be to create an additional independent witness; the same was true of the Gnostic Gospel of Thomas, which was increasingly cited. But what if Thomas were *not* an independent (or fully independent) witness, an issue bound up with its dating? What if John were viewed as almost entirely unhistorical? At least Paul was almost certainly an independent witness, because his major letters were all written before the 60s, the earliest decade for which the Gospels can be plausibly dated.[77]

The criterion of *Palestinian environment* could certainly help to avoid anachronism, but wasn't it at odds with the prong of double dissimilarity that looked for differences from conventional Judaism? The criterion of *coherence* seemed logical, but it was secondary, requiring a body of already authenticated material in order to function. And one scholar's tolerance for divergence, without calling it contradiction, varied widely from another's. What exactly was required to have consistency and to justify the application of the criterion of coherence?[78] Despite all these questions related to the criteria of authenticity, they largely reigned unchallenged during the new quest.

In addition to these questions about individual criteria was one larger issue that hovered above them all: Could any of them actually be used negatively—that is, to argue that if the criterion was not satisfied, Jesus could *not* have said or done the item in question? Many scholars were using them precisely in that fashion, but to do so required some

---

of weaknesses was D. G. A. Calvert, "An Examination of the Criteria for Distinguishing the Authentic Words of Jesus," *NTS* 18 (1972): 209–19.

77. On the relationship between Paul and the Jesus tradition, see esp. David Wenham, *Paul: Follower of Jesus or Founder of Christianity?* (Grand Rapids: Eerdmans, 1995).

78. Replying to these and related critiques were David Mealand, "The Dissimilarity Test," *SJT* 31 (1978): 41–50; Reginald H. Fuller, "The Criterion of Dissimilarity: The Wrong Tool?," in *Christological Perspectives: Essays in Honor of Harvey K. McArthur*, ed. Robert E. Berkey and Sarah A. Edwards (New York: Pilgrim, 1982), 42–48.

rather absurd assumptions: (1) Jesus never agreed with anything in the Judaism of his world, and the church never correctly captured the meaning or significance of his ministry; (2) unless two independent sources attest something, it cannot have happened; (3) Jesus in no way differed from his environment; (4) the Gospel writers included material they found flatly contradictory to other aspects of Jesus's ministry that they believed took place.[79]

Other criteria were therefore developed, but all had their strengths and weaknesses as well. In addition to those already noted, Robert Stein identified as commonly used the positive criteria of "Aramaic linguistic phenomenon," "tendencies of the developing tradition," "modification by Jewish Christianity," and "divergent patterns from redaction." For negative criteria, he added "environmental contradiction" and "contradiction of authentic sayings."[80] Aramaic linguistic phenomena, which could be subsumed under the criterion of Palestinian environment, refer to places where the Greek of Jesus's sayings looks like a more literal translation of an Aramaic original than one usually finds. Of course, this judgment is subjective: the Aramaic influence could still come from the early Aramaic-speaking Christian community, while the evaluation assumes we know enough Hellenistic Greek to know that it wouldn't have been normal for that era. We have already seen that the tendencies of the tradition are very unpredictable. Modification by Jewish Christianity could be a subset of dissimilarity from first-century Judaism and early Christianity—where something is too bold or striking not to be toned down in a later parallel account. Divergent patterns from redaction seems reasonably solid, but all editors vary their patterns at times. A specifically helpful version of this criterion could be when something was potentially quite embarrassing to the first Christians and yet allowed to remain in a Gospel. The two negative criteria correspond well to my comments in the next paragraph below. Still others added the criterion of *necessary explanation*, where one piece of the

---

79. See the thorough critique by Porter, *Criteria for Authenticity*, 69–102.
80. See esp. Robert H. Stein, "The 'Criteria' for Authenticity," in *Gospel Perspectives*, vol. 1, *Studies of History and Tradition in the Four Gospels*, ed. R. T. France and David Wenham (Sheffield: JSOT Press, 1980), 225–63.

Gospel tradition must be historical in order to make sense of another already recognized as historical.[81]

On top of all this, one overarching critique of all the criteria had to do with *the burden of proof*. Criteria of authenticity are needed only if one starts from a perspective of skepticism, doubting everything in a Gospel unless certain criteria are satisfied. But this is not the way historians have classically operated, especially when most events from the ancient world have far less documentation than those surrounding the life of Jesus. Instead, a text that purports to be a historical narrative is given the benefit of the doubt until it repeatedly shows signs of *inauthenticity*. If scholars take this tack, they focus primarily on anything that looks anachronistic or that flatly contradicts other historical testimony (as with the two negative criteria Stein identified). Where scholars disagree on whether differences amount to actual contradictions, proposed resolutions of the discrepancies have to be assessed before a final verdict is given.[82] David Strauss, in the nineteenth century, was one of the few writers of lives of Jesus to take that approach (on Strauss, see above, 5). Unfortunately, in many instances he did not interact with the most plausible resolutions of apparent contradictions (and in some cases these would emerge only later), so it is hard to be as confident as he was that the Gospels are riddled with intractable discrepancies.

A third approach became popular near the end of the new quest: the burden of proof is on every scholar to demonstrate whatever they are arguing for.[83] At first blush, this sounds like the fairest, most objective approach. But when one recognizes how much of ancient history has a comparatively small amount of testimony to assess, such an approach would actually lead to widespread agnosticism about the events routinely recorded in world history textbooks. The analogy from the world of American jurisprudence points to the better method: inno-

---

81. Including this, as well as offering a good survey and critique of most of the other criteria, is René Latourelle, *Finding Jesus through the Gospels: History and Hermeneutics*, trans. Aloysius Owen (New York: Alba House, 1979 [Fr. orig. 1977]), 215–41.

82. Stewart C. Goetz and Craig L. Blomberg, "The Burden of Proof," *JSNT* 11 (1981): 39–63.

83. Including Hooker, "Christology and Methodology," 485; Barbour, *Traditio-Historical Criticism*, 46.

cent until proven guilty beyond a reasonable doubt. In other words, accept the Gospels for what they claim to be until parts of them can be certifiably rejected.[84] And the issue of miracle is not a reason for wholesale rejection. For example, one ancient source with information about Caesar crossing the Rubicon (famous for being one of the most uncontestable facts of ancient Roman history) includes a miraculous element, which if discarded does not call into question the rest of the account (as parallels that lack the miracle demonstrate).[85]

Ahead of its time during the new quest was a collection of essays by somewhat more conservative German writers on proper methods for discovering the historical Jesus. Ranging widely throughout the Synoptic tradition, Ferdinand Hahn, Karl Kertelge, Fritzleo Lentzen-Deis, Franz Mussner, Rudolf Pesch, and Rudolf Schnackenburg refined the criteria of authenticity, stressed the connection between Jesus's words and deeds that would characterize the third quest (see below, 69–70), highlighted connections between oral and written traditions, tackled both the miracles and the passion of Jesus with particular vigor, and found historically reliable material in many places.[86] In the Spanish-speaking world, José Caba wrote a book integrating a high view of Scripture (and of the Catholic Church) with the new quest and its criteria and offered an excellent discussion of proper historical method throughout.[87] Québécois scholar René Latourelle did much the same for the French-speaking world.[88]

Various other lives of Jesus and related works appeared in the 1970s and 1980s. Not all were self-consciously adopting the methods or philosophy of the new quest, but they could not help having been influenced by it. S. G. F. Brandon and, to a lesser extent, George Buchanan revived Reimarus's thesis about Jesus as a Zealot, but few followed

---

84. Neil J. McEleney, "Authenticating Criteria and Mark 7:1–23," *CBQ* 34 (1972): 446.
85. Paul Merkley, "The Gospels as Historical Testimony," *EvQ* 58 (1986): 328–36.
86. Karl Kertelge, ed., *Rückfrage nach Jesus: Zur Methodik und Bedeutung der Frage nach dem historischen Jesus* (Freiburg: Herder, 1974).
87. José Caba, *De los Evangelios al Jesús histórico: Introducción a la cristología* (Madrid: Biblioteca de Autores Cristianos, 1971).
88. Surveyed and referenced in Latourelle, *Finding Jesus through the Gospels*. Arguably even more important was his later *The Miracles of Jesus and the Theology of Miracles* (New York: Paulist Press, 1988 [Fr. orig. 1986]).

them.[89] The development of liberation theology throughout the 1970s led to numerous theological but few exegetical studies. Two important exceptions were the work by Germans Luise Schottroff and Wolfgang Stegemann on Jesus's favoritism toward the poor, particularly in Luke, and the somewhat more balanced study by Uruguyan Juan Luis Segundo on the liberating role of the historical Jesus throughout the Synoptics.[90]

In Great Britain, Anthony Harvey utilized the concept of historical constraints as limiting how different Jesus could have been from others in his day and saw him fundamentally as a Jewish prophet, perhaps the greatest of all.[91] John Riches, on the other hand, stressed the ways in which he believed Jesus transformed Judaism, especially via his emphasis on enemy love and forgiveness of sinners.[92] The third quest would soon question if its predecessors had a sufficiently variegated picture of first-century Judaism and the extent to which love and forgiveness, even for the unlovely, was already known within it (see below, 82).

Gustav Aulén, a venerable Swede, published *Jesus in Contemporary Historical Research*, when he was ninety-four, and it was more perceptive than many works of younger scholars. His survey of key representatives of the landscape of the new quest can serve as a good summation of this section. Both continuity and discontinuity with his Judaic heritage characterized Jesus; his teachings polarized his listeners, leading to increasing discipleship and loyalty as well as increasing opposition and attack. The already-but-not-yet kingdom and the ethics that flowed from it formed the area of greatest agreement among new questers, while the question of the resurrection remained the most enigmatic. Historical-critical research could declare only that Jesus's

---

89. S. G. F. Brandon, *Jesus and the Zealots: A Study of the Political Factor in Primitive Christianity* (Manchester: Manchester University Press, 1967); George W. Buchanan, *Jesus: The King and His Kingdom* (Macon, GA: Mercer University Press, 1984).

90. Luise Schottroff and Wolfgang Stegemann, *Jesus and the Hope of the Poor*, trans. Matthew J. O'Connell (Maryknoll, NY: Orbis Books, 1986 [Ger. orig. 1978]); Juan L. Segundo, *The Historical Jesus of the Synoptics*, trans. John Drury (Maryknoll, NY: Orbis Books, 1985).

91. A. E. Harvey, *Jesus and the Constraints of History* (London: Duckworth; Philadelphia: Westminster, 1982).

92. John K. Riches, *Jesus and the Transformation of Judaism* (London: Darton, Longman & Todd, 1980).

disciples very early on believed that they had experienced the resurrected Christ. Notwithstanding these limitations, the critics of the quest, whether from fundamentalism or as the heirs of Lessing and Kähler, were entirely wrong on one point. *The quest for the historical Jesus is not superfluous. Rather, it must always remain a central task of the church of Jesus Christ.*[93]

## The Gospel of John

Students of the Fourth Gospel are accustomed to reading that it was the slim volume by Percival Gardner-Smith in 1938 that turned the tide from viewing the Gospel of John as dependent on and supplementary to the Synoptics to seeing it as a largely independent document.[94] That does not mean that scholars changed their minds equally quickly about the historical value of John's Gospel. Most didn't change their minds at all. *Most of those writing lives of Jesus paid scant attention to what was going on in Johannine research, in part because they already "knew" that the Fourth Gospel would be of little or no value for their endeavors.*

For Bousset, as the key representative of the history-of-religions school, the Fourth Gospel was rooted in the soil of Hellenistic mysticism.[95] Klausner mostly wrote it off, noting that the deists had preferred John "because it was more philosophical, contained fewer miracles, and placed more stress on Jesus' religious and ethical teaching than on his messianic claims."[96] This last statement seems backward; it was the Synoptics that focused more on Jesus's ethics. Still, we may forgive Klausner, the Jewish researcher, as the comparative newcomer to historical Jesus study. Klausner's own conclusion was that John's

---

93. See Gustaf Aulén, *Jesus in Contemporary Historical Research*, trans. Ingalill H. Hjelm (Philadelphia: Fortress, 1976 [Swed. orig. 1973]), esp. 157–63.
94. P. Gardner-Smith, *Saint John and the Synoptic Gospels* (Cambridge: Cambridge University Press, 1938).
95. Werner Georg Kümmel, *The New Testament: The History of the Investigation of Its Problems*, trans. S. MacLean Gilmour and Howard C. Kee (Nashville: Abingdon, 1972; London: SCM, 1973), 271.
96. Klausner, *Jesus of Nazareth*, 76.

Gospel was written in the middle of the second century, the product of a milieu in which Christians had no dealings with Jews and were extremely Philonic and philosophical rather than historical, although John may contain "a few historical fragments handed down to the author."[97] Case was open to more continuity between John and the Synoptics, thinking that John merely reflected a significant recasting of the first three Gospels.[98] Maurice Goguel examined the Fourth Gospel in more detail than many, but he nevertheless concluded that it is simply "a collection of independent incidents, selected in order to throw light on various aspects of Christian truth. It is a series of meditations on the Gospel story, set in a framework of narratives relating to John the Baptist and the story of the Passion." Fragments of historical incidents occur here and there.[99]

Herbert Braun, whose Jesus book was very black and white in terms of what in the Gospels was authentic and inauthentic, totally rejected John's historical value. Without any discussion, explanation, or defense, he pontificated, "The man Jesus *cannot* have spoken *both* like the Synoptic *and* like the Johannine Jesus; he did not speak like the Johannine Jesus."[100] Leslie Mitton, who was otherwise positive about a large portion of the Synoptics, opined, "The writer of the fourth gospel is the one who comes nearest to adopting this device, but it is almost certain that he used it quite consciously, ascribing to the historical Jesus what he knew were in fact words of the eternal Christ."[101] By "this device," Mitton meant prophetic words spoken in the early Christian community believed to have been inspired by the Risen Lord from heaven. While one doesn't hear this argument nearly as much today as in the twentieth century, both Bultmann and the new quest regularly accounted for all the "secondary" portions of the Gospels by assuming that early Christian prophets regularly mixed words they believed Jesus had revealed

---

97. Klausner, *Jesus of Nazareth*, 125.
98. Case, *Jesus*, 45.
99. Maurice Goguel, *The Life of Jesus*, trans. Olive Wyon (London: Allen & Unwin, 1933; repr., New York: AMS Press, 1976), 156–57.
100. Herbert Braun, *Jesus of Nazareth: The Man and His Time*, trans. Everett R. Kalin (Philadelphia: Fortress, 1979 [Ger. orig. 1973]), 18.
101. C. Leslie Mitton, *Jesus: The Fact behind the Faith* (Grand Rapids: Eerdmans, 1974), 50.

directly to them with the teachings of the historical Jesus and that the first readers of the Gospels would have understood this and not had a problem with it. Key studies at the end of the period of the new quest would largely refute this concept,[102] but until their appearance many scholars were able to view the alleged ancient practice of adding considerably to the core historical tradition of the Gospels (mostly in the Synoptics) as entirely innocuous, well intentioned, and compatible with Christian faith, and a few continued to do so even later.[103]

*While the almost wholesale rejection of John for historical Jesus research dominated the periods that have been called "no quest" and "new quest," there were always outliers.* William Sanday, in the first decade of the 1900s, mounted a vigorous defense of apostolic authorship, John's desire to supplement the Synoptics, plausible harmonizations of some of the more famous apparent contradictions, and related issues, updating his work first produced more than thirty years earlier.[104] Around the same time, J. Armitage Robinson published a series of lectures that highlighted numerous ways an aged apostle might select, stylize, and paraphrase what the Synoptics had to leave out once Mark had committed to narrating only one final trip to Jerusalem, and once Matthew and Luke had followed suit. Robinson highlighted similarities in most passages in John to key teachings or themes in the Synoptics, while acknowledging the ways the Fourth Evangelist meditated on and recast them. But Robinson insisted that it made no sense for one who highlighted the themes of truth and witness to have "knowingly offered us parable for fact, and . . . recorded with the most vivid and convincing realism scenes of Christ's life which he knew to be historically untrue."[105]

---

102. See esp. David Hill, *New Testament Prophecy* (London: Marshall, Morgan & Scott; Richmond: John Knox, 1979), esp. 160–85. See also James D. G. Dunn, "Prophetic 'I' Sayings and the Jesus Tradition: The Importance of Testing Prophetic Utterances within Early Christianity," *NTS* 24 (1978): 175–98.

103. See esp. M. Eugene Boring, *Sayings of the Risen Jesus: Christian Prophecy in the Synoptic Tradition* (Cambridge: Cambridge University Press, 1982); also, Boring, *The Continuing Voice of Jesus: Christian Prophecy and the Gospel Tradition* (Louisville: Westminster John Knox, 1991).

104. William Sanday, *The Criticism of the Fourth Gospel* (Oxford: Clarendon, 1905); cf. Sanday, *The Authorship and Historical Character of the Fourth Gospel* (London: Macmillan, 1872).

105. J. Armitage Robinson, *The Historical Character of St. John's Gospel* (London: Longmans, Green, 1908), 10. Very similar is E. H. Askwith, *The Historical Value of the Fourth Gospel* (London: Hodder & Stoughton, 1910).

I have already mentioned the works of Zahn and Schlatter as German counterparts (see, respectively, 25–26 and 45–46).

In 1923, Henry Scott Holland's work was posthumously published in a book longer than Robinson's but employing similar methods. Holland stressed even more than Robinson that Mark, and therefore Matthew and Luke to the extent that they followed him and adopted his overall structure, had to be very limited and selective in what they included. It was unthinkable that Jesus, the faithful Jew, would not have traveled to Jerusalem regularly at festival times, especially to avail himself of the advantage of the throngs that were present in order to instruct them. Holland also underlined the Jewish character of John's Gospel more than Robinson did, well in advance of the discoveries at Qumran of the beliefs and practices of the Dead Sea Scrolls' sect and their striking convergence at points with what had been thought to be very Hellenistic philosophy in John's Gospel.[106] In 1930, the prolific commentator Burton Scott Easton was also (cautiously) optimistic about retrievable historical detail from John.[107]

Considerably after Gardner-Smith, Arthur Cayley Headlam remained unconvinced of Johannine independence, continuing to insist that John was supplementing the Synoptics and certainly not superseding them. Sometimes he may even have been correcting them. Much of Headlam's discussion involves very subjective arguments about how various unparalleled episodes and details read like sober history. Problems with paralleled passages often led Headlam to compile and list the similarities between John and the Synoptics, followed by sheer affirmations that the differences are not as problematic as is often assumed.[108] Vincent Taylor asserted with more supporting evidence:

> That [John's] interpretation is legitimate, as compared, say, with the fantastic developments in the Apocryphal Gospels, is shown by three

---

106. H. Scott Holland, *The Fourth Gospel*, ed. Wilfrid J. Richmond (London: John Murray, 1923).

107. Burton Scott Easton, *Christ in the Gospels* (New York: Charles Scribner's Sons, 1930), 57–78.

108. A. C. Headlam, *The Fourth Gospel as History* (Oxford: Blackwell; New York: Macmillan, 1948).

things: (1) our knowledge of the Synoptic sayings with which he so often begins, (2) the many points of contact between the picture of the Johannine Christ and that presented by the Synoptists, and (3) the response his interpretation has evoked throughout the centuries, so that many Christians find themselves peculiarly "at home" with John, while appreciative of the worth of the Synoptics and the Pauline Epistles as a whole. To these considerations we may add the special Johannine traditions . . . such as the tradition concerning a pre-Galilean ministry, the extended treatment given to the Jerusalem ministry, the references to Annas, the data of the Last Supper, and the strong emphasis laid upon the reality of the humanity of Jesus, the divine Word who became flesh. One cannot hesitate to affirm that the Fourth Gospel contributes to a fuller appreciation of Jesus and his teaching than can be gained from the Synoptic Gospels read in isolation.[109]

In 1959, John A. T. Robinson penned a seminal essay titled "The New Look on the Fourth Gospel," a title that others would reuse in the decades ahead.[110] I will reserve comment on this "new look" for later (see below, 179–221). Independently, Angus John Brockhurst Higgins would write a short book on the historicity of the Fourth Gospel, with many of the same arguments as his predecessors.[111] What distinguished these scholars was their willingness to still find significant problems with both John's Gospel and the Synoptics. They were not writing on behalf of a conservative or traditional agenda. Indeed, in several instances, when they found John accurate, they decided the Synoptics had erred. It is unclear how much they knew about the new quest and how much they were intentionally following whatever they knew of it. But there was definitely a greater optimism about the use of John for historical purposes than the "received wisdom" that one so often encountered elsewhere, just as the new quest was willing to mine more of the Synoptics for their lives of Jesus than Bultmann had granted.[112]

---

109. Vincent Taylor, *The Life and Ministry of Jesus* (London: Macmillan, 1954; New York: Abingdon, 1955), 24.
110. John A. T. Robinson, "The New Look on the Fourth Gospel," *TU* 75 (1959): 338–50.
111. A. J. B. Higgins, *The Historicity of the Fourth Gospel* (London: Lutterworth, 1960).
112. By 1969, Harvey K. McArthur could suggest that "perhaps the current trend is to insist that there is more history in John than was believed a generation ago, but scholars continue

Up to this point, all the examples of a more positive view toward John's historical value have been English. But French Jesuit scholar Xavier Léon-Dufour, who elsewhere engaged in clear "new quest" discussion about the criteria of authenticity, compiled a succinct yet thorough catalogue of the kinds of details in John that could be trusted alongside those that probably should be suspected. His conclusions prove balanced: "Two extremes are to be avoided: one must not refuse to accept an event or a speech as historical on the pretext that John alone relates it, and one must not uncritically accept an event or speech simply because it is related in the gospel. The historian who is trying to find out the truth about Jesus of Nazareth must make use of the fourth gospel, but he must see it as a prolongation of the Synoptic tradition."[113]

## Conclusion

There never was a period of "no quest." The quest in Germany was significantly diminished, and questers around the world began to exercise more caution about psychologizing. But lives of Jesus continued to be written aplenty. Factors that substantially slowed the quest in Germany included two world wars and the closing of universities during one or both, the hiatus in cooperative international scholarship, and reduced opportunities for research. More significant even than these factors were the advent of form criticism and the linking of form criticism to Kähler's understanding of the relationship between the historical Jesus and the kerygmatic, biblical Christ by the most influential form critic, Rudolf Bultmann. Even when the new quest revived interest in the historical Jesus in Germany, it was still tinged with anti-Semitism, as even its criteria of authenticity demonstrated. Pride of place among them was the criterion of dissimilarity, which insisted on too much divergence between Jesus and the rest of Judaism. For these and other

---

to be cautious about determining precisely which elements are historical" (introduction to *In Search of the Historical Jesus*, ed. Harvey K. McArthur [New York: Scribner, 1969; London: SPCK, 1970], 10).

113. Xavier Léon-Dufour, *The Gospels and the Jesus of History*, trans. and ed. John McHugh (Paris: Desclée, 1967 [Fr. orig. 1963]), 105.

reasons, the new quest did much better in authenticating and determining the meaning of the sayings of Jesus than it did with understanding the significance of his life as a whole, and especially of his death and resurrection.

The new quest did not end with a blockbuster like the old one had with Schweitzer's review. Neither did anyone announce a "third quest" by using that for part of the title of their work like the new quest had. Nevertheless, the late 1970s and early 1980s introduced what at least merits the label "a new phase in the quest."[114] A. J. M. Wedderburn thinks that the new quest ended when scholars stopped reacting primarily to Bultmann.[115] In any event, by the late 1980s and early 1990s, scholars *were* speaking of a significantly different phase of Jesus research and calling it the "third quest." It is that story that the next three chapters present.

---

114. It is no coincidence that Werner G. Kümmel decided to collect the material from his regular literature reviews for *Theologische Rundschau*, which continued well after 1980, and combine those surveying the historical Jesus literature from the years 1950–80 as a discrete period. See his *Dreißig Jahre Jesusforschung (1950–1980)*, ed. Helmut Merklein (Bonn: Hanstein, 1985).

115. A. J. M. Wedderburn, *Jesus and the Historians* (Tübingen: Mohr Siebeck, 2010), 90–91.

# 3

# Launching the Third Quest with a Jewish Jesus

No one wrote a book announcing that they were starting a third quest for the historical Jesus. But at least by 1988, N. T. Wright was describing its beginnings.[1] The label quickly caught on, and soon most Jesus researchers were claiming the moniker, which eventually reduced its meaning to a chronological one: scholarship on the historical Jesus from the 1980s onward.[2] In fact, the term had come about because *new* trends were developing. Scholars recognized that it *was* legitimate, within clear parameters, to address questions not merely about the *authenticity* of portions of the Gospels but about the aims, purposes, goals, symbols, and "praxis" of Jesus given the likelihood that the broad strokes of the multiply attested parts of the Synoptic Gospels were not too unlike the actual Jesus of history.[3] They realized that it

---

1. Stephen Neill and Tom Wright, *The Interpretation of the New Testament, 1861–1986* (Oxford: Oxford University Press, 1988), 379.
2. See, e.g., the overviews by Maretha Jacobs, "'Historical Jesuses,' Their Movements and The Church," *Neot* 32 (1998): 405–23; John P. Meier, "The Present State of the 'Third Quest' for the Historical Jesus: Loss and Gain," *Bib* 80 (1999): 459–87.
3. For an excellent, later set of reflections on this fact, see Jordan Ryan, "Jesus at the Crossroads of Inference and Imagination: The Relevance of R. G. Collingwood's Philosophy of History for Current Methodological Discussions in Historical Jesus Research," *JSHJ* 13 (2015): 66–89.

was as legitimate and important to study the most probably historical deeds or activities of Jesus and not just his sayings. While they might not always be able to discover what actually happened, many of Jesus's miracles satisfied the authenticity criteria so well that some real events must have occurred that provoked the Gospel writers to pen their miracle narratives as they did. Interdisciplinary dialogue and training allowed Jesus research to make use of the best insights of the social sciences, especially sociology and cultural anthropology, and generate new theories about various portions of Jesus's ministry. Above all, attempts to banish anti-Semitism from Jesus research moved full speed ahead, so that "Jesus the Jew" went from being a shocking book title to a matter-of-fact label. *Interpreting Jesus squarely within his early first-century Palestinian Jewish-Christian milieu and as a keen, law-abiding Jewish holy man of some kind became the major contribution of the third quest.*[4]

As historical overviews of most kinds move increasingly close to the present, the resources available almost always grow exponentially. Historical Jesus study proves no different. We will have to cover more ground, even while being more selective in the studies we survey, since we do not yet have the advantage of a longer period over which to look back in order to see whose writings have stood the test of time. By referring to more lives of Jesus produced during a comparatively short period of time, we minimize the value of continuing a purely chronological survey, especially when fairly contemporaneous works bear no cause-and-effect relationship to one another. Already in the mid-1990s, Ben Witherington created a very helpful taxonomy of third-quest lives of Jesus.[5] In *Jesus and the Gospels*, I borrowed, modified, and supplemented his categories. Recognizing that almost all Jesus books covered both the teachings and the deeds of Jesus, I perceived that most to some degree prioritized either the deeds or the words of Christ. I then assigned ten descriptive labels, many of them from

---

4. See the helpful lists of characteristics in Craig A. Evans, "Assessing Progress in the Third Quest for the Historical Jesus," *JSHJ* 4 (2006): 35–54; Mark A. Powell, "'Things That Matter': Historical Jesus Studies in the New Millennium," *WW* 29 (2009): 121–28.

5. Ben Witherington III, *The Jesus Quest: The Third Search for the Jew of Nazareth* (Downers Grove, IL: InterVarsity, 1995).

Witherington, to the pictures of Jesus that resulted, with five in each major category. Under Jesus's deeds appeared "charismatic holy man," "eschatological prophet," "social reformer," "proactive peacemaker," and "marginalized Messiah." Under teachings were "sociopolitical liberator," "Cynic sage," "oriental guru," "messianic herald of the kingdom," and "incarnation of divine Wisdom."[6] I will reuse some of these labels in this chapter and the next, but not the two overall categories. The more I reflect on how blurry the dividing lines between activities and teachings can be, the less I find this twofold division to be as helpful.

Here, then, I am creating three topical categories in order to arrange the last roughly forty years of Jesus research into three chapters. Chapters 3 and 5 do, however, correspond very broadly to the two twenty-year periods into which 1980–2020 divide (1980–2000 in chap. 3, 2001–20 in chap. 5). Chapter 4 draws from all forty years but traces an approach that flourished the most in the 1990s. The rest of this chapter focuses on studies that intentionally located Jesus clearly on the landscape of the Palestinian Judaism of his day. Chapter 4 highlights what in many respects were throwbacks to the new quest or even to Bultmann, with Greco-Roman backgrounds playing a larger role than they have elsewhere. Chapter 5 focuses on Jesus research from within or at least moving in the directions of Christian orthodoxy, albeit with some interesting and important twists. It also includes some other outliers that defy easy categorization.

## Beginnings: Geza Vermes

Eventually becoming an Oxford don, *Geza Vermes* (1924–2013) was the son of ethnically Jewish parents who had converted to Roman Catholicism, in which religion they raised their son. As a young adult, however, he converted to his ancestral faith.[7] The more he studied Jesus

---

6. Craig L. Blomberg, *Jesus and the Gospels: An Introduction and Survey*, 3rd ed. (Nashville: B&H Academic; London: Inter-Varsity, 2022), 298–306.
7. Geza Vermes, *Jesus the Jew: A Historian's Reading of the Gospels* (London: Collins, 1973; Philadelphia: Fortress, 1981), 17.

of Nazareth, the more he was pained by how most of his Jewish contemporaries had vilified him, which in turn he believed was based on how Christendom had made Jesus into many things that could not be historically justified. *By finding it incomprehensible that staunchly monotheistic Jews could ever have viewed Jesus as deity, including Jesus's first Jewish followers, he sought to develop a historically defensible picture of Jesus that Jews could appreciate and even admire.*[8]

Vermes's first book on Jesus appeared in 1973 and stood out as something of an anomaly when it did. In fact, *Newsweek* magazine ran a story on it largely because of its surprising and controversial title, *Jesus the Jew*! Vermes would go on to pen four more book-length works on Jesus,[9] which (in 20/20 hindsight), if not initiating the third quest, at least primed the pump for those who would begin it. *Vermes took his cues from rabbinic traditions about other first-century charismatic Jewish healers in Israel.* Pride of place went to Hanina ben-Dosa and to Honi, who was given the nicknames of "the Rain-Maker" and "the Circle-Drawer." Both developed reputations for the effectiveness of their prayers in asking God for miracles, Hanina for various kinds of healings and exorcisms, and Honi for drawing a circle in the dirt and promising not to leave it until God answered his prayers for rain. Vermes believed that Jesus had learned how to tap into God's power, as it were, in an even more effective and uniquely helpful way. Combine that with the wisdom of his preaching, and Vermes likened Jesus to a *hasid* or *zaddik*, an especially "holy" or "righteous" man, like others in Judaism but by far the greatest example of this kind of person.[10]

Vermes, for the most part, does not discuss or explicitly employ the various criteria of authenticity developed and refined in the new quest. The Jewishness of Jesus seems to be his primary criterion, undoing the dissimilarity-from-Judaism criterion. That which he can conceive of an early first-century Palestinian Jew in Israel doing or saying, including what we might call Jewish exceptionalism, may well be authentic.

---

8. Geza Vermes, *Jesus and the World of Judaism* (London: SCM, 1983; Philadelphia: Fortress, 1984), 57. This book would be later revised and published as *Jesus in His Jewish Context* (Minneapolis: Fortress; London: SCM, 2003).

9. See notes 8, 13, 15, 19.

10. Vermes, *Jesus the Jew*, 223–24.

That which he cannot so envision cannot be.[11] He vehemently rejects Hengel's picture of numerous aspects of Greco-Roman thought and behavior infiltrating sectors of Jesus's milieu, though without any detailed rejoinder, so that he can proceed as he does.[12] He acknowledges that his appeal to individual teachings of Jesus may seem somewhat haphazard but promises a later book that will justify the choices he has made. In that later book, he stresses not only that a saying must be intelligible to Jesus's original Jewish audience but also that there are three either-or dichotomies that admit of no synthesis of perspectives: (1) either Jesus was a Jewish exclusivist or he was addressing the nations from the outset; (2) either he envisioned the parousia in the lifetime of his disciples or in the distant future; and (3) either he predicted his arrest, crucifixion, and "reported" resurrection or the disciples were taken by surprise by all of them.[13] The commonsense suggestions that, as Paul would later say, the gospel was to the Jew first but also to the Greek, that the parousia was imminent without necessarily being immediate, and that the disciples were stunned that such outrageous predictions did actually come true do not factor in Vermes's discussion in any significant way.

Perhaps the most recurring criticism of Vermes's portrait of Jesus as a holy and righteous miracle worker, teaching and healing his own people, is that it would scarcely have provoked his undeniable end: opposition from and gruesome execution by the religious and political authorities in the land.[14] To this he replies that Jesus simply found himself at the wrong place in the wrong way at the wrong time, and events escalated out of control. Perceptions of worst-case scenarios rather than genuine threats probably fueled the fires of the opposition.[15] While barely conceivable, it is not at all clear that this is the best answer to this question that can be given. As to the clearest example of

---

11. See Hilde Brekke Møller, *The Vermes Quest: The Significance of Geza Vermes for Jesus Research* (London: Bloomsbury T&T Clark, 2017), 47.

12. Vermes, *Jesus and the World of Judaism*, 26.

13. Geza Vermes, *The Authentic Gospel of Jesus* (London: Allen Lane, 2003; New York: Penguin, 2004), 375–89.

14. Vermes, *Jesus and the World of Judaism*, viii.

15. Geza Vermes, *The Religion of Jesus the Jew* (Minneapolis: Fortress, 1993), ix–x.

Jesus's self-understanding in the Gospels, the "Son of man" sayings, for Vermes no authentic "Son of man" saying was ever eschatological. The authentic sayings merely referred to someone who was a human being; "Son of man" was a circumlocution for "I."[16] Continuing research into this title, however, would make Jesus's use of Daniel 7:13 for the key background increasingly unavoidable.[17]

By the end of his life, Vermes was focusing less on the "charismatic holy man" picture of Jesus and more on Jewish backgrounds in general. He apparently recognized, to some degree, the tenuous links with Hanina and Honi because of the late dates of the relevant rabbinic sources, the paucity of detail they provide about these two men, and questions surrounding the historical reliability of the information that does appear. Or at least that was the growing reaction of others.[18] But Vermes rightly sensed that things had shifted with respect to "Jesus the Jew," and he had already written when the new millennium began that "with the arrival of the year 2000 the scene seems to be set for the next stage of the search for and understanding of the genuine Jesus."[19]

One can find enthusiastic support for the specific type of figure Vermes had proposed in works like one by Pierluigi Piovanelli, who factors in classic sociology as well in order to conclude that "the real 'genius' of this Jewish religious leader" consisted of "the social and spiritual empowerment 'beyond expectation' of the poor, the sick, and the sinners (men and women, children and slaves) of Israel." As recently as 2005, then, Piovanelli could predict that "we are only at the beginning of a new fruitful phase in the study of the historical Jesus through the lens of the Weberian charismatic ideal type."[20] Very similar statements, though without the explicitly sociological framework, can be found already coming from Irving Zeitlin, who wrote just after Vermes's

16. Geza Vermes, "The 'Son of Man' Debate," *JSNT* 1 (1978): 19–32.
17. See esp. Larry W. Hurtado and Paul L. Owen, eds., *"Who Is This Son of Man?" The Latest Scholarship on a Puzzling Expression of the Historical Jesus* (London: T&T Clark, 2011).
18. Møller, *Vermes Quest*, 220. Cf. later Eric Eve, "The Miracles of an Eschatological Prophet," *JSHJ* 13 (2015): 131–49, esp. 140–41.
19. Geza Vermes, *The Changing Faces of Jesus* (London: Allen Lane, 2000), 268.
20. Pierluigi Piovanelli, "Jesus' Charismatic Authority: On the Historical Applicability of a Sociological Model," *JAAR* 73 (2005): 423.

triad of most influential works.[21] Marcus Borg's contributions to the quest are reserved for the next chapter, but unlike most who placed Jesus in a sapiential category (as primarily a wise sage), Borg likewise recognized Jesus as one of the few men in history, and perhaps the greatest of them, who had a unique conduit or channel by which he could transfer God's healing power to others.[22] Amanda Witmer would later defend something similar, at least with respect to the exorcisms.[23] In terms of the broader category of Galilean charismatic holy man, one might include Bruce Chilton's *Rabbi Jesus* as well.[24] More recently, the works of André LaCocque and Amy-Jill Levine bear at least some resemblance to the aforementioned studies in terms of making Jesus *very* Jewish and rejecting whatever in the Gospels seems not to be as conventional.[25]

Vermes was hardly the first Jewish scholar to take great interest in Jesus, nor would he be the last.[26] He may have, for his day, been more influential than many others, but that is a fairly subjective assessment. He may have opened the door for others to feel freer to engage in the exercise without having to significantly criticize Jesus at some point.[27] He may have opened the door for others to go further in envisioning a Jesus with a Jewish messianic consciousness or to engage in the study that Christian scholars increasingly pursued with respect to the greater breadth or diversity of forms of monotheism in pre-70 Judaism (see also below, 217–20). Two Jewish scholars who came tantalizingly

---

21. Irving M. Zeitlin, *Jesus and the Judaism of His Time* (Oxford: Blackwell, 1988), esp. 45, 71.

22. Marcus J. Borg, *Jesus, a New Vision: Spirit, Culture, and the Life of Discipleship* (San Francisco: Harper & Row, 1987), 39–75.

23. Amanda Witmer, *Jesus, the Galilean Exorcist: His Exorcisms in Social and Political Context* (London: T&T Clark, 2012).

24. Bruce Chilton, *Rabbi Jesus: An Intimate Biography* (New York: Random House, 2000).

25. André LaCocque, *Jesus the Central Jew: His Times and His People* (Atlanta: SBL Press, 2015); Amy-Jill Levine, *The Misunderstood Jew: The Church and the Scandal of the Jewish Jesus* (New York: HarperOne, 2008).

26. For an overview, see Neta Stahl, ed., *Jesus among the Jews: Representation and Thought* (London: Routledge, 2012). From a little earlier period, cf. Donald A. Hagner, *The Jewish Reclamation of Jesus: An Analysis and Critique of Modern Jewish Study of Jesus* (Grand Rapids: Zondervan, 1984).

27. E.g., Zev Garber, ed., *The Jewish Jesus: Revelation, Reflection, Reclamation* (West Lafayette, IN: Purdue University Press, 2011).

close to affirming orthodox Christian theology within Judaism were David Flusser and Daniel Boyarin.[28] Even more dramatically, *Pinchas Lapide, an ordained Jewish rabbi, acknowledged that the evidence for Jesus's resurrection actually proved strong on purely historical grounds.* Nevertheless, he correctly pointed out that resurrection does not prove messiahship, much less divinity, since many Jews and Christians have believed that all God's people will one day be raised from the dead. And he simply found too much unfulfilled prophecy to countenance Jesus as the Messiah for Jews, whatever Gentiles might make of him. Yet he ended his study with the tantalizing comment that if, when the Messiah did come, it turned out to be Jesus, he wouldn't be entirely surprised![29]

### Jesus's Aims: Ben Meyer

A second key scholar who helped lay the foundations for the third quest is best known simply for one book.[30] *Ben F. Meyer* (1927–95), in his 1979 book *The Aims of Jesus*, provoked considerable conversation because of *his explicit intention to put back on the table what had been considered out of bounds for discussion for some time: a (cautious) delineation of Jesus's conscious goals or objectives in his ministry.*[31] Meyer, an American Roman Catholic scholar who taught for many years in Canada, wrote and demonstrated in detail about the likelihood that Jesus intended to restore or reconstitute the people of Israel. He walks his readers through the preparation by John the Baptist, who heralded both judgment and salvation for Israel, Jesus's proclamation of the reign of God, his "eschatological Torah," his choice of twelve apostles corresponding to the twelve tribes of Israel, his miracles as signs of God's reign, his table fellowship with sinners, his public de-

---

28. David Flusser, *Jesus*, 3rd ed. (Jerusalem: Hebrew University Magnes Press, 2001); Daniel Boyarin, *The Jewish Gospels: The Story of the Jewish Christ* (New York: New Press, 2012).

29. Pinchas Lapide, *The Resurrection of Jesus: A Jewish Perspective* (Minneapolis: Augsburg, 1982); Pinchas Lapide and Ulrich Luz, *Jesus in Two Perspectives: A Jewish-Christian Dialog* (Minneapolis: Augsburg, 1985).

30. Although see also Ben F. Meyer, *Critical Realism and the New Testament* (Allison Park, PA: Pickwick, 1989); Meyer, *Reality and Illusion in New Testament Scholarship: A Primer in Critical Realist Hermeneutics* (Wilmington, DE: Glazier, 1994).

31. Ben F. Meyer, *The Aims of Jesus* (London: SCM, 1979; San Jose: Pickwick, 2002).

bate and formulation of his mission, his entry into Jerusalem, and his temple-clearing actions.

In distinction from many of his predecessors, Meyer mounts a robust argument for the authenticity of the longer version of Peter's confession on the road to Caesarea Philippi in its Matthean form, showing how almost every phrase in Jesus's lengthier words of praise and promise in Matthew 16:16–19 reflects an Aramaic substratum and an Old Testament conceptual background.[32] While Jesus may well not have envisaged the church in all its elaborate institutionalization that Christians would later create, unlike for Loisy (on whom, see above, 6–7), he certainly laid the groundwork for an organized assembly of his followers to outlive him. One could too easily write Meyer off at this point as simply defending his Roman Catholic faith, but his understanding of this passage is still a long way from conventional Catholic "high church" elaboration.

For Meyer, because Jesus envisioned a restored Israel, one must come to grips with the seemingly failed prophecies of his imminent return. Restoration eschatology points to an answer. Jesus is speaking in symbolic mode. Just as most readers of the Gospels can fairly easily understand seeing the fulfillment of the ingathering of the Gentiles in the emergence of the Gentile wing of the church, even though the predicted centripetal mission (the nations flocking to Israel) was replaced with centrifugal mission (the Jewish apostles going to the nations), so also one must see the significant, even if partial, establishment of the kingdom through the church as the symbolic fulfillment of Jesus's coming in the short term, yet with more still to come.[33] At the same time, nothing in Meyer's work suggests that one can speak of Jesus's divinity, at least via historical methods. Jesus may have been a messianic, eschatological prophet, but no more, apart from simple affirmation by faith rather than history. Thus, Meyer's views, positive as so many of them are, come not with some knee-jerk conservative reaction to the excesses of liberalism but within his understanding of the limits of historiography and by a cautious use of the "indices" of historicity

32. Meyer, *Aims of Jesus*, 185–97.
33. Meyer, *Aims of Jesus*, 224–35.

(the expression Meyer prefers to "criteria"), which include discontinuity (with either Judaism or the early church because requiring both at the same time makes Jesus too anomalous), originality, personal idiom, resistive form (to the tendencies of tradition or redaction), multiple attestation, multiform attestation, and Aramaic substratum.[34] Meyer also correctly realizes that these indices can be used only positively to authenticate material and not negatively to dismiss it. Meyer sprinkles isolated references to key texts in John throughout his work, but like so many before him he does not significantly utilize the Fourth Gospel in his reconstruction of Jesus's aims.

Related to the more modest term "index" (as compared with "criterion") is Meyer's adoption of *the philosophical school of epistemology known as critical realism* and articulated in the years leading up to his scholarship particularly by the Canadian Jesuit theologian Bernard Lonergan.[35] Critical realism distinguished itself both from naive realism, which exaggerates the amount of secure knowledge about the past that the historian can attain, and from full-blown skepticism or postmodernism, which unnecessarily minimizes the amount of reasonably probable knowledge of the past that is attainable. A critical-realist position acknowledges that there are many degrees of probability about all the various things that one might want to affirm—in this case, about Jesus—but that there are enough things that can be said with a high enough level of confidence to avoid the amount of skepticism that still typically attached to the first two quests.

N. T. Wright would soon make critical realism far better known through his own series of works on the origins of Christianity,[36] but Meyer and Lonergan had already paved the way. Wright also pursued further Meyer's emphasis on understanding the aims and purposes, symbols and praxis of a person, so that all the individual sayings and deeds of Jesus had a framework into which they could fit. Timo Eskola would later author a narrative theology of the New Testament, unified

---

34. Meyer, *Aims of Jesus*, 85–87.
35. See esp. Bernard J. F. Lonergan, *Method in Theology* (London: Darton, Longman & Todd; New York: Herder & Herder, 1972).
36. See notes 87–89 below.

around the theme of the restoration of Israel.[37] Both he and Meyer would agree that, had the Jewish people been much more positive overall in their response to Jesus, God might well have ushered in a more literal fullness of his kingdom in their midst. But there was sufficient rejection and opposition within Israel to prevent that from happening, so that the church had to flourish as a largely Gentile institution and an alternative form of fulfillment of Jesus's aims and intentions.

### The Blockbuster: E. P. Sanders

No one is yet using the language of "the third quest" in 1985. Within no more than three years, people begin to do so. What happened in between? *E. P. Sanders* (1937–), who would teach at Oxford, McGill, and Duke Universities over an illustrious career, wrote a book titled *Jesus and Judaism*.[38] He did not speak of starting any new quest, but he built on patterns of scholarship perceivable in Vermes, Meyer, and others, and especially on his own previous research into Judaism *to further solidify the case for seeing Jesus as an eschatological prophet with hints of messiahship*. This bore perhaps the closest resemblance to Albert Schweitzer's Jesus in eighty years. But scholars had learned so much more about ancient Judaism in that period. Like Meyer, Sanders adopted restorationist eschatology as the appropriate conceptual framework for the historical Jesus. But he put forward several distinctive and controversial theses within this rubric that are still being discussed.

Sanders's work on Paul eight years earlier was even more of a blockbuster and widely considered as the catalyst for what has come to be called the "new perspective on Paul,"[39] although it probably should have been called the "new perspective on first-century Judaism." After a thorough survey of many ancient Jewish sources, Sanders became

---

37. Timo Eskola, *A Narrative Theology of the New Testament: Exploring the Metanarrative of Exile and Restoration* (Tübingen: Mohr Siebeck, 2015).
38. E. P. Sanders, *Jesus and Judaism* (Philadelphia: Fortress; London: SCM, 1985). See also Sanders, *The Historical Figure of Jesus* (London: Allen Lane; New York: Penguin, 1993).
39. E. P. Sanders, *Paul and Palestinian Judaism: A Comparison of Patterns of Religion* (Philadelphia: Fortress; London: SCM, 1977). For the story of the perspective, see James D. G. Dunn, *The New Perspective on Paul* (Tübingen: Mohr Siebeck, 2005; Grand Rapids: Eerdmans, 2008), esp. 1–97.

convinced that most Jews in Paul's (and Jesus's) world did not obey the law to "get saved" but to "stay saved" (to intentionally use anachronistic Christian terminology).[40] Children born into practicing Jewish families were raised as part of God's covenant people, affirmed their own membership in that elect group, and thus were already "in." But prolonged neglect, unrepentant disobedience, or willful apostasy could remove one from the covenant. There does not seem to have been anything like the Calvinist understanding of "the perseverance of the saints" (popularly called "eternal security") in ancient Judaism. Sanders believed, as a result, that the main dividing point between Paul and first-century Judaism was not over soteriology but over Christology—the identification of Jesus as the Messiah and our participation in him when we make him Lord.[41]

To the extent that Jesus even gave hints of a messianic self-consciousness, this would be a key point of division between Jesus and his other Jewish contemporaries as well. But the main points Sanders develops in his books on Jesus move in somewhat different directions. To begin with, one cannot overestimate the significance of the incident of Jesus clearing the temple for his "run-in" with the religious authorities. It was hardly a mere protest against corruption in God's house, but rather a symbolic announcement of his coming destruction of the temple (fulfilled in AD 70). At the same time, Jesus looked forward to the re-creation of a new, eschatological temple in a restored, purified Israel.[42] Sanders agreed with many of the points Meyer made about restoration but went beyond him at this juncture. For Sanders, Jesus's confrontation was largely with the Saducean leaders of Israel in Judea. The repeated Gospel portraits of Jesus's clashes with the Pharisees are overblown. Even if he disagreed with some halakah (the "traditions of the ancestors" that were not part of the written Torah), his agreement with and practice of the Mosaic law would have prevented disagreement on other matters from being as divisive as the Gospels claim.[43]

40. Sanders, *Paul and Palestinian Judaism*, 543–46.
41. Sanders, *Paul and Palestinian Judaism*, 447.
42. Sanders, *Jesus and Judaism*, 61–90.
43. Sanders, *Jesus and Judaism*, 245–69.

Sanders also stirred up considerable controversy by denying that Jesus called all individual sinners to repentance. Despite its use as a headline over Jesus's teaching ("Repent, for the kingdom of heaven has come near" [Matt. 4:17]), we see almost no examples of Jesus interacting with *individuals* and repeating those words. What was scandalous and *would* have led to fallout with Jewish leaders of all kinds was Jesus's willingness not merely to associate with the most outcast and the most notoriously wicked in his society ("sinner" can't be limited just to the first category),[44] but to do so and even to accept them at some level into his community without explicitly calling them to repentance.[45] Yet Sanders equivocates somewhat on this concept, so it has been hard to pin down exactly where he stands on it. Unlike some others who have highly stressed Jesus's Jewishness, though, he does imagine that Jesus could have conceived of a ministry to the Gentiles.[46]

At the end of his study, Sanders offers an exemplary taxonomy. Instead of just speaking of authentic and inauthentic material, he offers a list of statements about the historical Jesus that he deems "certain or virtually certain," "highly probable," "probable," "possible," "conceivable," and "incredible." What is exemplary is not necessarily what he puts in each category but the fact that he has so many gradations of probability, exactly as we should expect from a *historian*. In his first category appear the fact that Jesus shared the worldview of "Jewish restoration eschatology," that he began under John the Baptist, called twelve disciples, and expected a new (or at least) renewed temple and a coming eschatological era. He proclaimed God's kingdom, including its arrival among the wicked, did not explicitly oppose the law, and looked for the kingdom's establishment not by armed force but by God's miraculous intervention. It is highly probable that the kingdom he expected would have leaders (like this world's kingdoms do), the twelve tribes, and a functioning temple. Jesus's disciples regarded him as a king, and he accepted that designation, either implicitly or explicitly. It is probable that "he thought that the wicked who accepted his message would share

44. Sanders, *Jesus and Judaism*, 174–99.
45. Sanders, *Jesus and Judaism*, 200–208.
46. Sanders, *Jesus and Judaism*, 212–21.

in the kingdom even though they did not do the things customary in Judaism for the atonement of sin."[47] It is probable, too, that he did not emphasize the national character of the kingdom (contrast Vermes), since that had been the work allotted to John the Baptist. "Kingdom" language was multivalent, depending on Jesus's context.

It is possible that Jesus spoke about the kingdom in the visionary language of the Olivet Discourse (Mark 13 pars.) or as already present or both. It is conceivable that he envisioned that kingdom already present in his words and deeds, that he gave his death "martyrological significance," and that he identified himself with a "cosmic" Son of man. On the other hand, given Sanders's study of Judaism in detail, it is not credible that he was one of the *rare* Jews in his day who believed in "love, mercy, grace, repentance and the forgiveness of sin," that Jews in general or Pharisees in particular would kill people committed to such virtues, or that because of his ministry Jews' faith in their own divine election was somehow shaken to its core and Jewish religion destroyed.[48] Sanders also wants to forestall criticism that he falls victim to what others think Schweitzer tarnished his predecessors with: reconstructing Jesus in his (i.e., Sanders's) own image. Sanders explains, "I am a liberal, modern, secularized Protestant, brought up in a church dominated by low christology and the social gospel. I am proud of the things that that religious tradition stands for. I am not bold enough, however, to suppose that Jesus came to establish it, or that he died for the sake of its principles."[49]

Just about every detail of Sanders's picture of Jesus has been alternately commended or criticized by someone. It is hard to argue that any New Testament scholar in the world had more of an influence on the guild between the late 1970s and the beginning of the 1990s than he did, given his expertise and multiple writings in Jewish backgrounds, historical Jesus study, and Pauline research.[50] In the mid-1980s, David

---

47. Sanders, *Jesus and Judaism*, 326.
48. Sanders, *Jesus and Judaism*, 326–27.
49. Sanders, *Jesus and Judaism*, 334.
50. See also esp. E. P. Sanders, *Paul, the Law, and the Jewish People* (Philadelphia: Fortress, 1983); Sanders, *Jewish Law from Jesus to the Mishnah* (London: SCM; Philadelphia: Trinity

Wenham once summarized the two major endeavors of New Testament research at the time as "Jesus and Judaism" and "Paul and the Law,"[51] and both had burgeoned to the extent that they had precisely because of Sanders's work. In another context, one might proceed topic by topic, discussing the merits and influence of each of his major theses about the historical Jesus. Suffice it for our purposes to observe that one can no longer simply summarize first-century Judaism as people did before Sanders, even if one decides that he swung the pendulum too far away from the classic legalism that can be shown to have penetrated at least some first-century Jewish circles.[52] One cannot diminish the role of the temple clearing as the final catalyst for crucifying Jesus, even if one brings other factors into the mix more than Sanders did. One can no longer say that the "sinners" in Jesus's world were just the ʿam-hāʾāreṣ ("people of the land," untutored in the finer points of law keeping); at the very least they included the notorious and unrepentant morally wicked.[53] One can no longer convincingly claim that the Pharisees were Jesus's major antagonists, at least not in Jerusalem at the time of the crucifixion, even if one thinks that Jesus did have a few major spats with them, especially in Galilee. And it is difficult to deny the eschatological, prophetic, and even messianic dimension of Jesus's ministry, even if one would want to add other pieces into the puzzle of his identity (see chap. 5). The wording of this last statement is deliberately changed from "one can no longer" to "it is difficult to deny," because in the next chapter we will see a significant swath of scholarship that did deny precisely these things. But they did so very unconvincingly.

---

Press International, 1990); Sanders, *Judaism: Practice and Belief, 63 BCE–66 CE* (London: SCM; Philadelphia: Trinity Press International, 1992).

51. David Wenham, in the New Testament Study Group, Tyndale Fellowship Annual Conference, Cambridge, July 1986.

52. See, e.g., Dale C. Allison Jr., "Jesus and the Covenant: A Response to E. P. Sanders," *JSNT* 29 (1987): 57–78.

53. An important balancing approach on the topic of repentance is provided by Bruce D. Chilton, "Jesus and the Repentance of E. P. Sanders," *TynBul* 39 (1988): 1–18. For an excellent later synthesis of pros and cons of Sanders's perspective, see Mark A. Powell, "Was Jesus a Friend of Unrepentant Sinners? A Fresh Appraisal of Sanders's Controversial Proposal," *JSHJ* 7 (2009): 286–310.

## Other Key Supporters of Jesus the Eschatological Prophet

Even if Sanders's distinctive form of the "Jesus as eschatological prophet" thesis provoked lively debate, the overall category may be the most widely utilized in the guild today, especially when one is allowed to combine it with some form of messianic self-consciousness. But not all have taken that additional step. Three who did not, but who were still indebted to Sanders, as to Schweitzer well before him, stand out from the crowd. All three published their seminal historical Jesus works during less than a three-year period at the very end of the twentieth century.

### *Jesus the Ascetic and Millenarian Prophet: Dale Allison*

An important part of the motivation for Allison's *Jesus of Nazareth: Millenarian Prophet*[54] was to rebut the work of Dominic Crossan and related scholarship linked to the new-quest throwback that we will review in chapter 4, so we will have occasion to return to Allison. Here, however, the focus is on his positive alternative: Jesus as the type of prophet who announces the end of the world and the coming of a new age that is significantly different from this current age. Like Meyer, *Dale C. Allison Jr.* (1955–), who taught for many years at Pittsburgh Seminary but more recently has been at Princeton, is looking for an entire "paradigm" or "model" to account for the major emphases on Jesus in the Synoptic tradition. He observes that the following themes and motifs pervade Matthew, Mark, and Luke, form a coherent whole, and to some degree stand or fall together (and he meticulously documents all the main places they occur):

1. The kingdom of God
2. Future reward
3. Future judgment
4. Suffering/persecution for the saints
5. Victory over evil powers
6. A sense that something new is here or at hand

---

54. Dale C. Allison, *Jesus of Nazareth: Millenarian Prophet* (Minneapolis: Fortress, 1998).

7. The importance of John the Baptist
8. Reference to "the Son of man"
9. God as Father
10. Loving/serving/forgiving others
11. Special regard for the unfortunate
12. Intention as what matters most
13. Hostility to wealth
14. Extraordinary requests/difficult demands
15. Conflict with religious authorities
16. Disciples as students and helpers
17. Jesus as miracle worker[55]

Even without the application of any criteria of authenticity, the sheer frequency of references to these features, along with their coherence within a model of Jesus as "millenarian prophet," makes that model a prima facie hypothesis about Jesus's identity worth testing. Formal literary features or rhetorical strategies further develop the picture:

1. Parables
2. Antithetical parallelism
3. Rhetorical questions
4. Prefatory "amen"
5. The divine passive
6. Exaggeration/hyperbole
7. Aphoristic formulation
8. The unexpected or seemingly paradoxical[56]

Allison next develops five "indices" (following Meyer's lead with the label) to authenticate "individual complexes and topics": (1) if it illuminates or is illuminated by the hypothesis of Jesus as eschatological prophet; (2) if the early church seemed to struggle with it or tried to domesticate it (akin to the criterion of embarrassment); (3) if it is difficult to imagine it emerging in early Christianity (cf. one of the two prongs of dissimilarity); (4) if it contains one or more of the

55. Allison, *Jesus of Nazareth*, 46–48.
56. Allison, *Jesus of Nazareth*, 49–50.

formal features just itemized above; and (5) if it has "inconspicuous or unexpected connections" with other complexes or topics already authenticated (cf. the criterion of coherence).[57] There is necessarily some circular reasoning here, especially with (1), but the frequency of the presence of (2), (3), (4), or (5) in the list of recurring complexes or topics does provide some independent verification of the overall hypothesis.

Allison, like Sanders, stresses that this is not a re-creation of Jesus in his own image. Allison debunks the notion that the expectation of Christ's return was merely myth or metaphor, pointing out that the delay of the parousia would not have been the problem that it was unless the first Christians took it literally, as those whom Allison calls fundamentalists do, even though he dissociates himself from this category of Christian.[58] *He also adds an element not typically found in the "Jesus as eschatological prophet" model: an ascetic tinge.* This is not the asceticism of John the Baptist and certainly not that of some Christians in the history of the Orthodox and Catholic Churches. But he notes Jesus's countercultural disavowal of marriage personally in favor of the celibate life and his prohibitions against divorce for the sake of easy remarriage, both of which can lead to the complete or partial renunciation of the expression of sexual desire.[59]

### *Jesus as the Failed Apocalyptic Prophet: Bart Ehrman*

*Bart D. Ehrman* (1955–), longtime New Testament professor at the University of North Carolina in Chapel Hill, would come to be known in the twenty-first century as a scholar particularly eager to poke holes in conservative portraits of Jesus or approaches to critical method.[60] As a result, many atheists were shocked to see his book on the existence of Jesus appear in 2012, which robustly defended how much we can know about this first-century Jew and deriding those who would

---

57. Allison, *Jesus of Nazareth*, 52–54.
58. Allison, *Jesus of Nazareth*, 65.
59. Allison, *Jesus of Nazareth*, 175–210.
60. Particularly beginning with Bart D. Ehrman, *Misquoting Jesus: The Story Behind Who Changed the Bible and Why* (San Francisco: HarperSanFrancisco, 2005).

question that such a person ever lived.⁶¹ Had they paid closer attention to his earlier scholarship, they wouldn't have been surprised. In 1999, Ehrman had already published an entire book on Jesus similar to those by Sanders and Allison. *Ehrman prefers the term "apocalyptic prophet" for Jesus, and he also goes further than Sanders or Allison in this direction, by returning to Schweitzer in believing that Jesus thought the Son of man would come within a generation and was proved wrong by the passage of time.*⁶²

Like Allison, Ehrman recognizes a certain ascetic tendency in Jesus, though he does not make as much of it. But he rightly protests that Jesus wasn't particularly concerned to be a preacher of "family values," at least in the ways modern political and religious conservatives have sometimes understood that expression. As Ehrman phrases it, "He urged his followers to abandon their homes and forsake families for the sake of the Kingdom that was soon to arrive." He continues, "[Jesus] didn't encourage people to pursue fulfilling careers, make a good living, and work for a just society for the long haul; for him, there wasn't going to be a long haul. The end of the world as we know it was already at hand." Again, "The Son of Man would soon arrive, bringing condemnation and judgment against those who prospered in this age, but salvation and justice to the poor, downtrodden, and oppressed. People should sacrifice everything for his coming."⁶³ Schweitzer's interim ethic lives again!

## *A Misunderstood Apocalyptic Prophet: Paula Fredriksen*

The third in our triad of offshoots of the works of Schweitzer and Sanders is Paula Fredriksen's *Jesus of Nazareth, King of the Jews: A Jewish Life and the Emergence of Christianity.*⁶⁴ Paula Fredriksen (1951–) taught for much of her career at Boston University. Like Vermes,

---

61. Bart D. Ehrman, *Did Jesus Exist? The Historical Argument for Jesus of Nazareth* (New York: HarperOne, 2012).
62. Bart D. Ehrman, *Jesus: Apocalyptic Prophet of the New Millennium* (Oxford: Oxford University Press, 1999).
63. Ehrman, *Jesus*, 244.
64. Paula Fredriksen, *Jesus of Nazareth, King of the Jews: A Jewish Life and the Emergence of Christianity* (New York: Knopf, 2000).

she was brought up Roman Catholic and converted to Judaism as an adult. Like Schweitzer and Allison, she prefers the term "apocalyptic" to explain Jesus's views about the coming king or messiah. She does not believe that he accepted the ascription of Messiah himself, but his followers very early on linked him to it. She does not emphasize any particularly ascetic streak in Jesus but does highlight what we have not yet seen: a passion for purity. Jesus may have disagreed about halakic purity laws, but he obeyed and promoted those found in the Hebrew Scriptures. Unlike the others surveyed to date in this chapter, she adopts John's three-to-four-year chronology and a handful of other pieces of information from the Fourth Gospel.[65] Not only would a faithful Jew living in Israel make concerted efforts to go to Jerusalem each festival season, but also the Synoptic Gospels hint at his having been there repeatedly. This would explain why Pilate and Caiaphas would have known that Jesus was no true political threat. But the throngs at one fateful Passover time were whipped up into a frenzy over the seeming immediacy of the coming of God's kingdom that Jesus proclaimed, which could have jeopardized the stability of the nation of Israel and invited Roman intervention, so the political and religious leaders were willing to sacrifice Jesus for the preservation of the peace. This also explains how Jesus's disciples could stay and teach in Jerusalem after Jesus's death without being immediately executed as well.

Fredriksen is to be commended for taking a few steps in the direction of integrating the Fourth Gospel into her life of Christ. She still does not see any divine consciousness in Jesus, but she recognizes the need to implement what John Meier would call a criterion of necessary explanation (see below, 158). The distinction between the fate of Jesus and the fate of the apostles is the linchpin for her position.[66] As with almost everyone else in the second and third quests, she sees Jesus's kingdom proclamation as central; there was a combination of present and future dimensions to it; an ethical response was a requirement of its partial arrival and imminent completion; and the urgency of it all, not preservable in today's world, was governed by the presumed *soon*

65. Fredriksen, *Jesus of Nazareth*, 28–34.
66. Fredriksen, *Jesus of Nazareth*, 9.

coming judgment. *A particularly unique feature of Fredriksen's work that merits further elaboration is Jesus's concern for purity, including the purity of the temple—not overthrowing the Jewish purity laws or the temple, but genuine purity within the framework of Torah.*[67]

Other lives of Jesus could be loosely associated with these three, though without as many of the distinctives or quite the incisiveness that Allison, Ehrman, and Fredriksen brought to their works. One thinks particularly of Scot McKnight's very solid study *A New Vision for Israel: Jesus' Teachings in National Context*.[68] McKnight scarcely stops with the category of eschatological prophet, being an evangelical Christian himself. But this is the main thrust of his book, especially in terms of what he believes *historical* research can demonstrate. Interestingly, in more recent years, he has seemed to move more in the direction of a Martin Kähler, believing that historical Jesus studies per se cannot yield anything close enough to the biblical Christ to warrant the effort to engage in the endeavor in the first place.[69] McKnight may not be aware of how helpful his earlier historical Jesus study actually was!

## Jesus the Social Reformer or Proactive Peacemaker

The category of social reformer is a slippery one and could conjure up pictures of the social gospel of old (nineteenth- and early twentieth-century) liberalism. That is not how studies under this heading proceed. Rather, there is a recognition that Jesus's teaching, accompanied by the acclaim he accepted and the community of disciples he was forming, easily proved a threat to Rome. It was not that he called for some kind of armed or violent rebellion against the occupying troops. But in an empire where the Caesars claimed to be the providers of ultimate peace, filled with divine power and prerogatives, saviors of the people and deserving of service and sacrifice, along with worship that at least

---

67. Fredriksen, *Jesus of Nazareth*, 197–214.
68. Scot McKnight, *A New Vision for Israel: Jesus' Teachings in National Context* (Grand Rapids: Eerdmans, 1999).
69. Scot McKnight, "The Jesus We'll Never Know: Why Scholarly Attempts to Discover the 'Real' Jesus Have Failed and Why That's a Good Thing," *CT* 54 (2010): 22–26.

bordered on that which should be reserved for a god, any individual or movement that used similar language and made parallel claims risked being censored by the emperor. More serious persecution could easily result if initial prohibitions of repeating Christian claims or adopting Christian practices were not heeded.[70]

To use language that has been widely repeated in recent years, "If Jesus is Lord, then Caesar is not."[71] To the extent that the community of Jesus's followers, even already during his ministry, modeled a form of love, compassion, and concern for others not readily replicated elsewhere in the Roman Empire, they would have attracted negative attention from the authorities. To the extent that the Sadducee-dominated Sanhedrin wanted to keep the peace with Rome, the Jewish leadership could easily have gotten on board with Rome in wanting to silence Jesus. Various scholars have seen some of Jesus's teaching and deeds as sufficiently provocative to stir up the crowds or even just the Twelve—witness Jesus's cryptic reference to bringing swords in Luke 22:35–38.[72] While a few have seen Jesus as a sociopolitical liberator (see above, 59–60), *more have focused simply on the implicit threats to the social order begun by Jesus's teaching and behavior, demonstrating an alternate, more successful way to bring about what Rome claimed it had already accomplished.* Richard Horsley's numerous works deserve pride of place here,[73] with Warren Carter's a close runner-up, even though neither has written a formal life of Jesus per se.[74] Gerd Theissen and

---

70. For a good survey of "empire criticism" of the New Testament, which reads the texts in light of the potentially covert or at times even overt challenge to Rome that they might present, see Judith A. Diehl, "Anti-Imperial Rhetoric in the New Testament," *CurBR* 10 (2011): 9–52.

71. E.g., Scot McKnight and Joseph B. Modica, eds., *Jesus Is Lord, Caesar Is Not: Evaluating Empire in New Testament Studies* (Downers Grove, IL: IVP Academic, 2013).

72. On which, see I. Howard Marshall, *The Gospel of Luke: A Commentary on the Greek Text*, NIGTC (Grand Rapids: Eerdmans, 1978), 827; David E. Garland, *Luke*, ZECNT (Grand Rapids: Zondervan, 2011), 872.

73. Richard A. Horsley, *Jesus and the Spiral of Violence: Popular Resistance in Roman Palestine* (New York: Harper & Row, 1987; repr., Minneapolis: Fortress, 1993); see also Horsley, *Jesus and Empire: The Kingdom of God and the New World Disorder* (Minneapolis: Fortress, 2003); Horsley, *Jesus in Context: Performance, Power, and People* (Minneapolis: Fortress, 2008).

74. Warren Carter, *Matthew and the Margins: A Sociopolitical and Religious Reading* (Maryknoll, NY: Orbis Books, 2000). Cf. Carter, *Telling Tales about Jesus: An Introduction to the New Testament Gospels* (Minneapolis: Fortress, 2016); Carter, *Jesus and the Empire of God: Reading the Gospels in the Roman Empire* (Eugene, OR: Cascade Books, 2021).

Annette Merz's *The Historical Jesus* is a more proper historical Jesus book, and arguably they belong in this category the most, even though their portrait overlaps with others as well.[75]

Still other studies do not see any significant interaction between Jesus or his followers and Rome at all, even implicitly. But they still sense that he was trying to create a countercultural model of living in community, even while prioritizing pacifism, or at least proactive peacemaking. Glen Stassen, an evangelical ethicist, wrote in this area more than most and crossed over into biblical exegesis with his studies of the Sermon on the Mount and especially the antitheses in Matthew 5:21–48.[76] Stassen stressed that the structure of these six passages that contrast what Jesus's audience has "heard it said of old" with what he now declares to them is actually tripartite. After his contrasting teachings about what to do and what not to do, in five out of six instances Jesus gives examples of how to take proactive action to avoid conflict, confrontation, or hostility. Only the divorce logion is too short to have this third part, but Stassen speculates that 1 Corinthians 7:10–11 may preserve something of that particular "transforming initiative."[77]

Some writers in this category of proactive peacemaking have been explicitly Mennonite or Anabaptist (such as John Howard Yoder and Thomas Yoder Neufeld), in which believers avoid direct political engagement altogether.[78] It is certainly true that Jesus held no official position of any power in his society, nor did he instruct his disciples to aspire to one. But opportunities for an uncredentialed Jew in the early first-century Roman Empire were so limited as to make this observation potentially irrelevant to a discussion of Christian responsibilities in modern democracies. Nevertheless, writers from this perspective certainly bear inclusion along with the various perspectives in Witherington's classification system. Another scholar who probably

---

75. Gerd Theissen and Annette Merz, *The Historical Jesus: A Comprehensive Guide*, trans. John Bowden (Minneapolis: Fortress, 1998).

76. See esp. Glen H. Stassen, "The Fourteen Triads of the Sermon on the Mount (Matthew 5:21–7:12)," *JBL* 122 (2003): 267–308.

77. Stassen, "Fourteen Triads," 277.

78. John H. Yoder, *The Politics of Jesus*, 2nd ed. (Grand Rapids: Eerdmans, 1994); Thomas R. Yoder Neufeld, *Recovering Jesus: The Witness of the New Testament* (Grand Rapids: Brazos, 2007).

merits inclusion here is Etienne Trocmé.[79] Sean Freyne would appear to combine elements of the categories of social reformer and proactive peacemaker.[80]

Richard Horsley has involved the Gospel of John in some creative and significant ways in a coauthored book on Jesus.[81] Warren Carter has written an entire commentary of sorts on John from his "social reformer" perspective but without integrating it into any of his portraits of Jesus[82] (although his scholarship is focused less on the historical Jesus per se and more on highlighting the things about Jesus that promote Horsley's ideological interests). John Howard Yoder refers, however briefly, to eighteen texts in John but to eighty-three in Luke (which is also related to his recognition that Luke is more relevant for politics than John is).[83] Freyne also has eighteen texts in John but fifty-three from Mark.[84] Otherwise, most of our authors who find Jesus akin to a social reformer or a proactive peacemaker continue to focus primarily if not exclusively on the Synoptics.

In so doing, *a key text for several has been the parable of the workers in the vineyard (Matt. 20:1–16)*. The vast majority of church history has understood the landowner to stand for God and the point of the parable to focus on the unexpectedly gracious generosity of the landowner in paying all the laborers as if they had all worked a full day. William Herzog, on the other hand, finds this practice to be so intolerably unfair that he decides that the parable must describe a real-life picture of a corrupt landowner, like many in Jesus's day, designed to outrage his audience and start conversations about how they might counter such practices.[85] Other master-figures in several other parables can then be treated similarly. What is missed, however, is the "from the

---

79. Etienne Trocmé, *Jesus and His Contemporaries*, trans. R. A. Wilson (London: SCM, 1973 [Fr. orig. 1972]) = *Jesus as Seen by His Contemporaries* (Philadelphia: Westminster, 1973).

80. Sean Freyne, *Jesus, a Jewish Galilean: A New Reading of the Jesus Story* (London: T&T Clark, 2004).

81. Richard Horsley and Tom Thatcher, *John, Jesus, and the Renewal of Israel* (Grand Rapids: Eerdmans, 2013).

82. Warren Carter, *John and Empire: Initial Explorations* (London: T&T Clark, 2008).

83. Yoder, *Politics of Jesus*, 253–54.

84. Freyne, *Jesus, a Jewish Galilean*, 202–3.

85. William R. Herzog II, *Parables as Subversive Speech: Jesus as Pedagogue to the Oppressed* (Louisville: Westminster John Knox, 1994), 79–97.

lesser to the greater" dynamic of many of Jesus's parables (cf. explicitly in Luke 18:1–8), along with the fact that no character in any parable is intended to represent God (or anyone else) in *every* aspect, but merely in certain key aspects.[86] Had the landowner equalized the pay so that everyone got one-twelfth of a day's wage, that truly would have been unfair. But to give the first group of workers exactly what was agreed on and everyone else more than they expected is not unjust; it is a demonstration of lavish grace. Unfortunately, those who want God always to be nothing but fair are asking for their own damnation, since no one ever merits enough of God's favor for salvation, at least according to Jesus and his earliest followers.

### End of Exile: N. T. Wright

Like Sanders, N. T. Wright (1948–) stresses that his conclusions do not mesh with where he started, religiously speaking, and that the face of Jesus he sees is "disturbingly unlike" his own.[87] Like Sanders, Wright has been a key player in the new perspective on Paul, as well as in the third quest for the historical Jesus, though he is hardly in lockstep with all of Sanders's positions.[88] Unlike Sanders, Wright subscribes to the historic doctrines of the Christian faith, was the Anglican bishop of Durham rather than just a professor at multiple universities, and has a passion for helping the church worldwide be more obedient to the biblical gospel. Wright's most important (and largest) book on Jesus is titled *Jesus and the Victory of God*. It is the second in a series of large books he is writing, Christian Origins and the Question of God, four volumes of which have appeared to date.[89] The thesis of this Jesus book may perhaps be summarized in the single statement that *Jesus came*

---

86. See Craig L. Blomberg, *Interpreting the Parables*, 2nd ed. (Downers Grove, IL: IVP Academic, 2012), 185–87.
87. N. T. Wright, *Jesus and the Victory of God*, Christian Origins and the Question of God 2 (London: SPCK; Minneapolis: Fortress, 1996), xv.
88. For the fullest expression of his thought on Paul's theology, see N. T. Wright, *Paul and the Faithfulness of God*, 2 vols., Christian Origins and the Question of God 4 (London: SPCK; Minneapolis: Fortress, 2013).
89. N. T. Wright, *The New Testament and the People of God*, Christian Origins and the Question of God 1 (London: SPCK; Minneapolis: Fortress, 1992); Wright, *Jesus and the Victory*

*announcing the end of exile for God's people without a single Roman soldier having left his post among the occupying forces in Israel.*

Wright begins by discussing the highways of historical Jesus research coming from Schweitzer and Wrede, and he clearly prefers the former, at least in terms of a Jesus who promotes the arrival of the eschaton, even if in unexpected form. Wright also defends the importance of historical study and of a critical-realist epistemology (as with Meyer) that can support, even if not ultimately prove, a position of faith.[90] Wright further asks the necessary questions of praxis, story, symbol, and aims. His thesis starts from the conviction that Israel overall still felt itself to be in exile, even among the repatriated Jews no longer in the diaspora, because they were not living in the land in freedom from foreign powers in peace and prosperity. Where each of the leadership groups in Israel gave different assessments of why all the biblical promises to Israel remained unfulfilled, and therefore recommended different strategies to deal with the problem, Jesus simply announced that God had already dealt with it.[91] This required some fundamental redefinitions of key Jewish concepts: God was uniquely involved with Jesus and the Spirit, God's people were coterminous with Jesus's followers, salvation is more spiritual than political, the Messiah must die, and there are two stages to the messianic era to fulfill all of God's promises in him.

Two of the more controversial parts of Wright's presentation of Jesus involved corporate applications of his teachings that are usually taken more individually. For example, Wright saw the parable of the prodigal son as being first about the nation of Israel rather than a wayward person.[92] Related to that question is whether "end of exile" is a large enough theme to be the major point of Jesus's message about the kingdom of God having arrived.[93] Second, and possibly even more

---

*of God*; Wright, *The Resurrection of the Son of God*, Christian Origins and the Question of God 3 (London: SPCK; Minneapolis: Fortress, 2003); Wright, *Paul and the Faithfulness of God*.

90. Wright, *Jesus and the Victory of God*, 55; further articulated and defended in detail in Wright, *New Testament and the People of God*, 52–57.

91. Wright, *Jesus and the Victory of God*, esp. 428–30. For the other Jewish answers to these questions, see Wright, *New Testament and the People of God*, 167–214.

92. Wright, *Jesus and the Victory of God*, 125–31.

93. For a judicious discussion, see Michael F. Bird, "Jesus and the Continuing Exile of Israel in the Writings of N. T. Wright," *JSHJ* 13 (2015): 209–31.

criticized, was Wright's understanding of eschatology. For Wright, all the passages in the Gospels that have traditionally been taken to refer to the parousia refer to Christ's invisible coming in judgment in AD 70 through the Roman destruction of the temple and their decimation of Jerusalem. Wright certainly demonstrates that much of the eschatological or apocalyptic language in the Hebrew prophets did at times refer to national upheavals within the course of history.[94] But not all of Jesus's teachings mirror those prophetic declarations that closely, and Wright doesn't have an explanation for how the doctrine of Christ's second coming emerged almost immediately after Jesus's death and resurrection if he never taught it prior to his crucifixion.[95]

One of the highly distinctive features of Wright's presentation of Jesus is defended at length in an entirely separate volume, *The Resurrection of the Son of God*.[96] Rather than arguing that historians, by definition, cannot weigh in on what actually happened, Wright mounts a vigorous argument for the historicity of the resurrection. While many Jews looked forward to a bodily resurrection (Dan. 12:1–4) and therefore would have assumed that the Messiah, too, would be raised bodily at the end of the age, *what was unprecedented in the Gospels was the resurrection of someone believed to be the Messiah apart from the resurrection of all people.* The apparent inconceivability of such a separation speaks significantly against the invention of the accounts of Jesus's resurrection. Wright also notes how one can trace a messianic self-understanding of Jesus from his reply to the high priest when asked if he is the Messiah (Mark 14:62 pars.) backward through such events as the Last Supper, his question about how the Messiah could

---

94. Wright, *Jesus and the Victory of God*, 202–9; with Jewish backgrounds supplied and discussed in detail in Wright, *New Testament and the People of God*, 280–338.

95. For this and numerous other points of criticism and approval, see Carey C. Newman, ed., *Jesus and the Restoration of Israel: A Critical Assessment of N. T. Wright's "Jesus and the Victory of God"* (Downers Grove, IL: InterVarsity; Carlisle: Paternoster, 1999). On eschatology and the parousia, see esp. the chapter in that volume by Dale C. Allison Jr., "Jesus and the Victory of Apocalyptic," 126–41. For an even more appreciative review that still demurs on Wright's treatment of Jesus's eschatology, see Robert H. Stein, "N. T. Wright's *Jesus and the Victory of God*: A Review Article," *JETS* 44 (2001): 207–18.

96. See note 89 above. Part popularization and part application is the spinoff volume, N. T. Wright, *Surprised by Hope: Rethinking Heaven, the Resurrection, and the Mission of the Church* (New York: HarperOne, 2008; repr., London: SPCK, 2011).

be (merely) David's son (12:35–37 pars.), the parable of the wicked tenants (12:1–10 pars.), the temple incident (11:15–17 pars.), the cursing of the fig tree (11:12–14 pars.), the "triumphal" entry (11:1–11 pars.), Peter's confession on the road to Caesarea Philippi (8:27–30 pars.), his miracle-working and kingdom-teaching throughout his ministry, and finally the heavenly voice at his baptism (1:9–11 pars.).[97] And these are just the main highlights. In other words, it seems probable that Jesus recognized his messianic role already from the start of his public ministry.

## Other Supporters of Jesus the "Messianic Herald of the Kingdom"

Limiting our overview at this point to the first half of the third-quest period (recall above, 71) yields the writings of Leander Keck and Joachim Gnilka as representatives of those who stop short of defending a fully divine Jesus but nevertheless recognize his messianic consciousness at least implicitly.[98] Defending a more orthodox, historic Christian picture but still operating with contemporary historiographical canons are David Seccombe[99] and Edward Meadors. Indeed, Meadors's title is closest to Witherington's (which I have adopted for this section) in that he speaks of "the messianic herald of salvation."[100] Peter Stuhlmacher's and Markus Bockmuehl's comparatively brief studies fall somewhere in between the two pairs of scholars just mentioned, though both are clearly within a broadly conservative camp, and both offer very creative insights at numerous points.[101]

---

97. Wright, *Jesus and the Victory of God*, 489–537.

98. Leander Keck, *Who Is Jesus? History in Perfect Tense* (Columbia: University of South Carolina Press, 2000); Joachim Gnilka, *Jesus of Nazareth: Message and History*, trans. Siegfried S. Schatzmann (Peabody, MA: Hendrickson, 1997 [Ger. orig. 1990]).

99. David Seccombe, *The King of God's Kingdom: The Solution to the Puzzle of Jesus* (Carlisle: Paternoster, 2002).

100. Edward P. Meadors, *Jesus the Messianic Herald of Salvation* (Tübingen: Mohr Siebeck, 1995; Peabody, MA: Hendrickson, 1997).

101. Peter D. Stuhlmacher, *Jesus of Nazareth, Christ of Faith*, trans. Siegfried S. Schatzmann (Peabody, MA: Hendrickson, 1993); Markus Bockmuehl, *This Jesus: Martyr, Lord, Messiah* (Edinburgh: T&T Clark, 1994).

Witherington himself could be assigned to either of the two overarching categories, focusing more on the deeds of Christ in his *Jesus the Seer* and more on his words in his *Jesus the Sage*.[102] He places his view of Jesus within the category of "the incarnation of divine Wisdom," which I will discuss further in chapter 4. But his book *The Christology of Jesus* brings together perhaps the most helpful compendium of *implicitly* christological data in the Synoptics likely to be authentic, most of which are affirmed by many of the writers mentioned above who parallel, to one degree or another, Wright's approach to Jesus.[103] Sigurd Grindheim, more recently, has replicated most of Witherington's points and added a few more to the list.[104] Between them, we may itemize not merely such items as Jesus's use of "Abba" and "Amen," acknowledged already by Käsemann (see above, 40), but Jesus acting as God's final eschatological agent (see, e.g., Mark 8:38 pars.), his repeated references to having been "sent" by God in ways that seem unnatural for a merely human messenger (e.g., Matt. 15:24) or speaking of God as the one who sent him (e.g., Mark 9:37), his parallel language of "I have come to [do]" various heavenly ordained things (e.g., Luke 12:49 par.), his unique authority to forgive sins completely apart from the temple cult and its officiants (see esp. Mark 2:10 pars.), and his use of third-person-singular language to refer to himself, especially in his use of "Son of man," a rhetorical device known as illeism and found in the ancient Near East almost exclusively in the speech of monarchs or deities.[105]

Witherington adds three key features of Jesus's relationships with others that seem hard to explain apart from his having a very exalted view of his own identity. One involves his relation to John the Baptist. What feature of Jesus's self-awareness, for example, could have led him

---

102. Ben Witherington III, *Jesus the Seer: The Progress of Prophecy* (Peabody, MA: Hendrickson, 1999); Witherington, *Jesus the Sage: The Pilgrimage of Wisdom* (Minneapolis: Fortress, 1997).

103. Ben Witherington III, *The Christology of Jesus* (Minneapolis: Fortress, 1990).

104. Sigurd Grindheim, *God's Equal: What Can We Know about Jesus' Self-Understanding in the Synoptic Gospels?* (London: T&T Clark, 2011).

105. Roderick Elledge, *Use of the Third Person for Self-Reference by Jesus and Yahweh: A Study of Illeism in the Bible and Ancient Near Eastern Texts and Its Implications for Christology* (London: Bloomsbury T&T Clark, 2017).

to proclaim, "Truly I tell you, among those born of women there has not risen anyone greater than John the Baptist; yet whoever is least in the kingdom of heaven is greater than he" (Matt. 11:11)? He believes he has the ability and right to pronounce on the relative greatness of everyone who has ever lived, including the greatest human being to date, and then to add that all those associated with him are even greater. Or consider his attitude toward the Mosaic law. Jesus declares that he does not come to abolish it, but neither does he intend to preserve it all unchanged. Instead, he has come to fulfill it (Matt. 5:17–20). The six illustrations of this, which he proceeds immediately to offer, stress the differences from traditional interpretations of the law more than the similarities (vv. 21–48). In certain instances, they even seem difficult to limit to disagreement just with oral halakah but involve the written Torah as well (esp. vv. 33–34, 38–39). Little wonder that the crowds later respond that he spoke with a kind of authority that not even their official religious leaders could match (7:28–29). Finally, his authoritative calling of the twelve apostles (Mark 3:13–19 pars.), like his later sending them out on mission (6:7–13), paralleled by his still later sending of the seventy/seventy-two (Luke 10:1–20), reflects a remarkably high self-estimation as one who commands on behalf of God and communicates the divine will.[106]

A key player in the third quest, whom Witherington includes in his category of those supporting a "marginalized Messiah," is Roman Catholic scholar *John P. Meier* (1942–), who taught for many years at Catholic University of America and then at Notre Dame. Like Wright, he embarked on a huge multivolume project that grew with his research and has now produced five volumes spanning 1991–2016 with at least one more in the works.[107] Unlike any other historical Jesus scholar, Meier creatively envisioned a scenario that would curtail subjectivity at least to a significant degree and produce as much of a "consensus" document as could be possible in the current lay of the land. From the outset, he envisioned a group of scholars—one Catholic, one Protes-

---

106. Witherington, *Christology of Jesus*, 33–143.
107. John P. Meier, *A Marginal Jew: Rethinking the Historical Jesus*, 5 vols. to date (New York: Doubleday, 1991–2001; New Haven: Yale University Press, 2009–16).

tant, one Jewish, and one agnostic—confined to the basement of the Harvard Divinity School library in an "unpapal conclave" and not allowed to emerge until they had produced a consensus document about Jesus of Nazareth based on historical methods alone.[108] Recognizing that none of these hypothetical scholars would be able to say nearly as much collectively as each might want to say on their own, Meier read voluminously about what scholars of all these communities were writing about individual texts and sections of the Gospels, utilized to the best of his ability a consistent application of the standard criteria of authenticity, sifted between primary criteria and secondary indices, added the criterion of necessary explanation (especially with respect to how to account for Jesus's crucifixion), and wrote up his discoveries, with detailed endnotes after each chapter that sometimes significantly exceeded the lengths of the chapters themselves.

Volume 1 also set the stage with considerable prolegomena, including historical methodology, Jesus's cultural backgrounds, the relevant sources (esp. outside of the New Testament) and their relative values, and information about Jesus's birth and early years. Volume 2 devoted detailed study to the beginnings of Jesus's ministry, the life of John the Baptist, and the intersection of the two. It also contained nearly six hundred pages on the miracles of Jesus. While Meier was understandably cautious on authenticating any individual miracle, especially the nature miracles, the overall picture of Jesus as a miracle worker had so much to be said in its favor that to deny the criteria's positive application meant that, to be consistent, one should admit knowing virtually nothing about Jesus at all![109] Volume 3 dealt with Jesus's "companions and competitors," discussing in detail what we can know about the disciples and Jesus's interaction with them, as well as the various Jewish leadership groups and the nature of their varied opposition to Jesus. Like Meyer, Meier saw that one could not simply dismiss all evidence for Jesus having sown the seeds of an *organized* community of followers with at least a rudimentary hierarchy within it.[110] Volume 4 treated in

---

108. Meier, *Marginal Jew*, 1:1–2.
109. Meier, *Marginal Jew*, vol. 2, *Mentor, Message, and Miracles* (1994).
110. Meier, *Marginal Jew*, vol. 3, *Companions and Competitors* (2001).

detail Jesus's ethical teaching around the twin poles of law and love. Whatever else Jesus may have been doing, he was not merely promulgating a new law, nor was it sufficient to say that he entirely reaffirmed the existing law of Moses and challenged only its halakic accretions. Instead, love for God and fellow humans was central; it summarized everything and it redefined everything.[111] In short, even Meier's eclectic and ecumenical "consensus" document was clearly moving in the direction of recognizing an authoritative, messianic nature to Jesus's ministry, after the first four volumes.

Volume 5 surprised the readership that had been following Meier's work over the twenty-five years since its inception. Meier said that his conclusions surprised himself as well. But he was true to his avowed methodology and let the chips fall where they did. Instead of concluding that the parables of Jesus formed the very backbone of his teaching and the most undeniable core of authentic Synoptic tradition, the lack of any multiple attestation for a majority of the full, narrative parables led him to a verdict of *non liquet* ("not clear") for most of the texts.[112] In other words, his hypothetical conclave of five very diverse scholars (he had added a Muslim in vol. 4)[113] simply couldn't summon enough evidence to argue the case for authenticity. This didn't mean that the portion of the Gospels under scrutiny was *inauthentic*; it just meant that there was insufficient evidence to conclude that they were *authentic*. It would appear that his overtly prioritizing multiple attestation necessarily skewed the results, despite the parables satisfying numerous other criteria.[114] With all the christological titles, along with the events leading up to and including Jesus's passion, death, and resurrection still to be discussed, it is not clear where Meier's study will eventually land, even though it had seemed like it was leaning in the direction of a misunderstood Messiah. One hopes he will live long enough to

---

111. Meier, *Marginal Jew*, vol. 4, *Law and Love* (2009).
112. Meier, *Marginal Jew*, vol. 5, *Probing the Authenticity of the Parables* (2016).
113. Meier, *Marginal Jew*, 4:12.
114. See Blomberg, *Interpreting the Parables*. Cf. Klyne R. Snodgrass, "Are the Parables Still the Bedrock of the Jesus Tradition?" *JSHJ* 15 (2017): 131–46; Ruben Zimmermann, "Memory and Jesus' Parables: J. P. Meier's Explosion and the Restoration of the 'Bedrock' of Jesus' Speech," *JSHJ* 16 (2018): 156–72.

complete the project, but at the average rate that volumes have been appearing, it is difficult to know if that is a reasonable hope.

## But Where Is John?

One of the encouraging things about John Meier's work is his willingness to use the Gospel of John and use the identical criteria of authenticity with the Fourth Gospel as with the Synoptics. Of course, that means that much of John, too, must remain *non liquet*, but it also means that some sections merit inclusion with the authentic Synoptic material in legitimate Jesus research.[115] Nevertheless, even more so than in earlier eras, the vast majority of historical Jesus research in the first half of the third quest simply ignored John. It would seem that these questers tacitly agreed with Vermes at the very beginning of this period: "It is obvious to any religiously unbiased reader that if the Fourth Evangelist is right, his forerunners must be mistaken or vice versa."[116] Yet the only examples Vermes gives of these irreconcilable contradictions are the apparent differences between the length of Jesus's ministry and the date of the Passover. He does not mention, much less interact with, the well-known solutions to those two problems. He fails to observe that neither "contradiction," if accepted as such, would strike at the heart of who Jesus was or what he did. And he does not indicate where one might find this hypothetical "religiously unbiased" person! Other scholars acknowledged the potential value of parts of the Fourth Gospel for Jesus research but then proceeded not to utilize them in their own syntheses.[117] We have already noted above (88, 92) a sampling of those who gave it a token nod.

The answer to where John is during this period may in fact be found in the growing number of contributors to the "new look" on the Fourth Gospel (see further, chap. 6). Unfortunately, during this time, historical

---

115. See esp. the Johannine material about overlap between Jesus and John the Baptist and selected parts of certain Johannine miracles, both found in Meier, *Marginal Jew*, vol. 2. Volumes 3–5 do noticeably less with the Fourth Gospel.
116. Vermes, *Changing Faces of Jesus*, 8.
117. See, e.g., Juan L. Segundo, *The Historical Jesus of the Synoptics*, trans. John Drury (Maryknoll, NY: Orbis Books, 1985), 67.

Jesus research and the "new look on John" were two tracks of scholarship that seldom intersected. This would start to change some as the old millennium gave way to the new, but it has not altered the default model nearly enough. Meanwhile, there arose another development that must be discussed, which also produced a flurry of scholarship in the 1980s and 1990s. Because it chronologically coincided with the development of the third quest, many observers and even some of its practitioners simply lumped it together with this third quest. In reality, it had little to do with placing Jesus in a plausible Jewish context, but was either a continuation of the new quest, a throwback to the Bultmannian era, or some combination of the two, with a few new twists. But it garnered more public interest and awareness than any other part of historical Jesus research to date by intentionally courting media attention. This development will form our focus for chapter 4.

## Conclusion

The first twenty years or so of the third quest clearly saw a larger percentage of historical Jesus researchers locate him firmly within his Jewish milieu than at any previous point in the Jesus quests. Of course, one would not expect Jewish scholars, like Vermes, to view him as early Christianity did. Nevertheless, if not Vermes, at least several others, most notably Lapide, Flusser, and Boyarin, did at times move remarkably close to Christian beliefs. E. P. Sanders tried perhaps as hard as anyone to bracket his personal (liberal Christian) beliefs and follow what he saw as purely historical research. In many ways, one could assess his picture of Jesus by agreeing with what he affirmed—an eschatological prophet with possibly a messianic self-understanding—and by rejecting what he denied. The latter would include any serious conflict between Jesus and the Pharisees and Jesus's calling sinners to full repentance. Sanders also found the resurrection out of bounds for historical discussion. Numerous scholars have tweaked or modified Sanders's Jesus while staying within his "eschatological" framework, but sometimes, as with Allison, adding an ascetic twist.

Other investigators saw more of a "social reformer" or even "liberator" role for Jesus of Nazareth. None of them wrote a formal, comprehensive life of Jesus, but all in various ways showed how Jesus's kingdom-teaching and behavior posed an implicit threat to Rome by exposing the impotence of its ultimate claims. This would have been true even if Jesus were a proactive peacemaker, as a few other scholars argued.

N. T. Wright likewise recognized the implicit threat to Rome and, like Sanders, identified a major prophetic role for Jesus's ministry. He believed that too many scholars had mistaken Jesus's apocalyptic language for heavenly intervention and re-creation, when it referred to this-worldly sociopolitical upheavals. Jesus came announcing the end of exile but did not imply the removal of the occupying Roman troops. While his message had political implications—if Jesus was Lord, then Caesar was not—Satan and sin were the more serious opponents from which all people needed freedom. For Wright, Jesus's messianic intentions were inescapable, from the very beginnings of his ministry, as was the historicity of his resurrection. A variety of lives of Jesus produced around the same time or a little later anticipated or retained many features of Wright's portrait, but none captured the fascination of either the guild or the public in the way Wright's had.

John Meier's still-unfinished multivolume historical Jesus project outdoes any rivals by far in the scope of its coverage and the care in its methodology. Where he will end up, if he ever finishes the project, is still somewhat of a mystery, though his "marginal Jew" may well turn out to be a "marginalized Messiah." Intriguing among many things in his painstaking work is his willingness to use and to trust the Fourth Gospel from time to time. Otherwise, the vast majority of the third questers simply stopped even wrestling with John, and they either "decided" that earlier generations were right when they found him too different from the Synoptics to be credible or they realized that strategically they would be fighting an uphill battle if they chose to rely on John at all. Instead, they believed that the Synoptics afforded them an adequate "database" for the points about Jesus they wished to make.

.

# 4

# The Jesus Seminar and Its Kin: A Step Back in Time

The first time I saw a reference to the Jesus Seminar was in a Chicagoland newspaper in the spring of 1979.[1] I was working on my MA thesis in New Testament at Trinity Evangelical Divinity School. The article was short but talked about how *Robert W. Funk* (1926–2005), a University of Montana professor,[2] was hoping to organize a gathering of scholars to meet periodically to discuss the Gospels, section by section, and eventually vote on the likelihood that Jesus said or did the things attributed to him there. I thought that this would make an excellent reference in the opening paragraph of the introduction to my thesis, since I was comparing and contrasting the parables in the Gospel of

---

1. I believe that the article, a quite small one, was in the *Chicago Tribune*. Funk's planning, however, did not produce the kind of gatherings he envisioned until 1985 and the formation of the Westar Institute.

2. Funk was best known in those days for translating and editing Blass and Debrunner's standard Greek grammar: F. Blass and A. Debrunner, *A Greek Grammar of the New Testament and Other Early Christian Literature*, trans. and ed. Robert W. Funk (Chicago: University of Chicago Press, 1961). Specialists in Greek linguistic studies also knew his own offering: Robert W. Funk, *A Beginning-Intermediate Grammar of Hellenistic Greek*, 3 vols. (Missoula, MT: Society of Biblical Literature, 1973).

Thomas with those in the Synoptics and asking questions about their authenticity.[3] Both my first and second readers, however, objected to my use of that article because it was in a newspaper, not an academic source, and the project itself sounded to them like something silly and unlikely to get off the ground.[4] So I reworked my introduction and omitted the reference.

As the 1980s unfolded, however, such newspaper articles became more frequent. Eventually, the group of scholars that Funk convened became known as the Jesus Seminar, and by the 1990s, the results of their extensive, typically semiannual deliberations, were published in works that capitalized on all the media attention they had garnered. By that time, the project had very much established itself as a scholarly force to be reckoned with. But it had not emerged in a vacuum. Even as scholars in the 1980s were beginning the third quest for the historical Jesus based on fitting Jesus better into his Jewish background, seeing him as the culmination of the stream of Israelite prophets—often focusing more on his deeds than his sayings—eschewing the atomistic analysis that evaluated the authenticity of sayings in isolation from their larger contexts, and daring to address questions about his overall aims and intentions, another strand of scholarship was emerging that differed on every one of those topics.

*Instead of focusing on eschatology and apocalyptic, this strand highlighted the sapiential or wisdom-based elements in the Gospels, making Jesus primarily a sage.* This branch of historical Jesus inquiry often looked more to Greco-Roman backgrounds or at least to very Hellenistic Judaism than to Hebraic religion or Jewish backgrounds when it wanted to understand Jesus better. Some turned to Gnostic or other apocryphal "Christian" sources. *The most common depiction of Jesus based on known Greco-Roman religious or philosophical options was as a Cynic*—that school of thought that reveled in questioning established beliefs and morals, living a life of voluntary and sometimes itinerant poverty and beggary, relying on provisions from

---

3. Craig L. Blomberg, "The Tendencies of the Tradition in the Parables of the Gospel of Thomas" (MA thesis, Trinity Evangelical Divinity School, 1979).

4. My thesis supervisor was D. A. Carson and my second reader was Walter L. Liefeld.

others, and in extreme cases delighting in public behavior that most people thought belonged in private.[5] The first major proponent of Jesus as Cynic sage was *Burton L. Mack* (1931–2022), longtime Claremont professor, in his two books on Mark and Q,[6] for him the two earliest written accounts of Jesus and thus the best places to mine for the oldest traditions about him. *Marcus Borg* (1942–2015), who taught at Oregon State University, would combine Jesus the sage with Jesus the charismatic conduit of God's power,[7] while it fell to *John Dominic Crossan* (1934–), an Irish Catholic priest, teaching at DePaul University, to write a major study of Jesus, drawing also on sociological analysis of the first century and the earliest Jesus movement.[8] Not surprisingly, Borg and Crossan had already become cochairs of the Jesus Seminar. Robert Funk would also write a significant book, expanding on the "findings" of the Jesus Seminar before the start of the new millennium.[9] As a teenage fundamentalist pastor-in-training who moved ever further away from his roots,[10] his career was marked by increasing hostility to conservative scholarship.

Because all this was happening even as the studies discussed in chapter 3 were appearing, most observers subsumed these developments

---

5. For an excellent introduction to the ancient Cynic movement and its differences and independence from Christianity, see Marie-Odile Goulet-Cazé, *Cynicism and Christianity in Antiquity*, trans. Christopher R. Smith (Grand Rapids: Eerdmans, 2019).

6. Burton Mack, *A Myth of Innocence: Mark and Christian Origins* (Philadelphia: Fortress, 1988); Mack, *The Lost Gospel: The Book of Q and Christian Origins* (New York: HarperCollins, 1993).

7. Marcus J. Borg, *Jesus, A New Vision: Spirit, Culture, and the Life of Discipleship* (New York: HarperCollins, 1987).

8. John Dominic Crossan, *The Historical Jesus: The Life of a Mediterranean Jewish Peasant* (San Francisco: HarperSanFrancisco, 1991). A popularization of sorts appeared with Crossan, *Jesus: A Revolutionary Biography* (San Francisco: HarperSanFrancisco, 1994).

9. Robert W. Funk, *Honest to Jesus: Jesus for a New Millennium* (San Francisco: HarperSanFrancisco, 1996). Similar works that could have been surveyed in this chapter if this were a longer book include James Breech, *The Silence of Jesus: The Authentic Voice of the Historical Man* (Philadelphia: Fortress, 1983); F. Gerald Downing, *Christ and the Cynics: Jesus and Other Radical Preachers in First-Century Tradition* (Sheffield: JSOT Press, 1988); Stephen J. Patterson, *The God of Jesus: The Historical Jesus and the Search for Meaning* (Harrisburg, PA: Trinity Press International, 1998).

10. For a fuller biography of Funk's life, including this period, see Andrew D. Scrimgeour, "Tracking a Whirlwind: A Biography of Robert W. Funk," in *Evaluating the Legacy of Robert W. Funk: Reforming the Scholarly Model*, ed. Andrew D. Scrimgeour (Atlanta: SBL Press, 2018), 3–24.

under the third quest. They noted the Jesus Seminar's use of interdisciplinary research and the willingness to draw, sometimes heavily, on noncanonical sources, especially Gnostic or Gnostic-like ones, for the pictures of Jesus, and they began to attribute these traits to the third quest overall.[11] A few perceptive analysts, however, recognized that apart from publishing during the same time, these Jesus questers had little in common with the third-quest people introduced earlier. Some suggested that the Mack-Borg-Crossan-Funk trajectory was the natural continuation of the new quest, largely untouched by the distinctives of the real third quest.[12] Others observed that their methods were more of a throwback to the period of Rudolf Bultmann himself, with its atomistic, almost entirely form-critical analyses.[13] This chapter surveys these various developments and critiques the Jesus Seminar's "findings" particularly extensively because of the influence, especially at the popular level, that its work had at the time and, to some degree, still has. It ends by briefly reflecting on the proper place for the Christian apocrypha and on the role of John's Gospel in this throwback quest.

### The Myth of an Innocent Mack?

All the major proponents of Jesus the wise sage (rather than the messianic prophet) wrote multiple books overlapping in time with one another, which fostered mutual influence rather than a linear trajectory of development. *For Burton Mack, the historical Jesus was a Hellenistic Jew who was a dispenser of wisdom, more by means of short, enigmatic teachings and stories than by long discourses or monologues.* He resembled the Cynic sages who often were peripatetic or itinerant

---

11. E.g., John P. Meier, "The Present State of the 'Third Quest' for the Historical Jesus: Loss and Gain," *Bib* 80 (1999): 459–87, esp. 464–66.

12. Richard Hays, "The Corrected Jesus," *First Things* 43 (1994): 46. Closely reminiscent of Bornkamm is J. D. Crossan, "Divine Immediacy and Human Immediacy: Towards a New First Principle in Historical Jesus Research," *Semeia* 44 (1988): 21–40. Here Crossan, however, applies his criterion of immediacy to authenticate select sayings in the Gospel of Thomas.

13. Lane C. McGaughy, "The Search for the Historical Jesus: Why Start with the Sayings?," in *Finding the Historical Jesus: Rules of Evidence*, ed. Bernard B. Scott (Santa Rosa, CA: Polebridge, 2008), 72.

beggars and who sometimes used a common moneybag to store the meager resources that their followers and they had acquired. The wisdom they dispensed was not always solicited, but it was almost always very poignant and countercultural. Approximately half of a typical reconstruction of Q forms the most foundational "database" for the authentic Jesus sayings.[14]

Most of Mack's work, however, focuses on the history of Christian tradition after the earliest period of the historical Jesus. Mack was part of a definable subset of Gospels scholars who were intensely scrutinizing Q, and he wrote at a time when Gospels specialists were trying to reconstruct Q with as much precision as possible, comment on the resulting text, and determine what segment of early Christianity produced and valued it.[15] Reversing the "received wisdom" that if Q were not originally a homogeneous whole, the apocalyptic "half" must have predated the sapiential "half," Mack was arguing for a sapiential original. This left Jesus as a wise sage, but not a dispenser of judgment. Mark then inherited early Q-like material and narrativized his tradition while transforming it with apocalyptic. A later redaction of Q would do the same thing to this collection of Jesus's sayings.[16]

Mack asserts that it is with the innocence of the "myth" of new beginnings that Mark successfully inspired all later versions of the Gospel narrative. Building on Jewish and Christian frustration with Roman occupation and mistreatment, Mark created a foundational myth of Christian origins that justified the destruction of opponents with the violence that they had meted out to others. Mack is particularly interested in challenging, sociologically, the idea that one major predominant event must account for the birth and growth of Christianity and the formation of the Gospels. What if, he asks in essence, several fairly

---

14. Mack, *Lost Gospel*, 114–30. Cf. John S. Kloppenborg, *Q, the Earliest Gospel: An Introduction to the Original Stories and Sayings of Jesus* (Louisville: Westminster John Knox, 2008). For a critique of this stratification, see Dennis Ingolfsland, "Kloppenborg's Stratification of Q and Its Significance for Historical Jesus Studies," *JETS* 46 (2003): 217–32.

15. A significant portion of this research came from the International Q-Project, the findings of which are still being released in the multivolume series *Documenta Q*, ed. Paul Hoffmann et al., 22 vols. (Leuven: Peeters, 1996–).

16. Mack, *Lost Gospel*, 35–38, 41–49. See also F. Gerald Downing, *Cynics and Christian Origins* (Edinburgh: T&T Clark, 1992).

mundane events coalesced and were recounted in different ways orally and/or in writing until Mark created the "myth of innocence" that set everything else in motion?[17]

Of course, this leaves Mark's Gospel as the predominant originating event, so Mack has not escaped his vicious circle. And which is more likely: that a little known, probably Gentile writer with no formal literary or rhetorical training set all the events in motion to establish Christianity solidly, or that a wise Jewish sage (who was perhaps also an apocalyptic, prophetic messiah) did so? If Jesus were a Hellenized philosopher of any kind, we might be able to understand the ascriptions to him (only after his death, presumably) of "Son of God" and "Lord," which communicated in the Gentile world. But "Son of man" would have just sounded like a strange, circuitous way of talking about one's humanity, while "Messiah (Christ)" would have meant next to nothing. Why give him those titles?[18] What is more, there is very little evidence for any Cynic brand of philosopher in Israel, and particularly in Galilee, so who or what would turn someone into a "Jewish Cynic sage" in that part of the empire? One is virtually inventing a nonsensical category, as if someone today were to speak of an orthodox Jewish imam![19] Craig Keener observes that if Jesus was in fact a *Jewish* Cynic, he would be the only one we know of![20] The closest parallel to the Cynics is not found in anything Jesus did but in what he commanded his disciples to do when he sent them out without him, dependent on others to provide them with food. Yet even here the bag for provisions that was the signature possession of the itinerant Cynic is precisely what Jesus told both the Twelve and the seventy(-two) *not* to take (Mark 6:8 pars.; Luke 10:4). It would seem that it is Mack's reconstruction of Christian origins that is largely mythical. Given

17. Mack, *Myth of Innocence*, 353–57.
18. Nicholas Perrin, *Lost in Transmission? What We Can Know about the Words of Jesus* (Nashville: Thomas Nelson, 2007), 72.
19. Martin Hengel and Anna Maria Schwemer declare, "The view that Jesus was taught and 'enlightened' by Cynic itinerant philosophers [in Sepphoris] is too far-fetched. In a predominantly Jewish city Cynic teachers would hardly have found a fruitful sphere of activity, and in Galilean villages they would have encountered only incomprehension, indeed enmity" (*Jesus and Judaism*, trans. Wayne Coppins [Waco: Baylor University Press, 2019], 309).
20. Craig S. Keener, *The Historical Jesus of the Gospels* (Grand Rapids: Eerdmans, 2009), 19.

that Mack knew exactly what he was doing, it is also unlikely to have been innocent.[21]

## Meeting Borg Again for the First Time

Although Marcus Borg was brought up Lutheran, he left the Christian faith for about a decade as a young adult. When he returned, it was in large part due to a very special spiritual experience that he often referred to but, to my knowledge, never described publicly in any detail. He unflinchingly called himself a Christian but typically added that he was not an "exclusivist Christian." By that, he meant that he didn't claim to say that Jesus was the only way to God. Yet for those raised in Christian contexts, it made sense as the best way, and it might actually be the *best* way for everyone—but still not the *only* way.[22] Borg can readily be viewed as a Schleiermacher for the late twentieth and early twenty-first century. Very much convinced that some of the traditional dogmas of Christianity could not be intellectually defended in the modern world, he sought to repackage and preserve the core of the faith for what could have been called today's "cultured despisers" (on Schleiermacher, see above, 4).

We already noted in chapter 3 that part of Borg's picture of Jesus fits in with that of the charismatic holy man. Like Vermes, Borg believed that Jesus had a unique ability to be a conduit of God's power and holiness to others. In the published version of his doctoral dissertation, he dealt at length with the concept of purity and holiness in Judaism and Jesus, developing the concept that Jesus's holiness could be contagious and transmitted to others.[23] Still, the overall thrust of the volume had to do with the implicitly political effect of Jesus's ministry, the social

---

21. For these and related critiques, see esp. Gregory A. Boyd, *Cynic Sage or Son of God? Recovering the Real Jesus in an Age of Revisionist Replies* (Wheaton: Victor Books, 1995; repr., Eugene, OR: Wipf & Stock, 2010).

22. This paragraph is a composite of points I heard Borg make in two public dialogues I had with him, one at the Veritas Forum at Oregon State University in Corvallis in January 1996, and one at the Northwest Regional Evangelical Theological Society meetings at Multnomah College in Portland, Oregon, in February 2011.

23. Marcus J. Borg, *Conflict, Holiness and Politics in the Teaching of Jesus* (Lewiston, NY: Mellen, 1984), esp. 147.

transformation that a consistent outworking of his kingdom vision would create, along with the conflict caused en route.[24] Throughout all of his writings, he stressed a sapiential, largely noneschatological Jesus, strongly denying any apocalyptic significance to Jesus's favorite expression for himself as "Son of man."[25]

In 1987, Borg's *Jesus, A New Vision* cast him fully into the limelight in historical Jesus research. He sets up his book by contrasting his approach with two more common ones: the orthodox picture of Jesus as "the Messiah and the Son of God, the divine savior who was to die for the sins of the world," and the Schweitzerian tradition of the eschatological prophet.[26] What is his third image? Borg divides his book into two main sections corresponding to his answer. Jesus interacts with the Spirit and with culture. The second of these occupies double the space and is divided into double the number of chapters as the first.[27] Jesus's culture was the social world of early first-century Palestine, which he "radically criticized," "warned . . . of the historical consequences of its present path," and looked for "transformation in accord with an alternative vision."[28]

In the late 1980s and early 1990s, the Kellogg's company ran a variety of highly successful advertisements for its newest corn flakes with the slogan "Taste them again for the first time." It was a clever way of saying to people, in essence, "You know our product well, but with what we've added it will be as if you are just discovering them (and you'll find they're better than ever)." Or for adults who had not eaten corn flakes since their childhood, it would be a wonderful rediscovery. Borg (or his publisher) capitalized on that slogan for his 1994 book *Meeting Jesus Again for the First Time*.[29] For those who thought they knew the church's historic views of Jesus, and especially for those who were disenchanted with them, Borg wanted to reintroduce to them the

---

24. Borg, *Conflict, Holiness and Politics*, esp. 247–72.
25. Borg, *Conflict, Holiness and Politics*, esp. 223–37.
26. Borg, *Jesus, A New Vision*, 2–14.
27. Three chapters versus six, and 53 pages versus 113 (Borg, *Jesus, A New Vision*, 23–75, 77–189).
28. Borg, *Jesus, A New Vision*, 15–16.
29. Marcus J. Borg, *Meeting Jesus Again for the First Time: The Historical Jesus and the Heart of Contemporary Faith* (San Francisco: HarperSanFrancisco, 1994).

historical Jesus as he understood him and hopefully rekindle an enthusiasm for both Jesus and Christianity. As in his earlier works, but with a clearer organization of his material, he sums up his understanding of Jesus under four headings: *Jesus was "a spirit person," "a teacher of wisdom," "a social prophet," and "a movement founder."*[30] The diversity of these roles explains why it is hard to categorize Borg, and his composite picture is preferable to any of the others in this chapter because of how much it encompasses.

It seems, nevertheless, that Jesus as teacher of wisdom still wins out as the one of the four portraits that Borg returns to the most. That portrait occupies 50 of the 140 pages of *Meeting Jesus Again* and spans two full chapters, while none of the other three depictions takes up more than one chapter or 25 pages.[31] Not only was Jesus a purveyor of countercultural and subversive wisdom, especially in parables and aphorisms, but he was also in some way the Wisdom of God incarnate.[32] Here Borg comes very close to a more traditional form of Christology, but in rejecting a messianic Jesus he stops just short of its full-orbed form. He rightly stresses that many of the titles for Jesus must be taken as metaphors. Jesus is not a literal sheep when he is called "Lamb of God," he is not a morpheme formed in someone's throat or on their digital screen when he is referred to as the "Word of God," and he is not the biological result of the impregnation of Mary by an embodied heavenly Father with all the accompanying male anatomy when he is named the "Son of God."[33] But that does not make all predications about Jesus *merely* metaphorical, including the resurrection from the dead, as he seems to think.

## The Crossan That Spoke[34]

For many years, John Dominic Crossan was best known for his scholarship on the parables. An influential book called *In Parables: The*

30. Borg, *Meeting Jesus Again*, 30.
31. Borg, *Meeting Jesus Again*, 69–118.
32. "Sophia Become Flesh" (Borg, *Meeting Jesus Again*, 96).
33. Borg, *Meeting Jesus Again*, 118n54.
34. I borrow this play on words from Ben Witherington III, *The Jesus Quest: The Third Search for the Jew of Nazareth* (Downers Grove, IL: InterVarsity, 1995), 64.

*Challenge of the Historical Jesus*, published already in the 1970s, utilized a comparatively short-lived method in biblical scholarship known as structuralism to classify Jesus's parables into three main categories: parables of advent (the dawning of something new), parables of reversal (of the expected destinies of key characters), and parables of action (critical scenarios requiring urgent and resolute response). He then reflected on Jesus's message in light of those categories.[35] Less well-known books and articles continued to study one or more parables, as Crossan applied insights from subsequent poststructuralism, including both reader-response criticism and deconstruction.[36]

In 1988, Crossan surprised many in the scholarly world with a book titled *The Cross That Spoke: The Origins of the Passion Narrative*.[37] The second- or third-century apocryphal Gospel of Peter seemingly fills in gaps in the canonical narratives, including an actual description of the resurrection, in which Jesus and two men flanking him, depicted as angels, emerge from the tomb, with the two men's heads as high as the clouds and Jesus's appearing above the clouds. Behind them, apparently self-propelled, comes the cross. A voice speaks from the cross asking Jesus if, while his body lay entombed, he preached to the dead. He acknowledged that he had done so. Unlike most of the rest of even liberal scholarship, Crossan argued that this "Gospel" (which actually dealt only with Jesus's passion, death, and resurrection) existed in a basic form (though edited later) that predated the canonical passion narratives and was one of their sources. It was comparatively easy, then, for him to support the Jesus Seminar's conviction that the Gospel of Thomas also, whatever its original form, predated the canonical Gospels, perhaps dating to the 50s.[38]

---

35. John Dominic Crossan, *In Parables: The Challenge of the Historical Jesus* (New York: Harper & Row, 1973).

36. John Dominic Crossan, *The Dark Interval: Towards a Theology of Story* (Niles, IL: Argus, 1975); Crossan, *Cliffs of Fall: Paradox and Polyvalence in the Parables of Jesus* (New York: Seabury, 1980).

37. John Dominic Crossan, *The Cross That Spoke: The Origins of the Passion Narrative* (San Francisco: HarperSanFrancisco, 1988).

38. Robert W. Funk, Roy W. Hoover, and the Jesus Seminar, *The Five Gospels: The Search for the Authentic Words of Jesus* (New York: Macmillan, 1993), 18.

All this paved the way for Crossan's most famous and influential book, his large tome on the historical Jesus that first appeared in 1991.[39] In some ways, the most valuable part of the book is the first 200-plus pages, which give a vivid description of the history and sociology of first-century Palestinian Jewish disquiet with Rome.[40] There has been a lively debate about exactly how restless Jews were prior to the tumultuous decade of the 60s, but Crossan at least follows one significant branch of research when he stakes out his positions here (recall above, 59–60). His methodology for determining authentic Jesus material is more idiosyncratic. He depends a lot on the multiple attestation criterion but combines it with relying more heavily on earlier sources than on later ones. Both of those policies are fair enough, until he begins excluding material due to single attestation and dating numerous noncanonical sources a good century earlier than most scholars do, thereby making them independent from the canonical Gospels when they most likely depend on them instead (see below, 128–29).[41]

Thus, Crossan's earliest stratum for Gospel source material, which he dates between AD 30 and 60, are four of Paul's Letters that contain allusions to Jesus's teachings, the first edition of the Gospel of Thomas, the scraps of papyri known as the Egerton Gospel, the Fayyum fragment, the Grenfell and Hunt fragment, the Gospel of the Hebrews, Q, a collection of miracles now embedded in Mark and John, bits of an apocalyptic sermon now embedded in the Didache and Matthew 24, and the "Cross Gospel" underlying the Gospel of Peter, as noted above.[42] His second stratum, which he dates between 60 and 80, includes the Gospel of the Egyptians, the Secret Gospel of Mark (a document

---

39. Crossan, *Historical Jesus*. Crossan would go on to write an equally large volume, *The Birth of Christianity: Discovering What Happened in the Years Immediately after the Execution of Jesus* (San Francisco: HarperSanFrancisco, 1998), but it never became as influential.

40. Crossan, *Historical Jesus*, 1–224. Donald L. Denton Jr. concurs: "Where Crossan is most helpful is in application of sociological and interdisciplinary studies, but it is here he gives us less methodological reflection. Where he gives us more, with his criteria and tables, he applies less consistently and helpfully and the atomism is out of step with contemporary historiography" (*Historiography and Hermeneutics in Jesus Studies: An Examination of the Work of John Dominic Crossan and Ben F. Meyer* [London: T&T Clark, 2004], 77–78).

41. Crossan, *Historical Jesus*, 227–50.

42. Crossan, *Historical Jesus*, 427–29. Even from this first stratum alone, however, the historical Jesus can be shown to be considerably different from Crossan's. See Dennis

all but certainly shown to have been a modern forgery),[43] canonical Mark, Papyrus Oxyrhynchus 840, an expanded edition of the Gospel of Thomas, a collection of Gnostic dialogues, a Signs Gospel underlying John, and Colossians.[44] The third stratum of material, dated to between 80 and 120, includes Matthew, Luke, Revelation, 1 Clement, the Epistle of Barnabas, the Didache, the Shepherd of Hermas, the Epistle of James, the first edition of the Gospel of John, 1 Peter, 1 John, the letter of Ignatius to the Ephesians, and the letter of Polycarp to the Philippians.[45] He proceeds to itemize sources belonging to the years 120–50 as well, by which time he has included all relevant noncanonical sources, with heterodox ones all dated to a period prior to when most scholarship would actually date them.[46]

In reality, this taxonomy is not as stifling as one might imagine. Crossan uses the noncanonical material from time to time but only occasionally without at least some canonical support. Crossan acknowledges that he is "cheating," and on several occasions he includes what is only singly attested when it coheres with other material that is multiply attested.[47] It is more his sociological analysis that puts interesting and controversial spins on aspects from Jesus's life. Crossan envisions Jesus promoting nonviolent revolution in a revolutionary age. His vision for God's kingdom saw small groups of his followers living in countercultural, tightly knit, and loving community, demonstrating to a watching world that Rome did not have the last word on God, peace, and salvation. Like Wright, Crossan would resonate with a Jesus who was implicitly, even if not explicitly, critical of imperial power and authority.

Unlike Wright, Crossan does not see Jesus dying an atoning death as a substitute for humanity's sin, even if he was an exemplary martyr.

---

Ingolfsland, "The Historical Jesus according to John Dominic Crossan's First Strata Sources," *JETS* 45 (2002): 405–14.

43. Francis Watson, "Beyond Suspicion: On the Authorship of the Mar Saba Letter and the Secret Gospel of Mark," *JTS* 61 (2010): 128–70.

44. Crossan, *Historical Jesus*, 429–30.

45. Crossan, *Historical Jesus*, 430–32.

46. Crossan, *Historical Jesus*, 432–34. Hengel and Schwemer (*Jesus and Judaism*, 252) speak of Crossan's "source wizardry" and describe his divisions and dating as taking place "with an almost divinatory gift, paired with historical recklessness."

47. E.g., Crossan, *Historical Jesus*, 256, 346.

The resurrection accounts are pure metaphor for the affirmation that Jesus's vision, power, cause, and community live on. He probably did perform healings and exorcisms that appeared miraculous in his culture, but the more spectacular nature miracles are to be interpreted as parables—fiction that nevertheless teaches theological truth. *Crossan majors on the concept of "open commensality"—joyfully eating and fellowshiping with anyone, apart from the various traditional restrictions that Judaism with its purity laws typically imposed.*[48] Like the others we are surveying in this chapter, Crossan rejects apocalyptic material as a later addition to the Jesus tradition but sees the closest analogies to Jesus in Wisdom literature. Socioeconomically, Jesus was a peasant. "Jesus' Kingdom of nobodies and undesirables in the here and now of this world was surely a radically egalitarian one, and, as such, it rendered sexual and social, political and religious distinctions completely irrelevant and anachronistic."[49] In reality, even imagining, to say nothing of creating, an actual community of Jewish people living under Roman rule as egalitarian in *all* these ways is what is probably anachronistic![50]

Although Crossan does not make it as central to his portrait of Jesus as Mack does, Jesus again emerges as a peasant Jewish Cynic. One of Crossan's most famous and quoted descriptors appears in this context: Jesus's followers were "hippies in a world of Augustan yuppies."[51] While a "young, upwardly mobile" person in the ancient Roman Empire is also something of an anachronistic category, it is true that a small percentage of young adults were able to improve their lot in life, especially if they moved to Rome, and that this small percentage was nevertheless larger than in previous eras.

There is a curious methodological flaw in Crossan's approach that is repeated in Funk as well. The claim is made that legitimate historical Jesus research is done only by those who are willing to label a large number of passages in the Gospels as *inauthentic*.[52] The logic seems

---

48. Crossan, *Historical Jesus*, 332–48.
49. Crossan, *Historical Jesus*, 298.
50. C. H. Talbert, "Political Correctness Invades Jesus Research," *PRS* 21 (1994): 245–52.
51. Crossan, *Historical Jesus*, 421.
52. John Dominic Crossan, "Concluding Reflections: Reflections on a Debate," in *Will the Real Jesus Please Stand Up? A Debate between William Lane Craig and John Dominic Crossan*, ed. Paul Copan (Grand Rapids: Baker, 1998), 154–55.

to be that the more one doubts a historical source, the more likely one has very good reasons for not doubting it when arguing that a certain portion is authentic or historical. But this is not an approach used anywhere else in standard historical research. No one asks historians to demonstrate how much of the *Lives of Caesar* or *The Peloponnesian War* they reject before they will believe them about the parts they find historical. Crossan's students would have revolted and reported him to the administration had he applied this method to any historical essays he might have assigned them to write: if he believed what students wrote in certain places—and gave them good grades—only if they were demonstrably wrong in other major parts of their papers!

There is also a methodological inconsistency in Crossan's use of quite modernist approaches after years of promoting a variety of postmodernist ones. N. T. Wright penned an article-length book review of Crossan's *Historical Jesus* in which he likened Crossan's book to a young woman named Michelle who was trying to come to grips with her identity.[53] She knew that her author had flirted with all the latest versions of postmodernism, with which she had come to agree, only to discover that on her jacket were the words "The first comprehensive determination of who Jesus was, what he did, what he said."[54] That all sounded wholly modern; there was no indeterminacy or ambiguity there. But she realized that publishers often didn't even consult authors when creating book jackets. Still, the more she familiarized herself with her own contents, her own core identity, the more she realized that the book itself read like a very confident and demonstrable summary of the historical Jesus—to be accepted and believed to an extent that no other portrait of Jesus should. Finally, a critically realist suitor, representing Wright's epistemological preference, approached and began to woo her toward a better approach than either the supposed postmodernism of her author or the seeming naive realism of her contents and her jacket.

---

53. N. T. Wright, "Taking the Text with Her Pleasure: A Post-Post-Modernist Response to J. Dominic Crossan, *The Historical Jesus: The Life of a Mediterranean Jewish Peasant* (T & T Clark, Harper San Francisco [sic], 1991) (With Apologies to A. A. Milne, St Paul and James Joyce)," *Theology* 96 (1993): 303–10.

54. Wright, "Taking the Text with Her Pleasure," 304.

Wright's article, first delivered at a conference of the Society of Biblical Literature, is filled with clever word plays, allusions to other individuals and developments in the quests, and a rhetorical flair betraying its origin as an oral presentation, making it almost impossible to summarize adequately. For example, Wright reflects on the irony of the two men's positions in light of the middle names that each of them goes by. He has Michelle in a dream see that "there will be a man called Dominic who will claim that most Jesus material comes from Thomas; and he will be opposed by a man called Thomas who will claim that most Jesus material is Dominical."[55] While offered in good fun, Wright's review may have stung Crossan, for when he later reviewed Wright, he declared, "I find in your book a Jesus, a Judaism, and a God, all empty at the core, and hollow at the heart,"[56] a reaction echoed by almost no one else.

Ben Meyer's review of Crossan was the standard length and genre and was not first delivered orally. But his final detailed paragraph approximates Wright's skill in wordsmithing. Picking up on Crossan's confession that if his views on open commensality were wrong, the entire book would have to be redone, and that Jesus might not have been a Cynic social reformer, Meyer pens the following:

> For my part, I find here little evidence to support this description, but I would not recommend redoing the book. As it stands it is as good as it will ever be. In all these 500 pages of impeccable political correctness there is hardly one badly turned sentence. It is delightfully readable, the pace rapid, the text filled with useful information on recent anthropology, on the ancient world's social, economic, and political systems, on the Cynics, and so on. As historical-Jesus research, it is unsalvageable. Not that a long historical struggle has turned out to have been in vain, for there are no signs here of any such struggle's having taken place. Historical inquiry, with its connotations of a personal wrestling with evidence, is not to be found. There are

---

55. Wright, "Taking the Text with Her Pleasure," 305.
56. J. D. Crossan, "What Victory? What God? A Review Debate with N. T. Wright on *Jesus and the Victory of God*," *SJT* 50 (1997): 358. Wright's reply follows in "Doing Justice to Jesus: A Response to J. D. Crossan: 'What Victory? What God?,'" *SJT* 50 (1997): 259–79.

no recalcitrant data, no agonizing reappraisals. All is aseptic, the data having been freeze-dried, prepackaged, and labelled with literary flair. Instead of an inquiry, what we have here is simply the proposal of a bright idea. But, as Bernard Lonergan used to say, bright ideas are a dime a dozen—establishing which of them are true is what separates the men from the boys.[57]

Apart from rewriting the last clause so that it refers to separating the adults from the children, an important and not just a politically correct updating, it is hard to imagine what else to add.

## The Colorful Jesus Seminar

The first of the two major products of the Jesus Seminar was a book entitled *The Five Gospels: The Search for the Authentic Words of Jesus*, which appeared in 1993.[58] In almost identical format, five years later, the companion volume appeared, called *The Acts of Jesus: The Search for the Authentic Deeds of Jesus*.[59] The books printed a fresh, colloquial translation of the Gospels, passage by passage, in something that was dubbed the "Scholars Version," proceeding in order through Matthew, Mark, Luke, John, and the noncanonical, seemingly Gnostic, Gospel of Thomas. Each clause of each sentence of every text was colored either red, pink, gray, or black. Red meant that Jesus spoke the words or did what was recorded exactly as we have it. Pink meant that some liberties have been taken in narration but it's reasonably close to what Jesus did or said. Gray meant that some substantial liberties have been taken but there is still something left that resembles what he spoke or

---

57. Ben F. Meyer, review of *The Historical Jesus: The Life of a Mediterranean Jewish Peasant*, by John Dominic Crossan, *CBQ* 55 (1993): 576. A book that has not received nearly the attention it deserved, particularly because nothing on the front cover or title page would lead anyone to suspect that it contained contributions by Craig A. Evans, Amy-Jill Levine, Myrick C. Shinall Jr., Stephen J. Patterson, Robert J. Miller, Darrell L. Bock, David Wenham, and me, is Robert B. Stewart, ed., *The Message of Jesus: John Dominic Crossan and Ben Witherington III in Dialogue* (Minneapolis: Fortress, 2013).

58. See note 38 above.

59. Robert W. Funk and the Jesus Seminar, *The Acts of Jesus: The Search for the Authentic Deeds of Jesus* (San Francisco: HarperSanFrancisco, 1998).

accomplished. Black meant that the material did not at all correspond to the historical Jesus's words or deeds.[60]

What made news even in the popular press was that only 18 percent of Jesus's words and 16 percent of his deeds in all five Gospels were colored either red or pink, and that at times a version of a teaching of Jesus in Thomas was preferred to one in the canon.[61] Of the fifteen red sayings, most were pithy proverbs, parables, or aphorisms. Only one saying in Mark was colored red: Jesus's statement about giving to Caesar what was Caesar's and giving to God what was God's (Mark 12:17).[62] Seventy-five sayings were colored pink and about twice that number appeared in gray. All but five verses in John were colored gray or black.

Commentary on the voting, written by Robert Funk, appears below the portion of Scripture printed on each page, explaining the Jesus Seminar's rationale for their decisions. The coloring is based on the average of the scores of the votes cast. So a controversial passage that received half pink votes and half black votes would end up being colored gray. *The upshot is that Jesus turns out to be a "laconic sage," a wise person who spoke little but was well worth listening to when he uttered profound truths in one or a few sentences at a time.*[63]

When the first volume, on the sayings of Jesus, was published, there were seventy-four scholars in the Seminar who had a vote. At one time, the group had numbered over two hundred, but participants were largely self-selected, and many opted out over the years of meeting for a variety of reasons. Conservative scholars tended to leave because they sensed there were not enough of them for their views to significantly affect the results. The seventy-four who remained, in addition to Funk, Borg, and Crossan, included eleven who were leading Gospels scholars. Two of them were, at the time, broadly evangelical (Bruce Chilton and Ramsey Michaels). Approximately another twenty were recognizable

---

60. Funk, Hoover, and the Jesus Seminar, *Five Gospels*, 36–37.
61. E.g., the parable of the mustard seed in Gos. Thom. 20 and the parable of the wicked tenants in Gos. Thom. 65 (both paralleled in the canon), or the parable of the empty jar in Gos. Thom. 97 and the parable of the assassin in Gos. Thom. 98 (both unparalleled elsewhere).
62. Funk, Hoover, and the Jesus Seminar, *Five Gospels*, 102.
63. Funk, Hoover, and the Jesus Seminar, *Five Gospels*, 32.

as experienced New Testament scholars, usually fairly liberal, with a variety of other specializations. About forty were early-career scholars with at most a few publications to their names. Eighteen of those forty had no publications in peer-reviewed sources at that time. Of the seventy-four, only three were women.[64]

Religiously, the largest percentage were liberal Protestants, then liberal Catholics, then agnostics and atheists, and finally two Jewish scholars. Most were professors at universities, colleges, or seminaries. There was one pastor, three businessmen (funders of the Westar Institute, which hosted the scholarly gatherings), and one filmmaker, while three persons remained unidentified. The filmmaker's presence was due to original plans to make a movie about Jesus based solely on the material determined to be authentic, but such a movie never appeared. Almost all were North American scholars; what was particularly telling was that a full thirty-six (nearly half of the entire gathering) had a degree from and/or taught at one of three institutions: Harvard, Claremont, or Vanderbilt, three of the most religiously liberal institutions in the country at the time. Clearly, the Seminar's repeated claims to speak for a consensus of Gospels scholars was wildly exaggerated. Indeed, as we have already observed, the consensus among scholars in the mid-1990s was that the historical Jesus taught an eschatological message, while the Jesus Seminar was trying to *change* that consensus to the view that his message was noneschatological.[65]

Fortunately, the Jesus Seminar was very up front and open about its presuppositions and its methods. In fact, many of their conclusions could be found stated already in their presuppositions, printed and explained in detail in their overlapping but not identical introductions to their two volumes.[66] There are a number of ways one might pre-

---

64. The roster of fellows, with brief biographical information, appears in Funk, Hoover, and the Jesus Seminar, *Five Gospels*, 533–35. The research on the academic contributions of each was done in conjunction with my writing "The Seventy-Four 'Scholars': Who Does the Jesus Seminar Really Speak For?," *ChrRJ* 17, no. 2 (1994): 32–38.

65. See further J. C. Poirier, "On the Use of Consensus in Historical Jesus Studies," *TZ* 56 (2000): 97–107.

66. Funk, Hoover, and the Jesus Seminar, *Five Gospels*, 1–35; Funk and the Jesus Seminar, *Acts of Jesus*, 1–36. This was a key feature of their work that contradicted their professed quest

sent and critique these perspectives, but in keeping with the Seminar's own agenda, perhaps an interesting way of proceeding would be to categorize their viewpoints under four headings as well: those which could be colored red as almost certainly true, pink as probably true, gray as having some measure of truth but also noticeably misleading, and black as simply false.[67]

Under red, I list the following claims of the Jesus Seminar: Mark was written first, and Matthew and Luke adopted or modified his wording at many points. Jesus usually spoke in Aramaic, but the Gospels were written in Greek. There are varying degrees of how literally the Gospel writers quoted people's words, including those of Jesus. Detached objectivity is not a part of the historiographical process, and we can accept, with varying degrees of confidence, red, pink, and gray sayings into our historical Jesus "database." Almost as helpful, or pink, is the reminder that the Gospels are a complex mixture of tradition and redaction,[68] the probability of the Q-hypothesis, and the conviction that John came after the Synoptics and, at least at a literary level, was independent of them.

Gray matter, in the sense that each assumption or conclusion either *might* be true or *could* have a core truth underlying it despite misleading elements to it, includes the belief that the four Gospel writers were not Matthew, Mark, Luke, or John, that none of the Gospels was written before AD 70,[69] that oral tradition was very fluid,[70] that the early church invented material that was only partially based in tradition, that redactional material may be unhistorical,[71] that John is not as historical as the Synoptics,[72] that the supernatural is not a strictly "historical" cause

---

for some measure of objectivity in their method. See further Sean F. Everton, "What Are the Odds? The Jesus Seminar's Quest for Objectivity," *JSHJ* 13 (2015): 24–42.

67. See Blomberg, "Seventy-Four 'Scholars,'" 35–37.

68. This could be colored red, except for the fact that "redaction" for the Jesus Seminar automatically means "unhistorical."

69. These *are* the most common dates outside of evangelical scholarship; earlier ones are by no means required in order to demonstrate the authenticity of the Gospels' record, even if in certain ways they can enhance it.

70. The extent of the fluidity is what is at stake. See further below, 166–73.

71. The issue with both these points is again the way in which material was added and whether it cohered with the core of the passage already established.

72. John is freer in his wording and selection of material; what is debated is if he ever invents things out of whole cloth.

of anything,[73] that Jesus never interpreted his parables allegorically,[74] that he never directly declared who he was,[75] and that the burden of proof rests on each scholar making a case regarding authenticity.[76] In reality, there seem to be more things wrong than right with each of these claims, and space precludes a discussion of each one *ad seriatim*. But even if each one *was* completely true in the sense the Jesus Seminar intended it, the historic picture of Jesus would not *necessarily* be impugned (though it certainly might be).

Claims that must be colored black and rejected nevertheless remain. These include that Jesus more resembles a Cynic sage than any form of Palestinian Jewish figure; Jesus never engaged in extended dialogues or controversies; the Gospel of Thomas should be dated to about AD 50, so that Thomas's forms of paralleled sayings are often earlier or more authentic than their canonical parallels; wisdom material uniformly preceded apocalyptic in the developing tradition; and therefore Jesus is at times more Gnostic than orthodox.

Additional viewpoints never stated in a list of assumptions but repeatedly presented in the commentary on the Jesus Seminar's conclusions can be even more idiosyncratic. I will intersperse my responses with my listing of these claims: (1) According to Funk and company, no teaching is authentic that cannot be separated from its context and still be meaningful. At this point we are back to pure, early form criticism untampered by the next fifty years of scholarship. (2) No teaching can be authentic that is not pithy or parabolic. It could not have been remembered if it were longer, so the claim goes, despite massive disproof from the history of ancient education, rhetorical composition, and delivery.[77] (3) Anything with parallels in "common lore" is

---

73. One can define "historical" in such a way as to make this a truism, but that begs the question of whether appeal to the supernatural can ever be a "legitimate" approach.

74. Much depends on the definition of "allegory" utilized. See, in detail, Craig L. Blomberg, *Interpreting the Parables*, 2nd ed. (Downers Grove, IL: IVP Academic, 2012).

75. One could always be more direct, but the Jesus Seminar's definition of "directly" excludes a lot of material unnecessarily.

76. This viewpoint is widespread, and it is tempting to agree with it. But see above, 58–59.

77. See below, 166–68. See also Craig L. Blomberg, *Jesus and the Gospels: An Introduction and Survey*, 3rd ed. (Nashville: B&H Academic; London: Inter-Varsity, 2022), 132–33, and the literature there cited.

suspect because it might have originated there. So apparently Jesus never agreed with any accepted wisdom in his world. (4) Jesus said nothing to suggest any messianic consciousness; he could never have used "Son of man" as an exalted title (despite its use that way in Dan. 7:13).[78] (5) Jesus never taught about final judgment or God's wrath, since those topics are beneath the kind of enlightened person Jesus had to have been. This is quite the modern, politically correct imposition on a culture in which virtually every religious speaker or writer talked about final judgment at some point.[79]

(6) Jesus never debated anyone, engaged in conflicts or controversies, or compared his teaching with the law. Never mind that all Jewish teachers that we know much about in his world did all those things. (7) Jesus never worked miracles, prophesied, or even talked about his upcoming death. Here is pure antisupernaturalism in its rawest form, combined with a rejection of even the natural human propensity to project into the future, including projecting about one's personal destiny. (8) The current Gospel sequences of pericopes are fairly arbitrary. Not even Bultmann claimed this, and the entire discipline of redaction criticism overwhelmingly disproves this claim. (9) Meanwhile, other ancient sources impinging on the life of Jesus outside the Bible can be trusted implicitly.[80] The double standards applied are breathtaking!

## Jesus in a Funk

Remarkably, Robert W. Funk thought that Christianity was worth preserving but only in a radically revised form. His book *Honest to Jesus: Jesus for a New Millennium* capitalized on the intrigue surrounding the change in the calendar from 1999 to 2000 to narrate his vision for

---

78. See above, 73–74. See also Blomberg, *Jesus and the Gospels*, 638–41, and the literature there cited.

79. See Marius Reiser, *Jesus and Judgment: The Eschatological Proclamation in Its Jewish Context*, trans. Linda M. Maloney (Minneapolis: Fortress, 1997).

80. See further Darrell L. Bock, *The Missing Gospels: Unearthing the Truth behind Alternative Christianities* (Nashville: Nelson, 2006); Philip Jenkins, *Hidden Gospels: How the Search for Jesus Lost Its Way* (Oxford: Oxford University Press, 2001).

a better world.⁸¹ Most of the book is not about the historical Jesus, but about the methods utilized by the Jesus Seminar, with his occasional tweaking, and about what is wrong with much of current Jesus scholarship as well as the current church. Funk makes it clear that he believes his strand of the quest is a continuation of the new quest (or a "renewed quest"), whereas those whom Wright dubs the third questers may grant "the distinction between the historical Jesus and the creedal Christ" but show "no real interest in, or regard for, the Jesus of history beyond historical curiosity."⁸² At first, one might think that Funk is thinking solely of the more conservative wing of the third quest, but his next paragraph contains words that come close to defining the entire third quest that I described in chapter 3. "For third questers," Funk alleges, "there can be no picking and choosing among sayings and acts as a way to determine who Jesus was. Instead, one must present a theory of the whole, set Jesus firmly within first-century Judaism, state what his real aims were, discover why he died, when the church began, and what kind of documents the canonical gospels are." People like this are merely "pretend questers."⁸³ Of course, plenty of third questers ask these more holistic questions even while they separate certain sayings and deeds that are more probably authentic from those they find less so. Recall how Vermes, Meyer, Sanders, and Meier all explicitly did this. Richard Hays's words in this context are sharp but on target with the Jesus Seminar and Funk's trajectory of "findings":

> The depiction of Jesus as a Cynic philosopher with no concern about Israel's destiny, no connection with the concerns and hopes that animated his Jewish contemporaries, no interest in the interpretation of Scripture, and no message of God's coming eschatological judgment is—quite

81. Funk, *Honest to Jesus*, 306.
82. Funk, *Honest to Jesus*, 65. Bernard B. Scott (introduction to Scott, *Finding the Historical Jesus*, 6) would later argue the Jesus Seminar was a part of the third quest, or at least the third phase of the one quest for the historical Jesus, but when he described the characteristics of that third phase, conspicuously absent was anything about placing Jesus firmly into his Jewish milieu, the one feature that virtually everyone else comparing post-1980 historical Jesus scholarship with the new quest mentioned as the key distinguishing feature of the third quest.
83. Funk, *Honest to Jesus*, 64.

simply—an ahistorical fiction, achieved by the surgical removal of Jesus from his Jewish context. The fabrication of a non-Jewish Jesus is one particularly pernicious side effect of the Jesus Seminar's methodology. One would have thought that the tragic events of our [twentieth] century might have warned us to be wary of biblical scholars who deny the Jewishness of Jesus. . . . They are of course free to publish these views; however, their attempt to present these views as "the assured results of critical scholarship" is—one must say it—reprehensible deception.[84]

The historical Jesus, for Funk, was a deeply subversive Jesus if he was anything. In God's "domain," as Funk liked to call the kingdom, "family and tribal circles were greatly modified and enlarged, places and spaces took on new aspects, and seasons underwent drastic revision." In his gospel message, Jesus "was perpetually saying goodbye to the world he inherited." To enact this vision, "the players who populate his stories and aphorisms are at odds with the traditional cast of characters. God's estate was a vortex drawing into its swirling vacuum all the elements of the conventional drama."[85] Jesus was executed primarily by the Romans, with a bit of help from the highest Judean officials. After his execution, his disciples went home. There was no resurrection, only the glimpse of eternity and "what the world is really like," which led later to the formation of small communities of his followers "who organized their memories and convictions, and became a movement."[86] Citing Martin Kähler's century-old dictum that the Gospels are passion narratives with extended introductions, Funk argues that we should reverse that assessment: "The gospels are collections of parables and aphorisms, symbolic deeds and miraculous cures, with a passion appendix."[87]

Funk thus thinks this Jesus was "a secular sage who may have more relevance to the spiritual dimension of society at large than to

---

84. Hays, "Corrected Jesus," 47.
85. Funk, *Honest to Jesus*, 197. Robert J. Myles raises fascinating questions about to what extent numerous recent pictures of a subversive figure are actually the product of a capitalist ideology because they sell well ("The Fetish for a Subversive Jesus," *JSHJ* 14 [2016]: 52–70).
86. Funk, *Honest to Jesus*, 11, 223.
87. Funk, *Honest to Jesus*, 238.

institutionalized religion."⁸⁸ *He was a social deviant who "ate promiscuously with sinners, toll collectors, prostitutes, lepers, and other social misfits and quarantined people during his life." He "made forgiveness reciprocal," "condemned the public practice of piety," and "advocated an unbrokered relationship to God."*⁸⁹ Like Thomas Jefferson, who was one of Funk's heroes, one should (at least metaphorically) cut the miracles out of the Gospels and focus on the timeless truths of Jesus's authentic teachings, which are revolutionary. Unlike Jefferson, Funk is more supportive of undercutting historic Christian convention and morality.⁹⁰ Martin Hengel and Anna Maria Schwemer remark that Funk's work, like that of the Jesus Seminar more generally, "provides a truly progressive, politically correct picture of Jesus. It no longer has much to do with the historical reality."⁹¹

### The Proper Places for the Apocryphal Christian Sources

Not long after the proliferation of nonapocalyptic, sapiential Jesuses at the end of the twentieth century, the world experienced the *Da Vinci Code* phenomenon.⁹² Dan Brown's best-selling fiction, translated into dozens of the world's languages, has created the possibly unprecedented phenomenon of students in universities being taught a "history" of the early Christian movement that never existed. The council of Nicaea in 325, which actually convened to discuss trinitarian theology (with the Nicene Creed as its product), is said to have discussed what books belonged in the New Testament out of as many as seventy gospels alone! The Gospels of Philip and Mary supposedly demonstrate that Jesus had married Mary Magdalene. A Gnostic form of Christianity

---

88. Funk, *Honest to Jesus*, 302.
89. Funk, *Honest to Jesus*, 310–11.
90. Bruce Chilton and Craig A. Evans are fairly scathing in their description of Funk's attacks against anything that smacked of recognizable Christian faith and his heavy-handed leadership of the Seminar to push for results that satisfied his perspective as much as possible ("Jesus Seminar," in *Encyclopedia of the Historical Jesus*, ed. Craig A. Evans [New York: Routledge, 2008], 333–36).
91. Hengel and Schwemer, *Jesus and Judaism*, 195.
92. That is, the remarkable proliferation worldwide in English, and in dozens of translations, of Dan Brown, *The Da Vinci Code: A Novel* (New York: Doubleday, 2003).

allegedly predated orthodoxy. Through it all, Jesus is a purveyor of esoteric wisdom in keeping with the sapiential Jesus that ties the throwback quest together.

Elsewhere I have walked through the most important apocryphal or Gnostic documents for historical Jesus research, or at least that are alleged by some to be the most important ones.[93] Perhaps the key points to repeat here are that the dates assigned to them by both Crossan personally and the Jesus Seminar collectively are highly anomalous and almost certainly a century too early across the board. *While some scholars still cling to the notion that these documents provide independent and significant information about Jesus that is more reliable than canonical information, continued research into each of them is making this notion increasingly less likely.* The Gospel of Thomas remains a key exception to the generally unhelpful nature of this literature for knowing anything about the historical Jesus; for the Jesus Seminar, it was noticeably more valuable for the teachings of Jesus than the Gospel of John![94]

Just as Q defies simple categorization into wisdom or apocalyptic, causing scholars who want it to be one or the other to postulate two stages to its composition (as if the two strands could never cohere in one person's teaching), so also whenever people point out objectionable parts to the Gospel of Thomas, those tend to be assigned to a later stage in its formation (though we have no external evidence that there ever was more than one stage).[95] Classically, we see in Gospel of Thomas 53 what probably would be called anti-Semitism anywhere else it appeared, with the saying attributed to Jesus that if God had intended circumcision for baby boys, they would have emerged from their mothers' wombs already in that state. Even more dramatic is the misogyny (or at least androgyny) implicit in Gospel of Thomas 114 about how women can be saved—if they make themselves male. The proposal of two stages of composition quickly turns to special pleading. If a saying

---

93. Craig L. Blomberg, *The Historical Reliability of the New Testament: Countering the Challenges to Evangelical Christian Beliefs* (Nashville: B&H Academic, 2016), 559–608.

94. Funk, Hoover, and the Jesus Seminar, *Five Gospels*, 549–53.

95. See esp. April D. DeConick, *Recovering the Original Gospel of Thomas: A History of the Gospel and Its Growth* (London: T&T Clark, 2005).

doesn't fit the postulated theology of Thomas, excise it and attribute it to a later stage of redaction, rather than incorporate it and revise the postulated theology.

This is not to say that there may not be the occasional saying in Thomas that is unparalleled in the canon but in some form goes back to Jesus, just as scholars have suggested other authentic *agrapha* (from the Greek for "unwritten," meaning unwritten in the canonical Gospels)—in other apocrypha, quotations in the church fathers from no longer extant documents, Oxyrhynchus papyri, and certain textual variants in canonical passages.[96] Acts 20:35, of course, is the one canonical passage outside the Gospels that demonstrates that other sayings of the preresurrected Jesus not recorded in Matthew, Mark, Luke, or John continued to circulate. But none of these potential additions to our "database" of knowledge of his teachings turns Jesus into any kind of figure not already attested to in the canonical Gospels.[97]

Over the last decade and a half, additional documents potentially bearing on the Jesus of history have come to light. The so-called Gospel of Judas was a document we already knew about from ancient patristic references to it. It is just a rewrite of the last week of Jesus's life, turning Judas into a hero rather than a villain. Someone had to betray Jesus, so the argument goes, so that he would be arrested and crucified. The task is ignominious, but it will be rewarded in the life to come.[98] Even critics like Bart Ehrman are quick to stress that this tells us nothing about first-century events, only the issues pertaining to one heterodox sect in the late second century.[99] The so-called Gospel of Jesus's Wife was even less of a complete narrative, encompassing one scrap of papyrus with fragments of sentences in Coptic, including one that could be translated, "And Jesus said, 'My wife . . . ,'" at which point the text

---

96. See, e.g., the classic little book by Joachim Jeremias, *The Unknown Sayings of Jesus*, trans. Reginald H. Fuller (London: SPCK, 1957).

97. See esp. James H. Charlesworth and Craig A. Evans, "Jesus in the Agrapha and Apocryphal Gospels," in *Studying the Historical Jesus: Evaluation of the State of Current Research*, ed. Bruce Chilton and Craig A. Evans (Leiden: Brill, 1994), 479–533.

98. For the English translation, see Rodolphe Kasser, Marvin Meyer, and Gregor Wurst, eds., *The Gospel of Judas: From Codex Tchacos* (Washington, DC: National Geographic, 2006).

99. Bart D. Ehrman, *The Lost Gospel of Judas Iscariot: A New Look at Betrayer and Betrayed* (Oxford: Oxford University Press, 2006).

breaks off. After sensationalist claims were made, many of them only on the internet, painstaking analysis of the ink and the orthography, combined with the fact that all of the text could be accounted for as a pastiche of portions of sayings from the Gospel of Thomas, definitively demonstrated that the text on the papyrus was a modern-day forgery.[100]

In 2013, a group of about twenty self-appointed liberal scholars and church leaders who had repeatedly convened in what they dubbed the New Orleans Council, published *A New New Testament*, which included ten additional books along with the twenty-seven traditional ones.[101] Nine of the ten were Gnostic or Gnostic-like; the additional "Gospels" included the Gospel of Thomas, the Gospel of Mary, the Gospel of Truth, the first book of the Odes of Solomon, and Thunder: Perfect Mind. None of these texts, except for the Gospel of Mary, are even narratives; rather, they are collections of pseudo-Christian wisdom, often involving elaborate cosmologies, while Mary comprises just a fraction of a narrative. These works do contain the appealing concepts of discovering the divine wisdom, knowledge, and light within a person and fanning it into flame. People who come to understand hidden truths will rise above their circumstances in this life and the next. There is an individualism and a self-determination here that appeal to modern, Western humanity, which were not common in the ancient Mediterranean's religious worlds. There are *at times* more egalitarian roles for human beings in what was otherwise a very stratified culture, with males, Greeks and Romans, the freeborn, the wealthy, and adherents to state-sponsored religion normally rising above the rest of the people in status and privilege. Such partial egalitarianism is understandably attractive in today's world. But the documents were written too late, with theology too distinctive, for them to stand much chance of preserving otherwise unknown information about the historical Jesus and his teaching.[102]

---

100. See the entire issue of *New Testament Studies* 61, no. 3 (2015).
101. Hal Taussig, ed., *A New New Testament: A Bible for the Twenty-First Century Combining Traditional and Newly Discovered Texts* (New York: Houghton Mifflin Harcourt, 2013).
102. Craig A. Evans, "The Apocryphal Jesus: Assessing the Possibilities and Problems," in *Exploring the Origins of the Bible: Canon Formation in Historical, Literary, and Theological Perspective*, ed. Craig A. Evans and Emanuel Tov (Grand Rapids: Baker Academic, 2008), 147–72.

## The Role of the Fourth Gospel

As we round out this chapter, we must ask once again, "But where is John?" Mack does not even purport to take him into account, since his books are about Mark and Q. Borg, in *Jesus, A New Vision*, has a scant eleven references to John, most of them in endnotes.[103] Crossan has a good smattering of references to John, though not as many as to Thomas.[104] But most of the references have nothing to do with suggesting that something is historical in the Fourth Gospel, and we recall that even the earliest layer of Johannine material does not appear until Crossan's third stratum of Gospel sources (see above, 115–16). Funk has slightly more references to John than to Thomas, but both pale in comparison to the Synoptics.[105]

*It is the Jesus Seminar's voting that demonstrates the overwhelming disregard of John by the throwback quest when it comes to Jesus research.* I commented on their assessment of Jesus's sayings earlier. As one flips the pages of their book on his deeds, we discover that the "fellows" of the Jesus Seminar used pink to color the conclusion that Jesus was originally a disciple of John, as were some of Jesus's first followers. The first part of the incident of the temple clearing (John 2:15–16) appears in gray—not as reliable as its Synoptic counterparts—with the more distinctive remainder of the passage in black. A majority of 4:46–52 is similarly gray, as it bears some resemblance to the healing of the centurion's son in Q, which preserved that story more accurately. A majority of 5:1–9 is gray, too, given its partial resemblance to the Synoptic accounts of the healing of the paralyzed man in Capernaum. The short question in 7:15 by the Judeans about Jesus, which the Scholars Version translates, "This man is uneducated; how come he's so articulate?" is pink, since it is confirmed by information in the Synoptics. The core of the miracle in chapter 9 (vv. 6–7) is gray because it resembles information in Mark 8:22–26 and may have been the nucleus around which the rest of the account of the man born blind

---

103. Borg, *Jesus, A New Vision*, 216.
104. Crossan, *Historical Jesus*, 499–504.
105. Funk, *Honest to Jesus*, 336–39.

was invented. That Jesus was out of his mind (10:20) was not likely to have been invented, so something there must bear resemblance to an actual insult. So that verse, too, appears in the color gray.[106]

Somewhat surprisingly, bits of the buildup to the resurrection of Lazarus and part of the description of his coming out of the tomb are also gray; Funk explains that Meier's and Sanders's views influenced several fellows. The first six verses of the anointing scene (John 12:1–6) are similar enough to the Synoptics to be colored gray. When one comes to chapters 18–20, there is enough overlap with the Synoptics that more bits and pieces appear gray, in one case even pink (Jesus being handed over to Caiaphas), and the event of the crucifixion itself is red. Mary's encounter with the one she supposed to be the gardener at the tomb in the beginning of John 20, despite being a resurrection appearance, is, intriguingly, gray. Other than that, the deeds of Jesus throughout the Fourth Gospel are nothing but black.[107] One would never guess that by this time, the "new look on the Fourth Gospel" that John A. T. Robinson began (see above, 65) had been growing considerably for almost forty years. In fact, there is no indication in either of their big volumes that the Jesus Seminar overall was even aware of the extent to which the "new quest," which they claimed to be continuing, had authenticated a much greater number of Jesus's words and deeds.

## Conclusion

Most accounts of the third quest lump all the developments discussed in this chapter into the same categories as those discussed in chapter 3, substantially diluting whatever homogeneity the third quest might otherwise have. It is better to take the scholars discussed in this chapter at their word, as continuing the "new quest." At times, we might more accurately view them as a throwback to the Bultmannian "no quest" period (despite the problems attached to that label). It is not as fair to dismiss Marcus Borg's work in this fashion, because of the

---

106. Funk and the Jesus Seminar, *Acts of Jesus*, 365–407.
107. Funk and the Jesus Seminar, *Acts of Jesus*, 407–40, 470–71, 473–78, 486–91.

hybrid nature of his Jesus. However, the portraits sketched by Mack, Crossan, Funk, and especially by the Jesus Seminar overall certainly merit exclusion from the third quest, especially after Funk himself so strongly dissociated himself from it.[108] To be sure, Jesus *was* a wise teacher with some implicitly subversive elements to his teaching. But to almost entirely reject both the orthodox Jesus and the eschatological prophet Jesus and see little more than a laconic sage who uttered cryptic proverbs and parables, leaving others to figure them out, defies credibility. John Meier makes this insightful and humorous observation: "A tweedy poetaster who spent his time spinning out parables and Japanese koans, a literary aesthete who toyed with first-century deconstructionism, or a bland Jesus who simply told people to look at the lilies of the field—such a Jesus would threaten no one, just as the university professors who create him threaten no one."[109] Unfortunately, beginning students and uninformed laypersons often do not realize that there is no threat here, and so they abandon part or all of their faith as a result. It is crucial that they expose themselves to all sides of the issue and hopefully not take such needless steps.

---

108. Or perhaps, with Clive Marsh, "The Quests for the Historical Jesus in New Historicist Perspective," *BibInt* 5 (1997): 403–37, esp. 415–16, as part of a "postmodern quest."

109. John P. Meier, *A Marginal Jew: Rethinking the Historical Jesus*, 5 vols. to date (New York: Doubleday, 1991–2001; New Haven: Yale University Press, 2009–16), 1:177.

# 5

# Has the Third Quest Played Itself Out?

The twenty or so years since the turn of the millennium have continued to see a flurry of historical Jesus activity. A substantial majority of the full-length Jesus books, along with the most significant research on more specialized topics, appeared, however, between 2001 and 2011, with not nearly as much in the decade since. Claims have emerged that the third quest has done just about all that it can and that Jesus research should turn in different directions. The most conspicuous of these claims involve the criteria of authenticity: Are they being asked to do more than they are capable of, and should we move in different directions altogether in seeking the historical Jesus? Should we listen to the critics from the far right or the far left who disparage the endeavor as impossible, misguided, or both? In fact, the third quest has accomplished a lot in the last two decades, and a significant percentage of the criticism seems to come more from those who don't like the results than from any fatal flaws in the methodology. But there are new developments worth scrutinizing. This chapter, then, will consider the most important recent third-quest contributions; analyze methodological critiques about the overall enterprise, especially related to assessing authenticity; explore some promising new developments; and conclude with some observations about how far the quest has come.

## The Latest Third-Quest Portraits of Jesus

The most consistent observation about the more detailed and thorough treatments of the historical Jesus in the last twenty years is how many of them determine that Jesus really did present himself as, and that he was understood as claiming to be, Israel's Messiah. In other words, merely implicit Christology gives way to increasingly explicit Christology. As one might expect, there are still reasonable replicas or creative mutations of approaches we have seen before, along with outliers that don't really fit any category. A few in each of these categories I have mentioned earlier, when they related to earlier works, and I won't repeat references here. I will deal briefly with the outliers and repeat presentations first, though noting whatever creative differences they may exhibit, and then I will proceed to the most important studies.[1]

### *Outliers*

*Psychological Studies of Jesus.* It took almost a century, after Schweitzer largely "banned" the typically poorly applied psychology of the nineteenth century, for this genre to reemerge, at least as a full-fledged, legitimate discipline, rather than just a solitary, quirky study or two. It was exactly in 2001 when enough work had been done to merit Fortress Press's publishing of *Psychological Biblical Criticism*, by D. Andrew Killie, in its Guides to Biblical Scholarship series.[2] Precisely because we have so much more accurate and detailed information about historical and cultural backgrounds, and because psychology has made so many impressive strides since Sigmund Freud (1886–1939), scholars who are aware of what the Gospels do and don't purport to

---

1. See also Craig L. Blomberg and Darlene M. Seal, "The Historical Jesus in Recent Evangelical Scholarship," in *Jesus, Skepticism, and the Problem of History: Criteria and Context in the Study of Christian Origins*, ed. Darrell L. Bock and J. Ed Komoszewski (Grand Rapids: Zondervan Academic, 2019), 43–66.
2. D. Andrew Kille, *Psychological Biblical Criticism* (Minneapolis: Fortress, 2001).

tell us can utilize various forms of psychology with the potential of more accurate and useful results than their predecessors of a century or more ago could.[3]

A lot of reflection, for example, has gone into the question of what Jesus as an adult, presumably without Joseph living, would have experienced as "fatherless" in Galilee. This certainly could have enhanced his felt need for God as his heavenly father and a kingdom proclamation that so often centered on him in that role.[4] It could also have contributed to his sense of needing to play the part of a protector for other fatherless children or husbandless women.[5] Others have reflected on the extent to which it was believed Jesus was an illegitimate child—a *mamzer*, the Aramaic word for "bastard," with all the stigma that was associated with that label.[6] Would he have been forbidden to marry? Did he see himself as founding an alternative to the temple cult, in which he could not have participated?[7] The answers to these questions are not necessarily straightforward, but they are appropriate ones to ask. Examples could be multiplied in some detail.[8]

*The Refracted Jesus.* Anthony Le Donne has proposed an epistemology that is not as optimistic about recovering the historical Jesus as critical realism but is not as skeptical about it as typical postmodernism. He speaks of a mnemonic cycle of four steps that can occur in historical reflection. First, one begins with a mnemonic category

---

3. An excellent overview of key research is Bas van Os, *Psychological Analyses and the Historical Jesus: New Ways to Explore Christian Origins* (London: T&T Clark, 2011). See also James H. Charlesworth, "Should Specialists in Jesus Research Include Psychobiography?," in *Jesus Research: New Methodologies and Perceptions; The Second Princeton-Prague Symposium on Jesus Research*, ed. James H. Charlesworth with Brian Rhea, in consultation with Petr Pokorný (Grand Rapids: Eerdmans, 2014), 436–66.

4. John Miller, *Jesus at Thirty: A Psychological and Historical Portrait* (Minneapolis: Fortress, 1997), esp. 31–46.

5. Andries van Aarde, *Fatherless in Galilee: Jesus as Child of God* (Harrisburg, PA: Trinity Press International, 2001), esp. 135–54.

6. See Bruce D. Chilton, "Jésus, le *mamzer* (Mt. 1.18)," *NTS* 47 (2001): 222–27; Scot McKnight, "Calling Jesus *Mamzer*," *JSHJ* 1 (2003): 73–103.

7. Donald Capps, *Jesus: A Psychological Biography* (St. Louis: Chalice, 2000), 252–60.

8. For three other important sources, see Fraser Watts, ed., *Jesus and Psychology* (Philadelphia: Templeton Foundation Press; London: Darton, Longman & Todd, 2007); Roy M. Oswald and Arland Jacobson, *The Emotional Intelligence of Jesus: Relational Smarts for Religious Leaders* (Lanham, MD: Rowman & Littlefield, 2015); James R. Beck, *Jesus and Personality Theory: Exploring the Five-Factor Model* (Downers Grove, IL: InterVarsity, 1999).

of some significance. Second, this category undergoes a trajectory of refraction—some kind of modification of the image, which may or may not be considered a distortion of it. Third, this refraction leads to a new contemporary perception. Finally, the perception is relocated within the original mnemonic category.[9]

Le Donne uses the example of the title "Son of David." On several occasions in the Synoptics, people wanting or just having received healing acclaim Jesus with this title (Mark 10:47–48 pars.; Matt. 9:27; 15:22). But there is little obvious in Jewish backgrounds to make ordinary people associate the Messiah with miracles of physical healing. How did this come about? The category "Son of David" as the Messiah was certainly a significant one in people's memories. In Second Temple Judaism, traditions emerged that Solomon, David's most famous son, was in fact a healer and exorcist. So as Jesus's reputation in these areas grew, it would be natural to think of him as a Son of David. Did blind people, for example, really hail Jesus as "Son of David," or did the Jesus tradition associate the two because of the link with healing in Judaism at large? Both are possible. Did that association then lead Christians to associate more Old Testament texts with the Messiah than were originally intended to be?[10] Le Donne asks fascinating questions, but he has not followed up his studies with enough other examples to make for easier evaluation, nor have others done so.[11]

*The History-of-Religions School Redux.* Just as the Mack-Borg-Crossan-Funk trajectory of Jesus as a Cynic sage doesn't fit with the bulk of the third quest, neither do those who have recently tried to explain the exalted portrait of Jesus in the New Testament, especially in the Gospels, as the product of the imitation of Greco-Roman religion and mythology. But it does fit in with recent outliers. Best known, perhaps, is David Litwa's recent explanation for early Christianity's

---

9. Anthony Le Donne, *The Historiographical Jesus: Memory, Typology, and the Son of David* (Waco: Baylor University Press, 2009), 65–70.
10. Le Donne, *Historiographical Jesus*, 137–83.
11. Although see Anthony Le Donne, "Theological Memory Distortion in the Jesus Tradition," in *Memory in the Bible and Antiquity: The Fifth Durham-Tübingen Research Symposium (Durham, September 2004)*, ed. Loren T. Stuckenbruck, Stephen C. Barton, and Benjamin G. Wold (Tübingen: Mohr Siebeck, 2007), 163–77.

portrait of Jesus as "a Mediterranean god."[12] Litwa focuses particularly on the title "Son of God," but he goes beyond that to a variety of ways early Christians, both inside and outside the New Testament, drew, as he sees it, on Greco-Roman descriptions of deities to depict the exalted Jesus.

Some of the parallels, especially outside of the New Testament, are clear, and others are suggestive.[13] But even while Litwa acknowledges that there are Jewish concepts to be reckoned with as well, his focus lies almost entirely on the Greco-Roman world. The question remaining to be asked, especially about the Gospels, is whether Jewish backgrounds adequately explain the language used to describe Jesus and, if so, why we need to look farther afield, at least at the level of the historical Jesus. Technically, Litwa's study is not Jesus research, but it is easy for others who start where he does to subsequently conclude that there is no historical basis for various Gospel phenomena. Less careful scholars have often drawn parallels to Greco-Roman developments—for example, in Mithraism or the *Life of Apollonius*, which are simply too late to have influenced the Gospels, to say nothing of Jesus himself.[14] And the descriptions of these alleged parallels are often fairly imprecise.[15] The final step is taken when a zealous student of the literature without the requisite academic background, like Richard Carrier, then asserts that Jesus never existed.[16] Equally idiosyncratic are the writings of Thomas Brodie, who thinks that everything in the

---

12. M. David Litwa, *Iesus Deus: The Early Christian Depiction of Jesus as a Mediterranean God* (Minneapolis: Fortress, 2014). See also Michael Peppard, *The Son of God in the Roman World: Divine Sonship in Its Social and Political Context* (Oxford: Oxford University Press, 2011).

13. Litwa, *Iesus Deus*, 69–109.

14. See further Ronald H. Nash, *The Gospel and the Greeks: Did the New Testament Borrow from Pagan Thought?* (Phillipsburg, NJ: P&R, 2003), 133–38; Antonia Tripolitis, *Religions of the Hellenistic-Roman Age* (Grand Rapids: Eerdmans, 2002), 47–59; Loveday Alexander, "The Four among Pagans," in *The Written Gospel*, ed. Markus Bockmuehl and Donald A. Hagner (Cambridge: Cambridge University Press, 2005), 237.

15. See esp. Otto Rank, Lord Raglan, and Alan Dundes, *In Quest of the Hero* (Princeton: Princeton University Press, 1990).

16. Richard Carrier, *On the Historicity of Jesus: Why We Might Have Reason for Doubt* (Sheffield: Sheffield Phoenix, 2014). Against which, see Richard Gullatta, "On Richard Carrier's Doubts: A Response to Richard Carrier's *On the Historicity of Jesus: Why We Might Have Reason for Doubt*," *JSHJ* 15 (2017): 310–46.

Gospels was invented on the basis of the Old Testament to create a fictional Jesus as a profound symbol for how God can work through suffering-but-triumphant humanity, and Hal Childs, who ultimately finds "Jesus," like all religions' use of "God," to be another name for the unconscious dimension of humanity.[17] Justin Meggitt appears correct when he identifies this "quest for the non-historical Jesus" as "more ingenious than learned."[18]

*Jesus the Shaman.* A final outlier we will consider is Pieter Craffert's effort to liken Jesus to a Galilean shaman—one of "those religious entrepreneurs who enter controlled ASCs [altered states of consciousness] on behalf of their communities and perform certain social functions that center on healing, divination, and control of spirits."[19] Four key shamanic indicators ascribed to Jesus are (1) "a sense of divine identity: mystical transformations"; (2) "a disdain for sexual activities: an unmarried life of celibacy"; (3) "a sense of divine sonship: son of God the Father"; and (4) "a sense of divine knowledge: astral prophecy."[20] Being a shaman unifies all of Jesus's roles, including "prophet, teacher, rabbi, healer and exorcist."[21] It is interesting, though, that Craffert has virtually nothing to say about Jesus's passion and death—the one feature of Jesus's biography that the first Christians recognized as most important of all. The section on astral prophecy seems far-fetched, while early Christians, like Jews before them, would have most likely assigned the typical shamanic combination of traits to satanic influence, especially as they acknowledged that Satan and his minions could duplicate some of the functions of true religion.[22]

---

17. Thomas L. Brodie, *Beyond the Quest for the Historical Jesus: Memoir of a Discovery* (Sheffield: Sheffield Phoenix, 2012); Hal Childs, *The Myth of the Historical Jesus and the Evolution of Consciousness* (Atlanta: Society of Biblical Literature, 1998).

18. Justin J. Meggitt, "'More Ingenious Than Learned'? Examining the Quest for the Non-Historical Jesus," *NTS* 65 (2019): 443–60.

19. Pieter F. Craffert, *The Life of a Galilean Shaman: Jesus of Nazareth in Anthropological-Historical Perspective* (Eugene, OR: Cascade Books, 2008), 166.

20. Craffert, *Life of a Galilean Shaman*, 234–43.

21. Craffert, *Life of a Galilean Shaman*, 244.

22. For a more wide-ranging critique, see Christian Strecker, "'The Duty of Discontent': Some Remarks on Pieter F. Craffert's *The Life of a Galilean Shaman: Jesus of Nazareth in Anthropological-Historical Perspective*," *JSHJ* 11 (2013): 251–80.

## Key Third-Quest Models Repeated

*Jesus the Zealot.* Compared to Richard Carrier, Reza Aslan might be considered a biblical scholar, even though he is merely a well-read Muslim writer who wrote a best-selling popular-level account of Jesus as a freedom-fighter.[23] The picture is strikingly reminiscent of S. G. F. Brandon's from the new-quest era (see above, 59–60), though it has parallels in the third quest with those who find Jesus fairly revolutionary, confronting the Roman authorities and their surrogates to the extent that they perceived him as a real threat to the peace. Of course, the incident of the temple clearing always plays a key role in these depictions. Just as in Crossan's big historical Jesus book, the most helpful part of Aslan's work is his presentation of the historical background, especially concerning the other bandits, rabble-rousers, and would-be messiahs whom Josephus depicts in detail. The line can be a fine one between what behavior and teaching might have created superficial similarities to these other men who did lead groups of followers to fight against Rome and its henchmen (always eventually massacred), and what would have made Jesus a genuine threat. Douglas Oakman's book on Jesus's political aims could fit here or could be closer to Richard Horsley, depending on the section one is reading at the moment.[24]

*Jesus as Wisdom/Sophia.* If Aslan is a replica of Brandon, a group of writers depicting Jesus as Wisdom personified have produced a creative mutation of Jesus the dispenser of nuggets of wisdom that we saw in the throwback quest. They also contain parallels to Horsley's brand of Jesus the social reformer. Particularly popular in certain feminist circles, this version of the sapiential Jesus owes its flourishing to the major impetus of Elisabeth Schüssler Fiorenza in her numerous works. Schüssler Fiorenza made her mark particularly with her thesis that Jesus was an egalitarian who treated women and men equally and would have wanted his followers to do so as well, without

---

23. Reza Aslan, *Zealot: The Life and Times of Jesus of Nazareth* (New York: Random House, 2014).
24. Douglas E. Oakman, *The Political Aims of Jesus* (Minneapolis: Fortress, 2012).

a hierarchy that privileged men in any way.²⁵ For a few decades, the early church followed suit, but the cultural pressures soon became too much, and it reverted back to a form of hierarchicalism (sometimes called a "love patriarchalism" because it wasn't as heavy-handed as many non-Christian equivalents). The New Testament books where this is clearest are those for which mainstream scholarship has long argued for pseudonymity, allowing Schüssler Fiorenza and others who agreed with her to postpone the repatriarchalizing of Christianity for perhaps an additional generation. While a few feminists have written extensively about Jesus, no one within the guild has produced a work whose structure and genre resembles the lives of Jesus we have been surveying. But they have investigated at length the effect of the Greek word for "wisdom" (*sophia*) being feminine and the various ways Sophia was personified in Greek and Hellenistic Jewish literature, especially in light of Wisdom in the canonical Hebrew text of Proverbs being envisaged similarly (esp. chaps. 8–9).²⁶

A big part of the reason for the gap in feminist historical Jesus studies is the same as that for the gap in those from other advocacy perspectives. There is a barrage of studies that qualify as biblical or systematic theology from all these movements, but not nearly as much on the historical Jesus. Schüssler Fiorenza puts it about as bluntly as possible but also discloses the problem at the same time. She pontificates that "the refusal of the Third Quest to problematize its own methodological assumptions and ideological interests as well as its sophisticated advocacy of historical positivism corresponds to political conservatism." Again, "its universalizing discourse obfuscates that historians select and interpret archeological artifacts and textual evidence as well as incorporates them into a scientific model and narrative framework of

---

25. Elisabeth Schüssler Fiorenza, *In Memory of Her: A Feminist Theological Reconstruction of Christian Origins* (New York: Herder & Herder, 1983; London: SCM, 1995). For another advocacy emphasis, see Luise Schottroff and Wolfgang Stegemann, *Jesus and the Hope of the Poor*, trans. Matthew J. O'Connell (Maryknoll, NY: Orbis Books, 1986 [Ger. orig. 1978]).

26. E.g., Elisabeth Schüssler Fiorenza, *Jesus—Miriam's Child, Sophia's Prophet* (New York: Continuum, 1994). For a thorough critique of Schüssler Fiorenza's feminist exegesis, see Esther Yue L. Ng, *Reconstructing Christian Origins? The Feminist Theology of Elisabeth Schüssler Fiorenza; An Evaluation* (Carlisle: Paternoster, 2002).

meaning."²⁷ Having recently read or reread dozens of historical Jesus books from a wide period of time and from many diverse perspectives, I confess that I have not seen a single work to which she could be fairly referring. Jesus researchers regularly affirm exactly the things she criticizes them for not saying. For her, the real problem is that they do not start from a point of sociopolitical advocacy. In other words, unless the purpose of their research is to help the marginalized, poor, and oppressed, they shouldn't be writing books about Jesus. Later she explains that she sees the task of historical Jesus study as that of looking not for "what has happened" but for "what was historically possible."²⁸ If it is possible that Jesus was a liberator, then that is what we should say he was, apparently. But what if he weren't? Wouldn't the more honest thing be to say precisely that? Religiously, one might then wish to abandon Christianity or to never embrace it in the first place, rather than turning it into something it isn't. Fortunately, we are not faced with such a dilemma. We can and should affirm many of Schüssler Fiorenza's conclusions about Jesus and support many of the causes to which they lead without surrendering the quest for as much objectivity as the nature of the historical task will allow.²⁹

*Jesus and Nonviolence.* Simon Joseph has produced an important study of Jesus in the line of Etienne Trocmé, Thomas Yoder Neufeld, and those who have stressed his nonviolent and even pacifist nature (see above, 91–92).³⁰ Unlike most in this tradition, however, Joseph interacts in detail with the various source-critical distinctions scholars

---

27. Elisabeth Schüssler Fiorenza, "Critical Feminist Historical-Jesus Research," in *Handbook for the Study of the Historical Jesus*, ed. Tom Holmén and Stanley E. Porter, 4 vols. (Leiden: Brill, 2011), 1:526. Schüssler Fiorenza (526–27n52) cites numerous majority-world studies that third-quest scholars have ignored. But that is because such studies are not historical Jesus books. It is fine for her to decide that she doesn't like the genre and wants to write something else, but it is unfair for her to then turn around and criticize others for not doing what they didn't set out to do (except, of course, at the very macrolevel where someone might simply object to a whole genre of research as not adequately relevant).

28. Schüssler Fiorenza, "Critical Feminist Historical-Jesus Research," 535.

29. See, e.g., Ben Witherington III, *Women in the Ministry of Jesus: A Study of Jesus' Attitudes to Women and Their Roles as Reflected in His Earthly Life* (Cambridge: Cambridge University Press, 1987); Richard A. Horsley, *Jesus and the Powers: Conflict, Covenant, and the Hope of the Poor* (Minneapolis: Fortress, 2011).

30. Simon J. Joseph, *The Nonviolent Messiah: Jesus, Q, and the Enochic Tradition* (Minneapolis: Fortress, 2014).

make with the Synoptics, and especially with Q. While Joseph sees the nonviolent Jesus (roughly equivalent to the sapiential Jesus of Borg, Crossan, et al.) as dominating the Jesus of the Synoptics, there is still the minority strand of the apocalyptic Jesus who ushers in judgment, including with violence, in a manner Joseph finds simply incompatible with the other strand of thought.[31] The former must therefore represent the historical Jesus. The latter comes especially from 1 Enoch, which influenced the "Son of man" sayings portraying Jesus coming in judgment. In fact, the redactional contributions of the evangelists lead to viewing Jesus as fulfilling all the eschatological functions of Davidic, Danielic, Enochic, Adamic, and Isaianic messianism.[32] The key issue, of course, is whether the apocalyptic and the sapiential materials truly are at irreconcilable odds with each other. Most in the history of the church, like the final redactors of the Gospels, have thought otherwise. It is never easy to promote nonviolence throughout one's entire life, but knowing that God in Christ will eventually bring justice provides a huge motivation for making the attempt.[33]

*A Redefined Messiah.* A significant German scholar whose work could well be seen as carrying on the third-quest category of the "marginalized Messiah," but with considerable epistemological sophistication, is Jens Schröter.[34] Some probably would think that his work merits inclusion in our next section on even more important studies. If I keep it here, it is not to play down its value but to create a bridge to our next set of authors. At least Schröter's Jesus book is not nearly as big as the ones yet to be treated![35] What he finds authenticable is not quite as large an amount of material as for others who see the historical Jesus as a kind of messiah, but he works hard not to include in his portrait of

---

31. Joseph, *Nonviolent Messiah*, 144.
32. Joseph, *Nonviolent Messiah*, 125–95.
33. Ulrich Luz, *Matthew 21–28: A Commentary*, trans. James E. Crouch, ed. Helmut Koester, Hermeneia (Minneapolis: Fortress, 2005), 245; Klyne R. Snodgrass, *Stories with Intent: A Comprehensive Guide to the Parables of Jesus*, 2nd ed. (Grand Rapids: Eerdmans, 2018), 492.
34. Jens Schröter, *Jesus of Nazareth: Jew from Galilee, Savior of the World*, trans. Wayne Coppins and S. Brian Pounds (Waco: Baylor University Press, 2014 [Ger. orig. 2006]).
35. Shorter still and designed as introductions for wider audiences, and clearly fitting the "apocalyptic prophet" mold, are Cecilia Wassén and Tobias Hägerland, *Jesus the Apocalyptic Prophet*, trans. Cian J. Power (London: Bloomsbury T&T Clark, 2021 [Swed. orig. 2016]); Helen K. Bond, *The Historical Jesus: A Guide for the Perplexed* (London: T&T Clark, 2012).

Jesus that which does not clearly meet his criteria. He does find that the "Son of man" title with its messianic significance goes back to Jesus, but its meaning becomes clear only after Jesus's death. Jesus does accept the use of the title "Messiah/Christ" but significantly redefines it.[36] Schröter stresses the need to acknowledge a double refraction (using the term a little differently than Le Donne does)—that all historical knowledge is relative to some degree and that we never get behind the interpreted Jesus.[37] On the other hand, neither of these points requires "a material break between the concrete events and their subsequent interpretation," so that Lessing's ugly, broad ditch (see above, 3) also misleads. Instead, "the Gospels present the person of Jesus in precisely such a way that *in light of* his activity and fate the categories of interpretation applied to him are transformed and filled with new content. The interpretive narratives are thus prompted by historical recollections and stand therefore in connection with Jesus' activity."[38]

## *Major New Historical Jesus Books*

Particularly in the first decade of the twenty-first century, a surprising number of very important, comparatively large historical Jesus books appeared, arguably bringing the third quest to its culmination. We will focus on eight main works in this category here.

*Dunn Remembers Jesus.* In 2015, *James D. G. Dunn* (1939–2020) completed a three-volume collection of books in the Christianity in the Making series, the first of which was published in 2003 on the historical Jesus.[39] Dunn follows the classic organization of so many Jesus books, beginning with methodology, historical background, and sources utilized, and then proceeding to a roughly chronological study

---

36. Schröter, *Jesus of Nazareth*, 215–16.
37. Schröter, *Jesus of Nazareth*, 245–46.
38. Schröter, *Jesus of Nazareth*, 107. See also Jens Schröter, *From Jesus to the New Testament: Early Christian Theology and the Origin of the New Testament Canon*, trans. Wayne Coppins (Tübingen: Mohr Siebeck; Waco: Baylor University Press, 2013 [Ger. orig. 2007]), 107; Gerd Theissen, "Historical Scepticism and the Criteria of Jesus Research or My Attempt to Leap Across Lessing's Yawning Gulf," *SJT* 49 (1996): 147–76.
39. James D. G. Dunn, *Jesus Remembered*, Christianity in the Making 1 (Grand Rapids: Eerdmans, 2003).

of the major phases or facets of Jesus's life. On the one hand, Dunn is optimistic about finding authentic material in most of his categories, while believing that the resurrection raises certain questions that historians simply can't address.[40] But he insists that it is beyond reasonable doubt that the first witnesses *experienced* Jesus's resurrection and that the testimony we have enshrines their experience.[41] On the other hand, we have to always keep in mind that, by the very nature of history writing, *all that we have are collections of the ways in which Jesus was remembered.*[42]

Dunn himself states that his most distinctive contribution in the volume is his calling for a recognition that *oral tradition played a much larger role in the differences between Gospel parallels than is usually perceived.*[43] As in shorter writings elsewhere, he lobbies for the "default setting" in Gospels research to be the oral rather than the written mode.[44] He appeals to Kenneth Bailey's identification of "informal and controlled" tradition as the norm, rather than either "formal and controlled" (memorization) or "informal and uncontrolled."[45] Early Christian tradents frequently passed the teaching of Jesus along in ways that were free with respect to the actual wording but true to the gist of his meaning. Dunn argues for rehabilitating Jeremias's emphasis on our ability to recover the *ipsissima vox* (the very own voice) of Jesus, even if not the *ipsissima verba* (his very own words).[46] Anything that is both characteristic of Jesus in the Synoptics and distinctive from the surrounding culture is likely to go back to him. Dunn concludes that Jesus's self-understanding included seeing his ministry as one of

---

40. Dunn, *Jesus Remembered*, 825.
41. Dunn, *Jesus Remembered*, 861–62.
42. Dunn, *Jesus Remembered*, 129.
43. Dunn, *Jesus Remembered*, 6.
44. See esp. James D. G. Dunn, *The Oral Gospel Tradition* (Grand Rapids: Eerdmans, 2013), 41–79. See also David Wenham, *From Good News to Gospels: What Did the First Christians Say about Jesus?* (Grand Rapids: Eerdmans, 2018), 65–94; T. M. Derico, *Oral Tradition and Synoptic Verbal Agreement: Evaluating the Empirical Evidence for Literary Dependence* (Eugene, OR: Pickwick, 2016).
45. Dunn, *Jesus Remembered*, 205–10; Kenneth E. Bailey, "Informal Controlled Oral Tradition and the Synoptic Gospels," *AJT* 5 (1991): 34–54 (repr., *Them* 20 [1995]: 4–11).
46. Dunn, *Jesus Remembered*, 226; Joachim Jeremias, *New Testament Theology*, vol. 1, *The Proclamation of Jesus* (London: SCM; New York: Scribner, 1971), 3–29.

being the climactic, eschatological spokesman for God, in an intimate filial relationship with him, with an unparalleled authority over others, and the man playing the decisive role in bringing in the kingdom. He may legitimately be called messianic, but he was not a *royal* messianic figure in any conventional sense of that term.[47] Consideration of numerous doubly or triply attested passages, printed with their parallels in adjacent columns, shows how many differences remain. While scholars have quibbled with numerous details within Dunn's work, overall there has been great appreciation for his completion of a massive, meticulous undertaking.[48]

*Three Priests' Jesus. Armand Puig i Tàrrech* (1953–) is a Catalonian scholar who published, among other things, a technical monograph on the tradition history of the parable of the ten bridesmaids.[49] He by no means automatically accepts every part of the Synoptic tradition as authentically something Jesus did or said. In *Jesus: A Biography*, he works with the authenticity criteria of dissimilarity and coherence with the environment, embarrassment, multiple attestation, coherence, and what his translator calls "charactericity."[50] He authenticates largely the same material that Dunn does, independently from him. But as a Catholic priest, he also inserts, fairly unobtrusively, periodic theological reflection and contemporary applications for Christians. Almost certainly, this is the kind of hybrid work that Funk, Crossan, and others in their camp would pour scorn on as part of the "pretend quest" (see above, 127), but it is not obvious why it would merit that scorn. Readers can easily identify and bracket out this material and still assess for themselves the vast majority of the book, which involves standard historical Jesus research. For example, with respect to the resurrection, Puig i Tàrrech asserts that it "was an event that took place on the

---

47. Dunn, *Jesus Remembered*, 762.
48. An excellent anthology of appreciative yet thorough critiques appears as Robert B. Stewart and Gary R. Habermas, eds., *Memories of Jesus: A Critical Appraisal of James D. G. Dunn's "Jesus Remembered"* (Nashville: B&H Academic, 2010). For his response to a variety of criticisms, see James D. G. Dunn, "Eyewitnesses and the Oral Jesus Tradition," *JSHJ* 6 (2008): 85–105.
49. Armand Puig i Tàrrech, *La parabole des dix vierges (Mt 25,1–13)* (Rome: Biblical Institute Press, 1983).
50. Armand Puig i Tàrrech, *Jesus: A Biography* (Waco: Baylor University Press, 2011 [Span. orig. 2005]).

border between historical, empirical, provable reality and metahistorical reality, which is intuitively taken to be true and, for those who believe, asserted as necessary."[51]

A Spanish Catholic scholar, *José Pagola* (1937–), has written a book very similar to Puig i Tàrrech's.[52] While overall a little shorter, Pagola's work delves into the question of Jesus and purity in more detail than Puig i Tàrrech's and most other recent lives of Jesus. Pagola speculates that perhaps Jesus "had a very specific vision: what is holy does not need to be protected from contamination by a strategy of separation; on the contrary, those who are truly holy can spread purity and transform the impure. When Jesus touches the leper, he does not become impure; the leper becomes pure."[53] This explains Jesus's frequent meals with sinners, which form "one of Jesus' most unique and surprising characteristics, perhaps the one that most distinguishes him from all his contemporaries and from all the prophets and teachers of the past."[54] At the same time, Jesus does not criticize the purity code in any direct way. He simply acts with total freedom, on behalf of God, to treat people differently than others do. He approaches women "without hesitancy and relates to them openly," not looking at them "as a source of temptation or possible contamination." Many were no doubt attracted to him, and some even followed him in his itinerant ministry. Most of these may have been "single, unfortunate women who saw Jesus' travels as a way of living with greater dignity."[55]

Perhaps the most surprising contribution to this category is the three-volume series on Jesus's life and ministry by *Pope Benedict XVI*, the former cardinal *Joseph Ratzinger* (1927–).[56] Insisting that he is writing as the scholar Ratzinger (and indeed the research for the project began well before he was elected pope) and not with any papal authority, he works his way through the major events of Christ's life, well aware

51. Puig i Tàrrech, *Jesus*, 626.
52. José A. Pagola, *Jesus: An Historical Approximation*, trans. Margaret Wilde (Miami: Convivium, 2009 [Span. orig. 2007]).
53. Pagola, *Jesus*, 195.
54. Pagola, *Jesus*, 197.
55. Pagola, *Jesus*, 214.
56. Joseph Ratzinger (Pope Benedict XVI), *Jesus of Nazareth*, trans. Adrian J. Walker and Philip J. Whitmore, 3 vols. (New York: Doubleday, 2007–12).

of the major scholarly opinions of them. He is clearly willing to live with some gray areas; not every minor detail in the Gospels needs to be defended. But he also writes with an ecumenical spirit; a healthy smattering of Protestants and even the occasional evangelical scholar appear in his footnotes and bibliography. As with Puig i Tàrrech and Pagola, one can clearly delineate where he ends his historical-critical research and where he picks up the pen as priest and pastor. Unlike these other two writers, he also quotes patristic commentary fairly frequently. Referencing the contemporary German scholars Thomas Söding and Ulrich Wilckens, he asserts that the early testimony to the resurrection would have been utterly impossible had anyone been able to point to a body in a tomb.[57] Pastorally, Benedict hopes that each reader might follow Thomas and confess Jesus as Lord and God.[58]

*A Royally Jewish Messiah—Hengel and Schwemer.* One of the most prolific of recent German New Testament scholars, *Martin Hengel* (1926–2009), is also one of the most encouraging when it comes to Jesus research. Hengel, a longtime professor in Tübingen, and his former student Anna Maria Schwemer explain that they are not trying to argue for some innovative perspective but merely employing a barrage of criteria to determine if and how Jesus made any messianic claims. After detailed treatment of the relevant Jewish backgrounds, they find it undeniable that he did make such claims.[59] Hengel and Schwemer point out that form criticism neglected to highlight that "personal memory that is bound to an individual . . . can retain what has been seen and heard for decades."[60] They combine elements of sapiential with details of apocalyptic and argue for both in the one person of Jesus as "messianic teacher of wisdom."[61] By far the greatest impression Jesus made on his audiences "was as an exorcist and a healer." While parallels of different kinds outside the Gospels can be found to individual miracles of Jesus, "there is not really any

57. Ratzinger, *Jesus of Nazareth*, 3:254.
58. Ratzinger, *Jesus of Nazareth*, 3:xvii.
59. Martin Hengel and Anna Maria Schwemer, *Jesus and Judaism*, trans. Wayne Coppins (Waco: Baylor University Press, 2019 [Ger. orig. 2007]).
60. Hengel and Schwemer, *Jesus and Judaism*, 267.
61. Hengel and Schwemer, *Jesus and Judaism*, 397.

comparable collection of miracle stories, that is tied to *one* person, as in the Gospels. This must also have historical foundations in the person of Jesus."[62] Even the nature miracles cannot be regarded as "free inventions." There are historical incidents behind most of them. At the same time, "it is understandable that they were developed and intensified in the—kerygmatically conditioned—continual telling of them."[63]

For Hengel and Schwemer, Jesus is claiming messiahship that was not the kind that many were hoping for.[64] Our authors spend a much longer time than most discussing the resurrection accounts, even producing a harmonization of the disparate testimonies at the macrolevel, before concluding that the Gospels resist it on a microlevel.[65] On the other hand, they observe the restraint of description that occurs in the canonical texts in contrast with the later apocrypha. Earlier on, they have shown how virtually all the post–New Testament Christian literature is parasitic on the canonical texts, despite the more publicized claims to the contrary. Finally, in good Lutheran tradition, Hengel and Schwemer insist that "the high point of [the Gospels'] presentation remains the passion of Jesus, though it is illuminated by his resurrection."[66]

*Allison Redux.* Earlier, I discussed Dale Allison's medium-length treatment of the slightly ascetic apocalyptic Jesus, which he penned just before the turn of the millennium (see above, 84–86). Allison wrote a second, much larger volume, published in 2010, titled *Constructing Jesus: Memory, Imagination, and History*.[67] As the title suggests, Allison is scarcely averse to claiming that various parts of the New

---

62. Hengel and Schwemer, *Jesus and Judaism*, 491.
63. Hengel and Schwemer, *Jesus and Judaism*, 525.
64. See the favorable acknowledgment and assessment of this in Jostein Ådna, "The Messianic Claim of Jesus: An Appreciation and Appraisal of Martin Hengel's Portrayal of the Historical Jesus," in *The Mission of Jesus: Second Nordic Symposium on the Historical Jesus, Lund, 7–10 October 2012*, ed. Samuel Byrskog and Tobias Hägerland (Tübingen: Mohr Siebeck, 2015), 59–74.
65. Hengel and Schwemer, *Jesus and Judaism*, 685–87.
66. Hengel and Schwemer, *Jesus and Judaism*, 687.
67. Dale C. Allison Jr., *Constructing Jesus: Memory, Imagination, and History* (Grand Rapids: Baker Academic, 2010).

Testament Gospels do not reflect (or do not entirely reflect) the career of the historical Jesus. Yet his thrust here is a much more positive one. He notes that memory has been overly discredited in many modern studies or reports of others' studies. The gist of an event typically is remembered even when details aren't. Recurring, deeply embedded impressions are a better starting point for historical research than an atomistic collection of sayings satisfying stringent criteria, which may have little to do with one another.[68] Allison then notes thirty-two Synoptic sayings, all of which fit the theme of Mark 1:15, Jesus's announcement that the time of the kingdom was at hand, necessitating repentance and belief in the gospel. Many of these also involve the conquest of Satan.[69] Jesus thus forms a middle point between the preaching of John the Baptist and that of the early church, both of which agree on these particulars. It is, therefore, virtually undeniable that Jesus likewise would have held to the views in this apocalyptic material. We might call this the use of a double similarity criterion (see also below, 161–66).

A second kind of argument appeals simply to the barrage of Old Testament material used to explain the events of the last week, passion, and death (and to some degree the resurrection) of Jesus. With such a frequency here of citations and allusions to the Hebrew Scriptures across all four Gospels, noticeably greater than that found in the earlier portions of the evangelists' narratives, one must suggest that Jesus actually did fulfill prophecy, especially when one recalls the many kinds of fulfillment acceptable in ancient Judaism.[70] More specifically, the turn of the ages has indeed come. Allison highlights a series of additional facts to support an apocalyptic (rather than a sapiential) figure at the bedrock core of the historical Jesus material. These include his execution as king of the Jews, the function of the resurrection as turning Jesus into the *exalted* Son of man, the fact that the arrival of the kingdom of God requires the arrival of a king, the early Christian claims that Jesus sits at God's right hand, all the language of "someone

---

68. Allison, *Constructing Jesus*, 14.
69. Allison, *Constructing Jesus*, 33–43.
70. Allison, *Constructing Jesus*, 78–82.

greater than" the great figures of Jewish history, the use of "the coming one," and so on.[71]

Among many other excellent insights, Allison notes that no Christian that we know of ever called Paul a god, nor did *any* of Jesus's apostles or first followers ever make claims for themselves remotely close to those they ascribed to Jesus. The difference must have had something to do with who Jesus, Paul, and the others actually were. Allison concludes, "We should hold a funeral for the view that Jesus entertained no exalted thoughts about himself."[72] He summarizes his method as follows: "Instead of attempting to authenticate individual item after individual item, I have preferred, for the most part, to identify larger patterns across the sources and to seek for the best explanation."[73] Allison is clearly not starting from some prejudicial theological position and finding a Jesus made in his image, because much of his portrait could appear to be consistent with theological positions more conservative than those he has actually held.

*A Keener Jesus.* I suspect that the title *Craig S. Keener* (1960–), professor at Asbury Seminary in Kentucky, chose for his big Jesus book, *The Historical Jesus of the Gospels*, has put some people off reading it because it could sound like he is simply saying that the portraits in the canonical Gospels are entirely accurate. In that case, we would not need to construct a historical Jesus different from the Gospels' portraits. But what Keener is actually saying is that the Gospels contain enough historical material, and that noncanonical literature does not contain much authentic material about Jesus that is different from what the New Testament teaches, so that the Jesus of history does significantly resemble what we can read in large parts of Matthew, Mark, and Luke.[74] Much of Keener's book deals with collateral issues: the potential for great feats of memory in Jesus's oral culture, the fact that few people in antiquity wrote anything akin to a historical novel, and if they did, it was not about recent real-life people.[75] But as he deals with each main

---

71. Allison, *Constructing Jesus*, 225–51.
72. Allison, *Constructing Jesus*, 304.
73. Allison, *Constructing Jesus*, 460.
74. Craig S. Keener, *The Historical Jesus of the Gospels* (Grand Rapids: Eerdmans, 2009).
75. Keener, *Historical Jesus of the Gospels*, 77.

phase or topic in Jesus's life, Keener is also very explicit about how the standard criteria of authenticity support the positions he adopts.

On Jesus as a king, Keener observes, "Neither Pilate nor the disciples got the idea from each other; rather, it derived from a common ultimate source in Jesus himself. For later followers to invent such a title is inconceivable; it risked persecution against themselves for following the one executed for treason."[76] Moreover, there are no early Christian sources, not even the putative Q, that leave Jesus as just an earthly Messiah. The idea that Q represented a community that did not know of Jesus's suffering and death because it has no passion narrative is contradicted by its genre. It is mostly a sayings source. Some collections of Socrates's teachings don't mention his martyrdom either, yet no one imagines communities of Socratics who didn't know about it![77] Keener spends a healthy amount of time on the resurrection and concludes that whatever we do with the issue of divine causation, no one should doubt that Jesus's followers were sincerely and profoundly convinced that they had encountered him alive again in fully embodied form. This in turn cohered with his claim that God was establishing a new creation or world order, and with the disciples staking their lives, both in this age and in the coming one, on their convictions.[78]

*A Webb of Key Events: Taking Us Bock to Jesus the Messiah*. Pride of place in this compilation of recent, thorough studies of Jesus's life must go to an anthology edited by Darrell Bock and Robert Webb.[79] I should bracket my own contribution to this volume in giving that commendation, lest I sound simply self-serving, but the other eleven are excellent. The Institute for Biblical Research (IBR) commissioned

---

76. Keener, *Historical Jesus of the Gospels*, 266.
77. Keener, *Historical Jesus of the Gospels*, 306.
78. Keener, *Historical Jesus of the Gospels*, 348.
79. Darrell L. Bock and Robert L. Webb, eds., *Key Events in the Life of the Historical Jesus: A Collaborative Exploration of Context and Coherence* (Tübingen: Mohr Siebeck, 2009; Grand Rapids: Eerdmans, 2010). James Crossley, who affirms no Christian commitment at all, thinks that this anthology may be the strongest presentation of evangelical historical Jesus scholarship currently available, but then he uses this observation as a springboard to insist that, against some who have argued that it was a theologically disinterested quest, the third quest is in fact a very theologically interested quest almost in its entirety ("Everybody's *Happy* Nowadays? A Critical Engagement with Key Events and Contemporary Quests for the Historical Jesus," *JSHJ* 11 [2014]: 224–41).

a historical Jesus study group, which met annually throughout the first decade of the twenty-first century, to review drafts of contributors' chapters dealing with twelve key events (or types of events) from Jesus's life, where there seemed to be the potential for a good case, using the standard criteria of authenticity, for those events to have genuinely occurred. Chapters were revised and vetted multiple times. Ancient primary literature was required to be cited when statements were made about the historical or cultural contexts of the events. Darrell Bock, in turn, penned a popular-level volume summarizing the highlights of the scholarly tome that the study group had produced.[80]

The twelve events in question were Jesus's baptism by John; exorcisms, inaugurating the arrival of the kingdom and the defeat of Satan; the calling of the Twelve; table fellowship with sinners; the Synoptic Sabbath controversies; Peter's declaration about the identity of Jesus on the road to Caesarea Philippi; the royal entry into Jerusalem; the temple incident; the Last Supper; blasphemy and Jesus's "examination" before the Sanhedrin; the Roman "examination" and the crucifixion; and the empty tomb and Jesus's appearance in Jerusalem. As they apply the criteria of authenticity, enough study goes into the relevant background and context so that contributors may then reflect on the meaning of each event or cluster of activities as well.

The editors write the two chapters that frame all the others. At the beginning, Webb reflects at length on methodological and historiographical issues.[81] At the end, Bock adds a thorough summary. His conclusion merits a full citation:

> Summing up, the historical Jesus presented the kingdom of God and the opportunity for participation in it. Such participation involved a turning in repentance to reaffirm the covenantal responsibility God originally gave to Israel, something Jesus' participation in John the baptizer's baptism and the selection of the twelve introduced. Jesus' activity called for a restored people of God and a renewed relationship with God that

---

80. Darrell L. Bock, *Who Is Jesus? Linking the Historical Jesus with the Christ of Faith* (New York: Howard Books, 2012).

81. Robert L. Webb, "The Historical Enterprise and Historical Jesus Research," in Bock and Webb, *Key Events in the Life of the Historical Jesus*, 9–93.

was built upon his own authority. This new relationship, evidenced by the call to outsiders to come in, ultimately would reform the disciples' relationship to others, leading in directions of righteousness and reconciliation. With the privilege of being connected to God's rule came the rest of Jesus' teaching which we have not sought to corroborate in our study. This teaching called for the pursuit of a challenging personal and societal righteousness that honored God, reconfigured our role as God's creatures, and served as a contrasting paradigm to the world about how to live. This trajectory appears to cohere with what we have established. By acting to show this decisive era's arrival, Jesus affirmed his central role in its coming, calling on people to believe in what God was doing through him and, in doing so, to follow him. In this way, his actions spoke as loud [sic] as his words, giving his words presented in conjunction with such acts a context in which they could be illustrated and appreciated.[82]

If anything, this conclusion is understated in terms of what the various chapters have demonstrated individually. At the beginning of the book, the editors indicate this anthology's coherence with Hengel's emphases on Jewish backgrounds and Jesus as Messiah.[83] A very recent work, to date only in German, is Rainer Riesner's *Messias Jesus*, which is written very much within the trajectory of Hengel and Schwemer, with detailed excurses on archaeology and topography, and even a cautious use of the Fourth Gospel at key points.[84] A much briefer and less technical English equivalent of sorts is David Wenham's *Jesus in Context: Making Sense of the Historical Figure*.[85]

In light of all these recent third-quest studies, then, it is hard to agree with those who say that it has made little progress. But has it done all it can? And what about a fourth quest?

82. Darrell L. Bock, "Key Events in the Life of the Historical Jesus: A Summary," in Bock and Webb, *Key Events in the Life of the Historical Jesus*, 852.
83. Darrell L. Bock and Robert L. Webb, "Introduction to Key Events and Actions in the Life of the Historical Jesus," in Bock and Webb, *Key Events in the Life of the Historical Jesus*, 2–3.
84. Rainer Riesner, *Messias Jesus: Seine Geschichte, seine Botschaft und ihre Überlieferung* (Giessen: Brunnen, 2019).
85. David Wenham, *Jesus in Context: Making Sense of the Historical Figure* (Cambridge: Cambridge University Press, 2021).

## Questioning the Criteria

Morna Hooker's two little articles in the 1970s questioning the misuse of some of the authenticity criteria (see above, 55–56) had little effect on historical Jesus research in their day. Perhaps she was simply decades ahead of her time. Hooker never called for the abandonment of the criteria; she merely called for a greater awareness of what they can and cannot demonstrate. A glaring weakness in many studies was the frequent negative use of the criteria to argue for something in the Gospels as unhistorical. In 2012, Chris Keith and Anthony Le Donne coedited a small book of essays called *Jesus, Criteria, and the Demise of Authenticity*, crediting Hooker for her contributions and making it sound as if she had claimed somewhat more than she had.[86] Several essayists, including Keith in particular, conveyed the impression that recent developments in the study of the criteria invalidated their use altogether. Jesus research, as a result, had to turn in different directions.[87]

### *Understanding the Critique*

What precipitated this watershed claim? One factor was the observation that the criteria were developed by the old form critics and depended on the form-critical assumptions of relatively isolated sayings, stories, or small collections of them, circulating independently. Today that model has been largely debunked, so the criteria should be abandoned as well.[88] But it is not at all obvious how dissimilarity, multiple attestation, Palestinian environment, and coherence, to take just the most common four, cannot function positively to help authenticate material with or without the original form-critical model. One may have a

---

86. Chris Keith and Anthony Le Donne, eds., *Jesus, Criteria, and the Demise of Authenticity* (London: T&T Clark, 2012).

87. Esp. the editors of *Jesus, Criteria, and the Demise of Authenticity*: Anthony Le Donne, "The Rise of the Quest for an Authentic Jesus: An Introduction to the Crumbling Foundations of Jesus Research," 3–21; Chris Keith, "The Fall of the Quest for an Authentic Jesus: Concluding Remarks," 200–205.

88. Chris Keith, "The Indebtedness of the Criteria Approach to Form Criticism and Recent Attempts to Rehabilitate the Search for an Authentic Jesus," in Keith and Le Donne, *Jesus, Criteria, and the Demise of Authenticity*, 25–48. See also Keith, "The Narratives of the Gospels and the Historical Jesus: Current Debates, Prior Debates and the Goal of Historical Jesus Research," *JSNT* 38 (2016): 426–55.

slightly different list of what one deems to be independent sources, but that doesn't invalidate multiple attestation. Likewise, what is distinctive about Jesus remains distinctive, however the tradition was passed on. The same is true of that which fits a certain environment or coheres with sayings already authenticated. Elsewhere Keith wrote an article pitting the "Jesus-memory" approach against the "criteria" approach in another unnecessary either-or dichotomy, which in fact winds up affirming that "Jesus-memory" combines the best of form criticism with the best of the criteria of authenticity.[89] But Jesus-memory is a reminder that all ancient testimony about Jesus must be filtered through the lens of how people remembered him, form criticism postulates somewhat isolated pericopes being passed on in the tradition, and the criteria have to do with assessing authenticity. While each has been used in ways that affect one or two of the others, at heart each is dealing with a separate aspect of the oral tradition. To use a contemporary analogy, the way one takes notes throughout a semester of lectures, whether one studies each lecture largely in isolation from the others, and how well one recalls, synthesizes, and uses the information on an exam are not unrelated processes, but they are not three alternate ways of preparing for an examination. Each has its role to play and can be done well or poorly.[90] The same is true with original memories of Jesus, form-critical shaping in the oral tradition, and whether the final, written product can satisfy certain criteria of authenticity.

It also seems like it was the more skeptical contributors to the various quests who stimulated the writers in the Keith and Le Donne volume more than the works that this chapter has surveyed. There is no interaction with, nor even a mention anywhere in their work of, the historical Jesus studies of Bock and Webb, Keener, or Puig i Tàrrech, while Hengel, Schröter, and Pagola receive only passing mention.[91] The

---

89. Chris Keith, "Memory and Authenticity: Jesus Tradition and What Really Happened," *ZNW* 102 (2011): 155–77.

90. See further F. Gerald Downing, "Feasible Researches in Historical Jesus Tradition: A Response to Chris Keith," *JSNT* 40 (2017): 51–61; Michael Licona, "Is the Sky Falling in Contemporary Historical Jesus Research?," *BBR* 26 (2016): 353–68.

91. "Index of Authors," in Keith and Le Donne, *Jesus, Criteria, and the Demise of Authenticity*, 227–30.

contributors are understandably more worried about the negative use of the criteria, but that is no reason for jettisoning all positive use of them. The results of their positive use in these six (and other) historical Jesus books would certainly suggest that they continue to play an important role in Jesus research.

*Additional Criteria*

Throughout the third quest, various criteria were proposed in order to supplement or even partially replace the standard criteria of the new quest. John Meier introduced the criterion of "rejection and execution," or what might be called a "necessary explanation" for why Jesus was crucified. Unless one's life of Jesus gave a compelling explanation for why Jesus was so violently rejected and executed, it probably did not contain the right combination of authenticated material, or at least it did not interpret that material properly.[92] Meier also divided the standard criteria into two categories, primary and secondary, calling the latter "indices" that typically came into play only after utilizing the primary criteria. Meier labeled embarrassment, discontinuity, multiple attestation, coherence, and rejection and execution as the primary criteria, and "traces of Aramaic," "Palestinian environment," "vividness of narration," "the tendencies of the developing Synoptic tradition," and "historical presumption" (which is really not a criterion but rather the claim that the burden of proof is on everyone who makes a claim) as the secondary criteria or indices.[93]

Finnish scholar Tom Holmén argued for replacing the double dissimilarity criterion with what he called a "continuum approach."[94] Scholars should be looking for features of the Jesus tradition that can

---

92. John P. Meier, *A Marginal Jew: Rethinking the Historical Jesus*, 5 vols. to date (New York: Doubleday, 1991–2001; New Haven: Yale University Press, 2009–16), 1:177.

93. Meier, *Marginal Jew*, 1:168–84.

94. Tom Holmén, ed., *Jesus in Continuum* (Tübingen: Mohr Siebeck, 2012); cf. Holmén, ed., *Jesus from Judaism to Christianity: Continuum Approaches to the Historical Jesus* (London: T&T Clark, 2007). See also Jonathan Bernier, *The Quest for the Historical Jesus after the Demise of Authenticity: Toward a Critical Realist Philosophy of History in Jesus Studies* (London: Bloomsbury T&T Clark, 2016), 73–96, summarized on p. 158: "There is not rupture but, rather, continuity between Second Temple Judaism, Jesus's ministry, and the apostolic, and later, patristic churches."

be explained as the outgrowth of similar beliefs or behavior in the immediate environment from which Jesus emerged and that fairly directly led to early Christian tenets or practice in the same arenas. Dale Allison's work on constructing Jesus, as we have seen, built on that kind of continuum to highlight facets of the Synoptic Gospels that not only had this kind of continuity but also recurred frequently enough to be deemed characteristic of Jesus.[95] These scholars do not deny discontinuities between conventional Judaism and Jesus or between Jesus and the early church, but they focus on drawing plausible lines of development from Judaism to Jesus to the early church. Holmén gives a particularly detailed example with the concept of the temple in Jerusalem, which provoked Jesus's teachings about the destruction of the temple and the building of the church (Mark 13:1–2; Matt. 16:18)—which in turn lay behind early Christian reflection on the church as a temple and Christians as living stones (see esp. 1 Cor. 3:16–17; 6:19; Eph. 2:20–22; 1 Pet. 2:4–8).[96]

Robert Webb proposed "the criterion of inherent ambiguity," which arose out of repeated conversations in the IBR Historical Jesus Study Group. He defines it as follows: "Material that could be interpreted in two quite different ways—one positive and one negative—and that would require an explanation to help the audience avoid the negative viewpoint may be considered more likely to be authentic."[97] In some ways, this parallels the criteria of embarrassment and of tendencies against an evangelist's redaction. If the evangelists consistently want to depict Jesus in a positive light, but they present something that is quite ambiguous, presumably it is not invented, because they could have fashioned something they made up to appear wholly positive. Webb uses the triumphal entry as an illustration. Obviously the crowds

---

95. Allison, *Constructing Jesus*, throughout.
96. Tom Holmén, "Caught in the Act: Jesus Starts the New Temple: A Continuum Study of Jesus as the Founder of the *Ecclesia*," in *The Identity of Jesus: Nordic Voices*, ed. Samuel Byrskog, Tom Holmén, and Matti Kankaanniemi (Tübingen: Mohr Siebeck, 2014), 181–231.
97. Webb, "Historical Enterprise and Historical Jesus Research," 71. Partially parallel is the insistence by Tom Thatcher that ambiguous statements in the form of "Riddles, Wit, and Wisdom" are a key part of the authentic Jesus's teaching. See his essay so titled in Holmén and Porter, *Handbook for the Study of the Historical Jesus*, 4:3349–72.

cheering Jesus on were interpreting the event in a quite different light than Jesus (and his later biographers) did.[98]

Stanley Porter authored a book that split its time between, on the one hand, summarizing the quests and critiquing the standard criteria and, on the other hand, proposing three new criteria of authenticity. What Porter labeled "the criterion of Greek language and its context"[99] was not so much a criterion of authenticity as an attempt to determine those contexts in which it was likely that Jesus spoke Greek. In such instances, what we have in the Gospels could be not merely Jesus's *ipsissima vox* but his *ipsissima verba*, since they were written in Greek. Porter dubbed his second new criterion as that of "textual variance."[100] Those passages in which the vast textual tradition available to us shows a larger percentage of significant variation are more likely to have been modified over time than those in which the textual apparatus reveals fewer and less significant changes. Third, the criterion of "discourse features" suggests that those passages in which Jesus talks at some length, resembling a short homily in form, which may even be an abbreviation of a significantly longer address, have certain recurring syntactical distinctives.[101] These, once identified, can be what exegetes look for elsewhere in the Gospels' longer discourses as potential signs of the authentic Jesus. This last criterion somewhat resembles what Brian Wright terms the criterion of "Greek syntax."[102]

None of Porter's criteria has caught on much.[103] More people have used Holmén's continuum approach, though not necessarily with

---

98. Webb, "Historical Enterprise and Historical Jesus Research," 71–72.

99. Stanley E. Porter, *The Criteria for Authenticity in Historical-Jesus Research: Previous Discussion and New Proposals* (Sheffield: Sheffield Academic, 2000), 126–64.

100. Porter, *Criteria for Authenticity*, 181–209. Cf. Daniel B. Wallace, "Textual Criticism and the Criterion of Embarrassment," in Bock and Komoszewski, *Jesus, Skepticism, and the Problem of History*, 93–124.

101. Porter, *Criteria for Authenticity*, 210–37.

102. Brian J. Wright, "Greek Syntax as a Criterion of Authenticity: A New Discussion and Proposal," *CBQ* 74 (2012): 84–100.

103. Porter himself applied the criterion of Greek language and its context ("Luke 17.11–19 and the Criteria for Authenticity Revisited," *JSHJ* 1 [2003]: 201–24). But Sang-Il Lee thinks that the criterion assumes unidirectionality of translation from Aramaic into Greek without recognizing the possibility that the Greek of the Gospels, even where Jesus may have originally spoken in Greek, could still be the translation by the evangelist of the Aramaic that Jesus's original Greek utterance had to have been turned into in the oral tradition, if the first Christians were

that name (recall Allison), or the criterion of necessary explanation of the crucifixion. The most promising new direction was first suggested independently in 1996 by N. T. Wright and a pair of German scholars, Gerd Theissen and Annette Merz. It would then be significantly elaborated by Theissen in conjunction with Dagmar Winter in 2001. Wright referred to a *double dissimilarity and double similarity criterion*.[104] The Germans spoke of the *criterion of historical plausibility*, which they also divided into four parts. At the first level of division are "coherence and agreement"; at the second, "incoherence and disagreement." Under each of these come "plausibility of influence" and "plausibility of context." The plausibility of influence under coherence and agreement is labeled "plausible coherence of influence," while under incoherence and disagreement it is called "plausible influence contrary to the tradition." The plausibility of context under coherence and agreement is labeled "correspondence of context," while under incoherence and disagreement it is called "individuality of context."[105]

The terminology used by Theissen, Merz, and Winter is simply making more precise the kinds of similarity and dissimilarity we should look for in comparing Jesus both to his Jewish world and to early Christianity. Historical plausibility is just a more nuanced form of double similarity and double dissimilarity. In other words, when a saying or event from the Jesus tradition is at least plausible within an early first-century Palestinian Jewish context (and not anachronistic), and when emerging Christianity picked up on it in some noticeable way, and yet that saying or event also shows a considerable amount of distinctiveness over against both Judaism and early Christianity, then we have a very powerful criterion of authenticity. Various historical Jesus

---

living in a largely Jewish context (*Jesus and Gospel Traditions in Bilingual Context: A Study in the Interdirectionality of Language* [Berlin: de Gruyter, 2012], 55–58).

104. N. T. Wright, *Jesus and the Victory of God*, Christian Origins and the Question of God 2 (London: SPCK; Minneapolis: Fortress, 1996), 131–33.

105. Gerd Theissen and Annette Merz, *The Historical Jesus: A Comprehensive Guide*, trans. John Bowden (Minneapolis: Fortress, 1998), 116–18; Gerd Theissen and Dagmar Winter, *The Quest for the Plausible Jesus*, trans. M. Eugene Boring (Louisville: Westminster John Knox, 2002 [Ger. orig. 1997]).

scholars have applauded this as a good development.[106] It is insufficient to talk merely about the *dissimilarity* criterion or about a *continuum* approach; we need both simultaneously. Of course, by definition that will involve a smaller selection of details that will pass safely through the filter, and none of these scholars is suggesting that the criterion be used negatively to exclude that which doesn't make it through. But it does mean that we can have a very good reason for saying that something is likely to be authentic or historical if it passes muster with all four parts of the criterion.

What is fascinating is that Dagmar Winter, the scholar who developed historical plausibility as a tool in the greatest detail, was one of the very contributors to the anthology of essays that Keith and Le Donne edited.[107] While all the contributors to the slim volume were discontent with some current use of the standard criteria, the editors clearly were not just looking for viewpoints entirely consistent with their own more sweeping rejection of a criteria-based approach. Or perhaps they were only expressing their displeasure with the most common criteria while being open to trying out newer ones. Either way, it appears that historical plausibility has *not* been included among the tools they reject, to be discarded at the end of a cul-de-sac, as it were.[108]

### *Applying the Criterion of Historical Plausibility*

Five examples from the Synoptic tradition should help illustrate how historical plausibility works. The results are not dramatically different from what the other criteria validated, because Palestinian environment

---

106. Sean Freyne, *Jesus, a Jewish Galilean: A New Reading of the Jesus Story* (London: T&T Clark, 2004), 22, 172; Petr Pokorný, "Jesus as Feedback on His *Wirkungsgeschichte*," in *Jesus in Geschichte und Bekenntnis* (Tübingen: Mohr Siebeck, 2016), 36–38; Lee Martin McDonald, *The Story of Jesus in History and Faith: An Introduction* (Grand Rapids: Baker Academic, 2013), 44; Bengt Holmberg, "Futures for the Jesus Quests," in Holmén and Porter, *Handbook for the Study of the Historical Jesus*, 2:905–6.

107. Dagmar Winter, "Saving the Quest for Authenticity from the Criterion of Dissimilarity: History and Plausibility," in Keith and Le Donne, *Jesus, Criteria, and the Demise of Authenticity*, 115–31.

108. Tobias Hägerland is not part of the anthology but acknowledges many of the same weaknesses of the criteria, also proposing more nuanced uses rather than wholesale abandonment of them ("The Future of Criteria in Historical Jesus Research," *JSHJ* 13 [2015]: 43–65).

always had stood somewhat at odds with dissimilarity from Judaism and rarely did dissimilarity with emerging Christianity ever extend to the entire absence of a theme or passage's influence on the early church. One of the helpful by-products of historical plausibility, however, is the diminished need to rely on multiple attestation and the diminished likelihood that single attestation will automatically engender suspicion about the historicity of a given element in the Gospels.

*The kingdom of God.* Mark 1:14–15 uses as part of its "headline" over Jesus's ministry his announcement that the kingdom of God had drawn near. Remarkably, the actual expression "kingdom of God" appears nowhere in the Old Testament, and it is rare in Second Temple Jewish literature. Yet the concept of God as king permeates the Old Testament and subsequent Jewish writings. The expression "kingdom of God" appears sixty-four times in the Synoptics versus only fourteen times in Paul and three times in John. And the early church quickly lost sight of the original sociopolitical element of the kingdom. Thus, it is sufficiently Jewish to be credible in Jesus's context, yet sufficiently distinctive not to have likely been invented by someone else. It is not unknown in the early church, yet it hardly appears with the frequency and emphasis that it does in the Synoptics. All four parts of the historical plausibility criterion are satisfied.[109]

*Calling the Twelve (Mark 3:13–19 pars.).* It was standard practice for a rabbi to associate himself with disciples, so even if Jesus's role was more self-styled, it would have been natural for him to select a number of particularly close followers. And, as many in the third quest have observed, the number "twelve" is almost certainly designed to call to mind the twelve tribes of Israel, so that in some way Jesus is claiming to restore his nation. But no one has yet appealed to Jesus, wanting to follow him, and he has not selected from among a group of prize, potential students who hoped to study with him, as was typically the case. In the early church, numerous people function as followers of older or more mature Christians. Paul alone has Timothy and Titus singled out for special mention. Yet remarkably, even though the term

---

109. Theissen and Merz, *Historical Jesus*, 246–64. Cf. G. R. Beasley-Murray, *Jesus and the Kingdom of God* (Grand Rapids: Eerdmans, 1986).

*mathētēs* appears 262 times in the Gospels and Acts, it recurs nowhere else in the New Testament. It was not that it was reserved for followers of Jesus, because the book of Acts knows of disciples of Paul (Acts 9:25; 19:30) and of John the Baptist (19:1, 3). But apparently the specific kind of discipleship Jesus promoted became so associated with the Twelve that the church began to use other terms for those who trained under a different early Christian leader. Again, we have both similarity and dissimilarity with both Judaism and early Christianity.[110]

*Healings and exorcisms.* Isaiah 35:5–6 clearly predicted that miracles would accompany the eschatological ministry that came to be associated with the Messiah. Qumran and Jesus both picked up on this concept (Messianic Apocalypse [4Q521]; Matt. 11:5 par.). There were some parallels to Jesus's healings already in the miracles of Elijah and Elisha. Other signs and wonders were unprecedented, such as healing the blind. And no previous miracles in Jewish history were ever alleged to demonstrate that the kingdom of God had begun to arrive, as Jesus claimed the miracles demonstrated with him (Luke 11:20 par.). Neither was Satan's overthrow said to have begun, as in the aftermath of the sending of the seventy(-two) in Luke 10:18–19. Miracle-working and exorcistic activity continue throughout the New Testament, but after the earliest years of the Christian movement, they begin to wane noticeably. Despite the claims of some that these ended with the close of the New Testament, a fair number of reports continue through the third century.[111] But already in the latter portions of the New Testament and certainly beyond it, supernatural healings take on numerous functions without as consistently or explicitly pointing to the arrival of God's reign.[112]

*Pronouncement/conflict stories (e.g., Mark 2:1–3:6 pars.).* Every topic that appears in a pronouncement or conflict story in the Gospels fits a

110. Theissen and Merz, *Historical Jesus*, 213–17.
111. Cecil M. Robeck, *Prophecy in Carthage: Perpetua, Tertullian, and Cyprian* (Cleveland: Pilgrim, 1992).
112. Theissen and Merz, *Historical Jesus*, 281–313; Craig A. Evans, "Inaugurating the Kingdom of God and Defeating the Kingdom of Satan," *BBR* 15 (2005): 49–75; Graham H. Twelftree, *Jesus the Miracle Worker: A Historical and Theological Study* (Downers Grove, IL: InterVarsity, 1999).

common early first-century Jewish milieu: debates about forgiveness of sins, associating with sinners, fasting, keeping the Sabbath, corban laws and ritual purity, payment of taxes, the reality of the resurrection, and so on. No anachronisms appear here; in fact, some of these topics took on considerably less significance in the early church. Yet they did remain, even as the church, especially in the second century, often reverted to more legalistic practices. Gone was the full awareness of how radical Jesus's original teaching had been, which also explained its controversial nature. While some of the debates touched only issues of halakah in the oral Torah, others seemed to strike at something in the written law of Moses as well. The concept of "contagious holiness," which I spoke of earlier (see xix), was not often preserved. Significant dissimilarity and similarity with both Judaism and early Christianity once again emerges distinctly.[113]

*Redefining family (Mark 3:31–35 pars.).* In a strongly pro-family environment, Jesus's teaching about leaving family for the sake of ministry proved highly countercultural. Yet Jesus still affirms the fifth commandment of the Decalogue, about honoring one's father and mother (Mark 7:10 par.; 10:19 pars.). Still, when God's call conflicts with the clear teaching of Scripture, the believer has no choice but to follow God rather than fellow human beings. Paul will agree in 1 Corinthians 7, but he seemingly changes his mind in Ephesians 5. If we are not merely to punt and label Ephesians as pseudonymous, we must recognize both a new and an old dimension to Jesus's teaching throughout. Early church practice very quickly turned what at least sounded like a message of freedom into something much more conservative, rigid, or legal in nature. But, at least within the pages of the New Testament books, even at as solemn a gathering as the apostolic council, early Christian speakers can say, "It seemed good to the Holy Spirit and to us not to . . ." (Acts 15:28), without any whiff of legalism

---

113. Craig L. Blomberg, *Contagious Holiness: Jesus' Meals with Sinners* (Downers Grove, IL: InterVarsity, 2005); Blomberg, "The Authenticity and Significance of Jesus' Table Fellowship with Sinners," in Bock and Webb, *Key Events in the Life of the Historical Jesus*, 215–50; Simone Paganini and Boris Repschinski, "Kontinuität und Diskontinuität in der Reinheitsthematik von Judentum des weiten Tempels zum Neuen Testament," *ZKT* 134 (2012): 449–70.

being retained.[114] Good advice may be crucial, and we will continue to see passing references to the topics that dominated Jesus's repartee with the religious authorities. But Jesus offers no new law. The whole concept of contagious holiness that emerged out of controversy with the religious leaders fits only in a context concerned with ritual purity, but it shines a radically new light on the topic. After Pentecost, such debates disappear almost entirely, yet by the second century the pendulum has swung so that those who observe a day of rest, for example, are accused by some of being Judaizers![115]

None of this authenticates every detail in every passage in the Gospels that impinges on the issues discussed here. The criterion of historical plausibility cannot be that blunt a tool. But it does mean that substantial cores of the relevant passages most likely do reflect the kinds of things that characterized the public ministry of Jesus.

## More Global Factors Favoring the Conservation of the Jesus Tradition

Can we go further? Three developments beginning already during the new quest but continuing beyond it seem to hold out promise.

### *The Guarded Tradition*

We have already had occasion to encounter the topic of memorization in the ancient world. Most New Testament scholars today finally acknowledge the groundbreaking work of researchers like Birger Gerhardsson and Samuel Byrskog (see above, 50–51). But those who have not carefully studied it too easily dismiss it because it does not adequately explain the differences among the Synoptic parallels. Neither scholar ever claimed that memorization was an adequate explanation for all the Synoptic phenomena; rather, they merely asserted that it

---

114. Craig L. Blomberg, "The Christian and the Law of Moses," in *Witness to the Gospel: The Theology of Acts*, ed. I. Howard Marshall and David Peterson (Grand Rapids: Eerdmans, 1998), 397–416, esp. 407–10.

115. William Barclay, *The Plain Man's Guide to Ethics: Thoughts on the Ten Commandments* (Glasgow: Collins Fontana Books, 1973), 30–32.

was an important one that needed to be added into the mix, given its ubiquity as a method of education in both the Jewish and Greco-Roman worlds, given its role in the composition of public rhetoric, and given the obvious literary relationships among the Gospels as well.[116] One really needs to peruse the material surveyed by scholars like Craig Keener on how common remarkable feats of memorization occurred in what were predominantly oral cultures without the myriad of distractions we face in the modern world and without the myriad of resources to preserve information in print-based media that thereby make memorization unnecessary.[117]

Add to that how quickly the words and deeds of Jesus were deemed to be of great significance and even "holy,"[118] and the desire for careful preservation would have increased even more. By far the most recurring problem with those who would question the ancients' ability to remember large amounts of detail over a prolonged period is the use of experiments with modern, Westernized individuals.[119] Of course,

---

116. Birger Gerhardsson makes this particularly clear throughout *The Reliability of the Gospel Tradition* (Peabody, MA: Hendrickson, 2001; repr., Grand Rapids: Baker Academic, 2010). Cf. Samuel Byrskog, *Jesus the Only Teacher: Didactic Authority and Transmission in Ancient Israel, Ancient Judaism and the Matthean Community* (Stockholm: Almqvist & Wiksell, 1994). For Gerhardsson's reaction to the next two developments that I will discuss (flexible transmission with fixed limits and social memory), see Birger Gerhardsson, "The Secret of the Transmission of the Unwritten Jesus Tradition," *NTS* 51 (2005): 1–18. For appreciative but critical interaction with Gerhardsson's life work, see Werner H. Kelber and Samuel Byrskog, eds., *Jesus in Memory: Traditions in Oral and Scribal Perspective* (Waco: Baylor University Press, 2009).

117. Craig S. Keener, *Christobiography: Memory, History, and the Reliability of the Gospels* (Grand Rapids: Eerdmans, 2019), 420–37. For the methods used to hone memory, see Jocelyn P. Small, *Wax Tablets of the Mind: Cognitive Studies of Memory in Classical Antiquity* (London: Routledge, 1997), 81–137; for modern-day parallels that make the ancients' claims at least credible, see p. 128. Richard Bauckham shows how some New Testament scholars have wrongly interpreted contemporary research to claim that memory is generally unreliable ("The Psychology of Memory and the Study of the Gospels," *JSHJ* 16 [2018]: 136–55). "Personal event memory" under normal circumstances, and especially in very significant situations, is in fact generally trustworthy.

118. J. Arthur Baird, *Holy Word: The Paradigm of New Testament Formation* (Sheffield: Sheffield Academic, 2002), 46–63.

119. Of many possible examples, see April D. DeConick, "Human Memory and the Sayings of Jesus: Contemporary Experimental Exercises in the Transmission of Jesus Traditions," in *Jesus, the Voice, and the Text: Beyond the Oral and the Written Gospel*, ed. Tom Thatcher (Waco: Baylor University Press, 2008), 135–79, 269–70; J. C. S. Redman, "How Accurate Are the Eyewitnesses? Bauckham and the Eyewitnesses in Light of Psychological Research," *JBL* 129 (2010): 177–97.

we forget lots of things, garble others, and do this much too quickly, because we have not cultivated the skills of memory the way people in the ancient Mediterranean world did. A second major gaffe in most criticism of the guarded tradition hypothesis is the neglect of the fact that the disciples would have heard Jesus say much of what they recorded of his teaching most likely a few hundred times over the course of three years. If he indeed went throughout most of the towns and villages of Israel (Matt. 9:35), he certainly would not have invented a different way of phrasing his message in each new venue! Moreover, Jesus sent the Twelve out at least once (Mark 6:7–13), and likely more often (esp. if they were among the seventy[-two] in Luke 10:1–20) to replicate his ministry without him.[120] Long before even the shortest portion of a Gospel source was written down, the disciples would have practiced and perhaps already put in some stereotypic form what they wanted to communicate to others about his deeds and his words. The book of Acts gives the barest of summaries of early Christian preaching and teaching. But what would have been more natural or expected than that the apostles would continue both the form and the contents of their messages about Jesus immediately after his death and resurrection as they had previously?

### *Flexible Transmission with Fixed Limits*

I have also already introduced this category above (51–52). Studies go far beyond those by Kenneth Bailey, just in case his was flawed (as has been alleged but also rebutted).[121] In addition to A. B. Lord (see above, 51), Jan Vansina produced pioneering studies of a period of several de-

---

120. See esp. Gerd Theissen, "Jesus as an Itinerant Teacher: Reflections on Social History from Jesus' Roles," in *Jesus Research: An International Perspective; The First Princeton-Prague Symposium on Jesus Research, Prague 2005*, ed. James H. Charlesworth with Petr Pokorný (Grand Rapids: Eerdmans, 2009), 98–122.

121. For the challenge, see Theodore Weeden, "Kenneth Bailey's Theory of Oral Tradition: A Theory Contested by Its Evidence," *JSHJ* 7 (2009): 3–43; for the responses, see James D. G. Dunn, "Kenneth Bailey's Theory of Oral Tradition: Critiquing Theodore Weeden's Critique," *JSHJ* 7 (2009): 44–62; Craig S. Keener, "Weighing T. J. Weeden's Critique of Kenneth Bailey's Approach," *JGRChJ* 13 (2017): 41–78. Michael F. Bird endorses Bailey's approach but then supplements it with social memory (see note 128 below) ("The Formation of the Gospels in the Setting of Early Christianity: The Jesus Tradition as Corporate Memory," *WTJ* 67 [2005]: 113–34).

cades, particularly in traditional African contexts.[122] Prior to teachings or stories from great teachers becoming formally canonized—treated as uniquely authoritative in some way—there were still all kinds of checks and balances as storytellers "performed" their narratives in many different contexts. The freedom to abbreviate, omit, rearrange, select, add back in, explain, paraphrase, and so on, depending on the occasion, was always constrained by certain limits or fixed parameters. The storyteller who failed to include one of these lodestars or who significantly distorted its meaning might expect to be interrupted and corrected by others in the audience who also knew the epic tale.[123]

Rafael Rodríguez observes that "the programme of atomizing, de-contextualizing and recontextualizing snippets of the gospel tradition in order to critically reconstruct the 'historical Jesus' has been exposed as culturally and historically inappropriate."[124] In other words, the Jesus Seminar's approach, to take just the extreme example, fits neither the time nor the cultures of the ancient Mediterranean world. There is still a range of options for the forms of historiography or biography that the Gospels represent. "But the question of whether we ought to take them seriously as instances of the Jesus tradition has been answered. Unless we decide to give up the *historical* analysis of Jesus and of Christian origins, we have no other option."[125] Ruben Zimmermann also highlights the role of genre in the fixation of memory: "The form-bound memory is no longer completely free. Its wording may not be defined; however, the prominent characteristics and structures that place it into a genre are set. Thus we perceive a relative fixation of the linguistic form located between a freer oral memory and a memory set down literally in text."[126] Moreover, similar literature from the ancient Mediterranean world that deals with recent people and events tends

122. See esp. Jan Vansina, *Oral Tradition as History* (Madison: University of Wisconsin Press, 1985).
123. Paul R. Eddy, "The Historicity of the Early Oral Jesus Tradition: Reflections on the 'Reliability Wars,'" in Bock and Komoszewski, *Jesus, Skepticism, and the Problem of History*, 163.
124. Rafael Rodríguez, *Structuring Early Christian Memory: Jesus in Tradition, Performance and Text* (London: T&T Clark, 2010), 224–25.
125. Rodríguez, *Structuring Early Christian Memory*, 225.
126. Ruben Zimmermann, "Memory and Form Criticism: The Typicality of Memory as a Bridge between Orality and Literality in the Early Christian Remembering Process," in *The*

to be much more reliable than that dealing with the more distant past. "Researchers should neither treat the Gospels more skeptically nor demand from them greater precision than we would from comparable works of their era."[127]

## Social Memory

One of the most fascinating of the newer developments in the study of oral tradition is the discipline of *social memory*.[128] One seasoned practitioner, Alan Kirk, defines it this way: "First, the shaping of the individual by the social and cultural frameworks of the groups to which persons belong, and second, the shared cultural representations and artefacts (= *traditions*) that emerge from a community's commemorative activities."[129] We may all be familiar with ways in which certain authority figures can spin an account of very real events and repeat it in skewed fashion often enough until people who were eyewitnesses and who knew better begin to believe that's how things actually happened. Or a peer who was a fellow eyewitness of something has different memories from yours, and a conversation with that person leads to a new reconstruction of just what happened, whether it is more accurate than the one you had in the first place. All the changes, intentional and unintentional, that can occur to one's personal memory can occur to a group's memory of something in which all have participated. To the extent that events are recounted regularly and vividly, even people who were not originally present may start to think that they were. These

---

*Interface of Orality and Writing: Speaking, Seeing, Writing in the Shaping of New Genres*, ed. Annette Weissenrieder and Robert B. Coote (Tübingen: Mohr Siebeck, 2010), 143.

127. Craig S. Keener, "Assumptions in Historical Jesus Research: Using Ancient Biographies and Disciples' Traditioning as a Control," *JSHJ* 9 (2011): 26.

128. For an introduction to its application to Gospel studies, see Richard Bauckham, *Jesus and the Eyewitnesses: The Gospels as Eyewitness Testimony* (Grand Rapids: Eerdmans, 2006), 240–357. See also Robert K. McIver, *Memory, Jesus, and the Synoptic Gospels* (Atlanta: Society of Biblical Literature, 2011), 81–182; Michael F. Bird, *The Gospel of the Lord: How the Early Church Wrote the Story of Jesus* (Grand Rapids: Eerdmans, 2014), 95–113; Sandra Huebenthal, "'Frozen Moments'—Early Christianity through the Lens of Social Memory Theory," in *Memory and Memories in Early Christianity: Proceedings of the International Conference Held at the Universities of Geneva and Lausanne (June 2–3, 2016)*, ed. Simon Butticaz and Enrico Norelli (Tübingen: Mohr Siebeck, 2018), 17–43.

129. Alan Kirk, "Collective Memory/Social Memory," in *The Dictionary of the Bible and Ancient Media*, ed. Tom Thatcher et al. (London: Bloomsbury T&T Clark, 2017), 59.

and numerous other distortions of what happened can be caused by social memories.[130]

What is less commonly noted, however, are the remedial or rehabilitative possibilities of social memory.[131] One person forgets details that others can fill in. One person remembers something a certain way but changes their mind when enough other credible people disagree. When preserving truth is an important value and individuals within a group are willing to listen to one another, the collective results of everyone's memories may lead to a product that is better and more accurate than any single individual's memories.[132] When a narrative about a group of people is important to that group, especially in an oral culture, they will look for as many opportunities to retell it as they can. Public checks and balances intrude again, just as with the informal, controlled tradition discussed above. When a narrative is regularly recounted, even if in variant forms, newcomers to a community will quickly learn it and intuit which parts are fixed and which are flexible in retelling. If the group exists over time, so that original eyewitnesses increasingly give way to younger, newer members not originally present, the repeated narrative can be passed on with considerable accuracy, especially when it is institutionalized or ritualized in some way and when something in the group's ideology depends on it.[133]

---

130. For a good discussion of the distortions that can be created, written by someone aware of the positive constraints that can also be present, see Rodríguez, *Structuring Early Christian Memory*, 50–64.

131. On this generally conservative strand of social memory, see Samuel Byrskog, "A New Quest for the *Sitz im Leben*: Social Memory, the Jesus Tradition and the Gospel of Matthew," *NTS* 52 (2006): 319–36. Cf. James D. G. Dunn, "Social Memory and the Oral Jesus Tradition," in Stuckenbruck, Barton, and Wold, *Memory in the Bible and Antiquity*, 193–94. Dunn focuses on "how tradition functions in an oral society," "how repeated instruction can shape a life and become the life-blood of a community," "how tradition can serve as the actively continuing expression of a transforming encounter with the one remembered," and "how regular performance in quasi-liturgical contexts can sustain the substance and overall shape of what and who is remembered." He concludes, "These are the features I continue to find as hallmarks of the Jesus tradition in its character of 'the same yet different.' And these continue to persuade me that the Jesus tradition preserved in the Synoptic Gospels has been much more *retentive* than the various theories of social or cultural memory would seem to suggest."

132. See Jens Schröter, "Memory and Memories in Early Christianity: The Remembered Jesus as a Test Case," in *Memory and Identity in Ancient Judaism and Early Christianity: A Conversation with Barry Schwartz*, ed. Tom Thatcher (Atlanta: SBL Press, 2014), 95.

133. Barry Schwartz, "Where There's Smoke, There's Fire: Memory and History," in Thatcher, *Memory and Identity*, 7–37. Cf. Doron Mendels, "Societies of Memory in the Graeco-Roman

## Reflections

Paul Foster properly cautions against getting too excited about the guarded tradition, the flexible tradition with fixed limits, or social memory. He reminds us that they are not criteria themselves, but simply conditions of the oral tradition that at best might give us some optimism about the amount of authentic material we might recover.[134] The same is true if we buy into Richard Bauckham's arguments for multiple eyewitness traditions from the earliest stages of the tradition onward that preceded the composition of the first written Gospel sources.[135] None of these factors leads to an assessment of a specific saying of Jesus or passage in the Gospels, and they shouldn't be used as if they did.[136] On the other hand, Bauckham's reflections on memory, whether personal or collective, are still crucial. Among many important observations, he notes that memories of "exceptional or momentous events"—characterized by uniqueness, importance, emotion, and frequent rehearsal—are especially well retained.[137]

The key issue, however, is *repetition*. Even in our print-based culture today, many people at some point in their lives have large amounts of material memorized. It may be the lyrics and music to a group of their favorite songs, a long choral or theatrical performance, technical and other specialized information in their field, family stories from childhood, and much more. Some of it may have been formally memorized, some of it just remembered from dozens and even hun-

---

World," in Stuckenbruck, Barton, and Wold, *Memory in the Bible and Antiquity*, 151; Robert McIver, "Collective Memory and the Reliability of the Gospel Traditions," in Bock and Komoszewski, *Jesus, Skepticism, and the Problem of History*, 125–44.

134. Paul Foster, "Memory, Orality, and the Fourth Gospel: Three Dead-Ends in Historical Jesus Research," *JSHJ* 10 (2012): 198, 202. On the other hand, Foster's more sweeping rejection of these approaches as full-fledged cul-de-sacs goes too far. See Eric Eve, "Orality Is No Dead-End," *JSHJ* 13 (2015): 3–23; Stanley E. Porter and Hughson T. Ong, "Memory, Orality, and the Fourth Gospel: A Response to Paul Foster with Further Comments for Future Discussion," *JSHJ* 12 (2014): 143–64.

135. Bauckham, *Jesus and the Eyewitnesses*, 39–55.

136. This is what makes Chris Keith's pitting of social memory against the criteria of authenticity as two rival models hard to understand ("The Narratives of the Gospels and the Historical Jesus: Current Debates, Prior Debates and the Goal of Historical Jesus Research," *JSNT* 38 [2016]: 426–55). The two have different functions but can play complementary roles in Jesus research.

137. Bauckham, "Psychology of Memory," esp. 144–45.

dreds of episodes of recounting the information. Teachers, itinerant speakers, media celebrities, and others who regularly encounter diverse audiences reuse portions of talks as well as entire talks, sometimes with minor variations, but communicate the same material repeatedly. The least-appreciated feature in all the study of oral tradition in the first generation of the Jesus movement is the sheer frequency that his disciples, those they discipled, and so on, must have repeated, sometimes verbatim, sometimes just focusing on the gist, the same teachings and episodes from Jesus's life. Most of the skepticism about people's ability to preserve information that would have been readily deemed trustworthy by the cultural standards of the day evaporates when the "repetition factor" is taken seriously. Add to that the use of well-known mnemonic devices throughout the ancient Mediterranean world, and the possibilities of careful preservation of large amounts of material skyrocket.[138]

In an ancient oral culture in which memories were honed to such a greater degree than today, many ancient Middle Easterners like Jesus's disciples, with the proven ability to master large portions of the Hebrew Scriptures (or in the Greco-Roman world, the *Iliad* and the *Odyssey*) if they wanted to, could beyond any reasonable doubt have learned the gist of the words and deeds of Jesus as recorded in any of the Gospels.[139] Meanwhile, Kenneth Bailey reminds us of how he tried the children's game of "telephone" (an analogy to the oral tradition on which Bart Ehrman heavily relies)[140] with students in the Middle East from traditional subcultures and they couldn't understand the point of it, because they basically reproduced everything accurately![141] And all this still leaves room for all the factors that led to the variations among the Gospel accounts as we now have them.

138. Alessandro Vatri, "Ancient Greek Writing for Memory: Textual Features as Mnemonic Facilitators," *Mnemosyne* 68 (2015): 750–73.
139. Robert K. McIver, "Gist Memory: Memory, Gist and Verbatim," in Thatcher et al., *Dictionary of the Bible and Ancient Media*, 156–57. Cf. Small, *Wax Tablets of the Mind*, 223.
140. Bart D. Ehrman, *Jesus: Apocalyptic Prophet of the New Millennium* (Oxford: Oxford University Press, 1999), 51–52.
141. Kenneth E. Bailey, "Middle Eastern Oral Tradition and the Synoptic Gospels," *ExpTim* 106 (1995): 563–67.

## How Far Has the Third Quest Actually Come?

Lee McDonald, for many years professor at Acadia Divinity College in Nova Scotia, has written a very useful Jesus book that could easily have been included in my earlier survey in this chapter. Although a Protestant, his combination of historical research with faith reflection in some ways resembles the blend of the two in the Catholic works we noted above (147–49). At the conclusion of his study, he enumerates no fewer than twenty-eight details about Jesus's life (some of them composite) that can reasonably be said to be historical by the standard canons of Jesus research: Jesus (1) was a Jew; (2) was likely born in Bethlehem; (3) grew up in Nazareth in a lower-income family; (4) was the first person *known* to be called "rabbi"; (5) acknowledged the Hebrew Scriptures' authority; (6) regularly worshiped and studied in his local synagogue, practiced the ritual law, and celebrated the Jewish festivals; (7) learned the carpentry trade from Joseph; (8) at about thirty was baptized by John and identified with his message; (9) primarily ministered in the villages near the Sea of Galilee; (10) was a charismatic teacher and preacher who attracted crowds who began to think he was a prophet and even the Messiah; (11) called twelve disciples in order to establish a renewed Israel; (12) was known for remarkable healings and even had nature miracles attributed to him; (13) often associated with despised persons of various kinds; (14) proclaimed that God's kingdom had come in his ministry but was not yet fully present; (15) told his followers to love even the unlovely and forgive those who had sinned against them; (16) frequently spoke in short epigrammatic sayings or memorable parables; (17) was often at odds with the various religious authorities; (18) welcomed into his troupe of closest followers a Zealot and a tax collector—two classes of people who hated each other; (19) did not at first speak openly about his messianic role; (20) was welcomed as a messianic figure into Jerusalem at the beginning of the week in which he would be executed; (21) cleared at least one corner of the temple precincts of the money changers and their accoutrements; (22) was arrested and interrogated by the high priest, before whom he confessed that he was the Messiah and Son of God;

(23) left his disciples in surprise and despair at this turn of events that led to his execution; (24) was crucified; (25) was buried; (26) after which his tomb was found empty and reports began to circulate that he had been seen alive; (27) including one by his brother James, who became a believer in him as a result; and (28) within weeks was proclaimed as Messiah, Son of God, and Lord by his disciples both in and around Jerusalem as well as further afield.[142]

When one realizes that an impressive scholarly bibliography could be attached to each of these twenty-eight items arguing for their authenticity,[143] *it is hard to conclude that the third quest has not been worth the great amount of effort it has expended.* Of course, others' lists would be a little shorter, a little longer, or about the same length but with some substitutions.[144] Conspicuously absent from McDonald's list are Jesus's predictions of his suffering and death, his statements about the purpose of his crucifixion, and his vision of the coming destruction of the temple and the events surrounding the end of the age. Yet learned studies have made good cases for the authenticity of these events as well.[145] A burgeoning area of study in recent years that has not led to historical Jesus books per se but that makes even some of the most exalted Christology attributed to Jesus by others or even himself understandable in a monotheistic, Jewish context involves what

---

142. McDonald, *Story of Jesus*, 334–36. James H. Charlesworth itemizes no fewer than fifty-five such items ("The Historical Jesus: How to Ask Questions and Remain Inquisitive," in Holmén and Porter, *Handbook for the Study of the Historical Jesus*, 1:116–23).

143. See, e.g., throughout the bibliography of Keener, *Historical Jesus of the Gospels*, 604–713.

144. In addition to the works already cited in this chapter, see Gerald L. Borchert, *Jesus of Nazareth: Background, Witnesses, and Significance* (Macon, GA: Mercer University Press, 2011); James H. Charlesworth, *The Historical Jesus: An Essential Guide* (Nashville: Abingdon, 2008); Joachim Gnilka, *Jesus of Nazareth: Message and History*, trans. Siegfried S. Schatzmann (Peabody, MA: Hendrickson, 1997); Jonathan Knight, *Jesus: An Historical and Theological Investigation* (London: T&T Clark, 2004); Gerhard Lohfink, *Jesus of Nazareth: What He Wanted, Who He Was*, trans. Linda M. Maloney (Collegeville, MN: Liturgical Press, 2012); I. Howard Marshall, *Jesus at AD 2000* (Cambridge: Grove Books, 1999).

145. Hans F. Bayer, *Jesus' Predictions of Vindication and Resurrection: The Provenance, Meaning, and Correlation of the Synoptic Predictions* (Tübingen: J. C. B. Mohr, 1986); Rainer Riesner, "Back to the Historical Jesus through Paul and His School (The Ransom Logion—Mark 10.45; Matthew 20.28)," *JSHJ* 1 (2003): 171–99; David Wenham, *The Rediscovery of Jesus' Eschatological Discourse* (Sheffield: JSOT Press, 1984).

is called *divine identity Christology*.¹⁴⁶ If the third quest has played itself out, it is not because it has failed to accomplish what it set out to do but because it has covered pretty much all the bases—in the Synoptics' presentation of the life of Jesus.

## And the Gospel of John?

Yet where is John in all of this? If a case can be made even for the authenticity of some of the highest Christology in the Synoptics, where is the spinoff application to the unique details of the Fourth Gospel? With rare exceptions, it seems that the longer the various quests for Jesus continue, the more John is marginalized. For the most conservative of the questers, it is done for strategic reasons. Defending John opens up too many cans of worms and automatically weakens one's case in the minds of too many scholars.¹⁴⁷ Most others give some lip service to the occasional distinctive in John possibly being historical, but then they, too, proceed to leave the Fourth Gospel off to the side.¹⁴⁸ A few go into a little more detail about a slightly larger minority of John's Gospel that might be usable, akin to what we have seen in previous eras of Jesus research.¹⁴⁹ Some sound even more optimistic, but then don't develop their insights.¹⁵⁰ But overall, it seems to be taken as simply proven that the significant differences between John and the Synoptics can be explained only by arguing that theology has trumped history in the Fourth Evangelist's presentation of Christ.¹⁵¹ To read these large

---

146. Well surveyed in Andrew Ter Ern Loke, *The Origin of Divine Christology* (Cambridge: Cambridge University Press, 2017). More recent still is Andrei Orlov, *The Glory of the Invisible God: Two Powers in Heaven Traditions and Early Christology* (London: T&T Clark, 2019).

147. Keener (*Historical Jesus of the Gospels*, xxxiv) points people to his commentary on the Fourth Gospel (*The Gospel of John*, 2 vols. [Peabody, MA: Hendrickson, 2003]) for many places of probable historicity but believes he can make all the points he wants to about the historical Jesus just from the Synoptics; Bock and Webb (*Key Events in the Life of the Historical Jesus*) intentionally choose twelve events all from the Synoptics.

148. E.g., Puig i Tàrrech, *Jesus*, 27; Étienne Nodet, *The Historical Jesus? Necessity and Limits of an Inquiry*, trans. J. Edward Crowley (London: T&T Clark, 2008), 188.

149. E.g., McDonald, *Story of Jesus*, 106–21; Dunn, *Jesus Remembered*, 165–67.

150. E.g., J. R. Porter, *Jesus Christ: The Jesus of History, the Christ of Faith*, 2nd ed. (Oxford: Oxford University Press, 2007), 55.

151. E.g., James G. Crossley, *Jesus and the Chaos of History: Redirecting the Life of the Historical Jesus* (Oxford: Oxford University Press, 2015), 62; Robert T. Fortna, "The Gospel of

and immensely learned tomes, one would never guess that what John A. T. Robinson dubbed the "new look on the Fourth Gospel" over sixty years ago has become a significant lens through which many scholars peer. Apparently, the compartmentalization of scholarship has kept the two disciplines—historical Jesus research and Johannine studies—almost hermetically sealed off from each other. Or to change the metaphor, we appear to have two trains running on parallel tracks, too far from one another to be aware of the other's presence, each making remarkable progress toward their destinations, yet without many hints that either one values (or even knows) what the other is doing.

## Conclusion

If the exciting and provocative portions of the third quest pretty much all unfolded between 1980 and 2000, then a majority of the most solid, consolidating, and useful studies have appeared in the last twenty years, most of them from between 2001 and 2011. It may well be that there is little more to be said other than to reinforce these works with more detailed analyses of specific passages or themes. Of course, some authors will no doubt always propose iconoclastic theories, which in turn will require critique, and the continuation of the cycles of scholarship will be guaranteed. So, too, the criteria of authenticity have been scrutinized from almost every angle imaginable; new ones have been proposed and old ones jettisoned (or not, depending on the scholar). The double similarity and double dissimilarity criterion, alternately known as the criterion of historical plausibility, is by far the most promising of the new criteria. Study of the developing oral tradition has come a long way since the old form-critical days, with the guarded tradition hypothesis, flexible tradition within fixed limits, and social memory theories. No doubt there is good research still to be done in each of these and related areas.

---

John and the Historical Jesus," in *Finding the Historical Jesus: Rules of Evidence* (Santa Rosa, CA: Polebridge, 2008), 49–57; Pagola, *Jesus*, 426.

But what about John? Is the Fourth Gospel really, for all intents and purposes, as unusable for Jesus research as most historical Jesus questers either assume or explicitly declare? What has become of John A. T. Robinson's "new look"? A new look at the new look might yield some surprises. A lot has happened that one would never guess from reading the average Jesus book. It is finally time to turn to this parallel track of scholarship and see what has been developing. That will be the task of chapter 6.

# 6

# Foreshadowing the Fourth Quest: Rehabilitating the Gospel of John

Have there been three discrete quests for the historical Jesus? Yes and no. Yes, if the point is that researchers themselves have been aware of various changes in the overall quest, so that the labels have made sense to many of the participants. No, if the point is that only one approach, or even one ideologically aligned cluster of approaches, characterized each quest.[1] Did John A. T. Robinson initiate a "new look on the Fourth Gospel"? The same kind of twofold answer emerges. Many of the features of John's narrative that have today become widely acknowledged as probably historical appeared already in the minority of books that looked favorably on John's historicity in earlier eras. Still, some are new, and when the "new look" first appeared, most scholars believed

---

1. A. J. Godzieba, "From 'Vita Christi' to 'Marginal Jew': The Life of Jesus as Criterion of Reform in Pre-critical and Post-critical Quests," *LS* 32 (2007): 111–33; Fernando Bernejo Rucio, "The Fiction of the 'Three Quests': An Argument for Dismantling a Dubious Historiographical Paradigm," *JSHJ* 7 (2009): 211–53; Anthony Le Donne, "The Quest of the Historical Jesus: A Revisionist History through the Lens of Jewish-Christian Relations," *JSHJ* 10 (2012): 63–86. There are about as many alternative taxonomies as there are critics of the current quest; perhaps the best of them is the sevenfold division by Clive Marsh, "The Quests for the Historical Jesus in New Historicist Perspective," *BibInt* 5 (1997): 403–37.

John to be literarily independent of the Synoptics (see above, 61). *That much* was a decisive shift from the classic approach of the nineteenth and early twentieth centuries, when, as we have seen, John was believed to have known and depended on the written forms of Matthew, Mark, and Luke.[2]

Belief in full literary independence, however, would eventually give way to adherence to a third model: John was aware of the contents of the Synoptics and knew that his audience had some familiarity with them as well, but without strict literary dependence. In either of these last two models, would the same array of features in the Fourth Gospel meet the appropriate criteria of authenticity? Are the major Synoptic criteria adequate for examining John's Gospel or are new ones required? Over the last twenty years, thanks especially to the Society of Biblical Literature's "John, Jesus, and History" seminar, a whole raft of studies of this or that part of John have made excellent cases for authenticity (see below, 200–206), but there have been no extended syntheses of the composite results.

This chapter will survey highlights from the last sixty years or so of Johannine research favorable to the historicity of important portions of the Fourth Gospel. It is hard to know which is more remarkable: how much has been done in the "new look on John" or how much historical Jesus scholars have managed either to ignore it or to dismiss it out of hand! After the survey, I will then synthesize the point at which this branch of scholarship has currently arrived and propose two ways forward, one of which will be adopted in the rest of this book.

## The Historical Tradition of C. H. Dodd

Earlier in his career, the learned Welshman *C. H. Dodd* (1884–1973), who taught at both Oxford and Cambridge for significant stretches

---

2. The "Leuven school" reasserted Johannine dependence on the Synoptics, but they were in a small minority. See esp. the collection of papers discussing the topic in Adelbert Denaux, ed., *John and the Synoptics* (Leuven: Leuven University Press, 1992). For a recent anthology of studies of what John might have been doing to Mark if dependence is either presupposed or deemed to have been demonstrated, see Eve-Marie Becker, Helen K. Bond, and Catrin H. Williams, eds., *John's Transformation of Mark* (London: T&T Clark, 2021).

of his life, distinguished himself with his work on the parables of Jesus, all of which are in the Synoptic Gospels, along with studies in Acts and Paul.[3] Later in his career, he wrote two major works on the Gospel of John along with a commentary on John's Epistles.[4] Most relevant for our purposes is his *Historical Tradition in the Fourth Gospel*, published in 1963. Well into the heyday of belief in the literary independence of John from the Synoptics, Dodd examined, in four sections of five to seven chapters each, the "passion narrative," "the ministry," "John the Baptist and the first disciples," and "the sayings" of Jesus.[5] Where John and the Synoptics ran most obviously along parallel tracks, especially in sections one and three, Dodd showed that there were good reasons for accepting numerous distinctives of the Fourth Gospel's versions of events as historical. He found the same to be true of select passages in the main body of John, along with numerous smaller details, and he found numerous Synoptic parallels to individual sayings of Jesus, along with plausible ways of viewing the longer discourses of Christ in John as the Fourth Evangelist's expansion of shorter, authentic portions. These included parable-like teachings and other metaphors, along with sequences of sayings that lent themselves to elaboration.[6]

At the age of eighty-seven, Dodd published his last book, and it is a gem. *The Founder of Christianity* is as close as Dodd ever got to writing a historical Jesus book.[7] It is succinct, clear, written largely without footnotes citing other scholarship but obviously the product of very mature thinking. In numerous places, sayings or episodes from Jesus's life in John are interwoven into the otherwise largely topical

---

3. See esp. C. H. Dodd, *The Parables of the Kingdom* (London: Nisbet, 1935; New York: Scribner, 1936); also Dodd, *The Apostolic Preaching and Its Developments* (London: Hodder & Stoughton; New York: Harper, 1936); Dodd, *The Epistle to the Romans* (London: Hodder & Stoughton; New York: Harper, 1932).

4. C. H. Dodd, *The Interpretation of the Fourth Gospel* (Cambridge: Cambridge University Press, 1953); Dodd, *Historical Tradition in the Fourth Gospel* (Cambridge: Cambridge University Press, 1963); Dodd, *The Johannine Epistles* (London: Hodder & Stoughton; New York: Harper, 1946).

5. Dodd, *Historical Tradition in the Fourth Gospel*, ix–x.

6. Dodd, *Historical Tradition in the Fourth Gospel*, 315–420.

7. C. H. Dodd, *The Founder of Christianity* (New York: Macmillan, 1970; London: Collins, 1971).

survey of the main categories of Jesus's teaching and the stages of his adult ministry. They fit in well, appear unobtrusively, and do not create a synthesis with the Synoptics that is dramatically different from those by scholars who ignore John altogether. Because Dodd, with many, accepts John 6:15 as historical—when the crowds try to force Jesus into becoming their king—he does see that as a key turning point more so than many do, and he relates it to Jesus's withdrawal from Galilee, described only in Mark and Matthew (see Mark 7:24–8:30 par.). But the book is not sufficiently detailed to treat even all the *Synoptic* material that Dodd finds authentic, so it certainly does not come across as overloaded with Johannine excerpts.[8]

Dodd nowhere offers a list of John's verses, or any other literary units of thought, that he believes are either authentic or at least very deeply rooted in early tradition independent from the Synoptics. Had he done so, they would have comprised a very significant minority of the number of verses in the Fourth Gospel, but they would still have been a minority. A variety of historical Jesus scholars did pay lip service to Dodd, inferring in essence that what Dodd did was probably just about at the limit of how much Johannine material one could rehabilitate as likely to be historical. Typically, these scholars would not have been prepared to go nearly as far as Dodd did, but having acknowledged that they knew one might just be able to do that much, they then felt justified in not using John since it was still only a minority of the Fourth Gospel that Dodd employed.[9] After all, if similarity to (or coherence with) the Synoptics is a major criterion for Johannine authenticity, then by definition material added from John to a database formed from a larger portion of the Synoptics is not going to change the overall contents of one's synthesis of Jesus's life. In an important, lengthy essay recognizing all this, D. A. Carson asked the question "After Dodd, what?" and

---

8. John Painter nevertheless observes that here Dodd "made the Fourth Gospel more or less an equal partner with the Synoptics" ("The Fourth Gospel and the Founder of Christianity: The Place of Historical Tradition in the Work of C. H. Dodd," in *Engaging with C. H. Dodd on the Gospel of John: Sixty Years of Tradition and Interpretation*, ed. Tom Thatcher and Catrin H. Williams [Cambridge: Cambridge University Press, 2013], 279).

9. Craig R. Koester, "Progress and Paradox: C. H. Dodd and Rudolf Bultmann on History, the Jesus Tradition, and the Fourth Gospel," in Thatcher and Williams, *Engaging with C. H. Dodd*, 64.

set out a raft of methodological suggestions,[10] but apart from his own later commentary on the Fourth Gospel,[11] there didn't appear to be many people rushing to take him up on his proposals.[12]

## The Community of the Beloved Mirror-Readers: Louis Martyn and Raymond Brown

Not long after Dodd's book on historical tradition in John, two other scholars would compose discipline-defining studies. Taking his cue from John 9:22, on the excommunication from the synagogues of Jews who began to follow Jesus, *J. Louis Martyn* (1925–2015) of Union Seminary in New York City argued that this was unthinkable during Jesus's lifetime. It had to be the product of what happened sometime in the 80s or 90s of the first century, with the addition of the *birkat ha-minim* to the synagogue benedictions.[13] This Hebrew expression literally means "a blessing of the heretics," which was in fact a euphemism for a curse on them, enabling the pious Jew to avoid even uttering the word for "curse." The heretics were a broader category than just Christians, but they included them. They had to be *Jewish* Christians, of course, since local synagogues had no jurisdiction over Gentiles who were not worshiping with them.

About the same time, Martyn's colleague *Raymond E. Brown* (1928–98) was developing his theory of five stages to the composition of John's Gospel, only the first of which had some input from the apostle John.[14]

---

10. D. A. Carson, "Historical Tradition in the Fourth Gospel: After Dodd, What?," in *Gospel Perspectives*, vol. 2, *Studies of History and Tradition in the Four Gospels*, ed. R. T. France and David Wenham (Sheffield: JSOT Press, 1981), 83–145.

11. D. A. Carson, *The Gospel according to John*, PNTC (Leicester: Apollos; Grand Rapids: Eerdmans, 1991).

12. Indeed, J. S. King critiqued Carson in "Has D. A. Carson Been Fair to C. H. Dodd?," *JSNT* 17 (1983): 97–102, which then engendered D. A. Carson, "Historical Tradition in the Fourth Gospel: A Response to J. S. King," *JSNT* 23 (1985): 73–81. For an overview of Dodd's life and scholarly significance, esp. for Fourth Gospel research, see Beth M. Stovell, "C. H. Dodd and Johannine Scholarship," in *The Gospel of John in Modern Interpretation*, ed. Stanley E. Porter and Ron C. Fay (Grand Rapids: Kregel Academic, 2018), 101–17.

13. J. Louis Martyn, *History and Theology in the Fourth Gospel*, 3rd ed. (Louisville: Westminster John Knox, 2003 [orig. 1968]).

14. Raymond E. Brown, *The Gospel according to John I–XII*, AB 29 (New York: Doubleday, 1966), xxxiv–xxxix.

Mirror-reading was crucial for understanding the circumstances of the "Johannine community" at each stage, so that Jesus's staunch Pharisaic opponents stood for the later Jewish leaders who opposed Christianity, a character like Nicodemus represented Jews who were closet disciples of Jesus at a later date, and the woman at the well showed that there was even some Samaritan influence in the early church. Thus, the pattern continued. The theories were plausible, fit a lot of data, and even continued into the Epistles of John. In Brown's *The Community of the Beloved Disciple*, we can trace the trajectory from when secessionists began to leave the community (1 John), when they came back to try to take more people away (2 John), and when orthodoxy had become an embattled minority (3 John).[15]

It may well be that Martyn's and Brown's mirror-reading exercises were on target, or maybe only some of them were. But only if there are compelling reasons to reject the historicity of the narrative does mirror-reading require an either-or rather than a both-and approach. Only when there are reasons for saying that John's Gospel couldn't be recounting what happened during Jesus's life but could be referring *only* to analogous events at a later time and place does one have to reject the more natural interpretation: John included this historical information because it happened *and* was relevant to the churches he addressed that were facing similar issues.[16]

Little by little, the evidence for John's historical inaccuracy began to crumble. The assumption that the *birkat ha-minim* reflected a watershed moment in first-century Jewish history, at which point all synagogues began to excommunicate Christians, simply wasn't supported

---

15. Raymond E. Brown, *The Community of the Beloved Disciple: The Life, Loves, and Hates of an Individual Church in New Testament Times* (Mahwah, NJ: Paulist Press, 1979). For details of Brown's two major theories in the context of his career and an assessment of their significance, see Joshua W. Jipp, "Raymond E. Brown and the Fourth Gospel: Composition and Community," in Porter and Fay, *Gospel of John in Modern Interpretation*, 173–96.

16. The precise point that I. Howard Marshall was demonstrating for Luke, at the same time as Martyn and Brown were developing their hypotheses for John; see Marshall, *Luke: Historian and Theologian*, rev. ed (Downers Grove, IL: InterVarsity, 1988 [orig. 1970]). For John, see now Judith Christine Single Redman, "Eyewitness Testimony and the Characters of the Fourth Gospel," in *Characters and Characterization in the Gospel of John*, ed. Christopher W. Skinner (London: Bloomsbury T&T Clark, 2013), 59–78.

by the actual evidence. Rather, it was a gradual process of disfellowshiping that started at very different points at different places in the empire.¹⁷ Besides, none of the excommunication texts in John said anything about a practice outside of some of the synagogues in Jerusalem. It was much more likely that these were local, informal actions by select religious leaders such as might be envisioned in the very location where Jesus would soon be condemned to die. The other reason the two-level reading of Martyn seemed so attractive to many is that it appeared that one didn't need to deal with the anti-Semitism (or at least anti-Judaism) that seemed to be implied by some of Jesus's more hostile behavior toward key Jewish leaders or by John's sweeping indictments of "the Jews" at various places in his Gospel.¹⁸ These were just ciphers for the hostility between Christian and non-Christian Jews at the end of the first century. However, it turned out that the notion of an empire-wide ban of Christian Jews decreed in the synagogues in the late first century was much more condemning of Judaism than the idea of a handful of local assemblies much more unofficially taking hostile actions of the kind that have regularly occurred in the history of religion.¹⁹ It would take a few more decades, though, before this understanding would take root on a more widespread basis.

## The Priority of John A. T. Robinson

The early 1960s through the early 1970s was a turbulent decade—the Vietnam War, the civil rights movement in the United States, the Red Guard in Germany, the Russian invasion of Czechoslovakia, an unusual

---

17. An excellent, succinct rebuttal appears in Tobias Hägerland, "John's Gospel: A Two-Level Drama?," *JSNT* 25 (2003): 309–22. On the excommunication issue, see esp. Jonathan Bernier, *Aposynagōgos and the Historical Jesus in John: Rethinking the Historicity of the Johannine Expulsion Passages* (Leiden: Brill, 2013); Edward W. Klink III, "Expulsion from the Synagogue: Rethinking a Johannine Anachronism," *TynBul* 58 (2008): 99–119; Martinus C. de Boer, "Expulsion from the Synagogue: J. L. Martyn's History and Theology in the Fourth Gospel Revisited," *NTS* 66 (2020): 367–91.

18. For both the problem and a good solution, see esp. Stephen Motyer, *Your Father the Devil? A New Approach to John and "the Jews"* (Carlisle: Paternoster, 1997). Cf. Jonathan Numada, *John and Anti-Judaism: Reading the Gospel in Light of Greco-Roman Culture* (Eugene, OR: Pickwick, 2021); Raimo Hakola, *Identity Matters: John, the Jews, and Jewishness* (Leiden: Brill, 2005).

19. Carson, *Gospel according to John*, 370–72.

number of assassinations of key religious and political figures in several countries, and so on. This decade also birthed secular feminism, the sexual revolution, hippies, and widespread experimentation with hallucinogenic drugs and catapulted rock music into the center stage of popular culture. In retrospect, it shouldn't have been the surprise that it was that this was the decade of Vatican II, a veritable theological revolution within the Roman Catholic Church, and the era of certain radically liberal Protestant church leaders. One of those was *John A. T. Robinson* (1919–83), bishop of Woolwich in England, who also lectured at Cambridge University. His book *Honest to God*, released in 1963, became an international best seller, as he defended a somewhat impersonal view of God (much like Tillich's "Ground of Being"), low Christology (questioning the full divinity of Jesus), and situation ethics (denying all absolute moral principles).[20] Robinson tended to be either loved or vilified,[21] but few were prepared for what he would write in the 1970s and 1980s.

By 1976, Robinson had turned to a totally different topic, with the publication of his *Redating the New Testament*.[22] In it, he argued that every book from Matthew to Revelation was written prior to the destruction of Jerusalem by the Romans in AD 70. Even very conservative scholars had regularly dated the Johannine literature (the Gospel, the three Epistles, and Revelation) to the 80s or 90s, and most of the academic guild put quite a few other books into the period of 70–100 as well. One of Robinson's main arguments was the absence of any reference to the fall of Jerusalem, except in the form of a few predictions. He was well along the way to completing a follow-up book on the Gospel of John when he passed away. His Cambridge colleague J. F. Coakley edited and completed the work, which was published two years later, in 1985.[23] Here Robinson argued not only that the Fourth Gospel

---

20. John A. T. Robinson, *Honest to God* (London: SCM; Philadelphia: Westminster, 1963).
21. David L. Edwards, ed., *The "Honest to God" Debate: Some Reactions to the Book "Honest to God"* (London: SCM; Philadelphia: Westminster, 1963).
22. John A. T. Robinson, *Redating the New Testament* (London: SCM; Philadelphia: Westminster, 1976).
23. John A. T. Robinson, *The Priority of John*, ed. J. F. Coakley (London: SCM, 1985; Oak Park, IL: Meyer-Stone, 1987).

probably predated 70 but also that it was still literarily independent enough of the Synoptics to be considered "prior" to them. Sometimes this meant that the contents reflected older traditions; sometimes, that they were simply more authentic or historical.[24]

Robinson defended these conclusions with a composite of the sorts of arguments and evidence from the scholars we surveyed during the period of the supposed "no quest": Holland, Headlam, Higgins, Askwith, and Robinson's uncle, J. Armitage Robinson (see above, 63–65). He noted places where the Fourth Evangelist, seemingly tangentially, offers clues to solve puzzles raised but not addressed in the Synoptics, but also the reverse "interlocking"—where John can presume his audience's knowledge of the Synoptics so that he leaves things unexplained that would otherwise puzzle readers who had only the Gospel of John (see further below, 191–92).[25] I am not aware if Robinson's interest in the priority of John had anything to do with his low Christology in *Honest to God*; one would think that the two emphases would work at cross-purposes with each other. Perhaps Robinson was just a bit of an impish iconoclast.[26] Nevertheless, the last chapter of *The Priority of John*, a quite lengthy one, turned to the Christology of the Fourth Gospel and argued that it wasn't necessarily as "high" as most in church history have understood it to be. The great "I am" statements all involve metaphorical predicates (bread of life, vine, good shepherd, etc.) that do not necessarily point to deity. "I and the Father are one" (John 10:30) can easily refer to oneness in mind, will, and purpose, not any ontological unity. Making himself "Messiah" meant precisely that: arrogating to himself a title that only others were meant to bestow on someone—at least that was what some strands of Judaism believed.[27] In other words, for Robinson, one does not have to see John's Christology as anything like later creedal declarations on the two natures of Christ or on the relationships of the members of the Trinity, so it would help Robinson's agenda if John, so interpreted, were earliest or most faithful to Jesus.

24. Robinson, *Priority of John*, 1–35.
25. Scattered about Robinson, *Priority of John*, 158–295.
26. See Stanley E. Porter, "John A. T. Robinson: Provocateur and Profound Johannine Scholar," in Porter and Fay, *Gospel of John in Modern Interpretation*, 171.
27. Robinson, *Priority of John*, 343–97.

Two reasons why Robinson's work did not have more of an effect on the academy probably stem from this strange juxtaposition of perspectives. First, conservative scholars have usually followed early church tradition when it comes to the authorship of New Testament books, and little in that tradition suggests a date earlier than the end of the first century. Liberal scholars have relied more on internal evidence, but then there is little in John to challenge their conviction that John *does* exhibit a high Christology but does so because he represents how Christian thinking had developed by the end of the first century, not as it was at its outset.[28] Second, conservatives were thrilled to have someone rehabilitate the origins and trustworthiness of John as much as Robinson seemed to do, but then his low Christology made them wonder if committing to the rest of his arguments compelled them to accept this final plank in his platform.[29]

## Polar Opposites: Is Maurice Casey True? and Richard Bauckham for All Christians

In the decade 1991–2000, several small studies appeared that bolstered or supplemented Robinson's arguments for John's reliability,[30] but much

---

28. For one representative example, see Jörg Frey, *The Glory of the Crucified One: Christology and Theology in the Gospel of John*, trans. Wayne Coppins and Christoph Heilig (Waco: Baylor University Press, 2018 [Ger. orig. 2013]).

29. Porter ("John A. T. Robinson," 166) stresses how "out of sync" the final chapter of *The Priority of John* is with the rest of the book, making the connection between the two parts by no means necessary.

30. Stephen Barton, "The Believer, the Historian, and the Fourth Gospel," *Theology* 96 (1993): 289–302; Craig L. Blomberg, "To What Extent Is John Historically Reliable?," in *Perspectives on John: Method and Interpretation in the Fourth Gospel*, ed. Robert B. Sloan and Mikeal C. Parsons (Lewiston, NY: Mellen, 1993), 27–56; Alfonso de la Fuente, "Trasfondo cultural del cuarto evangelio," *EstBíb* 56 (1998): 491–501; E. Earle Ellis, "Background and Christology of John's Gospel," in Sloan and Parsons, *Perspectives on John*, 1–25; Antonio García Moreno, "Autenticidad e historicidad del IV Evangelio," *ScrTh* 23 (1991): 13–67; Thomas D. Lea, "The Reliability of History in John's Gospel," *JETS* 38 (1995): 387–402; Francis J. Moloney, "The Fourth Gospel and the Jesus of History," *NTS* 46 (2000): 42–58; D. Moody Smith, "Historical Issues and the Problem of John and the Synoptics," in *From Jesus to John: Essays on Jesus and New Testament Christology in Honour of Marinus de Jonge*, ed. Martinus C. de Boer (Sheffield: JSOT Press, 1993), 252–67; Marianne Meye Thompson, "The Historical Jesus and the Johannine Christ," in *Exploring the Gospel of John: In Honor of D. Moody Smith*, ed. R. Alan Culpepper and C. Clifton Black (Louisville: Westminster John Knox, 1996), 21–42; David Wenham, "A Historical View of John's Gospel," *Them* 23 (1998): 5–21.

Johannine scholarship remained unaffected by these. *Maurice Casey* (1942–2014), professor in Nottingham, would soon argue for a very early date and Aramaic substratum for Mark's Gospel,[31] and he swung the pendulum to the opposite extreme with the Fourth Gospel. He unequivocally gave a negative answer to the rhetorical question that formed the title of his book *Is John's Gospel True?* but went much further than most other scholars had. The majority had insisted on seeing John as at least a very worthwhile work of Christian theology, even if considerable license had to be taken with history to produce it. Casey argued that John's Gospel was theologically as well as historically false.[32] Then he went one big step further, warning that it was also theologically dangerous, especially with its anti-Semitic portrait of "the Jews," a sweeping indictment that could hardly have applied to all or even most first-century Jews in Jesus's world.[33] At least he acknowledged evangelical scholarship, which Johannine scholars hadn't always done, but he then proceeded in some detail in his opening chapter to both mock and dismiss the scholarship of people like D. A. Carson and me, who dared to suggest that a large portion of John might be authenticable by the best of historical methods.[34]

Casey's work, published in 1996, would not stay at the forefront of Johannine scholars' attention for very long, because of the work edited by *Richard Bauckham* (1946–), professor in St. Andrews and Cambridge, titled *The Gospels for All Christians*, which appeared two years later. The overall thesis of this anthology was sweeping: we should not think, as redaction criticism had been doing for the previous forty years, of distinctive or discrete Christian communities to which each Gospel was originally addressed, with their distinctive contents or theological emphases particularly appropriate for the needs of those communities. Rather, the Gospels were from the

---

31. Maurice Casey, *The Aramaic Sources of Mark's Gospel* (Cambridge: Cambridge University Press, 1998).

32. Maurice Casey, *Is John's Gospel True?* (London: Routledge, 1996).

33. Casey, *Is John's Gospel True?*, esp. 229.

34. Casey, *Is John's Gospel True?*, 4–29. Cf. Carson, *Gospel according to John*, 177–78; Craig L. Blomberg, *The Historical Reliability of the Gospels*, 2nd ed. (Downers Grove, IL: IVP Academic; Nottingham: Apollos, 2007), 216–19. Casey was, of course, referring to the first edition of my book, published in 1987.

outset designed to be disseminated widely, even if of necessity there was one copy that was initially sent to the church in a specific location (as patristic evidence itself claims).[35] Contributions to the volume discussed the mechanics of book production, the (largely well-to-do) buyers who were the target audience, the speed of dissemination, the nature of the Gospels more generally, and the like. Probably the most significant chapter was one of Bauckham's own essays, "John for Readers of Mark."[36] Despite the appearance of literary independence from the Synoptics, John himself must have known not only Mark but quite possibly Matthew and Luke also, and he must have presupposed that many of his readers were familiar with many of the contents of Mark. This doesn't necessarily mean that they had ever seen a scroll of Mark's Gospel, but they may well have heard it read out in church or at least heard many of its episodes passed on or summarized by word of mouth.

As evidence, Bauckham provides a series of examples of passages that would have been mystifying to readers of John's Gospel unless they had additional knowledge like that found in Mark. For example, in John 3:24 we read the parenthetical comment that when Jesus and John were simultaneously baptizing in the countryside, "this was before John was put in prison." Yet up to this point the Fourth Gospel has said nothing about John the Baptist being imprisoned, nor does it do so later. Mark 6:14-29, on the other hand, has an extensive narrative about John's imprisonment and execution, which probably would have been well known in early Christian circles.[37] Or consider John 11:2, where again the Fourth Evangelist adds a parenthetical comment on Mary of Bethany being the same Mary "who poured perfume on the Lord and wiped his feet with her hair." Once again, nothing has been

---

35. Richard Bauckham, ed., *The Gospels for All Christians: Rethinking the Gospel Audiences* (Grand Rapids: Eerdmans, 1998). A number of printed references to this work give its publication date as 1997, probably because Amazon has that (unless you click on the copyright page of the book to see what it actually says). Amazon is a big bibliographic help, but it makes mistakes often enough in titles, spellings of names, dates, etc. that one must always check inside the actual book.

36. Richard Bauckham, "John for Readers of Mark," in Bauckham, *Gospels for All Christians*, 147-71.

37. See Bauckham, "John for Readers of Mark," esp. 152-55.

said about this event thus far in John's Gospel. In this case, John does go on to narrate the event one chapter later (12:1–8). Still, that offers no help to the first-time reader or listener here in chapter 11, and one might have expected a future conditional (this is the Mary "who would pour perfume . . . and wipe . . ."), since chronologically it hasn't happened yet when Jesus is about to raise Lazarus. Intriguingly, Mark, however, without naming Mary, recounts the story and describes Jesus announcing that "wherever the gospel is preached" her action will be retold "in memory of her" (Mark 14:9). Even if there is some hyperbole there, Jesus's prediction suggests an even more widespread awareness than just what would come about because Mark wrote it down. John could very easily, as a result, have assumed that his churches would have heard about the anointing.[38]

What Leon Morris had already called "interlocking" works in both directions.[39] Sometimes John doesn't write in a way that requires a knowledge of Mark or its contents for understanding; sometimes John includes material that helps explain a Synoptic puzzle, not in a straightforward redactional sense, but in a more tangential way. Of all the "false witness" that someone could have invented and charged Jesus with, why choose the claim that he predicted he would destroy the temple and rebuild it in three days (Mark 14:58)? Nothing that Jesus has said to the crowds or to the authorities anywhere in the Synoptics even remotely suggests this. Jesus did tell his disciples privately that a day was coming when no temple stone would be left upon another (Mark 13:2). Yet nothing appears there about three days or about rebuilding the temple at any point. John 2:19, however, has a remarkably close parallel, in which Jesus declares, "Destroy this temple, and I will raise it again in three days." Tellingly, John says that Jesus's conversation partners misunderstood him and that even the disciples didn't grasp what he meant until after his resurrection (2:21–22). So a teaching like John 2:19 could easily have become garbled and turned into false but

---

38. See Bauckham, "John for Readers of Mark," 162–65.
39. Leon Morris, *Studies in the Fourth Gospel* (Grand Rapids: Eerdmans; Exeter: Paternoster, 1969), 33–63.

potentially persuasive witness.⁴⁰ Examples of this kind of interlocking could be multiplied at length.⁴¹

Not surprisingly, reaction to the Bauckham volume was quite mixed. Wendy Sproston North spoke for those who remained largely unconvinced.⁴² The thesis probably was too sweeping, and "both-and" theories weren't much considered. Too much redaction criticism fit too well. I later wrote an article on how the early church fathers actually support a chastened form of audience analysis as in redaction criticism, but that scarcely precludes the intention that the churches most directly addressed proceeded to make copies of their Gospel and send them elsewhere, with each new destination repeating the process.⁴³ Hughson Ong has added the point that much of what we attribute to the audience of a Gospel is more appropriately ascribed to the community *from* which that Gospel arose.⁴⁴ But Sproston North swings the pendulum too far in the opposite direction. She correctly argues that Bauckham has not proved that John was necessarily envisaging all Christians as potential addressees, but she should more clearly acknowledge that he *has* made his case that John is assuming awareness of Mark (or something very like Mark) on the part of his audience.⁴⁵ Writers like Leon Morris a generation ago and Lydia McGrew quite recently have offered even more such evidence (see notes 39, 41 above).

Jörg Frey speaks for many by rejecting interlocking in principle. He thinks that it violates the cardinal rule of interpreting each Gospel in

---

40. Jörg Frey rejects this because he doesn't understand why the witness would be called false if Jesus did predict the rebuilding of the temple (*Theology and History in the Fourth Gospel: Tradition and Narration* [Waco: Baylor University Press, 2018], 90). However, the two statements are using different meanings of the word "temple" (metaphorical vs. physical), while the blatantly false part is that *Jesus* threatened to destroy either temple. He spoke only of what would happen if and when his body was destroyed.

41. See also Lydia McGrew, *The Eye of the Beholder: The Gospel of John as Historical Reportage* (Tampa: DeWard, 2021), 240–68.

42. Wendy E. Sproston North, "John for Readers of Mark? A Response to Richard Bauckham's Proposal," *JSNT* 25 (2003): 449–68.

43. See Craig L. Blomberg, "The Gospels for Specific Communities *and* All Christians," in *The Audience of the Gospels: The Origin and Function of the Gospels in Early Christianity*, ed. Edward W. Klink III (London: T&T Clark, 2010), 111–33.

44. Hughson Ong, "The Gospel from a Specific Community but for All Christians: Understanding the Johannine Community as a 'Community of Practice,'" in *The Origins of John's Gospel*, ed. Stanley E. Porter and Hughson T. Ong (Leiden: Brill, 2016), 101–23.

45. Sproston North, "John for Readers of Mark?," 449.

its own context and that it allows one to bypass questions of source criticism and the literary relationships among the Gospels.[46] But this is to misunderstand how it works. Bauckham has subsequently written an excellent theology of John's Gospel, while Morris penned a major commentary on John in his day.[47] Both engaged in source criticism and studied historical backgrounds to John's Gospel in detail. Neither derives their findings from a "harmonizing" approach that blurs the distinctions among the Gospels. But once they have done what they can according to standard scholarly canons of research, they recognize that the Synoptics formed part of the historical background for John. They realize that it was unlikely that John and his audience were unaware of the major points of the Synoptic kerygma two generations after the dissemination of information about Jesus. The observations about interlocking reinforce and confirm these already probable assumptions. Frey may conclude that "in this procedure, historical methodology—not to mention common sense—is sacrificed in favor of the aprioristic principle of defending the alleged historical 'truth' of all biblical accounts."[48] But, in so doing, he misrepresents both the process and the motive, and it is his approach that sacrifices common sense. As small and interconnected as the early Christian movement was, the notion that a collection of churches, which had received potentially more apostolic ministry than any other (in and around Ephesus) for several decades, would be utterly unaware of any of the main contours of the Jesus tradition that the Fourth Gospel didn't record defies credibility.[49]

## The Historical Reliability of Craig Blomberg's Gospel of John

Shortly after both Wright and Theissen and Merz had outlined their double dissimilarity and double similarity criterion (see above, 161),

---

46. Frey, *Theology and History in the Fourth Gospel*, 90–91.
47. Richard Bauckham, *Gospel of Glory: Major Themes in Johannine Theology* (Grand Rapids: Baker Academic, 2015); Leon Morris, *The Gospel according to John*, rev. ed. (Grand Rapids: Eerdmans, 1995).
48. Frey, *Theology and History in the Fourth Gospel*, 91.
49. See all the other essays in Bauckham, *Gospels for All Christians*, esp. Michael B. Thompson, "The Holy Internet: Communication between Churches in the First Christian Generation," 49–70.

I (1955–), a longtime Denver Seminary professor, thought that it would be fascinating to apply the criterion on a widespread fashion to the Gospel of John, especially since I saw no sign of anyone else who was doing so. I worked through the Fourth Gospel, pericope by pericope, and while not every passage was amenable, the criterion worked well with at least some part of a sizable majority of the pericopes overall. It then dawned on me that there might be interest, in some circles at least, for a book that followed the format of a commentary, beginning with an extended introduction and then moving through the Gospel section by section and sometimes verse by verse, but addressing only historical questions.[50] I did not for one moment deny the rich theological contribution and the frequent literary artistry in John's Gospel, but others had written and were continuing to write excellent works in those arenas.[51] Yet no one, to my knowledge, was asking predominantly historical questions about what in each pericope caused some scholars to question its historicity, along with asking what grounds there might be for supporting historicity. Not all of those questions and their responses involved double dissimilarity and double similarity; often other criteria came into play. Yet double dissimilarity and double similarity played an important role throughout. The result was a very intentionally one-sided "commentary" that was skewed in the direction of asking historical questions.

I was grateful that a number of scholars, including some not already in my "evangelical" camp, recognized the volume as worthy of serious interaction, whether or not they were always convinced by a given position.[52] Unfortunately, the three most common reactions I received, in ascending order of frequency and vehemence, might be paraphrased

---

50. Craig L. Blomberg, *The Historical Reliability of John's Gospel: Issues and Commentary* (Downers Grove, IL: IVP Academic, 2001).

51. At the time, particularly useful were George Beasley-Murray, *Gospel of Life: Theology in the Fourth Gospel* (Peabody, MA: Hendrickson, 1991); D. Moody Smith, *The Theology of the Gospel of John* (Cambridge: Cambridge University Press, 1995); R. Alan Culpepper, *Anatomy of the Fourth Gospel: A Study in Literary Design* (Philadelphia: Fortress, 1983). Today, out of a plethora of options, see esp. Bauckham, *Gospel of Glory*; Paul A. Rainbow, *Johannine Theology: The Gospel, the Epistles and the Apocalypse* (Downers Grove, IL: IVP Academic; Nottingham: Apollos, 2014); Warren Carter, *John: Storyteller, Interpreter, Evangelist* (Peabody, MA: Hendrickson, 2006).

52. For one example of each, see Brian D. Johnson, "The Jewish Feasts and Questions of Historicity in John 5–12," in *John, Jesus, and History*, ed. Paul N. Anderson, Felix Just, and Tom Thatcher, 3 vols. (Atlanta: Society of Biblical Literature, 2007–16), 2:124–25; Helen K.

in the following ways: (1) Blomberg is a "maximalist," a position as unlikely as the "minimalist" one, since truth is always in the center;[53] (2) Blomberg's argument depends on the position of apostolic authorship that he took in his introduction, and we all know that has been disproved;[54] (3) Blomberg thinks that Jesus cleansed the temple twice, which is so ludicrous a notion that it tempts us to write off the entire volume![55]

The more reviews I perused, the more I wondered how much of my book my critics had actually read. Observation (1) was true insofar as I had stated from the outset that I was not writing a full-orbed commentary but embarking on an investigation of a specific historical hypothesis to see where it might lead me—namely, that there were credible arguments for the historicity of much more of John's Gospel than was usually realized.[56] Truth is not always found at the midpoint between two extremes, but, given that I explicitly did *not* presuppose the inerrancy or inspiration of the Gospel, my results scarcely were at the extreme end of any spectrum. Comment (2), on the other hand, was simply false. Yes, in the introduction I argued that apostolic authorship had *not* been disproved and that good arguments still supported it, but I explicitly said that other theories of authorship could also create a climate favorable to historical reliability and that aged apostles could have faulty memories.[57] My commentary section was going to be based on criteria of authenticity, not on the presumption of apostolic authorship.[58]

---

Bond, "At the Court of the High Priest: History and Theology in John 18:13–24," in Anderson, Just, and Thatcher, *John, Jesus, and History*, 2:317.

53. Andrew T. Lincoln, in essence, sets Casey and me at opposite ends of the spectrum and then recommends his own middle-of-the-road position in *Truth on Trial: The Lawsuit Motif in the Fourth Gospel* (Peabody, MA: Hendrickson, 2000), 49–50. For fuller exegetical details, see throughout Lincoln, *The Gospel according to Saint John*, BNTC (London: Continuum; Peabody, MA: Hendrickson, 2005).

54. Frey, *Theology and History in the Fourth Gospel*, 78n85; Mark A. Matson, "Current Approaches to the Priority of John," *SCJ* 7 (2004): 97. Matson thinks that apostolic authorship is "a far more crucial issue" for me than for Robinson, but in fact the reverse would seem to be more accurate.

55. Frey, *Theology and History in the Fourth Gospel*, 89; Casey, *Is John's Gospel True?*, 11–13. Dodd (*Historical Tradition in the Fourth Gospel*, 157n2) had already declared that postulating two cleansings "is the last resort of a desperate determination to harmonize Mark and John at all costs."

56. Blomberg, *Historical Reliability of John's Gospel*, 66–67.

57. Blomberg, *Historical Reliability of John's Gospel*, 40–41.

58. Blomberg, *Historical Reliability of John's Gospel*, 63–66.

Charge (3) becomes "curiouser and curiouser" (with apologies to *Alice in Wonderland*) the more I read it. To begin with, once again, I have never defended the theory of two temple cleansings to the exclusion of alternatives, nor have I ever come down on one side of the debate and said that it is the solution I definitely prefer. I have repeatedly explained that I have no problem with the theory that John has topically relocated the one Synoptic temple cleansing to a very early period in Jesus's ministry.[59] I can even understand, though I find it much less likely, the idea that the Synoptics relocated the Johannine incident because they had only one Passover in their narrative with which they could associate it. Second, I am aware of the dangers of artificial harmonization as much as anyone, but I am also aware of the inappropriate rejection of *all* harmonization when studying biblical history, because most complex historical events involving multiple narratives from different points of view sooner or later disclose places where harmonization is the most logical explanation of divergences.[60]

The two accounts of the temple cleansing form one such example. We will return to John's version in the next chapter; here, I may be brief. It *would* be self-contradictory to claim that Jesus celebrated two Last Suppers. It is bizarre to consider him raising Jairus's daughter twice, just to account for the apparent discrepancies between the accounts in

---

59. Blomberg, *Historical Reliability of John's Gospel*, 87–91. See Blomberg, *Historical Reliability of the Gospels*, 216–17; at one place (219n66) I say that "I am inclined to agree" with Darrell L. Bock's language (*Jesus according to Scripture: Restoring the Portrait from the Gospels* [Grand Rapids: Baker Academic; Leicester: Apollos, 2002], 427) that two cleansings may be "slightly more likely" (one could hardly be more tentative, I would have thought); Blomberg, *The Historical Reliability of the New Testament: Countering the Challenges to Evangelical Christian Beliefs* (Nashville: B&H Academic, 2016), 194–95; Blomberg, *Jesus and the Gospels: An Introduction and Survey*, 3rd ed. (Nashville: B&H Academic; London: Inter-Varsity, 2022), 369–70. In the second edition, Darrell L. Bock and Benjamin I. Simpson, *Jesus according to Scripture: Restoring the Portrait of the Gospels,* 2nd ed. (Grand Rapids: Baker Academic, 2017), 539–40, shift to favoring one temple cleansing.

60. Craig L. Blomberg, "The Legitimacy and Limits of Harmonization," in *Hermeneutics, Authority, and Canon*, ed. D. A. Carson and John D. Woodbridge (Grand Rapids: Zondervan; Leicester: Inter-Varsity, 1986), 165, 168, 173. Cf. Robinson, *Priority of John*, 27: "Harmonization has got a bad name; and clearly there can be quite uncritical harmonization. Yet if one is dealing with several genuinely independent accounts, each going back, however accurately or inaccurately, to the event, then it is legitimate to ask how they can be correlated and combined." The same is true even for dependent sources, if a redactor's changes were intended not to correct but merely to supplement.

Matthew and Mark, which are otherwise located in similar contexts and identical locations.[61] Either of these notions would indeed deserve Gerald Borchert's label of a "historiographical monstrosity."[62] One can have only one "last" of any kind of event, and Jesus could not have celebrated two consecutive Passover meals and two Last Suppers. The idea of having to raise a person multiple times in this life also suggests a certain impotence on the part of the miracle worker, despite the amazing feat, and that so many details would be identical each time seems unlikely in the extreme.

But are two outbursts of anger at what Jesus believed to be behavior that defied God's will for the temple precincts, once near the beginning of his public ministry and once at the end, with most of the details described in the two accounts *differing* from one another, really that unbelievable? On the assumption that one temple clearing made no lasting difference to the practices Jesus objected to, is it that inconceivable that he might do something similar again after two or three years? If we imagine that even one such incident must have led to Jesus's downfall, then there are problems even in Mark's account. No one arrests Jesus on the spot, nor for several more days. The event *was* a catalyst for the leaders' scheming to put Jesus to death (Mark 11:18), but so was his teaching on the Sabbath early in his ministry, according to Mark (3:6), and nothing came of that. An early protest in one corner of the temple precincts would have raised serious questions in people's minds about how such a self-styled rabbi thought he could do such a thing, but here was an individual who was already working many miracles (John 2:23). He merited very close scrutiny to see what else might develop, but precisely because no long-term damage was done, his action might have been tolerated. A second such incident would have "upped the ante" considerably, however, and demonstrated that he was literally "shameless" (not affected by the cultural standards of honor and shame).[63]

---

61. As argued by Andreas Osiander in the first half of the sixteenth century. See Robert H. Stein, *Difficult Passages in the Gospels* (Grand Rapids: Baker, 1984), 12.

62. Gerald L. Borchert, *John 1–11*, NAC (Nashville: Broadman & Holman, 1996), 160.

63. E. Randolph Richards, "An Honor/Shame Argument for Two Temple Clearings," *TJ* 29 (2008): 19–43. See also Allan Chapple, "Jesus' Intervention in the Temple: Once or

Perhaps this reconstruction is implausible. But exegetes should pursue the discussion by pointing out what exactly they find implausible and why, rather than just summarily dismissing it with overblown rhetoric. Let me repeat myself, since I have so often been misrepresented in the past: I do *not* know if "two cleansings" is the best solution and am *not* suggesting here that it is. But serious scholars have proposed it as such, and they do not deserve to be written off as unworthy of serious interaction. If it turns out that either John or Mark has thematically relocated a very different version of events, precisely because the largely different details in the two accounts could mesh well with each other, I have no difficulty in accepting that explanation. I just marvel at the unwillingness of so many ever to give reasons for *why* the idea of two discrete protests by Jesus, framing his ministry, is so ludicrous.

At any rate, far more important than a decision on this single issue are the overall results of my study. Using the double similarity and double dissimilarity criterion as well as other methods of historical inquiry, and not once suggesting a conclusion that no one else had also come to, even relatively recently, I suggested that the following portions of John 1–11 had a strong likelihood of being historical: (1) the overlap in the ministries of Jesus and John the Baptist; (2) the raft of titles people use of Jesus in John 1, but probably meaning only that they are acclaiming him as Messiah, given the titles' varied uses in Second Temple Judaism; (3) a core event in Cana involving a comparison and contrast between ritual purification and the new joy of the kingdom that Jesus offers, especially in light of Jesus's parable or metaphor of new wine requiring new wineskins (Mark 2:22 pars.); (4) Jesus anticipating a new metaphorical temple; (5) a conversation with a key leader of the Pharisees named Nicodemus about new birth; (6) Jesus having a ministry of baptism in addition to John; (7) the bulk of the dialogue with the Samaritan woman and its aftermath; (8) a healing similar to that of the centurion's servant/son in Q, whether John 4:46–54 is narrating the same event or a separate one; (9) the

---

Twice?," *JETS* 58 (2015): 545–69; Colin Humphreys, "The Last Days of Jesus in John and the Synoptics: The Evidence from Astronomy and Chronology," in Anderson, Just, and Thatcher, *John, Jesus, and History*, 3:283–98.

core of the account of the healing of the paralyzed man by the pool of Bethesda; (10) the parable of the apprentice's son and a chiastically structured set of claims to which it naturally led; (11) a feeding event outside of Bethsaida, with a midrashically structured message related to it in the Capernaum synagogue later; (12) the unbelief of Jesus's brothers; (13) claims about living water and the light of the world in conjunction with a celebration of the Feast of Tabernacles; (14) claims to be God's unique agent without anything that can fairly be labeled anti-Semitic; (15) the curing of a blind man in conjunction with washing in the pool of Siloam; (16) limited local disfellowshiping of Jewish followers of Jesus from Jerusalem synagogues; (17) teaching on Jesus as the good shepherd and the gate for the sheep; (18) purification in the context of Hanukkah; (19) a dramatic event involving the reanimation of Lazarus, brother of Mary and Martha, that afforded yet another key prompt for certain religious leaders to plot Jesus's demise.[64]

In chapters 12–21, I included the following as probably historical: (20) an anointing at Bethany and the so-called triumphal entry; (21) a footwashing; (22) teaching in the upper room focusing especially on the coming ministry of the Holy Spirit, Jesus's coming death but also his vindication, and the outworking of love as an entire self-giving to others; (23) the predictions of coming hostility against the disciples; (24) a final prayer with petitions strikingly reminiscent of "the Lord's Prayer"; (25) key events in the passion narrative, including the uniquely Johannine information about Rome taking capital punishment away from the Jewish leadership, the hearing before Annas and the involvement of Roman as well as Jewish soldiers; (26) certain unique features in the resurrection narrative such as Mary Magdalene seeing Jesus as a gardener, the fear and doubt of the disciples, and Peter's "recall" matching his call (three times to match his threefold denial).[65] In referring to each episode on that list, I am well aware that historical methods alone do not allow one either to corroborate or to disconfirm many individual details, which is why I have phrased them as generally as I have. I also realize that individual scholars' views of the miraculous

---

64. Blomberg, *Historical Reliability of John's Gospel*, 286–88.
65. Blomberg, *Historical Reliability of John's Gospel*, 288–90.

inevitably color their opinions of what happened with Jesus's apparent miracles, which in the Fourth Gospel are regularly called signs. In 2001, however, when my book came out, I was unaware of anyone else who had tried to push the argument for historicity, *essentially on historical grounds*, as far as I had, at least since the rise of the new quest. That would all soon change.

### John, Jesus, and Paul Anderson

Important book-length studies would continue to appear, strengthening the case for individual portions of John or for his historicity in general, but not nearly as often as in smaller journal articles.[66] Other contributions appeared in edited collections like John Lierman's *Challenging Perspectives on the Gospel of John*.[67] A very important singly authored work was Richard Bauckham's *The Testimony of the Beloved Disciple: Narrative, History, and Theology in the Gospel of John*. His chapter on Johannine historiography is perhaps the most relevant for this study.[68] In it he shows that in various ways John more resembles ancient Greco-Roman historiography than the Synoptics do. But pride of place must go to a small, unobtrusive seminar that began at the Society of Biblical Literature in 2001, masterminded by *Paul Anderson* (1956–), longtime professor at George Fox University in Oregon. Little by little, an impressive array of Johannine scholars would give papers at the seminar from a wide variety of perspectives, but almost all of them recognized that *historical* study was supporting at least a few snippets of John not usually acknowledged as authentic in historical

---

66. Mention should be made here at the very least of D. Moody Smith, *The Fourth Gospel in Four Dimensions: Judaism and Jesus, the Gospels and Scripture* (Columbia: University of South Carolina Press, 2008), 47–118. See also Smith, "Jesus Traditions in the Gospel of John," in *Handbook for the Study of the Historical Jesus*, ed. Tom Holmén and Stanley E. Porter, 4 vols. (Leiden: Brill, 2011), 3:1997–2039. Surveys of the developments, however, began to appear, showing that the trend to rehabilitate John was gaining notice. See esp. Gilbert van Belle, "The Return of John to Jesus Research," *LS* 32 (2007): 23–48.

67. John Lierman, ed., *Challenging Perspectives on the Gospel of John* (Tübingen: Mohr Siebeck, 2006). Particularly significant was Richard Bauckham, "Messianism according to the Gospel of John," in Lierman, *Challenging Perspectives on the Gospel of John*, 34–68.

68. Richard Bauckham, *The Testimony of the Beloved Disciple: Narrative, History, and Theology in the Gospel of John* (Grand Rapids: Baker Academic, 2007), 93–112.

Jesus research. Many of the presenters went well beyond suggesting just a handful of bits of additional material (see below, 203–5).

Anderson himself would author a major contribution to the topic, which appeared in 2006, called *The Fourth Gospel and the Quest for Jesus: Modern Foundations Reconsidered*.[69] In it, he describes in detail what he calls the "dehistoricization" of John and the "dejohannification" of Jesus.[70] Many of the reasons for these two trends were not related to straightforward historical analysis, and Anderson calls for a reversal of both trajectories. He makes it clear that he is not interested just in trying to authenticate as much of the Gospels as possible, because he believes that in several instances the historicity of something in John that can be vindicated will make a corresponding element in the Synoptics appear less accurate.[71]

Anderson also recognizes that most of the common solutions to either the Synoptic problem or the relationship between John and the Synoptics have been not nearly complex enough. Every major solution to these problems has outliers where the theories of the interrelationship of the Gospels don't work well. Instead of simply looking for the theory with the fewest outliers, unless hypotheses are mutually exclusive (e.g., Luke depended entirely on Matthew vs. Matthew depended entirely on Luke), they should be combined where they are based on solid evidence. Thus, there had to be a common fund of oral tradition that all the Gospels drew on, even as each would naturally have had access to some unique traditions. For some time it has been recognized that oral traditions didn't suddenly "shut down" the moment the first Gospel (or any written predecessor) was composed. Because of the interconnectedness of the many streams of earliest Christian tradition, these would have naturally influenced one another, even before any of them was written down as well as after they were. The date of the final form of a Gospel has no necessary correlation to the age of any tradition that it contains, since some oral traditions circulated

---

69. Paul N. Anderson, *The Fourth Gospel and the Quest for Jesus: Modern Foundations Reconsidered* (London: T&T Clark, 2006).
70. Anderson, *Fourth Gospel and the Quest for Jesus*, 46–74, 74–97.
71. Anderson, *Fourth Gospel and the Quest for Jesus*, esp. 180–89.

longer than others. Some would have been preserved better than others, and careful preservation, while often related to the amount of elapsed time, wasn't always so related. One tradition might be preserved very carefully for a long time, and another modified much more even in a shorter time. Anderson, therefore, coins another word to speak about streams of tradition that mutually influenced one another: they were "interfluential."[72] Later, more narrowly focused studies would demonstrate how John may have relied on pre-Markan tradition and Mark may have utilized pre-Johannine tradition.[73] Similar relationships can plausibly be postulated between any pair of Gospels.[74]

In the latter part of his book, Anderson itemizes the most significant uniquely Synoptic contributions to the historical Jesus quest and the rationale for including them. He does the same for those attested by both the Synoptics and John, and he highlights uniquely Johannine contributions. Listed in this last category are Jesus's ministry alongside John the Baptist and the resulting "prolific availability of purifying power"; the temple clearing as the inaugural sign of Jesus's ministry; his travels to and from Jerusalem and multiyear ministry; the early events in his public ministry (John 2–4); his favorable reception among women, Samaritans, and Gentiles; the "archaeological realism" in Jesus's ministry in Judea; the Lord's Supper as a "common meal" just before Passover; and Jesus's teaching about "the way of the Spirit and the reign of Truth."[75]

Three volumes of papers from the "John, Jesus, and History" seminar have been published to date, after an inordinately long wait for volume 3 to appear.[76] Anderson insists that three more volumes are

---

72. Anderson, *Fourth Gospel and the Quest for Jesus*, esp. 101–12. See the elaboration in Anderson, "Interfluential, Formative and Dialectical: A Theory of John's Relation to the Synoptics," in *Für und wider die Priorität des Johannesevangeliums: Symposion in Salzburg am 10. März 2000*, ed. Peter Leander Hofrichter (Hildesheim: Olms, 2002), 19–58.

73. See esp. Craig L. Blomberg, "The Sayings of Jesus in Mark: Does Mark Ever Rely on a Pre-Johannine Tradition?," in Porter and Ong, *Origins of John's Gospel*, 81–98; cf. Paul N. Anderson, "Incidents Dispersed in the Synoptics and Cohering in John: Dodd, Brown and Johannine Historicity," in Thatcher and Williams, *Engaging with C. H. Dodd*, 176–202.

74. Anderson, *Fourth Gospel and the Quest for Jesus*, 112–25.

75. Anderson, *Fourth Gospel and the Quest for Jesus*, 154–73.

76. Anderson, Just, and Thatcher, *John, Jesus, and History*, vol. 3.

forthcoming, but they, too, seem unusually delayed.[77] For our purposes, volumes 2 and 3 contain the most relevant studies. Anderson has also coedited a large volume with Alan Culpepper, *John and Judaism: A Contested Relationship in Context*, with several contributions that impinge on our topic.[78] Finally, the *Journal for the Study of the Historical Jesus*, begun in 2003, has published several articles (at times with rejoinders) in support of significant use of John for Jesus research. Studies published in one of these various outlets, supporting segments of John's Gospel, make good cases for the trustworthiness of (1) imagery that portrays Jesus as a king of Israel, even if in unexpected form;[79] (2) the putting out of Jesus followers from certain Jerusalem synagogues;[80] (3) contextual limitations behind Jesus's most vitriolic anti-Jewish rhetoric to specific individuals or groups of Jews, making it an intramural or "in-house" debate;[81] (4) Jesus having disciples from Bethsaida;[82] (5) the probability that Bethesda and Siloam were *mikvaot* (ritual immersion pools), making the events described there more understandable and probable;[83] (6) Jesus's role as a baptizer;[84] (7) various aphorisms of Jesus embedded in John;[85] (8) parable-like

---

77. See the list of forthcoming volumes in Paul N. Anderson, "Why the Gospel of John Is Fundamental to Jesus Research," in *Jesus Research: The Gospel of John in Historical Inquiry*, ed. James H. Charlesworth with Jolyon G. R. Pruszinski (London: Bloomsbury T&T Clark, 2019), 15–16.

78. R. Alan Culpepper and Paul N. Anderson, eds., *John and Judaism: A Contested Relationship in Context* (Atlanta: SBL Press, 2017).

79. Jan G. van der Watt, "'Is Jesus the King of Israel?': Reflections on the Jewish Nature of the Gospel of John," in Culpepper and Anderson, *John and Judaism*, 39–56.

80. Jonathan Bernier, "Jesus, Ἀποσυνάγωγος, and Modes of Religiosity," in Culpepper and Anderson, *John and Judaism*, 127–33. Cf., more fully, Bernier, *Aposynagōgos and the Historical Jesus in John*.

81. Paul N. Anderson, "Anti-Semitism and Religious Violence as Flawed Interpretations of the Gospel of John," in Culpepper and Anderson, *John and Judaism*, 265–311.

82. Mark Appold, "Jesus' Bethsaida Disciples: A Study in Johannine Origins," in Anderson, Just, and Thatcher, *John, Jesus, and History*, 2:27–34.

83. Urban C. von Wahlde, "The Pool of Siloam: The Importance of the New Discoveries for our Understanding of Ritual Immersion in Late Second Temple Judaism and the Gospel of John," in Anderson, Just, and Thatcher, *John, Jesus, and History*, 2:155–73. See also von Wahlde, "The Pool(s) of Bethesda and the Healing in John 5: A Reappraisal of Research and of the Johannine Text," *RB* 116 (2009): 111–36.

84. Joan E. Taylor and Federico Adinolfi, "John the Baptist and Jesus the Baptist: A Narrative Critical Approach," *JSHJ* 10 (2012): 247–84; Graham H. Twelftree, "Jesus the Baptist," *JSHJ* 7 (2009): 103–25.

85. Linda McKinnish Bridges, "Aphorisms of Jesus in John," *JSHJ* 9 (2011): 207–29; R. Alan Culpepper, "Jesus Sayings in the Johannine Discourses," in Anderson, Just, and Thatcher,

sayings;[86] (9) the metaphors involved in John's unique "I am" sayings;[87] (10) the use of "Son of God" for Jesus;[88] (11) Jesus's *exalted* self-designation as "Son of man";[89] (12) distinctive elements in the account of the anointing of Jesus;[90] (13) Semitic language and syntax within the speech of Jesus;[91] (14) the role of Jesus as God's agent;[92] (15) the role of John the Baptist as a witness;[93] (16) the discussion with the woman at the well about living water and her subsequent role as an evangelist to her townspeople;[94] (17) the Bethany family of Mary, Martha, and Lazarus;[95] (18) the resurrection of Lazarus as a catalyst for Jesus's death;[96] (19) the essence of the footwashing incident;[97] (20) distinctive features of Pilate's examination of Jesus;[98] (21) the portrayal of the

---

*John, Jesus, and History*, 3:353–82. Cf. already C. H. Dodd, "Some Johannine 'Herrenworte' with Parallels in the Synoptic Gospels," *NTS* 2 (1955): 75–86. Reinhard Nordsieck identifies no fewer than thirty sayings of Jesus at the core of his teachings in John, out of which larger wholes could have been constructed (*Johannes: Zur Frage nach Verfasser und Entstehung des vierten Evangeliums; Ein neuer Versuch* [Neukirchen-Vluyn: Neukirchener Verlag, 1998], 60–68).

86. Ruben Zimmermann, "Are There Parables in John? It Is Time to Revisit the Question," *JSHJ* 9 (2011): 243–76.

87. Paul N. Anderson, "The Origin and Development of the Johannine *Egō-Eimi* Sayings in Cognitive-Critical Perspective," *JSHJ* 9 (2011): 139–206.

88. Peder Borgen, "Observations on God's Agent and Agency in John 5–9: Tradition, Exposition, and Glimpses into History," in Anderson, Just, and Thatcher, *John, Jesus, and History*, 3:423–38.

89. Benjamin J. Reynolds, "The Johannine Son of Man and the Historical Jesus: John 9:35 as a Test Case," in Anderson, Just, and Thatcher, *John, Jesus, and History*, 3:459–68.

90. Tim Ling, "John, Jesus, and Virtuoso Religion," in Anderson, Just, and Thatcher, *John, Jesus, and History*, 3:271–82.

91. Steven A. Graham, "Semitic Language and Syntax within the Speech of the Johannine Jesus," in Anderson, Just, and Thatcher, *John, Jesus, and History*, 3:407–21.

92. Borgen, "Observations on God's Agent and Agency in John 5–9," 435.

93. Robert L. Webb, "Jesus in Relation to John 'the Testifier' and Not 'the Baptizer': The Fourth Gospel's Portrayal of John the Baptist and Its Historical Possibilities," in Anderson, Just, and Thatcher, *John, Jesus, and History*, 3:215–30. See also Mary Coloe, "John as Witness and Friend," in Anderson, Just, and Thatcher, *John, Jesus, and History*, 2:45–61.

94. Jo-Ann A. Brant, "The Geopolitics of Water and John 4:1–42," in Anderson, Just, and Thatcher, *John, Jesus, and History*, 3:245–58.

95. Richard Bauckham, "The Bethany Family in John 11–12: History or Fiction?," in Anderson, Just, and Thatcher, *John, Jesus, and History*, 2:185–201.

96. Derek M. H. Tovey, "On Not Unbinding the Lazarus Story: The Nexus of History and Theology in John 11:1–44," in Anderson, Just, and Thatcher, *John, Jesus, and History*, 2:213–23.

97. Jaime Clark-Soles, "Of Footwashing and History," in Anderson, Just, and Thatcher, *John, Jesus, and History*, 2:255–69. See also David Wenham, "Paradigms and Possibilities in the Study of John's Gospel," in Lierman, *Challenging Perspectives on the Gospel of John*, 1–13, esp. 10–13.

98. Warren Carter, "Jesus and Pilate: Memories in John's Gospel?," in Anderson, Just, and Thatcher, *John, Jesus, and History*, 3:59–76; Craig S. Keener, "'What Is Truth?': Pilate's

Jewish feasts;[99] and (22) ritual purification as pervasive in the earliest stratum of the Gospel tradition.[100]

Still other recent journal articles, contributions to similar anthologies, or individual monographs have bolstered support for (23) Jesus as the divine bridegroom;[101] (24) eating Jesus's flesh and drinking his blood as a graphic but plausible metaphor for intimate association with him in his death;[102] (25) sayings of Jesus about doing God's works;[103] (26) quite a number of Jesus's "Amen, Amen" sayings;[104] (27) Jesus's use of the concepts of light and truth;[105] (28) the use of discourse analysis to demonstrate cohesion in places typically ascribed to awkward seams tying different sources together;[106] (29) the Upper Room Discourse understood in light of rhetorical and dramatic principles of the day;[107] (30) Synoptic-like sayings of Jesus scattered about the Farewell Discourse, which overall is unified by a broadly chiastic structure;[108] and (31) the "parable" of the vine and the branches.[109] Étienne Nodet

---

Perspective on Jesus in John 18:33–38," in Anderson, Just, and Thatcher, *John, Jesus, and History*, 3:77–94.

99. Johnson, "Jewish Feasts and Questions of Historicity in John 5–12," 117–29.

100. Gary Burge, "Siloam, Bethesda, and the Johannine Water Motif," in Anderson, Just, and Thatcher, *John, Jesus, and History*, 3:259–69.

101. Ruben Zimmermann, "Jesus—the Divine Bridegroom? John 2–4 and Its Christological Implications," in *Reading the Gospel of John's Christology as Jewish Messianism: Royal, Prophetic, and Divine Messiahs*, ed. Benjamin Reynolds and Gabriele Boccaccini (Leiden: Brill, 2018), 358–86.

102. Jan Heilmann, "A Meal in the Background of John 6:52–58?," *JBL* 137 (2018): 481–500.

103. Peter W. Ensor, "The Johannine Sayings of Jesus and the Question of Authenticity," in Lierman, *Challenging Perspectives on the Gospel of John*, 14–33. See further Ensor, *Jesus and His "Works": The Johannine Sayings in Historical Perspective* (Tübingen: Mohr Siebeck, 1996).

104. R. Alan Culpepper, "The AMHN, AMHN Sayings in the Gospel of John," in Sloan and Parsons, *Perspectives on John*, 57–101.

105. Elizabeth W. Mburu, *Qumran and the Origins of Johannine Language and Symbolism* (London: T&T Clark, 2010), esp. 74.

106. David I. Yoon, "The Question of Aporiai or Cohesion in the Fourth Gospel: A Response to Urban C. von Wahlde," in Porter and Ong, *Origins of John's Gospel*, 219–38.

107. George Parsenios, "How and in What Ways Does John's Rhetoric Reflect Jesus' Rhetoric?," in Charlesworth with Pruszinski, *Jesus Research*, 83–95. See also George L. Parsenios, *Rhetoric and Drama in the Johannine Lawsuit Motif* (Tübingen: Mohr Siebeck, 2010).

108. Johannes Beutler, "Synoptic Jesus Tradition in the Johannine Farewell Discourse," in *Jesus in Johannine Tradition*, ed. Robert T. Fortna and Tom Thatcher (Louisville: Westminster John Knox, 2001), 165–73.

109. P. R. Choi, "'I Am the Vine': An Investigation of the Relations between John 15:1–6 and Some Parables of the Synoptic Gospels," *BR* 45 (2000): 51–75.

believes that "John is closer to the facts in the narrative parts, but he has retained only what is prone to a metaphorical meaning; the identity of Jesus is especially revealed by some of the discourses."[110] Only a refusal to cross *intra*disciplinary boundaries can account for the continued appearance of historical Jesus studies that largely or entirely ignore the Gospel of John, a situation even more ironic when one sees how frequently the third quest has utilized *inter*disciplinary study entirely outside of biblical scholarship.[111] If that explanation fails, one wonders if anything other than sheer bias against the Fourth Gospel can explain the lacuna.

## Jesus as Mirrored in James Charlesworth

Longtime Princeton professor, editor of the major English translation of the Old Testament Pseudepigrapha, and a veteran biblical archaeologist, *James Charlesworth* (1940–) has also published numerous studies on the Gospel of John. He has updated several of these and combined them with new essays to form his recent book *Jesus as Mirrored in John: The Genius in the New Testament*.[112] Already in 2010, he was heralding a "paradigm shift," as more and more scholars were using John for Jesus research despite the demurral of other highly influential authors of historical Jesus books.[113] In this new volume, he ranges from discussions of the huge amounts of topographical, geographical, and circumstantial detail in John that has been corroborated, especially surrounding the pools of Bethesda and Siloam; the logic of John 5:16–18 depending on a literal reading of Genesis 2:2 that could suggest that God continued to work on the Sabbath; the amount of detail, once assumed to be

---

110. Étienne Nodet, *The Historical Jesus? Necessity and Limits of an Inquiry*, trans. J. Edward Crowley (London: T&T Clark, 2008), 188.

111. One of the very defining traits of the third quest is its use of multidisciplinary studies. See esp. Halvor Moxnes, "Jesus in Discourses of Dichotomies: Alternative Paradigms for the Historical Jesus," *JSHJ* 13 (2015): 130–52; Moxnes, "The Historical Jesus: From Master Narrative to Cultural Context," *BTB* 28 (1998): 135–49.

112. James H. Charlesworth, *Jesus as Mirrored in John: The Genius in the New Testament* (London: Bloomsbury T&T Clark, 2019).

113. James H. Charlesworth, "The Historical Jesus in the Fourth Gospel: A Paradigm Shift?," *JSHS* 8 (2010): 3–46.

Hellenistic, that has parallels of varying degrees in the Essene Jewish literature from Qumran; the Old Testament backgrounds and symbolism of the serpent lifted up in the wilderness (John 3:14); the location of Bethany beyond the Jordan; and the possibility of a first edition of John that was written before AD 70. Much less plausible is his defense of Thomas as the author of the Gospel,[114] and somewhat tangential is his theory that the Fourth Gospel depends on the Odes of Solomon.[115]

Appearing only months before *Jesus as Mirrored in John* was Charlesworth's edited volume of the proceedings of the third Princeton-Prague symposium.[116] All three volumes were devoted to Jesus research, including a couple of essays involving the Fourth Gospel in volume 1.[117] The third volume, however, was devoted entirely to the value of John for historical Jesus study. Here Charlesworth himself gives a good summary of six main reasons John has been so little utilized in this fashion: (1) it was believed to be the last of the four Gospels; (2) it was for so long viewed as dependent on the Synoptics; (3) it is too theologically developed; (4) it is not interested in history because it focuses on spirituality; (5) it is too cumbersome to combine with the Synoptics and could lead to anachronism; (6) historical Jesus work thus far has been largely limited to the Synoptics.[118] To counter these rationales, Charlesworth argues, in essence, that (1) there may have been multiple editions of John, with the earliest at least as early if not earlier than the Synoptics; (2) it is now widely held that John is independent of the Synoptics even if with considerable knowledge of their contents; (3) we are

---

114. Elaborated in an entire book on the authorship of John: James H. Charlesworth, *The Beloved Disciple: Whose Witness Validates the Gospel of John?* (Valley Forge, PA: Trinity Press International, 1995).

115. Elaborated in an entire book: James H. Charlesworth, *Critical Reflections on the Odes of Solomon: Literary Setting, Textual Studies, Gnosticism, the Dead Sea Scrolls and the Gospel of John* (Sheffield: Sheffield Academic, 1998).

116. Charlesworth with Pruszinski, *Jesus Research*.

117. James H. Charlesworth, "From Old to New: Paradigm Shifts Concerning Judaism, the Gospel of John, Jesus, and the Advent of Christianity," in *Jesus Research: An International Perspective; The First Princeton-Prague Symposium on Jesus Research, Prague 2005*, ed. James H. Charlesworth with Petr Pokorný (Grand Rapids: Eerdmans, 2009), 56–72; Carsten Claussen, "Turning Water to Wine: Re-reading the Miracle at the Wedding in Cana," in Charlesworth with Pokorný, *Jesus Research*, 73–97.

118. James H. Charlesworth, "Introducing the Focus of the Third Princeton-Prague Symposium: John in Jesus Research," in Charlesworth with Pruszinski, *Jesus Research*, 1.

more appreciative than ever of how highly developed the Synoptics are too, but that does not stop us from mining them for historical material; (4) the very fact John wrote a Gospel and not some other literary form suggests at least some interest in history, and it is a false dichotomy to pit history against spirituality; (5) anachronism is a danger with the Synoptics also, but scholars can take effective measures to guard against it; and (6) just because we've regularly relied almost solely on the Synoptics doesn't make it optimal (Charlesworth actually calls it a case of the blind leading the blind!).[119]

Paul Anderson's offering in the Charlesworth volume lays out as fully and clearly as anywhere his current understanding of John, which has evolved slightly from his full book on the topic (see above, 201–2).[120] One section that is new involves the dangers of *not* using John for Jesus research: he might actually contribute something important; he has many mundane details, sometimes more than the Synoptics do, which are not obviously motivated by theology; if John contradicts the Synoptics occasionally, as Anderson believes he does, there may be good reasons for preferring John to the Synoptics.[121] Anderson also believes that new criteria of authenticity need to be developed, and he suggests several. Rather than multiple attestation as previously used, and similar to Dale Allison's continuity approach (see above, 150–52), he proposes "corroborative impression." Instead of either dissimilarity or embarrassment, he prefers a broader criterion of "primitivity," and instead of the standard use of "coherence" to reinforce only that which has already been authenticated (what he calls "closed portraiture"), he prefers "open coherence," which more creatively looks for what naturally fits with other authentic material even if not in lockstep fashion. Finally, although he calls it another criterion, it really is his epistemological perspective: instead of either "supranaturalism" or "dogmatic naturalism," he supports "critical realism."[122]

---

119. Charlesworth, "Introducing the Focus of the Third Princeton-Prague Symposium," 1–2.
120. Anderson, "Why the Gospel of John Is Fundamental to Jesus Research." See also Anderson, "On 'Seamless Robes' and 'Leftover Fragments'—A Theory of Johannine Composition," in Porter and Ong, *Origins of John's Gospel*, 169–218.
121. Anderson, "Why the Gospel of John Is Fundamental to Jesus Research," esp. 23–29.
122. Anderson, "Why the Gospel of John Is Fundamental to Jesus Research," 42–43.

## Philipp Bartholomä's Discourse Analysis

A very distinctive publication is the slightly revised PhD thesis of *Philipp Bartholomä* (1980–), who now teaches in Giessen, Germany, first submitted to the Evangelische Theologische Faculteit in Leuven, Belgium.[123] There is no question that the largest segment of John's Gospel, which remains relatively untouched by even the latest round of scouring for potentially historical content, is the extended discourse material. Long stretches of a synopsis of the four Gospels show no parallels in the Synoptics whenever Jesus is giving one of his lengthier messages, whether in public as in his several visits to Jerusalem at festival times or privately to the disciples in the upper room with his Farewell Discourse. As a result, Bartholomä chooses Jesus's dialogues with Nicodemus (John 3:1–21) and the Samaritan woman (4:1–30), discourses on the bread of life (6:22–59) and the light of the world (8:12–59), the so-called first farewell address (14:1–31), and Jesus's postresurrection words to his disciples (20:11–29).[124]

Bartholomä then scours the Synoptics with a fine-toothed comb. He divides each Johannine discourse into individual sentences and sometimes individual clauses. If he finds significant verbal parallelism in a Synoptic teaching of Jesus, he gives the sentence or clause in John a score of 2; if there is less significant but still observable verbal parallelism, he scores it a 1; if there is none, he gives it a 0. Then he does the same thing for conceptual parallelism. Every portion of every discourse is given a composite score that he indicates with the forms [0/0], [0/1], [0/2], [1/1], [1/2], or [2/2], with the first number standing for amount of verbal parallelism and the second for the amount of conceptual parallelism.[125] For example, dividing the words of Jesus in John 3:1–21 into 32 such linguistic units discloses 19 examples of verbal parallelism and 30 of conceptual parallelism. Only 3:14a and 3:21a are scored with [0/0]. On the other hand, Jesus's discrete sayings in 4:1–30, which fall

---

123. Philipp F. Bartholomä, *The Johannine Discourses and the Teaching of Jesus in the Synoptics: A Contribution to the Discussion Concerning the Authenticity of Jesus' Words in the Fourth Gospel* (Tübingen: Francke, 2012).
124. Bartholomä, *Johannine Discourses*, 107–334.
125. Bartholomä, *Johannine Discourses*, 83–91.

into 14 linguistic segments, find only 3 verbal parallels in the Synoptics. But 10 of the 14 do contain conceptual parallels. The discourses in chapters 6, 8, and 14 all contain significantly more parallelism than this, and in 20:11–19, 11 of 20 linguistic units contain verbal parallelism while another 6 have at least conceptual parallelism.[126]

Bartholomä repeatedly reminds his reader that he does not claim to be demonstrating that Jesus actually spoke any portion of any of these six discourses. Rather, he is showing that there are insufficient linguistic reasons for *rejecting* the Johannine Jesus for being too different from the Synoptics to have spoken these discourses.[127] Peter Ensor adds that "90% of Jesus' Johannine vocabulary either also occurs in his Synoptic speech, or, failing to occur there, also fails to occur in the Johannine literature outside dominical [Jesus'] speech (a fact which weighs against that vocabulary being particularly Johannine)."[128] And George Parsenios adds that the longer discourses in John contain many pointed, epigrammatic statements of the kind that one finds in more discrete locations in the Synoptics.[129] The older form-critical model of the tradition ever attaching accretions to itself is not the only explanation of this; the Synoptics could reflect tradition that had already begun to separate out longer discourses into their constituent elements, or Jesus himself could have used proverbial-like wisdom in many contexts, both with and without larger contextual material.

Why, then, do readers of John so consistently come away with the impression that John's Jesus is just too different in his style from the Synoptic Jesus to be the same person? The answer is fairly straightforward: the overall *style* is considerably different. But Bartholomä stresses that this is frequently the case when one compares two or more ancient writers recounting the words of a historical figure. It was considered *appropriate* method to put those words in one's own linguistic styles and forms.[130] The amount of what we might call "paraphrase" has no

126. Bartholomä, *Johannine Discourses*, 415–28.
127. Bartholomä, *Johannine Discourses*, 409–14.
128. Ensor, "Johannine Sayings of Jesus," 20.
129. Parsenios, "How and in What Ways Does John's Rhetoric Reflect Jesus' Rhetoric?," 91.
130. See esp. Gary Knoppers, "The Synoptic Problem: An Old Testament Perspective," *BBR* 19 (2009): 11–34.

bearing on the accuracy of the *contents* of an individual's reported speech. The Fourth Evangelist also has a smaller vocabulary for these paraphrases, so that key words and expressions reappear more frequently than in the Synoptics, adding to that sense of a different style.[131] When we see that a writer like Josephus even varies *his own* style from one account of a historical period or recorded speech to another account of that same period or speech,[132] we should hardly balk when John and the Synoptics vary in the same way.

## Why Else *Is* John So Different?

Still, despite all that we have seen, John is different. How are we to respond to that? Must we choose either John or the Synoptics as our primary "database" for historical Jesus research? If the fourth quest asks for parity between the two in principle, it seems as though its participants assume that once all the appropriate criteria are applied, John will still be the junior partner in terms of the amount contributed to our understanding of Jesus. This may turn out to be the result of the exercise, but should it be assumed in advance? Exactly why do John and the Synoptics vary to the extent that they do and in the ways that they do, and can John be trusted historically despite those differences? No fewer than fourteen additional points may help provide some answers.[133]

First, *we cannot underestimate the power of the triple tradition to reinforce the impression of difference.* Once Matthew and Luke decided to incorporate a significant majority of Mark into their Gospels, even while adding considerably more material, the stage was set that would all but guarantee that any subsequent, largely independent Gospel writer would seem very different. In terms of literarily independent witnesses, nevertheless, the "score" is not 3 to 1, but 1 to 1, the

---

131. Bartholomä, *Johannine Discourses*, 345–53.
132. Cf. Josephus's *Jewish War* with those portions of his *Jewish Antiquities* that overlap with it. For the same phenomenon in Plutarch's *Lives*, see Michael R. Licona, *Why Are There Differences in the Gospels? What We Can Learn from Ancient Biography* (Oxford: Oxford University Press, 2017), 23–109.
133. For these points, I rely heavily on Blomberg, *Jesus and the Gospels*, 256–63.

Synoptics versus John.[134] Had a fifth writer, like the author of the Coptic Gospel of Thomas, produced a connected narrative of key details from Jesus's life and death, we might well be talking about Thomas versus the four Synoptics, not perceiving John as that much different from Matthew, Mark, and Luke by comparison.

Second, *critics tend to underestimate the power of a Gospel's overall outline to dictate what was included and what was excluded.* For example, how could the most dramatic resurrection of all—that of Lazarus—be found only in John if it really occurred? The answer may stem solely from Mark's decision to include only one time in which Jesus ministers in Judea—when he is immediately en route to the Passover during which he would lose his life. Once Matthew and Luke accept at least that much of Mark's outline, none of the three has a place for the Lazarus story, since it occurred in Judea, near Jerusalem, yet during Jesus's penultimate sojourn there (John 11:1–45). That they all included at least one resurrection story anyway (Jairus's daughter in all three Synoptics, and the widow of Nain's son in Luke as well) would have largely offset the lack of the account of Lazarus's resurrection. Conversely, the one key truth that older views seeing direct literary dependence by John on the Synoptics correctly recognized was that he was desiring to supplement more than repeat their contents.[135]

Third, *the examples of interlocking (John inadvertently explaining the Synoptics or vice versa) remind us of how much must necessarily be left out of any biography, modern or ancient.* That these coincidences seem undesigned, and arise tangentially or in passing, helps us recall that much more was going on than any of the Gospels ever narrates. John 21:25, though no doubt hyperbolic, is a good reminder that Jesus said and did much more than any Gospel could include in a single scroll, and that even the omission or inclusion of an entire literary

---

134. See Anderson, "Why the Gospel of John Is Fundamental to Jesus Research," 15–16, 25–27.

135. Even today, Wendy E. Sproston North argues that John knew all three Synoptics, identifying places where he appears to reuse one of them in the same ways that he reuses his own material or Old Testament texts or imagery (*What John Knew and What John Wrote: A Study in John and the Synoptics* [Lanham, MD: Rowman & Littlefield, 2020]).

form such as parables or exorcism accounts still leaves an evangelist with plenty to narrate.[136]

Fourth, *the unique circumstances of a late first-century Christian community in and around Ephesus, bedeviled by the twin challenges of hostility from local Jewish leaders and the growth of Gnostic or Gnostic-like false teaching in the vicinity, certainly would have dictated the choices of material to include or leave out, to emphasize or to play down.* John's high Christology, on the one hand, combined with the emphasis on the humanity of Jesus, on the other, certainly fits this setting.[137] But that is quite different from saying that it was invented for this context.

Fifth, *historical trustworthiness in antiquity simply was not defined by the standards of precision to which we are so accustomed in today's world.* This extends to people's reported speech. We need not hesitate to acknowledge the distinctive style of Jesus's speech in the Fourth Gospel or to attribute it largely to John himself. But that issue must remain separate from the question of whether the content of Jesus's teachings in John are faithful to the gist of his original proclamation.[138]

Sixth, we dare not overlook what at least some scholars in every phase of the quest(s) have acknowledged: *John includes so many more details of time, place, custom, and landscape than the Synoptics do, and these have been proven right many times over.*[139] When we combine that observation with the realization that historical novels as we

---

136. On which, see Zimmermann, "Are There Parables in John?"; André van Oudtshoorn, "Where Have All the Demons Gone? The Role and Place of the Devil in the Gospel of John," *Neot* 51 (2017): 65–82.

137. For the latter, see esp. Udo Schnelle, *Antidocetic Christology in the Gospel of John: An Investigation of the Place of the Fourth Gospel in the Johannine School*, trans. Linda M. Maloney (Minneapolis: Fortress, 1992 [Ger. orig. 1987]).

138. Which is also tied to the specific genre of John, on which point various scholars have stressed the features John shares more with drama than with history, while remaining within the accepted range of the latter. See esp. Derek Tovey, *Narrative Art and Act in the Fourth Gospel* (Sheffield: Sheffield Academic, 1997). See also Jo-Ann A. Brant, *Dialogue and Drama: Elements of Greek Tragedy in the Fourth Gospel* (Peabody, MA: Hendrickson, 2004); Harold W. Attridge, "The Gospel of John: Genre Matters," in *The Gospel of John as Genre Mosaic*, ed. Kasper Bro Larsen (Göttingen: Vandenhoeck & Ruprecht, 2015), 27–45; George L. Parsenios, "The Silent Spaces between Narrative and Drama: *Mimesis* and *Diegesis* in the Fourth Gospel," in Larsen, *Gospel of John as Genre Mosaic*, 85–97.

139. I have gathered together perhaps the most important examples in Blomberg, *Historical Reliability of the New Testament*, 189–229.

think of them were unknown in the ancient Middle East (recall above, 152), it goes a long way toward showing that John thought he was writing history or biography. The details of what happened in the contexts so carefully presented should at least, then, carry a presumption of authenticity.

Seventh, *despite the largely Johannine style of Christ's words in the Fourth Gospel, there are at least 145 words used only by Jesus in John that suggest that Jesus's style was not consistently identical with John's.*[140] It is difficult to know if Jesus's words to Nicodemus end after 3:13, 3:15, or 3:21, but there are few other places where similar ambiguities remain. The "Johannine thunderbolt" in Matthew 11:25–27 and parallel sounds remarkably like Jesus's teaching in John and yet happily coexists in Matthew and Luke with more characteristic Synoptic "Jesus-talk."[141]

Eighth, *the numerous misunderstandings of Jesus by others in the Fourth Gospel that are corrected only with the passage of time (usually after the resurrection) belie the claim that post-paschal understanding was being read back into Jesus's original speech so that the two are no longer distinguishable.*[142] His claim about "destroying this temple" in 2:19 is the classic example, but there are plenty of others, including his teaching in the upper room for his closest followers at a time when one might have anticipated the greatest clarity (14:5, 8, 22; 16:17–18). In fact, Tom Thatcher uses phenomena like these to make the claim that John shows more historical interest in Jesus than the Synoptics do. He explains what he means by this:

> The Gospel of John was born out of a desire to portray Jesus as a figure from the past and to keep him locked in that past, to draw a bold line between present Christian experience and the events of "the beginning," to suppress the living memory of Jesus and replace that memory with a

---

140. H. R. Reynolds, *The Gospel of John*, vol. 1 (New York: Funk & Wagnalls, 1906), cxxiii–cxxv.

141. On the pervasive influence of the language and concepts of this passage in John, see John W. Pryor, "The Great Thanksgiving and the Fourth Gospel," *BZ* 35 (1991): 157–79.

142. D. A. Carson, "Understanding Misunderstandings in the Fourth Gospel," *TynBul* 33 (1982): 59–91. See also Tom Thatcher, *The Riddles of Jesus in John: A Study in Tradition and Folklore* (Atlanta: Society of Biblical Literature, 2000).

fixed image of a person who lived and died decades earlier. The Jesus of the Fourth Gospel is an intentionally historical figure, one whose image is explicitly conflated with Christian faith and the Jewish Scriptures, but whose memory is no longer solely dependent on the work of the Spirit and no longer subject to the vicissitudes of tradition and the needs of the moment.[143]

Ninth, *many of the details in John more accurately fit pre-70 conditions in Palestine than anywhere at the end of the first century and would not likely have been invented in the form we have them at that later date.* These range from details about the annual festivals to the wide variety of messianic titles (esp. in John 1) that later tended to have greater overtones of divinity. Later in the Gospel, the prophet like Moses forms perhaps the clearest example.[144]

Tenth, *several of Jesus's longer discourses in John appear to be crafted after the form of Jewish midrash*[145] *and/or utilize extended chiasmus.*[146] Neither of these forms is unique to early first-century Judaism, but one might have imagined their diminished use, the more the gospel message moved away from strictly Jewish circles. A diverse collection of other linguistic forms in these discourses betrays a Jewish or Semitic style, diction, or theological background. None of these features proves that Jesus was their creator, but the possibility that he might have been can only increase along the way.

Eleventh, *even as John contains more details of time and place than do the Synoptics, a number of them seem to have little or no theological motivation.* When we recall that the ancients typically did not combine meticulous concern for historical accuracy in the framework of a piece of literature with fictional events to carry the plot line, our overall confidence in historicity can only increase. I have mentioned

---

143. Tom Thatcher, *Why John Wrote a Gospel: Jesus-Memory-History* (Louisville: Westminster John Knox, 2006), 165.
144. See esp. Bauckham, "Messianism according to the Gospel of John," 34–68 (reprinted in Bauckham, *Testimony of the Beloved Disciple*, 207–38).
145. Peder Borgen, *Bread from Heaven: An Exegetical Study of the Concept of Manna in the Gospel of John and the Writings of Philo* (Leiden: Brill, 1965).
146. See esp. Wayne Brouwer, *The Literary Development of John 13–17: A Chiastic Reading* (Atlanta: Society of Biblical Literature, 2001).

many of the archaeological corroborations of details at one point or another in our surveys of the various quests and will not repeat them here, but fuller catalogues are available.[147] And again it is important to stress that most of this information appears tangentially, not as part of a coordinated effort to enable us to reconstruct either a chronology or an itinerary of Jesus's ministry.

Twelfth, *the Fourth Evangelist is contextualizing the gospel for a somewhat Jewish but largely Hellenistic audience*, even apart from the specific threats it is receiving from the local synagogue and emerging Gnosticism. "Eternal life," for example, communicates much better than the "kingdom of God." But lest that be seen as an utter distortion of Jesus's original message, we must recall how in Matthew 19, verse 16 and verses 23–25 show the interchangeability in certain contexts of "eternal life," "kingdom of heaven," "kingdom of God," and salvation. It is also important to see that the concept of God's kingship appears in numerous ways in the Fourth Gospel, even though the term appears in only three verses (John 3:3, 5; 18:36).[148]

Thirteenth, *we must acknowledge that statements that form part of a typical list of the clearest statements of high Christology in John, from the vantage point of 20/20 hindsight, typically utilize metaphors that were not always grasped that clearly when they were first spoken.* The "I am" statements with predicates ("bread of life," "good shepherd," "true vine," etc.) illustrate this well. When we realize that passages like 8:25 and 10:25 show a lack of understanding on the part of Jesus's closest followers, and that even when they say that he is finally speaking clearly (16:29–30) it would seem that they still don't fully grasp matters (vv. 31–33), we had better exercise caution in our descriptions of how explicit Jesus's self-revelation was.[149] Rainer Riesner proposes that John has drawn on the form of Synoptic "I am" statements

---

147. See esp. Urban C. von Wahlde, "Archaeology and John's Gospel," in *Jesus and Archaeology*, ed. James H. Charlesworth (Grand Rapids: Eerdmans, 2006), 523–86.

148. Beth M. Stovell, *Mapping Metaphorical Discourse in the Fourth Gospel: John's Eternal King* (Leiden: Brill, 2012). Cf., from a very different, postcolonial perspective, Sehyun Kim, *The Kingship of Jesus in the Gospel of John* (Eugene, OR: Pickwick, 2018).

149. Going too far in the opposite direction, but adequately making the point about the metaphors, is Yung Suk Kim, *Truth, Testimony, and Transformation: A New Reading of the "I Am" Sayings of Jesus in the Fourth Gospel* (Eugene, OR: Cascade Books, 2014).

(e.g., Mark 6:50 pars.; 13:6 pars.) plus parallel Synoptic imagery to the predicates (e.g., Jesus searching for the lost sheep [Luke 15:3–7] or telling his would-be followers to enter through the narrow gate [Matt. 7:13–14], etc.) for his form of "I am" statements.[150]

Fourteenth, *despite numerous scholarly reminders that themes like bearing testimony and telling the truth need not refer solely or even primarily to historical truth,*[151] *it is still difficult to square their frequency in John with theories that the Fourth Gospel was largely invented as pious fiction.* What F. F. Bruce opined forty years ago still rings true: "John presents the trial and execution of Jesus, as he presents everything else in his record, in such a way as to enforce his theological *Leitmotiv*: Jesus is the incarnate Word, in whom the glory of God is revealed. But the events which he presents in this way, and preeminently in the events of the passion, are real, historical events. It could not be otherwise, for the Word became flesh—the revelation became history."[152]

The major issue still not addressed here is the *overall*, composite high Christology. It is one thing to explain one or several "I am" sayings with a predicate as more metaphorical in its original context than we often remember it is. It is another thing to traverse the Gospel of John from start to finish with its lofty prologue equating Jesus with the *logos* ("Word"), who "was God" even in the very beginning (1:1), who also uttered the great "I am" without a metaphorical predicate (8:58), who claimed oneness with the Father (10:30) and was worshiped by Thomas with the confession "My Lord and my God" (20:28). Surely *this* John cannot be squared with the Synoptics, or so the standard argument goes.

Again, the parallel but nonintersecting tracks of historical Jesus and Johannine research are largely to blame for exacerbating this perception. The *divine identity Christology* highlighted especially by Larry

---

150. Rainer Riesner, *Messias Jesus: Seine Geschichte, seine Botschaft und ihre Überlieferung* (Giessen: Brunnen, 2019), 457.
151. See esp. Lincoln, *Truth on Trial*.
152. F. F. Bruce, "The Trial of Jesus in the Fourth Gospel," in *Gospel Perspectives*, vol. 1, *Studies of History and Tradition in the Four Gospels*, ed. R. T. France and David Wenham (Sheffield: JSOT Press, 1980), 18.

Hurtado and Richard Bauckham from different but complementary perspectives[153] has become more and more well known in Synoptic and in historical Jesus research but has only quite recently begun to affect Johannine studies. Most contemporary comparisons in Johannine research between John and the Synoptics are still comparing John as it is viewed today with the Synoptics as they were characterized a generation or more ago, perspectives still held by many but whose numbers are steadily decreasing. Both the implicit and the titular Christology of the historical Jesus, as we have seen (above, 97–98, 136), have changed the perspective of a significant number of third questers to something much more compatible with the Johannine portrait.

Two quite recent works suggest that rapprochement can become even closer. From the Synoptic side, Andrei Orlov has studied the baptismal and transfiguration accounts in light of the Jewish "two powers in heaven" motif.[154] The transfiguration imagery is firmly rooted in that of Moses seeing God's glory on Mount Sinai, while Orlov believes that the baptismal imagery owes more to Ezekiel's revelations by the Kebar River in Babylon than has often been realized. Although Orlov is more interested in the origins and meaning of the theological motifs, his contribution is to plant them firmly in Jewish backgrounds, even while demonstrating that the monotheism reflected in them left room for a second divine power, closely related to but still distinct from Yahweh. Binitarianism is again shown to be a thoroughly Jewish concept.[155]

Ruben A. Bühner looks at a broader array of New Testament texts, including Johannine ones. His title discloses his thesis: *Messianic High Christology: New Testament Variants of Second Temple Judaism.*[156]

---

153. See esp. Larry W. Hurtado, *One God, One Lord: Early Christian Devotion and Ancient Jewish Monotheism*, 3rd ed. (London: Bloomsbury T&T Clark, 2015); Richard Bauckham, *Jesus and the God of Israel: God Crucified and Other Studies on the New Testament's Christology of Divine Identity* (Grand Rapids: Eerdmans, 2010).

154. Andrei A. Orlov, *The Glory of the Invisible God: Two Powers in Heaven Traditions and Early Christology* (London: Bloomsbury T&T Clark, 2019). This theme was first investigated particularly by Alan F. Segal, *Two Powers in Heaven: Early Rabbinic Reports about Christianity and Gnosticism* (Leiden: Brill, 2002).

155. See also Larry W. Hurtado, *Lord Jesus Christ: Devotion to Jesus in Earliest Christianity* (Grand Rapids: Eerdmans, 2005).

156. Ruben A. Bühner, *Messianic High Christology: New Testament Variants of Second Temple Judaism* (Waco: Baylor University Press, 2021).

Bühner devotes successive, detailed chapters to Philippians 2:6–11, Mark 14:61–65, Luke 1:26–38, and Revelation 4–5, climaxing with a study of Jesus as the *logos* in John 1:1–18. Key Second Temple texts used for comparison include 11Q Melchizedek, 4 Ezra, the Jewish reception history of Psalm 110, 4Q Son of God, and the Parables of Enoch, along with scattered texts on the divine Word. While the various New Testament texts move beyond what is claimed in the Second Temple Jewish literature, in every case they build on it. No other religious background or period is needed to account for the early messianic developments, and the developments are more readily imaginable before AD 70 than afterward.

With respect to historical Jesus research, Bühner draws two conclusions, carefully understated. First, "that a man in the first century CE who proclaimed himself a man approved by God, who claimed to possess a special divine authority, and who was thought to have inherited some kind of divinity was ultimately sentenced to death because the Jewish authorities considered his divine claims to be blasphemous . . . is not implausible in historical terms."[157] Second, "we also have to reconsider the commonly held view that no claim regarding Jesus's divinity could have had any basis in his lifetime. Instead, the hope for a superhuman messiah was part of the diverse discourse of Second Temple messianism."[158] So Bühner decides that it is "also possible, therefore, that a Jew in the first century CE was already believed during his lifetime to have some divine authority or to be an otherwise superhuman figure."[159] The implications for the Gospel of John should be obvious: "The depiction of Christ as divine can no longer be thought to be the categorical difference between early Jewish Messianism and New Testament Christology,"[160] so that "it is not impossible in historical terms that a Jew in the first century CE was believed to be one such otherworldly or otherwise superhuman figure, even within his own lifetime."[161]

157. Bühner, *Messianic High Christology*, 190.
158. Bühner, *Messianic High Christology*, 190–91.
159. Bühner, *Messianic High Christology*, 191.
160. Bühner, *Messianic High Christology*, 200.
161. Bühner, *Messianic High Christology*, 201.

## Conclusion

The "new look on John" has come a long way since it was declared by John Robinson to have begun. C. H. Dodd, of course, gave it its biggest early emphasis. Many studies, large and small, some better known than others, have advanced the cause ever since. But it has been the prolonged existence of the "John, Jesus, and History" seminar of the Society of Biblical Literature that really established the new look as a serious endeavor meriting attention. The diversity of scholars who have participated and the wide range of topics and passages they have covered join hands with studies in other recent anthologies, the occasional monograph, and an entirely new journal (*Journal for the Study of the Historical Jesus*) to demonstrate the breadth of possibilities for authenticating key portions of most of the major pericopes or themes in the Fourth Gospel.

The most significant contrary argument focuses on how John simply remains so different from the Synoptics. This, of course, is a very subjective assessment—so different compared to what? There is a plethora of reasons why John is different in what he selects to narrate and what themes he chooses to highlight in his editing of material shared with the Synoptics, especially Mark, which doesn't necessarily affect historicity. Once one recognizes the appropriateness in ancient history and biography of putting others' speech in one's own idiolect, the question of John's distinctive style no longer has much to do with our assessment of his Gospel's historicity. Once we pore over conceptual and not just verbal parallels, the amount of John not found in some form in the Synoptics shrinks dramatically. We also must remember that so much of John's distinctiveness is due simply to the fact that we have three Gospels so remarkably like one another, and that the differences between John and Mark, for example, are not that distinctive when compared with other largely independent historical or biographical sources treating the same figure or time in the ancient Mediterranean world.

I resonate, then, with Paul Anderson's initial call for a fourth quest for the historical Jesus based on giving John and the Synoptics parity as potential sources for Jesus research. I agree with his more recent claim that such a fourth quest has already begun. Indeed, even a review article out of Germany acknowledges its existence, describes its development, and prognosticates about its future.[162] But what might a full-orbed Jesus book of the fourth quest look like? What might a few chapters of such an endeavor resemble on a smaller scale? The rest of this book will tackle the second of these questions after ever so briefly making a few observations in reply to the first.

---

162. Folker Siegert, "Die 'vierte Suche' nach dem historischen Jesus: Zur Einbeziehung des Johannesevangeliums in die Jesusforschung," *TLZ* 138 (2013): 525–36.

# 7

# Purification, Baptism, and Transformation in John 1–4

The fullest treatment of the historical Jesus with the methodology of the fourth quest would articulate one's chosen criteria of authenticity, determine what was most likely authentic from the Synoptics, assess what was most likely authentic from John, and then devise a way to integrate the two. As with many historical Jesus books of the first three quests, such a study could proceed chronologically through Jesus's life, as best as we can reconstruct it, combining the historically probable information from both John and the Synoptics at each stage. A variation of this approach would be to take the large, middle period of Jesus's ministry and deal with his teachings and actions more topically, since it is often difficult to reconstruct an actual sequence of events with any high degree of probability. This is not, as many would argue, because the Synoptics regularly contradict both one another and the Fourth Gospel in their placement of material but because the references to time and place in all four Gospels are too often too imprecise for scholars to create one and only one chronological arrangement of the material.[1]

---

1. See Craig L. Blomberg, *Jesus and the Gospels: An Introduction and Survey*, 3rd ed. (Nashville: B&H Academic; London: Inter-Varsity, 2022), 319–23.

Some collections of Jesus's sayings may be composite in origin, while numerous subsections illustrating his deeds are arranged thematically. Sometimes a Gospel writer changes the setting from one pericope to the next without alerting readers, or without alerting them right away.[2]

English (and other modern-language) translations of the Gospels often use words like "then" or "now," which first suggest a chronological relationship between pericopes, even in just one Gospel, but which can also imply logical or topical connections, not in purely chronological order. Sometimes these and other synonyms translate the Greek words *kai*, *de*, or *nyn*, which have considerable built-in ambiguity of meaning beyond their initial dictionary entries ("and," "but," and "now," respectively). Even words that more commonly suggest a chronological order, like *tote* ("then"), as also in English may denote a logical rather than a chronological succession of passages.[3] It is not, then, that it is impossible to create a chronological harmony of the four canonical Gospels with every passage from every one of the books placed in a plausible sequence; it is rather that there are multiple ways to do so.[4] Thus, a partly topical historical Jesus work, like those based on the Synoptics alone,[5] could proceed from the events surrounding Jesus's birth and infancy to his teaching in the temple at age twelve, to the beginnings of his ministry in John 2–4, to the beginnings of his Galilean ministry in all four accounts, to the Sermon on the Mount/Plain. But then one could discuss the major details of Jesus's year-or-more public ministry with successive treatments of controversy or conflict stories, short teachings or proverbs, parables and other extended metaphors,

---

2. See Craig L. Blomberg, *The Historical Reliability of the Gospels*, 2nd ed. (Downers Grove, IL: IVP Academic; Nottingham: Apollos, 2007), 168–71.

3. See the entries to each of these words in any of the standard lexica of the Greek of the New Testament and other literature of that time, esp. BDAG.

4. Cf. several of the standard harmonies of the Gospels, ancient and modern. See esp. Robert L. Thomas and Stanley N. Gundry, eds., *The NIV Harmony of the Gospels, with Explanations and Essays* (San Francisco: HarperSanFrancisco, 1988); George W. Knight, *A Simplified Harmony of the Gospels, using the Text of the HCSB* (Nashville: Holman, 2001).

5. As with many of the works we have surveyed belonging to the third quest. Cf. also works from the genre "lives of Christ," which organize *all* the material of the Synoptics (or of the four Gospels) in order to comment on it. One of the best known over the past generation, despite (or perhaps because of?) its classic dispensationalist orientation, is J. Dwight Pentecost, *The Words and Works of Jesus Christ: A Study of the Life of Christ* (Grand Rapids: Zondervan, 1980).

miracles and their aftermath, and longer discourses or dialogues. That which is most likely to be authentic in John could be interspersed and integrated with comparable Synoptic material.

Requiring somewhat less work would be a book that gathered the most probably authentic Synoptic material, summarizing and arranging it, along with the most probably authentic Johannine material, summarizing and arranging it. Reflections on both comparisons and contrasts, similarities and differences, could then follow.[6] Integration of the two could then take place at the level of broad themes rather than the specific details of individual passages. Still other outlines could be envisioned. Just as the second and third quests often eschewed combining the material of the three Synoptics into one cluttered synthesis of the life of Jesus that blurred the distinctions of each Gospel, so that the last sixty-plus years have focused on hearing each evangelist in his own right,[7] now the most probably authentic bits could be rejoined to their counterparts in the other Gospels to create a combined Gospels' portrait and swing the balance of scholarship back to a mediating position between the two poles.[8]

Unlike older lives of Christ, a treatment of Jesus in this vein would intentionally bracket and omit numerous details that simply don't have as strong support as others do. *This need not imply that these other events didn't happen; it merely implies that the purely historical evidence for them is not as strong.* As a result, we wouldn't enter them into our databases of authenticable actions and sayings of Jesus. Once the project was complete to this point, we would look for patterns of Jesus's teaching and behavior that might highlight or emphasize certain dimensions of his ministry or play down others, especially where the church has not always preserved the same priorities that Jesus did. We would see if the main themes emerging about who Jesus was and

---

6. Cf., in part, the organization of I. Howard Marshall, *New Testament Theology: Many Witnesses, One Gospel* (Downers Grove, IL: IVP Academic, 2004).

7. See esp. the works on each Gospel in the Biblical Theology of the New Testament series (Grand Rapids: Zondervan, 2009–).

8. Again an analogy from New Testament theology comes to mind. See, e.g., how Udo Schnelle devotes sections both to the historical Jesus and to the individual evangelists in *Theology of the New Testament*, trans. M. Eugene Boring (Grand Rapids: Baker Academic, 2009). See also Craig L. Blomberg, *A New Testament Theology* (Waco: Baylor University Press, 2018).

how we should understand him varied at all from typical ecclesiastical portraits, just as other quests have done.⁹

Paul Anderson's detailed studies have suggested to him some initial findings that could emerge from such a project in which John is given parity with the Synoptics. He organizes them under the four revised criteria of authenticity that he has proposed (see above, 208). Under "primitive memory" he includes "Jesus as a Jewish rabbi teaching his band of followers," "the privileging of women," "a non-ritualizing religious leader," "informal views of the church and its leadership," and "transformative encounters and their impressions." Under "corroborative impression" we read of John the Baptist and Jesus both "challenging ritual means of purity," multiple callings of disciples gradually and in stages over a period of time, a prophetic temple incident probably occurring early in Jesus's ministry, healings on the Sabbath, and Jesus as the eschatological prophet. For "critical realism" he lists "the Galilean prophet and his ambivalent receptions in Judea," "Roman occupation and its consequences," "popularism and its liabilities," "the Last Supper as a common meal," and numerous details surrounding the crucifixion and final days of Jesus. Finally, he unpacks "open coherence" with the categories of "Jesus and parabolic instruction about the leadership of God," "Jesus and the gifting of the Spirit," "embracing the neglected and the marginalized," "rejecting violence as the way of the kingdom," and "the love commands as radical faithfulness to the ways of God." Each of these specific examples of what each criterion could authenticate is then further elaborated with explanations and illustrations.¹⁰

More succinctly, Anderson concludes the essay in which he presents this material by rehearsing a conversation he had with Marcus Borg in 2010. Borg had asked him, If a fourth quest did emerge as

---

9. There would no doubt be some similarities between this and classic lives of Christ, except that the goal would not be to incorporate everything in all four Gospels, just those items that had the strongest case for historicity.

10. Paul N. Anderson, "The John, Jesus, and History Project and a Fourth Quest for Jesus," in *Jesus, Skepticism, and the Problem of History: Criteria and Context in the Study of Christian Origins*, ed. Darrell L. Bock and J. Ed Komoszewski (Grand Rapids: Zondervan Academic, 2019), 259–64.

Anderson desired, how much would it lead to a distinctive portrait of Jesus that previous quests had not uncovered? In other words, would there be significant emphases *not normally* present in historical Jesus studies based solely or almost solely on the Synoptics? Anderson's reply included such items as "a fuller understanding of Jesus and his ministry, the elevated place of women around Jesus, a familial and egalitarian ecclesiology, a concern for authentic spirituality, and a view of continuing revelation."[11] Anderson has been researching and writing a fourth-quest historical Jesus book along these lines, and it may even be in print a little before this book is.[12] Whenever it appears, it will surely be a landmark work and a milestone in Jesus research worthy of celebration.

My goals in the rest of this book are much more modest. I would like to follow up on only one of Anderson's topics, the first that he listed under "corroborative impressions," that of "challenging ritual means of purity."[13] I do not intend to use his criteria; they are comparatively new to me and I am not skilled in their application. In fact, I would need to study them in considerably greater detail in order to determine which ones I would *want* to use. My interest in Jesus as purifier came via a different methodology, one that is not as fashionable today as it was earlier in my career. But fashions come and go, and methodological development is not linear, as we have seen. I will rely heavily on the criterion of authenticity sometimes known as "cutting against the grain" (of a Gospel writer's major redactional emphases). At the height of redaction criticism, it was quite popular;[14] it continues to figure heavily in the work of scholars like John Meier, whose quest has now spanned more than three decades.[15] As long as one uses it only positively and not also negatively (to exclude material that doesn't satisfy it), this criterion remains a powerful tool.

---

11. Anderson, "John, Jesus, and History Project," 264.
12. Paul N. Anderson, in personal conversation, January 2022. His book is being published by Eerdmans.
13. Anderson, "John, Jesus, and History Project," 260.
14. Today, see Jörg Frey, *Theology and History in the Fourth Gospel: Tradition and Narration* (Waco: Baylor University Press, 2018), 103.
15. John P. Meier, *A Marginal Jew: Rethinking the Historical Jesus*, 5 vols. to date (New York: Doubleday, 1991–2001; New Haven: Yale University Press, 2009–16), 1:168–71.

The process of applying this criterion proceeds roughly as follows. First, take a specific Gospel pericope and identify the most obvious or influential redactional emphases. These are compiled by familiarizing yourself with the most consistent ways in which one Gospel writer edits his sources along with themes or features that simply recur most often in that Gospel. In short, one looks for what is dominant and distinctive to a specific writer. Second, bracket those emphases—topics, stylistic features, or formal elements—and see what remains. Recognize those stripped-down pericopes or core accounts as the best candidates for an origin in the early Jesus tradition preceding the composition of the Gospel or even in Jesus himself. Third, apply whatever other criteria seem appropriate, whether double similarity and double dissimilarity, multiple attestation or multiple forms, or others. If enough of these are satisfied, we may have reached bedrock historical Jesus material.[16] Of course, the exercise is as much an art as a science, and different individuals' levels of criteria satisfaction will vary. Still, there will at least be some methodological consistency to the process.[17] Finally, look through all the bedrock material and see if there are recurring emphases. Consider whether any of these differ from what practitioners of the other quests have highlighted the most. If you find any, the exercise may have been worthwhile. If they dovetail with what the emerging fourth quest is stressing that previous quests didn't, even better. You are likely to be on to something that is of value rather than merely idiosyncratic.

The perceptive reader will recognize a tension inherent in this process. Every detail in a pared-down passage is also a part of the entire, original passage. If a recurring element, concept, or topic appears frequently in the pared-down texts, it is clearly present in the complete

---

16. I did some of this in Craig L. Blomberg, *The Historical Reliability of John's Gospel: Issues and Commentary* (Downers Grove, IL: IVP Academic, 2001). See also Frey, *Theology and History in the Fourth Gospel*, 103; Sean Freyne, "Jesus and the Galilean 'Am Ha'arets: Fact, Johannine Irony, or Both?," in Paul N. Anderson, Felix Just, and Tom Thatcher, eds., *John, Jesus, and History*, 3 vols. (Atlanta: Society of Biblical Literature, 2007–16), 2:139. There are also striking parallels to the methodology of Thomas Kazen, *Jesus and Purity Halakhah: Was Jesus Indifferent to Impurity?* (Stockholm: Almqvist & Wiksell, 2002; repr., Winona Lake, IN: Eisenbrauns, 2010), 41, 197–98.

17. In most instances, I do not go into detail applying these other criteria, because I have already done so in Blomberg, *Historical Reliability of John's Gospel*.

passages as well. Why then not identify it as a redactional theme and eliminate it along with the others? The answer is that elements that stand out in stripped-down passages don't necessarily seem at all major when they are surrounded by undeniably redactional material. Near the start of my career, I illustrated this principle in a somewhat different exercise of separating tradition from redaction in Luke's travel narrative. Most readers observe that Luke 9:51–18:14 contains quite a few parables. But it is only when the parables unique to this section of Luke are isolated that one sees an elaborate but clear chiastic (inversely parallel) structure. Luke appears to have thematically associated the remaining teachings (and a few deeds) of Jesus in this section with the parables with which they had something important in common. But it is those larger themes that strike the reader of the final form of Luke much more so than the underlying structure of what may well have been a written (or at least oral) parable source.[18]

Of course, presumably every evangelist believed in everything he wrote, so that a full-orbed theology of a Gospel writer must consider every detail of every passage. But while the tasks overlap, determining the theology of an evangelist is not entirely the same as determining his redactional contributions; the latter is a more limited endeavor.[19] *I also cannot stress enough that my labeling a theme as redactional does not mean I believe that it is inauthentic or unhistorical.* Unless a Gospel writer could not possibly have accessed reliable information (not present in his demonstrable sources) from any other sources, written or oral, or, should any of the authors turn out to *have* been eyewitnesses, from his own memory, then we can never say that redactional could not also be historical.[20] We have to at least allow for the possibility. Conversely, there is always the chance that something that satisfies several key criteria of

---

18. Craig L. Blomberg, "Midrash, Chiasmus, and the Outline of Luke's Central Section," in *Gospel Perspectives*, vol. 3, *Studies in Midrash and Historiography*, ed. R. T. France and David Wenham (Sheffield: JSOT Press, 1983; repr., Eugene, OR: Wipf & Stock, 2003), 217–61.

19. See esp. I. Howard Marshall, *Luke: Historian and Theologian*, rev. ed. (Downers Grove, IL: InterVarsity, 1988 [orig. 1970]); and the painstaking outworking of this principle in Marshall, *The Gospel of Luke: A Commentary on the Greek Text*, NIGTC (Grand Rapids: Eerdmans, 1978).

20. Another point recognized by I. Howard Marshall. See Craig L. Blomberg, "Luke: I. H. Marshall on Historical Redaction," *EvQ* 93 (2022): 1–16. From the perspective of social-memory theory and applied to John 1, see Rafael Rodríguez, "What Is History? Reading John 1 as Historical Representation," *JSHJ* 16 (2018): 31–51.

authenticity is nevertheless unhistorical for different reasons altogether. We are always dealing in probabilities rather than certainties.

Still, there are enough patterns of both tradition and redaction, of both what is more and what is less likely to be trustworthy on sheer historical grounds, especially in the Gospel of John, to undertake the experiment. I will proceed through the Fourth Gospel sequentially, focusing on each instance of purity, especially ritual purity. I will not woodenly retrace every step in the process described above, lest this turn into a far bigger book than it was designed to be, but I will highlight the key findings of undertaking the process. We will see that in not a single case is the topic of purity a dominant one. Never does it rise above what literary critics would call a motif and become a full-fledged theme. In every instance, other topics prove more important to John. Sometimes they even create the perception of some tension with what is said or implied about purity. Nevertheless, especially when the more dominant topics are stripped away, a remarkably recurring pattern emerges. It is consistent with, but not identical to, Synoptic treatments. It suggests that the topic was noticeably more important to the historical Jesus than most treatments in any of the three quests have indicated.[21] It also has ramifications for contemporary Christianity that are too little noticed. The rest of this chapter will trace my findings through the first four chapters of the Gospel of John. Chapters 8 and 9 will do the same for the rest of the Gospel and consolidate my findings. Chapter 10 will then make comparisons with Synoptic data, while my conclusion will not only summarize the argument but also suggest some contemporary significance.

## What Was John's Baptism All About? (John 1)

The Gospel of John begins with a prologue, usually taken as spanning the book's first eighteen verses. It does not contain information about

---

21. There have been studies of it in Johannine scholarship, but they have not yet recognized the full significance of the motif for historical Jesus research. See esp. Larry Paul Jones, *The Symbol of Water in the Gospel of John* (Sheffield: Sheffield Academic, 1997); Wai-Yee Ng, *Water Symbolism in John: An Eschatological Interpretation* (New York: Peter Lang, 2001); Seung-In Song, *Water as an Image of the Spirit in the Johannine Literature* (New York: Peter Lang, 2019).

Jesus's earthly life but alludes to creation "in the beginning" (1:1). The preexisting Word of God, not identified as Jesus until verse 17, was God's agent in creating the universe (v. 3). The incarnation is mentioned in verse 14, but without any accompanying details about Jesus's life. Many theories have been put forward about the prologue's composition: Did it evolve in stages of tradition-critical development?[22] Was it written entirely by the author of the Fourth Gospel, perhaps even after the rest of the book had been completed?[23] However these questions are answered, there is little doubt that key themes in the book are identified here at the outset: the deity of Christ; light versus darkness; Jesus's incarnation for the entire world; his rejection by many of his own people but acceptance by some of them and by other people; the importance of belief, which leads to a new, spiritual birth; a contrast with but also fulfillment of the law; and Jesus as God's Son, not as just another one of the children of God but in closest relationship with the Father. On top of all of these is the very distinctive use of the title *logos* ("Word") for Jesus, found nowhere else in the Gospel outside of 1:1–18.[24]

Tucked into this prologue are two snippets of text about a man named John (vv. 6–8, 15). The second one especially seems to interrupt the narrative, so that several important translations put it in parentheses (NRSV, ESV, NIV, CSB). For a variety of scholars, these references provide a key clue to unlocking a chiastic structure in verses 1–18.[25] Peter Williams, however, has revived an ancient interpretive tradition of seeing the body of the Gospel beginning already in verse 6, where the first reference to John appears.[26] Either way, this John is introduced

---

22. Of such theories, perhaps the strongest is that of Ed L. Miller, *Salvation History in the Prologue of John: The Significance of John 1:3–4* (Leiden: Brill, 1989).

23. On the likelihood of the prologue in its current form being composed to introduce the major themes of the Gospel, perhaps even after the writing of the rest of the Gospel, see Ed L. Miller, "'In the Beginning': A Christological Transparency," *NTS* 45 (1999): 587–92.

24. See esp. Daniel Boyarin, "The Gospel of the Memra: Jewish Binitarianism and the Prologue to John," *HTR* 94 (2001): 243–84. For a broader study of the wide-ranging foundations afforded by this concept, see John Ronning, *The Jewish Targums and John's Logos Theology* (Peabody, MA: Hendrickson, 2010).

25. See R. Alan Culpepper, "The Pivot of John's Prologue," *NTS* 27 (1980): 1–31; Jeffrey Staley, "The Structure of John's Prologue," *CBQ* 48 (1986): 241–64; Stephen Voorwinde, "John's Prologue: Beyond Some Impasses of Twentieth-Century Scholarship," *WTJ* 64 (2002): 15–44.

26. Peter J. Williams, "Not the Prologue of John," *JSNT* 33 (2011): 375–86.

as if the audience already knows who he is.[27] Indeed, throughout the Fourth Gospel this John is never called the Baptist, as he is in the Synoptics. In addition, John the apostle never appears by name at all, even though "the sons of Zebedee" do (21:2), so the author clearly knows of John the apostle, son of Zebedee. By never mentioning him by name, however, he does not have to distinguish him from the Baptist, and the Baptist may simply be called John.

This John continues to appear throughout verses 19–40, but the attention gradually turns more and more to Jesus, and after verse 40 John does not reappear until 3:23. The Fourth Gospel knows about and refers to John's ministry of baptism, but the primary emphasis is on his role as a witness to point people to Jesus.[28] Three times in two verses (vv. 19–20) we are told that John bore testimony (from the Gk. *martyreō*) or acknowledged (from *homologeō*) that Jesus rather than he was the Messiah. Indeed, every time John is mentioned in this Gospel, his ministry is tied to witness.[29] There is enough emphasis throughout chapter 1 on who John is *not*, as well as on who he was, to make one suspect that at least some in the intended audience were overly exalting John.[30] Acts 19:1–7 discloses a group of apparent believers nearly thirty years later in Ephesus who are still followers of John rather than Jesus. Second-century Christian testimony discloses that some of John's disciples, like some scribes and Pharisees who had been baptized by him, began claiming John as the Messiah (Ps.-Clem., *Rec.* 1.54, 60). It is not unreasonable, therefore, to imagine some people of this nature in or around the churches in Ephesus toward the end of the

---

27. John F. McHugh, *A Critical and Exegetical Commentary on John 1–4*, ed. Graham N. Stanton, ICC (London: T&T Clark, 2009), 121.

28. See esp. Jean Daniélou, *The Work of John the Baptist*, trans. Joseph A. Horn (Baltimore: Helicon, 1966), 90–102; Robert L. Webb, "Jesus in Relation to John 'the Testifier' and Not 'the Baptizer': The Fourth Gospel's Portrayal of John the Baptist and Its Historical Possibilities," in Anderson, Just, and Thatcher, *John, Jesus, and History*, 3:215–30. See also Dietrich-Alex Koch, "Der Täufer als Zeuge des Offenbarers: Das Täuferbild von Joh 1,19–34 auf dem Hintergrund von Mk 1,2–11," in *The Four Gospels, 1992: Festschrift Frans Neirynck*, ed. F. Van Segbroeck et al., 2 vols. (Louvain: Peeters, 1992), 2:1963–84.

29. Marianne Meye Thompson, *John: A Commentary*, NTL (Louisville: Westminster John Knox, 2015), 30.

30. See esp. Craig S. Keener, *The Gospel of John: A Commentary*, 2 vols. (Peabody, MA: Hendrickson, 2003), 1:388–91.

first century as well.[31] In a world in which antiquity of religious belief closely paralleled its credibility, that John began his ministry prior to Jesus's could have carried a lot of weight, especially for those who were baptized by John. It is thus the Fourth Gospel that has John explicitly clarify that Jesus actually existed before him (1:15) and then repeat the point almost verbatim (v. 30).[32]

The Fourth Gospel can scarcely not talk at least a little about John as a baptizer, and the three clearest and most extensive points of contact with the Synoptic tradition are John's use of Isaiah 40:3 to describe his ministry (John 1:23), how he is unworthy even to untie the straps of the sandals of the one who is coming (v. 27), and the comparisons of his current water baptism with the Messiah's future Spirit baptism (v. 33). But John's baptismal ministry is barely described; it is introduced, as we have seen, as if the Fourth Gospel's readers already knew about it. His baptism with water is significant enough for priests and Levites to come from Jerusalem to question him (v. 19), but it hardly represents one of the Fourth Gospel's major theological emphases here. The baptism of Jesus himself, important for all three Synoptists, does not appear at all in John. The Spirit's descent in verse 33 may allude to the identical event as Mark 1:10 and parallels—the Spirit as a dove descending on Jesus at his baptism—but without providing the explanatory framework that the Synoptics offer. That John's baptism occurs in the Jordan River (v. 28) affords another link with the Synoptics, but nothing is made of it. The location of Bethany beyond the Jordan is uncertain,[33] as is whether this means that John used the Jordan River, as the Synoptics assert, or other immersion pools of some sort.

---

31. Andrew T. Lincoln, *The Gospel according to Saint John*, BNTC (London: Continuum; Peabody, MA: Hendrickson, 2005), 101.

32. Leon Morris, *The Gospel according to John*, rev. ed., NICNT (Grand Rapids: Eerdmans, 1995), 96.

33. For an equation of Bethany with Batanea, see Rainer Riesner, "Bethany beyond the Jordan (John 1:28): Topography, Theology and History in the Fourth Gospel," *TynBul* 38 (1987): 29–63. On the other hand, Michele Piccirillo believes that either Bethabara or Wadi al Kharrar, just east of the Jordan across from Judea, is a more probable location ("The Sanctuaries of the Baptism on the East Bank of the Jordan River," in *Jesus and Archaeology*, ed. James H. Charlesworth [Grand Rapids: Eerdmans, 2006], 433–43). There is also a textual question here, since many, typically later, manuscripts read "Bethabara," rather than "Bethany," although virtually all translations today have rejected the support of the KJV and NKJV for the former and opted for the latter.

The focus of the Fourth Gospel's narrative is unrelentingly christological throughout John 1. Jesus is confessed by those who encounter him with a barrage of titles that seem astonishing for people to utilize this early in the ministry: "the Lamb of God" (1:29–36),[34] "God's Chosen One" (v. 34), "Messiah" (v. 41), "Son of God," and "king of Israel" (both in v. 49). Given the background of each of these terms, however, they may all coalesce around the concept of messiah without at this point sounding any overtones of divinity.[35] How do John and his ministry of baptism fit into all of this? Carl Kazmierski summarizes the various portraits of John found in the four Gospels under five headings: "prophet and evangelist," "apocalyptic preacher of judgment," "Elijah," "forerunner to the Messiah," and "witness to the Messiah." Only the last of these is dominant in the Fourth Gospel.[36]

John, as a popular and influential baptizer, thus cuts against the grain of the theological emphases of John 1. We cannot determine the purpose of his baptism from this chapter alone. That the priests and Levites are his first questioners could point to matters of ritual purity, since they oversaw this area of Jewish life.[37] By what authority was he immersing people in water, apart from the officially sanctioned *mikvaot* or immersion pools, so prevalent in Jerusalem, as well as dotting the landscape of Israel? Apparently, some people expected the Messiah to baptize, perhaps based on the prophecy in Ezekiel 36:25–27 on the role of water in the coming age for cleansing Israel from its impurities.[38] But if John denied playing this role, or others that could be equated with it, what was he doing? A good number of studies on the historical John see his role as fundamentally that of helping to purify the people of Israel, preparing them for their coming

---

34. J. Ramsey Michaels believes that neither gentleness nor a willingness to be sacrificed forms the core of this text or accounts for this title's use, but rather the concept of purity does so (*The Gospel of John*, NICNT [Grand Rapids: Eerdmans, 2010], 110).

35. See Francis J. Moloney, *The Gospel of John*, SP (Collegeville, MN: Liturgical Press, 1998), 56; Edward W. Klink III, *John*, ZECNT (Grand Rapids: Zondervan, 2016), 152.

36. Carl R. Kazmierski, *John the Baptist: Prophet and Evangelist* (Collegeville, MN: Liturgical Press, 1996), 115–17.

37. Herman Ridderbos, *The Gospel according to John: A Theological Commentary*, trans. John Vriend (Grand Rapids: Eerdmans, 1997), 63.

38. Michaels, *Gospel of John*, 102.

Messiah.[39] Because water helped to physically cleanse people and objects, it had long been understood as instrumental in the process of metaphorical or ritual cleansing as well. Faithful Jews had to immerse themselves in cleansing pools whenever they became ritually unclean and whenever they wanted to enter the temple precincts (see also below, 164).

Rabbinic Judaism would insist on immersion in water as a ceremony to mark a Gentile proselyte's incorporation into the family of the children of Israel. While many scholars doubt that this practice can be dated to a pre-70 era, Craig Keener has supplied six reasons why he thinks it can and should be: (1) The widespread presence of *mikvaot* from the Hasmonean period onward shows the prevalence of ritual immersion, and it is "inconceivable" that the major change from being an unclean Gentile to a clean Jew would not have been marked by immersion in water. (2) At the end of the first century, Epictetus speaks of proselyte baptism for those becoming Jews as if it is already well known. (3) The Mishnah refers to a debate on the topic between the houses of Shammai and Hillel, pushing matters back to an early date. (4) The probably late-first-century Sibylline Oracles refer to Gentiles knowing the Jewish practice of baptisms when turning from sins. (5) Most other initiation rituals in the religions of the Roman Empire of Jesus's day included ceremonial washings. (6) The undeniable frequency of ritual immersions in the rabbinic era is not likely to have been derived either from Christianity or from Greco-Roman religion but probably depends on earlier Jewish washings.[40] It is hard, therefore, not to see purification or cleansing from various forms of impurity as deeply embedded in any ritual involving the washing in water at the time of John the Baptist.

It also seems likely that John's Gospel is responding to an overemphasis on baptism in the context of its composition. Scholars debate whether this forms part of what should be called an antisacramentalist

---

39. Walter Wink, *John the Baptist in the Gospel Tradition* (Cambridge: Cambridge University Press, 1968), 90; Joan E. Taylor, *The Immerser: John the Baptist within Second Temple Judaism* (Grand Rapids: Eerdmans, 1997); Cornelis Bennema, "Spirit-Baptism in the Fourth Gospel: A Messianic Reading of John 1,33," *Bib* 84 (2003): 35–60; Catherine M. Murphy, *John the Baptist: Prophet of Purity for a New Age* (Collegeville, MN: Liturgical Press, 2003), esp. 83–84, 141–43.
40. Keener, *Gospel of John*, 1:446–47.

tendency in the Fourth Gospel, but in any event the author is obviously not trying to emphasize baptism, especially when he leaves out all mention of Jesus himself being baptized.[41] That he still preserves several references to John's ministry of baptism makes them very likely to be historical, especially when viewed as purification rites. Marianne Meye Thompson elaborates on the reasons for viewing them in this fashion, noting that the Septuagintal background of key words, descriptions of baptism elsewhere in the New Testament, other Jewish understandings of immersion and of John's ministry, and the meaning in the closest Greco-Roman parallels all support a view of the Baptist that sees him as providing ritual cleansing for the people of Israel.[42]

Catherine Murphy's study of the historical John the Baptist concludes that John was "recalling Jews to a long prophetic tradition of coherence between ritual practice and moral obligation. Absent this association, it is unlikely that he would have been intelligible to first-century Jews, unlikely too that he would have gathered a movement at all."[43] Joel Marcus carries this a step further, believing that John saw baptism as a "sacrament of salvation," bringing genuine purification, as well as preparing for the coming Messiah.[44] This, then, fits the continuum approach, which I discussed earlier (see above, 158–59), because Acts discloses the early church likewise maintaining a very close connection between baptism and the forgiveness of sins, beginning already in 2:38. Thus, although witness or revelation is the main purpose of the Fourth Evangelist's inclusion of material about John the Baptist, "its aspect of cleansing, which is naturally evoked by βαπτίζω, has never completely disappeared."[45]

---

41. Keener, *Gospel of John*, 1:441–42; Jörg Frey, "Baptism in the Fourth Gospel, and Jesus and John as Baptizers," in *Expressions of the Johannine Kerygma in John 2:23–5:18: Historical, Literary, and Theological Readings from the Colloquium Ioanneum 2017 in Jerusalem*, ed. R. Alan Culpepper and Jörg Frey (Tübingen: Mohr Siebeck, 2019), 87–116, esp. 113–15.

42. Marianne Meye Thompson, "Baptism with Water and with Holy Spirit: Purification in the Gospel of John," in *The Opening of John's Narrative (John 1:19–2:22): Historical, Literary, and Theological Readings from the Colloquium Ioanneum 2015 in Ephesus*, ed. R. Alan Culpepper and Jörg Frey (Tübingen: Mohr Siebeck, 2017), 59–78.

43. Murphy, *John the Baptist*, 142.

44. Joel Marcus, *John the Baptist in History and Theology* (Columbia: University of South Carolina Press, 2018), 80.

45. Bennema, "Spirit-Baptism in the Fourth Gospel," 39.

This aspect of John's ministry is multiply attested in Mark, Q, L, John, and Acts, making it core material. John himself appears nowhere in the rest of the New Testament, where Jesus has supplanted him in significance. John's baptism fits the double similarity and double dissimilarity criterion well, with ritual immersions in Judaism preceding John and appearing in early Christianity immediately after Jesus. Yet no other Jewish purification ceremony symbolized the repentance of Israel to prepare for its Messiah, and John's baptism is not identical with Christian baptism, as Acts 19:1–7 poignantly demonstrates. John's ministry in John 1 stands a good chance of having a solid historical core.

### Why Stone Water Jars for the Rite of Purification? (John 2:1–12)

John 2 begins with Jesus's famous miracle of turning water into wine at a wedding in Cana of Galilee. This is his first recorded miracle, although John always calls them "signs"—pointers to who Jesus is and to the necessity of believing in him. Topics of recurring interest to John in verses 1–11 include these signs, the nonarrival (and later the arrival) of "his hour," and the other details beside signs in verse 11: glory and belief.[46] References to Mary, the mother of Jesus (though never by name), also fit, complete with what appears as a slightly strained relationship between Jesus and his family,[47] though these scarcely appear often enough to merit the label of a theme.

Overall, the narrative is so abbreviated that the miracle itself is never narrated. No statement ever asserts that Jesus changed water into wine. Instead, this extraordinary event is relegated to a subordinate clause: "the water that had been turned into wine" (v. 9). At the same time, John slows down long enough to tell us that the liquid was initially contained in "six stone water jars, the kind used by the Jews for ceremonial washing, each holding from twenty to thirty gallons" (v. 6). Stone jars

---

46. See Richard Bauckham, *Gospel of Glory: Major Themes in Johannine Theology* (Grand Rapids: Baker Academic, 2015).
47. On the dialogue between Jesus and his mother here, Keener (*Gospel of John*, 1:505) observes, "She approached him not as her son but as a miracle worker; he replies not as her son but as her Lord."

and ritual baths have both been discovered at Khirbet Qana, so we see verisimilitude in the account and may assume there were law-abiding Jews in ancient Cana.[48] What was John's purpose in recording all this detail in what is otherwise so sparse a narrative? The number and size of the water jars suggest one or more wealthy families were involved in the wedding.[49] Since the water jars had been filled to their brim, an astonishing amount of wine was produced (between 120 and 180 gallons). But even more intriguing is the jars' function. Why tell us that they were *hydriai* ("water jars") used *kata ton katharismon tōn Ioudaiōn* ("for the cleansings of the Jews") or that they were *lithinai* (made from "stone")? Stone jars were preferred to pottery because they were not subject to contamination and impurity the way earthenware vessels were (Lev. 11:33). Water jars did not have to be filled with water, but by telling us that they were, John emphasizes their contents. Even the expression "the water that had been turned into wine" succeeds in telling the reader a third time that Jesus began with water. Verse 9 goes on to add, using a more expansive phrase, that the servants knew where the wine had come from: "The servants who had drawn the water knew."

Verse 10 turns the miracle story, at least in part, into a pronouncement story. Instead of having Jesus make the climactic declaration, however, John tells us that the master of the banquet does: "Everyone brings out the choice wine first and then the cheaper wine after the guests have had too much to drink; but you have saved the best till now." Just as Jesus's wine contrasts with conventional wedding wine, including in the order in which the various wines were served, his wine is clearly superior to the water from the jars for ceremonial washing, pure as it was.[50] One thinks of the extended metaphor or mini-parable

---

48. Rainer Riesner, *Messias Jesus: Seine Geschichte, seine Botschaft und ihre Überlieferung* (Giessen: Brunnen, 2019), 126. Riesner also notes that, after considerable debate, this seems to be the correct site for ancient Cana.

49. Jonathan L. Reed, "Stone Vessels and Gospel Texts, Purity and Socio-Economics in John 2," in *Zeichen aus Text und Stein: Studien auf dem Weg zu einer Archäologie des Neuen Testaments*, ed. Stefan Alkier and Jürgen Zangenberg with Kristina Dronsch and Michael Schneider (Tübingen: Francke, 2003), 400–401.

50. Thompson writes, "The blessings of this age follow and surpass the bounty of earlier blessings. The move is not lateral, from the old reality of 'Judaism' to a parallel and new reality in Jesus, outside of Judaism; rather, the move is forward, from Scriptural hope and expectation to the extravagant provision expected in the coming age" (*John*, 62).

of Mark 2:22 and parallels, creating the multiple attestation of a concept: "And no one pours new wine into old wineskins. Otherwise, the wine will burst the skins, and both the wine and the wineskins will be ruined. No, they pour new wine into new wineskins."[51] There is no criticism here of the ritually pure water of Judaism, or of the old wine that the old wineskins presumably contained, but there is an affirmation of the arrival of something even better. Wine was a frequent symbol for joy in the Old Testament and Second Temple Judaism (see esp. Ps. 104:15; Zech. 10:7) and probably functions that way here too. Large quantities of wine are also part of the great abundance prophesied of the eschatological age (Joel 3:18; Amos 9:13–14). Just as grace was added to grace already given in John 1:17, a new level of rejoicing is appropriate with the presence of Jesus, even beyond the joy attached to the other most festive occasions in Israel.[52] As both Gerry Wheaton and Karen Jobes observe, that Jesus transforms the contents of the vessels suggests not supersession or replacement but rather working within the elements of Judaism in fulfilling them.[53]

Luke 5:39, however, adds to the little parable of the wineskins the ironic comment that no one after drinking old wine wants the new. People claim that the old is better. Jesus's opponents similarly wanted just to preserve all their traditions, much like the banquet master in John 2:10 notes with his comment about the invitees preferring inferior wine after they are a little drunk.[54] If Jewish practice emphasized the ritual law beyond what Scripture itself required, there could be some implied polemic in both passages. But the "holy water" in the purification jars itself is what changes. Something already good becomes far better. In Dorothy Lee's words, "At Cana the water possesses cultic

---

51. See further Craig L. Blomberg, "The Miracles as Parables," in *Gospel Perspectives*, vol. 6, *The Miracles of Jesus*, ed. David Wenham and Craig Blomberg (Sheffield: JSOT Press, 1986; repr., Eugene, OR: Wipf & Stock, 2003), 333–37.

52. See Ruben Zimmermann, "Jesus—the Divine Bridegroom? John 2–4 and Its Christological Implications," in *Reading the Gospel of John's Christology as Jewish Messianism: Royal, Prophetic, and Divine Messiahs*, ed. Benjamin Reynolds and Gabriele Boccaccini (Leiden: Brill, 2018), 381.

53. Gerry Wheaton, *The Role of Jewish Feasts in John's Gospel* (Cambridge: Cambridge University Press, 2015), 58; Karen H. Jobes, *John through Old Testament Eyes: A Background and Application Commentary* (Grand Rapids: Kregel Academic, 2021), 60.

54. Michaels (*Gospel of John*, 152) finds Luke 5:39 to be the closest parallel to John's account of the comment by the master of ceremonies.

overtones and therefore already speaks of a purification that is more than the cleanliness of the body. Yet its ritual use for washing changes dramatically in the Johannine narrative. . . . Water is now on the way to becoming a symbol, but it does not yet function in its own right; strictly speaking, the symbolism that emerges is the wine, miraculously transformed."[55] While scholars typically adjudicate on the believability of the miracle itself, employing other than historical criteria, the remaining details in the passage—the location and nature of Cana, the potentially embarrassing nature of Jesus's interaction with his mother, the kind and size of jars used, the nature of the wedding itself, and the use of "the third day" as more likely historical than symbolic—all contribute to the story's probable historicity.[56]

As in chapter 1, then, purification does not rise to a level of Johannine redaction or even emphasis. But it is clearly there in the earliest stratum and probably played a larger role in the original meaning of Jesus's actions than the Fourth Evangelist intimates. Ruben Zimmermann observes that early rabbinic tradition associated consecration with both the engagement and the wedding of a couple.[57] John appropriates the account of the wedding that Jesus attends and preserves a christological focus, as throughout his Gospel—it is the wine that *Jesus* provides that saves the day. But other details suggest a more variegated initial focus—compassion, joy, abundance, glory, detachment, and transformation[58]—with a special place for purification.[59]

### Temple Trauma (John 2:13–22)

After an unspecified time, Jesus goes up to Jerusalem for a Passover festival. But nothing suggests that this occurred two or three years later,

---

55. Dorothy Lee, *Flesh and Glory: Symbolism, Gender, and Theology in the Gospel of John* (New York: Crossroad, 2002), 67.
56. Carsten Claussen, "Turning Water to Wine: Re-reading the Miracle at the Wedding in Cana," in *Jesus Research: An International Perspective; The First Princeton-Prague Symposium on Jesus Research, Prague 2005*, ed. James H. Charlesworth with Petr Pokorný (Grand Rapids: Eerdmans, 2009), 73–97, esp. 90–95.
57. Zimmermann, "Jesus—the Divine Bridegroom?," 277.
58. Karl T. Cooper, "The Best Wine: John 2:1–11," *WTJ* 41 (1979): 364–80.
59. Urban C. von Wahlde places purification at the very "earliest stratum of the Gospel" here (*The Gospel and Letters of John*, 3 vols., ECC [Grand Rapids: Eerdmans, 2010], 2:83).

after most of the other events of chapters 3–12, as it would have had to if it represented the incident in the temple assigned by the Synoptics to the last week of Jesus's life. Nothing in the Johannine pericope seems out of place at an early stage of Jesus's public ministry. A faithful Jewish man within a reasonable distance from the temple was expected to participate in the three key annual festivals: the Day of Atonement, the Feast of Tabernacles, and Passover. That Jesus "found" (from Gk. *heuriskō*) people in the temple engaging in the commercial activity that until recently had gone on in the Kidron Valley[60] fits a first trip to the temple during his early ministry. The command in verse 16 could suggest that all this activity was occurring in the Court of the Gentiles, where non-Jewish sympathizers and God-fearers could worship Yahweh, a task now made much more difficult by the cacophony of noises and bustle that the marketplace would have created (cf. Mark 11:15–17 pars.).[61]

The traditional title given to this episode, "the temple cleansing," is thus reasonably appropriate for the Johannine account,[62] certainly more so than it is for the Synoptic story, where the coming destruction of the temple comes more to the fore.[63] Something like the whip of cords, unique to John's account, would have been necessary to get the larger animals to move. Psalm 69:9a ("Zeal for your house consumes me") is a natural Scripture to be remembered in this setting. Once Jesus's Davidic ancestry has been established, the typological application

---

60. Victor Eppstein, "The Historicity of the Gospel Account of the Cleansing of the Temple," *ZNW* 55 (1964): 42–58.

61. Riesner, *Messias Jesus*, 304. Riesner notes the difficulty of the two cleansing accounts, rejects the "more than improbable harmonizing solution that there were two temple actions" (*mehr als unwahrscheinliche harmonistische Lösung, dass es zwei Tempelaktionen gegeben habe*), and then proceeds to show how each fits perfectly into its own historical context and that the Johannine incident was probably on a small enough scale not to have demanded the intervention of the authorities! So what is "more than improbable"?

62. John A. T. Robinson, *The Priority of John*, ed. J. F. Coakley (London: SCM, 1985; Oak Park, IL: Meyer-Stone, 1987), 185.

63. A view now particularly associated with E. P. Sanders, *Jesus and Judaism* (London: SCM; Philadelphia: Fortress, 1985), 61–75. Cf. more recently, Cecilia Wassén, "The Use of the Dead Sea Scrolls for Interpreting Jesus's Action in the Temple," *DSD* 23 (2016): 280–303. For the minority view, which sees even the Synoptic account as still more a purification than a warning or threat, see Craig A. Evans, "Jesus' Action in the Temple: Cleansing or Portent of Destruction?," *CBQ* 51 (1989): 237–70; Evert Jan Vledder, "Was Jezus' optreden in de tempel een reiniging?," *HTS* 61 (2005): 593–617. Historically, of course, this was the majority perspective.

is quite straightforward. And David wouldn't have been foreseeing the destruction of the tabernacle or of the temple that Solomon would build. The quotation is not likely to have been invented and placed on Jesus's lips, because it does stand in a little tension with John 2:19. There Jesus refers to himself as the new temple, whereas here he is the one who is zealous for the current building.[64]

The request for a sign fits Johannine redaction, but no miracle is provided even if one is predicted. No one on the spot recognized that this was about the resurrection; only his disciples ever did, and then only after its fulfillment. The local authorities would naturally ask him by what authority he could cause this disruption, even if it affected only one small corner of the court. Only at this point (v. 19) do Johannine concepts and language really begin—not just with the theme of signs (which could have been John's rewording in verse 18 of their request for a miracle), but with Jesus fulfilling Jewish institutions and with his words not being understood until after the resurrection, and then sometimes only with the help of Scripture (vv. 20–22). The garbled false testimony against Jesus at his trial about him claiming that he could destroy the temple and raise it in three days (Mark 14:58 par.) makes good sense as a twisted reference to a claim dimly recalled from two to three years earlier.[65] The very precise reference to forty-six years, finally, creates a limited window of time in which John claims that the temple cleansing occurred. The rebuilding of the temple under Herod the Great began in 20–19 BC, so the latest this could have occurred was AD 28,[66] two years too early to fit even the earlier (and more probable) date for the crucifixion in 30. Not surprisingly, a considerable number of those who have participated in the "new look on John" or in the "John, Jesus, and History" projects accept the authenticity of a core of this pericope as having occurred at the outset of Jesus's ministry.[67]

---

64. Cf. Thompson, *John*, 72.
65. Robinson, *Priority of John*, 125–31; see also McHugh, *John 1–4*, 202; Gonzalo Rojas-Flores, "From John 2.19 to Mark 15.29: The History of a Misunderstanding," *NTS* 56 (2009): 22–43.
66. Robinson, *Priority of John*, 130–31.
67. Paul N. Anderson, *The Fourth Gospel and the Quest for Jesus: Modern Foundations Reconsidered* (London: T&T Clark, 2008), 158–61; James F. McGrath, "'Destroy This Temple,'" in

There is also a fair amount of agreement that, in its original context, whatever else Jesus may have intended, purification of the temple for right worship was central. Trade in areas reserved for holier activities was viewed as an act of desecration.[68] Removing the traders was necessary for reconsecrating it and could be seen as fulfillment of one textual tradition of Zechariah 14:21.[69] Malachi 3:1–4 may be even more important as scriptural background. There the Lord will suddenly "come to his temple" (v. 1). Central to God's ministry there is his purifying activity: "He will sit as a refiner and purifier of silver; he will purify the Levites and refine them like gold and silver. Then the Lord will have men who will bring offerings in righteousness, and the offerings of Judah and Jerusalem will be acceptable to the Lord, as in days gone by, as in former years" (vv. 3–4).[70] Not surprisingly, various scholars label John 2:13–22, even in its final form, as the purification of the temple.[71] Stripped of possible Johannine redaction, or at least emphases, it fits that label even more.

The Synoptic accounts of the temple cleansing focus more on the coming judgment on the temple.[72] They fit the late date in Jesus's ministry, when it is less likely that he is merely trying to reform Judaism. But at the beginning of his ministry, a goal of reformation proves more probable. As we noticed earlier, credible cases can be made for John and the Synoptics both narrating the same temple incident, with plausible explanations for its occurrence at either the beginning or the end of Jesus's ministry. Either John is locating it chronologically and the Synoptics topically, or it is the other way around. Yet a credible case can also be made for two different incidents. The more that the one looks like an attempted reformation and the other the announcement

---

Anderson, Just, and Thatcher, *John, Jesus, and History*, 2:39; von Wahlde, *Gospel and Letters of John*, 2:97–98. Much more cautiously, see Paula Fredriksen, "The Historical Jesus, the Scene in the Temple, and the Gospel of John," in Anderson, Just, and Thatcher, *John, Jesus, and History*, 1:249–76.

68. George R. Beasley-Murray, *John*, 2nd ed., WBC (Nashville: Nelson, 1999), 39.
69. Thompson, *John*, 71.
70. Robinson, *Priority of John*, 85.
71. See esp. Francis J. Moloney, "Reading John 2:13–22: The Purification of the Temple," *RB* 97 (1990): 432–52.
72. See, e.g., Andrew T. Le Peau, *Mark through Old Testament Eyes: A Background and Application Commentary* (Grand Rapids: Kregel Academic, 2017), 203–6.

of coming destruction, the more one might be inclined to opt for two separate events. One of the very reasons that one can envision a single temple incident without John contradicting the Synoptics is also a good reason for seeing two: the details apart from the barest of essentials are so different in the two traditions that they don't contradict each other, but neither do they really go with each other very much at all![73]

## Born of Water and the Spirit (John 3)

The "now" that appears in several translations at the beginning of John 3:1 (ESV, NASB, NET, NIV, NRSV) translates the simple Greek word *de*, a loose connective and mild adversative that need not have any temporal connection with what precedes it. Still, Jesus's apparent distrust of Nicodemus's welcoming overture based on the signs that he knew Jesus had worked dovetails nicely with Jesus's distrust of the Jerusalem crowds' signs-based faith in 2:23–25. Thus, 3:1 is naturally taken as occurring not long after the events of chapter 2. There are references in the rabbinic literature to more than one Nicodemus in the ben Gurion family, so the name and role of Jesus's conversation partner is not improbable.[74] Many commentators have taken the heart of Jesus's claims to Nicodemus in verses 3–8 as based on authentic teaching, especially since they begin with verse 3, on not seeing the kingdom of God without being born again. This is a rare use of "kingdom" in John and echoes Synoptic teaching like that in Matthew 18:3: "Unless you change and become like little children, you will never enter the kingdom of heaven."[75] Seeing or entering the kingdom cuts very much against the grain of John's preference for his somewhat equivalent language about eternal life.

---

73. Lydia McGrew, *The Eye of the Beholder: The Gospel of John as Historical Reportage* (Tampa: DeWard, 2021), 283–96. Cf. also her methodological discussion in McGrew, "Time and Narrative: Clarity and Chronology in Reading the Gospels," *JGRChJ* 17 (2021): 62–87.

74. Richard Bauckham, "Nicodemus and the Gurion Family," *JTS* 47 (1996): 1–37.

75. Barnabas Lindars, *The Gospel of John*, NCB (London: Oliphants, 1972; Grand Rapids: Eerdmans, 1981), 48, 150–51. It has also been deemed authentic by virtue of its use of the (double) "Amen" formula to introduce it. See R. Alan Culpepper, "The AMHN, AMHN Sayings in the Gospel of John," in *Perspectives on John: Method and Interpretation in the Fourth Gospel*, ed. Robert B. Sloan and Mikeal C. Parsons (Lewiston, NY: Mellen, 1993), 101; J. Ernest Davey, *The Jesus of St. John: Historical and Christological Studies in the Fourth Gospel* (London: Lutterworth, 1958), 55.

Some critics insist that Jesus can't have spoken anything like this, because there is no Hebrew or Aramaic word that can communicate the double meaning of *anōthen* ("again" and "from above") in verse 3. But there is nothing in the immediate context that requires Jesus to have meant "from above"; Nicodemus clearly takes Jesus's words as referring to a second, physical birth and discerns nothing heavenly or metaphorical about it (v. 4). It may simply have been fortuitous for the Fourth Evangelist to have a Greek word available that had a second meaning that fit nicely into the context, given the topics Jesus will address in verses 12–15. In fact, Jesus himself calls everything up to this point in their conversation "earthly things," asking how Nicodemus will understand heavenly things if he can't fathom the simpler topics (v. 12).[76]

Because of Jesus's refusal to accept the topic of Nicodemus's opening gambit,[77] it is hard to know if verse 5 intends to answer Nicodemus's subsequent question directly. But even if it adds meaning to being born *anōthen*, verse 5 still explains what is involved in a second birth—being born of "water and the Spirit"—especially as it repeats the expression "the kingdom of God." Someone reading the Fourth Gospel sequentially might easily recall the teaching of John in 1:33, in which John baptized with water, but there was one coming who would baptize with the Spirit.[78] A modified form of Granville Sharp's rule suggests that the Fourth Evangelist believes that Jesus's words in 3:5 are referring not to two separate births, each of which could be represented by a baptism, but to one birth "of water and the Spirit." Here it is not the lack of a second article before the second noun that tips us off, since both nouns are anarthrous (*ex hydatos kai pneumatos*). Instead, it is the lack of the repetition of the preposition "of" (*ek*) that suggests that the two nouns should be taken as closely related.[79] If Ezekiel 36:25–27

---

76. See further D. A. Carson, *The Gospel according to John*, PNTC (Leicester: Apollos; Grand Rapids: Eerdmans, 1991), 191n1.
77. On which, see F. Peter Cotterell, "The Nicodemus Conversation: A Fresh Appraisal," *ExpTim* 96 (1985): 237–42.
78. Cf. Keener, *Gospel of John*, 1:605.
79. Jobes, *John through Old Testament Eyes*, 80. Cf. Lincoln, *Gospel according to Saint John*, 150. This also renders less likely the idea of Timothy D. Foster that "born of water" refers

was likely in the background in John 1:33, it is all the likelier the key to understanding 3:5.[80] Jesus is not talking primarily either about John's baptism or later Christian baptism, which would lead to the doctrine of baptismal regeneration. Even less likely is the idea that "born of water" has something to do with the physiology of natural birth (as a euphemism for semen or a reference to the mother's water breaking).[81] Instead, the historical, literary, and grammatical data all converge to support the interpretation that Jesus is referring to the inward cleansing that God works through his Spirit in human hearts when they turn to him. That this may (and even should) be then symbolized by baptism is very appropriate, but that is not Jesus's primary thrust.

Verse 6 next contrasts what is born of the flesh with what is born of the Spirit. Now Jesus probably *is* contrasting physical and spiritual birth. Nicodemus thought of a second physical birth in verse 4; Jesus explained in verse 5 that he was talking about a spiritual one. Each birth produces offspring according to the likeness of the parents, either physical or spiritual. None of this should surprise Nicodemus, given the teachings of the Hebrew Scriptures (v. 7). Still, the new purification by the Spirit comes with surprises. Like the wind, where it will blow or whom it will touch cannot always be predicted (v. 8).[82]

How much longer John views Jesus as speaking, after Nicodemus's exasperated outburst in verse 9, dictates where one inserts closing quotation marks after verse 15 or verse 21.[83] A minimalist approach to a historical core of this passage could assign most everything after the back-and-forth dialogue of verses 1–9 to later redaction.[84] From this point on, key Johannine themes dominate: testimony, the earthly versus

---

to the exodus, which Nicodemus as an archetypal Jew would have "experienced" vicariously as part of Israel ("John 3:5: Redefining the People of God," *BBR* 27 [2017]: 351–60).

80. See esp. Linda L. Belleville, "'Born of Water and Spirit': John 3:5," *TJ* 2 (1981): 125–41.

81. As for Ben Witherington III, *John's Wisdom: A Commentary on the Fourth Gospel* (Louisville: Westminster John Knox, 1995), 191–93. Witherington nevertheless has a good discussion of all the major options.

82. On which, see Karl O. Sandnes, "Whence and Whither: A Narrative Perspective on Birth ἄνωθεν (John 3,3–8)," *Bib* 86 (2005): 153–73.

83. Most recent commentators end the quotation after verse 15; many recent translations still end it after verse 21.

84. See Rudolf Bultmann, *The Gospel of John: A Commentary*, trans. G. R. Beasley-Murray, ed. R. W. N. Hoare and J. K. Riches (Oxford: Blackwell; Philadelphia: Westminster, 1971), 132.

heavenly contrast, Jesus's "lifting up" (the crucifixion as exaltation), belief, and eternal life. Verses 16–21, which may well not even be intended to depict Jesus's words, add John's characteristically realized eschatology, his contrast between light and darkness, and his emphasis on truth. None of this has much of anything to do with purification, which further confirms the likelihood of a traditional origin for much, if not all, of verses 1–9.

Verses 22–36 introduce a scene change, as Jesus and his disciples leave Jerusalem for the Judean countryside (v. 22). Here we are introduced for the first time to the fact that Jesus, too, had people baptized. For those already familiar with the main contents of the four Gospels, this comes as a surprise because the Synoptics never even hint at such a ministry, and John makes nothing more of it after 4:3. However, given the identical call to repentance in view of the arriving kingdom that Matthew assigns both the Baptist and Jesus (Matt. 3:2; 4:17), if the one man baptized, it would have been natural for the other one to do so too.[85] Since, in the Fourth Gospel, Jesus's first disciples come out of John's orbit of followers, their continuing to baptize would be even more natural. Yet the very fact that Jesus is assembling followers separate from John's disciples leads to the two having separate ministries (v. 23), and there are changes ahead.

By necessity, after John is imprisoned, Jesus must go his separate way, and the Synoptics will introduce key differences between John and him (see esp. Matt. 11:16–19 par.). But the Fourth Evangelist notes that he is still narrating events before the Baptist's imprisonment (John 3:24). Here is a classic example of why it seems highly probable that this writer can assume his audience's knowledge of many of the events narrated only in the Synoptics, because nowhere else does he expound on this imprisonment the way they do (esp. Mark 6:14–29).[86] John 3:25, nevertheless, comes as a surprise, with its cryptic disclosure that an argument developed between some of John's disciples and a certain Jew over the matter of ceremonial washing. Who was this mystery

---

85. Witherington, *John's Wisdom*, 209–10.
86. Richard Bauckham, "John for Readers of Mark," in *The Gospels for All Christians: Rethinking the Gospel Audiences*, ed. Richard Bauckham (Grand Rapids: Eerdmans, 1998), 152–53.

man,[87] what was the argument about, and why was it with John's disciples? One could easily imagine it being between someone Jesus had just baptized and one or more of John's baptizands about the relative merits of the two ministries of purification. It is attractive to envision the washing in view (the Gk. has simply *peri katharismou* ["about cleansing"]) as a comparison and contrast between John's and Jesus's baptisms.[88] Still, what little elaboration we receive in verse 26 notes only the increasing numbers of individuals flocking to Jesus rather than to John, while John's reply focuses on the need for Jesus to become greater and for John to recede in significance (vv. 27–30).

The term *katharismos* occurs only six other times in the New Testament. In Luke 2:22, it refers to the ritual purification by animal sacrifice for Mary forty days after the birth of Jesus. Mark 1:44, with its parallel in Luke 5:14, denotes the ceremonial cleansing for the leprous man Jesus healed, again by temple sacrifice. We have already seen the same word used in John 2:6. Hebrews 1:3 mentions the purification for sins that God's Son accomplished, which goes beyond merely ritual to moral purification but does not exclude ritual purification in the process. In 2 Peter 1:9, finally, Christ's work on the cross is again in view, with the reference to those who have forgotten their cleansing from past sins. It is highly likely, therefore, that something about ritual purity is the subject of the debate here in John 3.[89]

Considerable attention has been devoted to trying to determine if John was part of the old or the new age, since Christians appropriated the two-era scheme of Jewish thought. Data from both John and the Synoptics variously fit into each of the ages, and the best reply no doubt is that John straddled the two. It is only later Christians' desire

---

87. An important textual variant has John disputing with "Jews," in the plural, but this is the less well-supported reading among the earliest manuscripts and appears to be avoiding some of the questions surrounding the singular. See John W. Pryor, "John the Baptist and Jesus: Tradition and Text in John 3.25," *JSNT* 19 (1997): 15–26. Pryor nevertheless thinks that the debate was originally with Jesus himself (*Iēsou*), which John changed to "a Jew" (*Ioudaiou*). Yet no other positive evidence clearly supports this theory.
88. Rodney A. Whitacre, *John*, IVPNTC (Downers Grove, IL: InterVarsity, 1999), 96; von Wahlde, *Gospel and Letters of John*, 2:152.
89. C. H. Talbert, *Reading John: A Literary and Theological Commentary on the Fourth Gospel and the Johannine Epistles*, rev. ed., RNT (Macon, GA: Smyth & Helwys, 2005), 111–12; Lincoln, *Gospel according to Saint John*, 160.

to neatly schematize history that raises the question of the moment of the end of the old and the beginning of the new. Even apart from John's ministry, various texts written by one of the four evangelists can be seen as taking the incarnation, Jesus's baptism, crucifixion, resurrection, ascension, and Pentecost all as the key time of the shift in the ages.[90] Given that John was six months older than Jesus and began his ministry before Jesus did, he clearly lived in the old age but then lived long enough to see at least some of the beginnings of the new.

The key takeaway from this discussion, then, is that there is no reason to suppose that John's and Jesus's baptisms were markedly different at the outset.[91] There is no indication anywhere in the Gospels, Acts, or the rest of the New Testament that Jesus's twelve apostles were baptized, and yet baptism proved central to their ministry as others turned to Jesus as their Lord. The most probable explanation is that those who were baptized by John never submitted to any additional initiatory immersion, while the rest were baptized by Jesus or his first followers and never asked to submit to fully "Christian" baptism.[92] Baptism from Pentecost onward certainly took on added significance, with the arrival of the Spirit in power, yet if the basic meaning of the immersion in water remained a ceremonial cleansing,[93] we can understand why reimmersion was not required. The more that Christian theology stressed new-age versus old-age divisions of history, the less this would be the case. But as long as the sense of a ritual purification for the imminent fulfillment of God's plans dominated people's thinking, the less it mattered exactly which of these forms of baptism one had experienced. The less it mattered, the more we can appreciate why jealousy could occur over Jesus's increased following at John's expense.[94]

90. Ridderbos (*Gospel according to John*, 144) explains that the shift in the ages was "gradual."
91. Morris, *Gospel according to John*, 209–10; Murphy, *John the Baptist*, 143; Frey, "Baptism in the Fourth Gospel," 113.
92. Niclas Förster observes that in P. Oxy. 840 the circle of the disciples is said to have been baptized while Jesus was still alive ("Jesus der Täufer und die Reinwaschung der Jünger," *NTS* 64 [2018]: 470). Förster believes that the text is a fragment of a lost Jewish-Christian Gospel, which may well represent very early tradition at this point.
93. Jey J. Kanagaraj, *John*, NCCS (Eugene, OR: Cascade Books, 2013), 36; Thompson, *John*, 92–93.
94. Moloney, *Gospel of John*, 105. Already in the nineteenth century, E. W. Hengstenberg pointed out the potential for a situation like that described in 1 Cor. 1:14–17 and mused about

As in the first part of John 3, there is a crucial literary seam that may or may not mark the end of the speaker's words. Verses 31–35 repeat the almost identical cluster of themes that occurs in verses 16–21 and may very well reflect the Fourth Evangelist's own commentary on the Baptist's words in verses 27–30. John had likened his role to that of a best man attending to a bridegroom, with Jesus as the bridegroom. But verses 31–35 expand the conversation to again contrast the heavenly with the earthly, to speak of testimony, truthfulness, the Spirit's ministry, the Father's love for the Son, belief, and who will and won't receive eternal life.[95] We quickly move a considerable distance away from the topic of ceremonial washings with which this half-chapter began. We also confirm that if any of this section is historical, it must be that first part, on the topic of ritual purity.[96]

## Water and Spirit in Samaria (John 4:1–44)

The first four verses of John 4 set the stage for the long narrative of Jesus's dialogue with the Samaritan woman by the well. These verses pick up where 3:22–23 left off in the middle of the apparent rivalry between Jesus and John (4:1). John clarifies that it was not Jesus but his disciples who performed the baptismal ceremony on behalf of their master. Perhaps this was to prevent anyone from inappropriately claiming privilege or status because Jesus had immersed them himself (cf. the probable explanation of the rival factions in Corinth, along the lines of which Christian leader baptized various others [1 Cor. 1:12–14]).[97] Perhaps by Jesus delegating this authority to his closest followers, people were kept from getting the wrong understanding of the role of baptism and tying it too closely to salvation. At least it keeps the focus on Jesus's person, as throughout so much of John,

---

how boastful some might have become had they been baptized by Jesus himself (*Commentary on the Gospel of St. John*, 2 vols. [Edinburgh: T&T Clark, 1865 (Ger. orig. 1861)], 1:195).

95. For all the structural parallels between the two "halves" of John 3, see Jeffrey Wilson, "The Integrity of John 3:22–36," *JSNT* 3 (1981): esp. 37.

96. Beasley-Murray, *John*, 49.

97. Gerald R. Borchert notes that the clarification in 4:2 matches the relative priorities of 1 Cor. 1:14–17 (*John 1–11*, NAC [Nashville: Broadman & Holman, 1996], 199).

rather than on his actions.⁹⁸ If John's ministry took place predominantly in Judea, leaving for Samaria and then Galilee would have brought Jesus out of the jurisdiction of a majority of the Pharisees, who were increasingly becoming his critics. A withdrawal to Galilee, by way of the quickest route, through Samaria, makes perfect sense in this context (v. 3).

The criterion of embarrassment makes this information about Jesus's own baptismal ministry, even if through his disciples, almost certainly historical.⁹⁹ It fits no known Johannine distinctive, seems to keep Jesus on John's "level," and leads to what appears to be a competition between these two early Christian teachers, or at least between their followers. Older commentators often identified verse 2 as a later redactional addition to the Gospel, thinking that it created a contradiction with 3:22.¹⁰⁰ A clarification to avoid a misunderstanding seems more likely, and it could just as easily have come from the same person who penned 3:22. In a world of indelible ink and costly manuscript material, one didn't just erase written texts, and crossing things out (which did happen) made them look sloppy. Simply clarifying yourself further on in a document was much tidier. It was common enough to talk about a person doing something through their agents, so it was not as if John had erred in his first, less precise statement that Jesus baptized. More recent commentators have thus much more commonly taken Jesus's baptizing ministry, even if through his disciples, as another key historical element remaining in John.¹⁰¹

Cleansing imagery is important in verses 4–44 also. In the encounter with the Samaritan woman at the well, Jesus asking to drink of water

---

98. See Bernadeta Jojko, *Worshiping the Father in Spirit and Truth: An Exegetico-Theological Study of Jn 4:20–26 in the Light of the Relationships among the Father, the Son and the Holy Spirit* (Rome: Editrice Pontificia Università Gregoriana, 2012), 85.

99. Meier (*Marginal Jew*, 2:122) calls this "perhaps the best New Testament example of how the criterion of embarrassment works," with Jesus submitting to John in a baptism that was for repentance from sin (though Jesus could have been identifying with his people and confessing the nation's corporate sin, or simply showing solidarity with John's ministry). Whatever the explanation, it certainly was awkward in an early Christian context that was rapidly exalting Jesus as the sinless savior.

100. Classically, C. H. Dodd, *Historical Tradition in the Fourth Gospel* (Cambridge: Cambridge University Press, 1963), 211.

101. Frey, "Baptism in the Fourth Gospel," 107; Beasley-Murray, *John*, 52.

from a Samaritan bucket, presumably poured into a Samaritan cup, risked ritual uncleanliness right at the outset.[102] Then Jesus seizes on a conversation about literal thirst to introduce his metaphor of living water that eternally satisfies. The woman's initial reactions to Jesus seem as dense as Nicodemus's had been, but she does not give up on the dialogue as he did.[103] At first, she thinks that Jesus is talking about actual water—understandable when one realizes that "living water" was an expression for flowing (rather than stagnant) water, and already associated with various kinds of purity. Whatever she was thinking, her replies enable Jesus to focus on his role as greater than that even of Jacob, to whom the well had been attributed. But verses 7–15 are just the first part of the conversation and not Jesus's main points. Those will come in the rest of the passage, as Jesus confronts the woman's background (vv. 16–18) and they debate about where holy worship should occur (vv. 19–24). Here appear more realized eschatology (v. 23), the need for "worship in the Spirit and in truth" (v. 24), and the identity of the Messiah (vv. 25–26).[104]

A minimalist approach to historicity could again dismiss all these as characteristically Johannine emphases. But verses 4–15 remain more intractable, closely resembling the Synoptics' portrait of Jesus as a friend of sinners and seeker after the "least, last, and lost." The conjunction of the "living water" imagery and the woman's perception of Jesus as a prophet recalls Joel 2:23 and Hosea 10:12, which argues at least for a very Jewish origin of the account.[105] When the disciples return, their conversation with Jesus occasions his metaphorical comments about special food to eat. Here, though, there is nothing specifically about

---

102. Peter F. Ellis, *The Genius of John: A Composition-Critical Commentary on the Fourth Gospel* (Collegeville, MN: Liturgical Press, 1984), 69.

103. This is just one of numerous contrasts between the two characters, defying conventional expectations. See further Craig L. Blomberg, "The Globalization of Biblical Interpretation—A Test Case: John 3–4," *BBR* 5 (1995): 1–15.

104. For a detailed history of interpretation, see Janeth Norfleete Day, *The Woman at the Well: Interpretation of John 4:1–42 in Retrospect and Prospect* (Leiden: Brill, 2002). More briefly, see David S. Dockery, "Reading John 4:1–45: Some Diverse Hermeneutical Perspectives," *CTR* 3 (1988): 127–40.

105. Hannah S. An, "The Prophet like Moses (Deut. 18:15–18) and the Woman at the Well (John 4:7–30) in Light of the Dead Sea Scrolls," *ExpTim* 127 (2016): 469–78. She notes that Qumran made this collocation as well.

cleansing. As the Samaritan woman goes away, she takes the message of her experience with her. Some of her hearers believed based on her testimony alone; others came to see Jesus for themselves and then believed.

There is actually nothing explicitly about purification in Jesus's metaphor of living water either.[106] The main point is about quenching thirst, both literally and spiritually. But living water *was* needed for any form of ritual purification, so we cannot separate the two meanings altogether. When we recognize that the woman's marital history would at the least have aroused suspicions among her townspeople that she was at fault, and that many Jews appear to have regarded Samaritan women as always ritually unclean (cf. m. Nid. 4:1),[107] we realize that she *might* have needed both ceremonial and moral purification. Still, that perception may be unjustified. Despite centuries of assumptions by male commentators that all five of her failed marriages were all due to divorce, and to divorce that was unjustified, and that her current situation of living with a man furthered her sin, nothing in the text requires this interpretation. She could easily have been the victim of a series of unscrupulous men and, in a world where women regularly needed men for protection, found that the best she could do with her sixth was live together with him.[108] But whatever the realities, perceptions often outweigh them, and those perceptions probably would have led to the assumption that she needed both moral and ritual purification. To whatever degree the lack of any reference to ritual purification means

---

106. J. Duncan M. Derrett nevertheless argues that the woman *was* metaphorically purified by Jesus's word, which then enabled her to lead others to faith in him as well, thereby also purifying them ("The Samaritan Woman's Purity [John 4:4–52]," *EvQ* 60 [1988]: 291–98). That some part of Jesus's new usage of the metaphor of "living water" included it flowing onward from the woman to others with its life-giving power is defended in more detail by Cesar Motta Rios, "'Águas vivas' no Evangelho segundo João, na Bíblia Hebraica e nos manuscritos do Mar Morto: Entre continuidades e diferenças," *EstTeo* 57 (2017): 157–70.

107. Jonathan Bourgel, "John 4:4–42: Defining a Modus Vivendi between Jews and the Samaritans," *JTS* 69 (2018): 39–65, esp. 45–49.

108. See further Alice Mathews, *A Woman Jesus Can Teach: Lessons from New Testament Women Help You Make Today's Choices* (Grand Rapids: Discovery House, 1991), 24–26. Gail R. O'Day and Susan E. Hylen suggest that the woman may have been "caught in a situation of levirate marriage (see Deut. 25:5–10; Luke 20:27–33), in which the last male of the family has refused to marry her" (*John*, WestBC [Louisville: Westminster John Knox, 2006], 53).

that Jesus is pointing away from that need, he would also be setting the stage for Jews and Samaritans embracing one another more readily.[109]

All the accompanying details in John 4 about Samaritans more generally fit what we know from other sources from antiquity: the intense rivalry with the Judeans, the dispute about the central location for worship, and differing expectations of a messiah, to name the main ones.[110] This makes it likely that other details in the account were carefully preserved as well. By the end of the first century, John may also have been casting a side glance at Rome repeatedly throughout his Gospel, as Jo-Ann Brant explains, with respect to chapter 4: "Jesus' assertion of the sovereignty of God brings him into conflict with the Roman emperor's claims to bring all good things: peace, security, roads, wine, bread and circuses, and not least running water. When the Fourth Gospel names living water as one of the divine gifts that he brings, it points to the principle of open access to resources essential for life and worship, perhaps the central tenet of the proclamation of the historical Jesus."[111]

As for John's and Jesus's relationship, with which John 4 began, some have gone further than I have and spoken of Jesus as beginning his career as a disciple of John, or of other ways in which he viewed himself as an inferior and only gradually came to the conviction of his superiority.[112] Such schemes certainly would fit the criterion of embarrassment, but they go beyond anything the text even hints at. On the other hand, Mary Coloe presents excellent balance with her conviction that the overall depiction "of John and Jesus engaging in similar and contemporary baptizing ministries is quite probable, as is its description of Jesus' first disciples coming from the ambit of John."[113]

---

109. Susan Miller, "The Woman at the Well: John's Portrayal of the Samaritan Mission," in Anderson, Just, and Thatcher, *John, Jesus, and History*, 2:73–82, esp. 75–80. Brent Neely highlights Jesus's crossing over traditional interpersonal boundaries without preconditions, but with sensitivity and yet confidence ("Jesus at the Well [John 4.4–42]: Our Approach to the 'Other,'" *Theology* 121 [2018]: 332–40).

110. See esp. Reinhard Pummer, "Samaritans, Galileans, and Judeans in Josephus and the Gospel of John," *JSHJ* 18 (2020): 77–99.

111. Jo-Ann A. Brant, "The Geopolitics of Water and John 4:1–42," in Anderson, Just, and Thatcher, *John, Jesus, and History*, 3:258.

112. See esp. Meier, *Marginal Jew*, 2:403–60.

113. Mary Coloe, "John as Witness and Friend," in Anderson, Just, and Thatcher, *John, Jesus, and History*, 2:53.

We learn nothing else new in John's Gospel about John the Baptist. Subsequent references always refer back to the early period of his ministry (5:33, 35, 36; 10:40, 41); we do not learn anything more about further activity. No other hint appears of Jesus baptizing at all. Some have argued, therefore, that the practice died out for a while, especially once John was imprisoned, only to be revived by the first followers of Jesus after the descent of the Spirit at Pentecost.[114] A better solution may be to recognize the probability that ritual immersion continued, thus explaining its recurrence in Acts. But it was not yet full-orbed Christian baptism; the Fourth Evangelist himself recognizes preresurrection and postresurrection distinctions in the ministry of the Spirit (cf. 14:17 with 20:22). At the redactional level, John is nonsacramental; he may even be a bit antisacramental. So any hints of a larger role for baptism probably are traditional.

Employing similar logic, Joan Taylor and Federico Adinolfi detect hints of a baptismal ministry of Jesus even in Mark's narrative: the constant presence of water, often in combination with wilderness places, crowds, and teaching (and healings), all of which replicate features of John's activity. Mark is more interested in the coming ministry of the Spirit, and so he does not explicitly talk about baptism during Jesus's ministry. But the law was still binding on Israel, so that each person Jesus healed could have needed immersion for purification. A few times Jesus can send people to the temple, but baptism in water for those who began to follow him after their healing would have accomplished the same thing in his mind. Taylor and Adinolfi thus conclude that "the narrative pattern of Mark reflects historical memory, even when in Mark's rhetoric the baptizing activity of Jesus is not explicitly mentioned."[115]

## Healing as Purification (John 4:45–54)

The final pericope in John 4 narrates the healing of the nobleman's son (vv. 45–54). Nothing of ritual purification appears in it, nor is any

---

114. See esp. Graham H. Twelftree, "Jesus the Baptist," *JSHJ* 7 (2009): 103–25.
115. Joan E. Taylor and Federico Adinolfi, "John the Baptist and Jesus the Baptist: A Narrative Critical Approach," *JSHJ* 10 (2012): 284.

water present. Still, our immediately preceding review reminds us that the son was cleansed from a form of impurity through his healing; for all we know, either he or his father (or both) may have been baptized. The account certainly states that the father "and his whole household believed" because of this, the second of Jesus's signs "after coming from Judea to Galilee" (vv. 53–54).[116] Debates about historicity are bound up with decisions about the relationship of this passage to the healing of the centurion's son in Q (Matt. 8:5–13; Luke 7:1–10). The situation is somewhat like the debate over the accounts of the temple cleansing. If John and Q are telling the same story, they are recording such different portions of the episode that they don't create contradictions, but they do tilt things in the direction of separate events.[117] If that is the case, multiple attestation of concepts supports authenticity.

## Conclusions

John is introduced not as a baptizer but as a witness to Jesus, yet his role in ministry eventually comes out. The baptism of Jesus is never narrated, but it turns out that he baptizes others, at least through his disciples. He deliberately turns into wine water put in huge stone vessels that ensure ritual purity, though the Fourth Evangelist is mostly interested in the miracle—as a sign. Jesus really does perform a temple cleansing, and he does so at the beginning of his public ministry, whatever implications that has for the similar Synoptic event. The authentic core of his interaction with Nicodemus, if we must limit ourselves to a core, is about the spiritual cleansing provided by the new birth that belief in Jesus brings. John graciously acknowledges that his role as a baptizer must shrink in comparison to Jesus's overall public roles. Does that mean there was a time when Jesus's disciples baptized even more than John did? Jesus offers a Samaritan woman living water—ritually pure and spiritually satisfying for eternity, though the Gospel writer overall is more interested in her acceptance of Jesus as Messiah

---

116. See esp. Whitacre, *John*, 115–16.
117. Ridderbos, *Gospel according to John*, 174–75; Morris, *Gospel according to John*, 254–55; Carson, *Gospel according to John*, 234.

and her role as an evangelist to her own townspeople. A (probably) Gentile nobleman's son is healed; for the Gospel writer, it is Jesus's second sign, but at root it provides ritual and spiritual wholeness, for the boy but also for all who believe based on his healing.

Issues of purity, especially ritual purity, appear explicitly or implicitly throughout John 1–4. They never reflect the evangelist's main points, which often focus on very different issues. At the very least, they do not represent his most obvious or characteristic theological interests. John's baptism emerges out of the context of ritual purity but comes to symbolize repentance in the moral arena. Jesus deliberately transforms ritually pure water into wine, as an act not of supersession but of the fulfillment of the old in the new. A temple incident still holds the possibility of effecting true cleansing, even if the long-term results will not be what Jesus desired. With Nicodemus, Jesus applies water imagery, previously used for John's baptism, to symbolize new birth by the Spirit. This metaphorical use builds on already well-known Old Testament precedent. But John continues his ministry of ritual immersion, and Jesus replicates it through his disciples. Even with a Samaritan woman under a shroud of suspicion of immorality, whether deserved or not, he develops the theme of living water as an eternal alternative to all temporal refreshment. Yet salvation remains from the Jews. With this woman, it results in spiritual healing with probable social implications; with the nobleman's son, it produces temporal health, which in turn leads to spiritual wholeness.

Thus far Jesus has done nothing that cannot be contained within the bounds of at least some forms of first-century Judaism. Even when he most focuses on the newness of what he brings, it is by transforming the old rather than abolishing or superseding it. By claiming baptism akin to that of John, he utilizes but adds to an existing form of ritual immersion (whether proselyte baptism specifically existed then). But he hints at changes with the future arrival of the Holy Spirit in new forms. Unless all questions about the chronological relationship between Johannine and Synoptic information are simply removed from the table as off limits, it appears that we have not yet arrived at the period of Jesus's ministry often referred to by students of the Synoptics as the great Galilean ministry, unless at the very end if 4:46–54 is a version of the story that Matthew and Luke also record. John 5–10, on the other hand, will overlap with that period, even while primarily presenting Jesus's trips to Jerusalem that punctuate it. Will Jesus's perspectives on purity remain the same, or will they change in any way? It is this topic to which our next chapter must turn.

# 8

# Purification Starting to Change in John 5–11

As we saw earlier, numerous historical Jesus scholars of past eras were fascinated by possible stages or phases in Jesus's ministry. At least one key turning point in his public career seemed crucial to postulate. For Ernest Renan in the nineteenth century, it was the Galilean springtime—the period of success and popularity—giving way to the more somber period of opposition culminating in the road to the cross (Mark 10:1 pars.). For Albert Schweitzer in the early twentieth century, Jesus traded his conviction that the kingdom of God was so imminent that the "Son of man" would arrive before the disciples had finished the mission that he sent them on in Israel (Matt. 10:23) for the belief that he had to go to Jerusalem to die to bring it about himself. Certainly, Luke sets up two relatively equally balanced portions of Jesus's ministry before and after Jesus's resolutely setting out to go to Jerusalem to the fate that he knew awaited him there (Luke 3:1–9:50; 9:51–18:34).[1]

---

1. Key works on Luke's central section include Paul Barnett, *Following Jesus to Jerusalem: Luke 9–19* (Milton Keynes: Paternoster, 2012); David P. Moessner, *Lord of the Banquet: The Literary and Theological Significance of the Lukan Travel Narrative* (Minneapolis: Fortress, 1989); Helmuth L. Egelkraut, *Jesus' Mission to Jerusalem: A Redaction-Critical Study of the Gospel of Luke 9:51–19:48* (Frankfurt: Peter Lang, 1976).

But what of Jesus's relationship to John the Baptist? Was there ever a change there? The Synoptics record the imprisoned Baptist sending some of his disciples to ask Jesus point-blank if he is the Coming One (Luke 7:18–23 par.). Jesus does not directly answer but quotes Isaiah 35:5–6, noting that the miracles of the messianic age were being performed in that very day. In other words, John should recognize him as the one to whom he had testified, even if God had not shown John that he would be imprisoned, which detention had led to his doubts.[2] Jesus himself goes on to contrast people's reactions to the two special men by likening John to an ascetic who "came neither eating bread nor drinking wine" and by likening himself to a more festive person who "came eating and drinking" (Luke 7:33–34).[3] Since the Synoptics also portray John and Jesus as more similar than dissimilar at the outset of their ministries (cf. Matt. 3:2 with 4:17), it is reasonable to view their divergence as a later development, perhaps largely only after John's imprisonment (or at least only after the greater geographical separation of the two men).[4]

In this light, John 3:24 may have had another purpose besides being a merely chronological marker. The seemingly parallel ministries of John and Jesus described in verses 22–23 obviously took place before John's imprisonment, since he was never released before his execution. When else *could* such a ministry have occurred? Perhaps the Fourth Evangelist is stressing that Jesus so resembled John only before John's imprisonment; after that point, Jesus began to do certain things differently. One of those things could well have been to give up having new followers baptized. It is rather extraordinary not to hear a word about Jesus or his disciples baptizing anyone anywhere in Matthew, Mark, or Luke. Yet those three Gospels narrate *no* incidents about Jesus's public activity in the months leading up to his "great Galilean ministry," so we have no reason to expect Jesus to baptize. Even if there are hints,

---

2. Jesus's reply strikingly parallels the use of Isa. 35:5–6 at Qumran (Messianic Apocalypse [4Q521]).

3. See further Craig L. Blomberg, *Interpreting the Parables*, 2nd ed. (Downers Grove, IL: IVP Academic, 2012), 262–67.

4. John P. Meier, *A Marginal Jew: Rethinking the Historical Jesus*, 5 vols. to date (New York: Doubleday, 1991–2001; New Haven: Yale University Press, 2009–16), 2:130–63.

for example in Mark (see above, 255), of baptisms during the height of Jesus's public popularity, perhaps they were relegated to a noticeably lesser role in Jesus's overall ministry than in the earliest stages, when he was still in touch with John prior to his arrest.[5]

Why might this playing down of baptism's role have begun after John's imprisonment? Roger Amos has recently suggested that *we should consider dividing Jesus's ministry into an initial phase in which he hoped to reform institutional Judaism, followed by the rest of his ministry in which he focused more on forming a countercultural community of Jews who welcomed and included among their number the most ostracized and marginalized people within Israel.*[6] Whatever the extent that this proves persuasive for the whole of Jesus's public career, it fits reasonably well the information we discover in John as the months progress and Jesus's conflict with the Jewish, and especially Judean, leaders continues to grow. Once baptism no longer features in the Fourth Gospel's narrative about Jesus, while his involvement in events triggered by or at least involving issues of ritual purity continues, his building on and transformation of that foundation of purity appears to give way increasingly to one of merely setting up an alternative model, parallel to what Amos sees in other areas.

This phase continues until the end of the Gospel, but another turning point occurs after John 11. Chapter 11:55–57, as we will see (below, 288–89), contains the last reference to even the perception that Jesus might be concerned to keep ritual laws of purity. Throughout John 5–11 there are no further depictions of Jesus or his disciples baptizing; whether they continued to do so is beyond our ability to determine (recall above, 248–49). But even where there are hints of the Jewish law and traditions on this topic, Jesus ever more clearly is distancing himself from any literal obedience to them. Increasingly, he points to the coming ministry of the Spirit in a person as the functional but greater equivalent to being in a state of ceremonial purity. It also becomes increasingly more difficult to refer to his aims or goals as merely those

---

5. See Graham H. Twelftree, "Jesus the Baptist," *JSHJ* 7 (2009): 103–25, esp. 122–24.
6. Roger Amos, *What Was Jesus Hoping to Achieve?* (Eugene, OR: Wipf & Stock, 2021).

of institutional reform. Rather, as he fulfills the Scripture, he ushers in a new age of greater grace and truth (recall 1:17).

Commentators have regularly recognized two main sections in the body of the Fourth Gospel. Frequently, they have been identified as chapters 2–12 and 13–20 and called the Book of Signs and the Book of Glory.[7] Seven miracles signifying Jesus's identity punctuate the plot of the first main section, while Jesus's suffering and death revealed as Christ's glorification feature heavily in the second part. Because the death and resurrection of Lazarus (chap. 11) also foreshadow Jesus's own death and resurrection, it would be possible to place the break between the two main halves of John after chapter 10. A compromise occasionally adopted sets off chapters 11–12 by themselves (or just one of those two chapters) as a transitional section.[8] A division after chapter 11, however, seems to be the best; 12:1 marks a clear shift in time and place. No more miracles ensue, and all events from here on lead inexorably to the cross.[9]

That there is disagreement on this suture and that most scholars would place the break after chapter 12 demonstrate at the very least that John is not concerned to highlight a sharp break in his narrative. If we sense an underlying shift with respect to questions of purity, it, too, is somewhat gradual and not obviously a redactional seam. It is interesting that all three Synoptics more clearly feature the point at which Jesus "set his face to go to Jerusalem" (Luke 9:51 NRSV, ESV; but cf. also Matt. 19:1; Mark 10:1) for his fateful Passover there. John is vaguer about whether Jesus ever returns all the way northward after his sojourns away from Jerusalem and its environs when he finished ministering during Hanukkah (John 10:40–42) or again after his time in Bethany (11:1, 18) with Mary, Martha, and Lazarus (vv. 54–57). Nevertheless, 12:1 makes it clear that he has returned again to Bethany. From this point on, John's narrative drives relentlessly to the crucifixion, with

---

7. Esp. influenced by Raymond E. Brown, *The Gospel according to John: Introduction, Translation, and Notes*, 2 vols., AB (Garden City, NY: Doubleday, 1966–70).

8. See esp. D. A. Carson, *The Gospel according to John*, PNTC (Leicester: Apollos; Grand Rapids: Eerdmans, 1991), 106–7.

9. Gerald L. Borchert, *John 1–11*, NAC (Nashville: Broadman & Holman, 1996); Borchert, *John 12–21*, NAC (Nashville: Broadman & Holman, 2002).

Jesus exclusively in and around Jerusalem. *This seems to confirm the decision to keep chapter 12 with chapters 13–20.*

### Jesus or the Pool of Bethesda? (John 5)

Chapter 5 begins with a passage that links much more explicitly to the themes of washing and cleansing than 4:43–54 did. We are back in the world that permeated 1:19–4:42. The difference is that John is more interested in what Jesus did on those occasions when he went up to Jerusalem at one of the major annual festivals of Judaism. His main theological focus will be to present Jesus as the fulfillment of those festivals.[10] This, too, leads to an identification of at least chapters 5–10 as the next major section of his Gospel. No festival appears in conjunction with the raising of Lazarus in chapter 11, except a proleptic look ahead to the coming Passover, which will form the setting of chapters 12–20, at the very end of the chapter (vv. 55–57). But the reawakening of Jesus's dear friend to live in this world forms the climactic sign of the seven, so chapter 11 should be kept with chapters 5–10.[11]

John 5 is the one and only example of Jesus going to Jerusalem at festival time where we are not told the specific festival (v. 1). This is most likely because *what will become important here is Jesus's healing on the weekly holy day—the Sabbath—not the seasonal festival, whichever one it was.* As he does elsewhere (esp. 9:14), the narrator withholds this information at the outset of the account in order to create a more dramatic disclosure after the miracle and to change the direction of the story (v. 9b).[12] The debate about the Sabbath that ensues is where John's theological emphases lie. The healing is simply the context for the debate; if there is traditional material at all in John 5,

---

10. See Francis J. Moloney, *The Gospel of John*, SP (Collegeville, MN: Liturgical Press, 1998), 164; Brian D. Johnson, "'Salvation Is from the Jews': Salvation in the Gospel of John," in *New Currents through John: A Global Perspective*, ed. Francisco Lozada Jr. and Tom Thatcher (Atlanta: Society of Biblical Literature, 2006), 98.

11. E.g., Leon Morris, *The Gospel according to John*, rev. ed., NICNT (Grand Rapids: Eerdmans, 1995), 473.

12. See J. Ramsey Michaels, *The Gospel of John*, NICNT (Grand Rapids: Eerdmans, 2010), 294–95.

it is most likely found in this miracle story.[13] The focus in the portion of the narrative about a miraculous healing, however, is on the pool of Bethesda. Verse 2 introduces it and creates several exegetical problems in so doing. John uses the present tense: "Now there *is* in Jerusalem . . . a pool, . . . which is surrounded by five covered colonnades [lit., "having five stoa"]." After the destruction of much of the city in AD 70, this would no longer be true. Is this an indication that the Gospel should be dated to the 60s? Is this a use of the historical present in John to make a narrative more vivid? Both suggestions have been proposed, and both have been disputed.[14] Uncertain, too, is the exact name of the pool. The two major textual variants beside "Bethesda" are "Bethzatha" and "Bethsaida."[15] Fortunately, none of these conundrums have to be solved in order to discuss the significance of the location.

*Recent archaeology has confirmed beyond most reasonable doubt that the pool was a giant* mikveh. *Most likely, it was the major body of "living water" to the north of the temple that travelers to Jerusalem would stop at to immerse themselves and be cleansed prior to participating in the portions of the festivals when they went into the temple precincts and were required to be in a state of ritual purity.*[16] There were two parts to the area, a lower pool and an upper pool, each forming roughly a square, with four stoa surrounding the combined area and a fifth portico down the middle, separating the two pools. In other words, it was a rectangular area divided into two adjacent squares; hence, the "five covered colonnades" of verse 2.[17]

13. L. T. Witkamp, "The Use of Traditions in John 5:1–18," *JSNT* 8 (1985): 19–47. But Witkamp shows that it is not as simple as many proponents of the Johannine signs source had argued, with John simply taking a self-contained miracle story from his source and appending the Sabbath controversy to it; he has crafted his material in 5:1–9 as well.
14. See Murray J. Harris, *John*, EGGNT (Nashville: B&H Academic, 2015), 104.
15. For "Bethesda" as the most likely original reading, see David J. Wieand, "John V.2 and the Pool of Bethesda," *NTS* 12 (1965–66): 392–404. See also Robin Thompson, "Healing at the Pool of Bethesda: A Challenge to Asclepius?," *BBR* 27 (2017): 67–68.
16. Urban C. von Wahlde, "The Pool(s) of Bethesda and the Healing in John 5: A Reappraisal of Research and of the Johannine Text," *RB* 116 (2009): 111–36.
17. Craig R. Koester, "The Healing at the Pool of Bethesda (John 5:1–18): A Study in Light of the Archaeological Evidence from Bethesda, Jewish and Greco-Roman Practice, and the Johannine Narrative," in *Expressions of the Johannine Kerygma in John 2:23–5:18: Historical, Literary, and Theological Readings from the Colloquium Ioanneum 2017 in Jerusalem*, ed. R. Alan Culpepper and Jörg Frey (Tübingen: Mohr Siebeck, 2019), 243–73.

Despite the use of the pool particularly at festival times, there were also some syncretistic views, even associated with pagan gods, about the water as a healing shrine. An intermittent spring most likely caused the water to periodically bubble up, leading to the notion that these were times when special healing powers were available in the water.[18] All of this is spelled out in a widely attested later textual variant spanning verses 3b–4: "And they waited for the moving of the waters. From time to time an angel of the Lord would come down and stir up the waters. The first one in the pool after each such disturbance would be cured of whatever disease they had." Although almost certainly not what John originally wrote, this later scribal addition may well reflect the actual beliefs of at least some of the unwell persons who waited by the pool. Something along these lines seems necessary in order to make sense of the crippled man's complaint in verse 7 that he had no one to help him into the water when it was stirred. Thus, he never could be the first person in the pool.[19]

On this occasion, Jesus does not utilize the pool at all. Had he merely helped the man in, there would have been no reason for the man to attribute any healing he might have received to Jesus. So Jesus bypasses the alleged curative powers of the pool and commands him simply, "Get up," which he currently could not do. In addition, he is to pick up his mat and walk (v. 8), presumably taking it somewhere else because he no longer needs to wait by the side of the pool.

"At once" the man does so and demonstrates that he is cured (v. 9a). Now the lesson is clear. Jesus can provide physical healing, which is so important for this man's overall well-being. Might he have returned to Bethesda for ritual purification later? Might one of Jesus's followers have baptized him in the process? Neither is impossible, but nothing even hints at their occurrence. *John's concern is to show Jesus's superior ability to make someone whole.*[20] Later, Jesus *will* employ a

---

18. Urban C. von Wahlde notes that this is the common view but prefers an explanation involving the "intermittent opening of the sluice gate in [a] conduit to replenish or purify the water in the southern pool" (*The Gospel and Letters of John*, 3 vols., ECC [Grand Rapids: Eerdmans, 2010], 2:218–19).

19. Thompson, "Healing at the Pool of Bethesda," 75–77.

20. The concept of *hygiēs* ("healthy, well, sound") permeates the passage, recurring in verses 6, 9, 11, 14, 15. Patricia Bruce identifies it as the thread that ties the miracle story

*mikveh* in healing a blind man (9:7), but here he is demonstrating his own healing power as a superior alternative to whatever healing powers the water of Bethesda ever had or was ever believed to have. As we have noted, it appears that John the Baptist has at least been imprisoned by this point (see above, 190). It is time, as a result, for Jesus to move in somewhat different directions from using literal water to symbolize cleansing.

In terms of historical authenticity, the location and its implications are accurately described.[21] The heart of the miracle story echoes words from Jesus's healing of the paralyzed man in Capernaum (Mark 2:1–12) verbatim, with the command to pick up his mat and walk. Because very few scholars would equate these two episodes, multiple attestation may again come into play for some measure of corroboration. Even more significantly, the Fourth Evangelist now finally declares that all this happened on a Sabbath (v. 9b). From the Jewish leaders' viewpoint, someone who had been disabled for thirty-eight years, presumably unchanged for much of that time, could easily wait one more day. Jesus could have chosen to cure him on the first day of the new week; he would have been every bit as healthy, and even the most religiously scrupulous could rejoice. Obviously, Jesus has chosen to provoke the authorities deliberately. Not surprisingly, the rest of the chapter discusses the aftermath of this choice. Jesus observes that God himself works on the Sabbath, as he creates and sustains life (v. 17). But that never precluded him from giving the fifth commandment, to remember the Sabbath and keep it holy, including by not working (Exod. 20:8–11). The only way Jesus's observation could be relevant is if he were somehow associating himself too closely with God. That apparently is what the leaders did infer, because they plotted his death even more as a result (v. 18).[22]

---

together ("John 5:1–18 The Healing at the Pool: Some Narrative, Socio-Historical and Ethical Issues," *Neot* 39 [2005]: 43).

21. Markus Sasse, "Beobachtungen zum Verhältnis von Archäologie und Exegese am Beispiel der Ausgrabungen am Teich Betesda in Jerusalem (Joh 5)," in *Zeichen aus Text und Stein: Studien auf dem Weg zu einer Archäologie des Neuen Testaments*, ed. Stefan Alkier and Jürgen Zangenberg with Kristina Dronsch and Michael Schneider (Tübingen: Francke, 2003), 259.

22. For the appropriate nuancing, see Carson, *Gospel according to John*, 249–50. See also John W. Pryor, *John, Evangelist of the Covenant People: The Narrative and Themes of the*

The rest of chapter 5 forms an uninterrupted discourse by Jesus, which falls into two parts. Verses 19–30 unfold with an extended chiastic outline and defend Jesus's behavior by him claiming to do nothing but what he sees his heavenly Father do and what the Father delegates to him. The climactic center of the structure is the twice repeated "double Amen" saying about resurrection to eternal life in verses 24–25.[23] Because such sayings have often been viewed as an authentic core to Jesus's teaching in John,[24] and because all twelve verses hang together as a tightly knit unit, this may all reflect Jesus's response on this occasion. That he defends himself by a kind of subordinationism rather than with overly high Christology further supports this conclusion.[25]

Verses 31–47 are a bit more disjointed; those who suggest composite origins could make a stronger case for a later addition here. Yet the whole section does loosely hang together around the theme of testimony or witnesses in Jesus's favor: John (the Baptist), the Scriptures, the Father, and Moses (again through the Scriptures).[26] Verses 39–40 epitomize the central tenet of the Fourth Gospel with respect to the Scriptures: they point to Jesus.[27] Not agreeing with this, the biblical scholars of the day readily reject him. Mention of John the Baptist reintroduces the theme of his primary role in this Gospel, that of witness or testifier (vv. 33–34). The assumption that by this time John has

---

*Fourth Gospel* (London: Darton, Longman & Todd; Downers Grove, IL: InterVarsity, 1992), 26–27.

23. Albert Vanhoye, "La composition de Jean 5,19–30," in *Mélanges bibliques en homage au R. P. Béda Rigaux*, ed. Albert Descamps and André de Halleux (Gembloux: Duculot, 1970), 259–74.

24. R. Alan Culpepper, "Jesus Sayings in the Johannine Discourses," in *John, Jesus, and History*, ed. Paul N. Anderson, Felix Just, and Tom Thatcher, 3 vols. (Atlanta: Society of Biblical Literature, 2007–16), 3:353–82.

25. Steven M. Bryan shows that Jesus's whole point is to refute those who claim that he heals on the Sabbath apart from doing simply what the Father empowers him to do ("Power in the Pool: The Healing of the Man at Bethesda and Jesus' Violation of the Sabbath [Jn. 5:1–18]," *TynBul* 54 [2003]: 7–22).

26. J. D. Atkins shows how the logic of these verses is illuminated by the teaching of Deut. 18–19 on the eschatological prophet like Moses distinguished from false prophets ("The Trial of the People and the Prophet: John 5:30–47 and the True and False Prophet Traditions," *CBQ* 75 [2013]: 279–96). See also Thomas W. Simpson, "Testimony in John's Gospel: The Puzzle of 5:31 and 8:14," *TynBul* 65 (2014): 201–18.

27. Craig L. Blomberg, *A New Testament Theology* (Waco: Baylor University Press, 2018), 624–25.

been imprisoned and perhaps even executed seems to be confirmed, because Jesus speaks of John's light as a lamp that burned and illuminated (past tense), which was appreciated for a time, a time that now appears to be over (v. 35).[28] We should not be surprised, then, that this chapter contains nothing overt about ceremonial cleansing, and that the one place with key implications for ritual purification is rejected in favor of Jesus's direct cure.

## No Cleansing in the Wilderness (John 6)

At first blush, John 6 contains nothing that is relevant to our topic. Most of the chapter involves Jesus feeding the five thousand and delivering the Bread of Life Discourse in the Capernaum synagogue. There are parallel trajectories, however, between Jesus's development of "living bread" and the "living water" motif he has previously introduced. Intriguingly, verse 35 declares that just as those who come to Jesus as the bread of life will never again hunger, neither will they ever again thirst. One doesn't slake one's thirst by eating bread, so the application of the second metaphor is a bit jarring. It is possible that the water that eternally satisfies, having already been introduced, became the locus for the development of the concept of the bread of life, which was then added to it and elaborated.[29] *At any rate, the implied presence of water in this verse provides at least a tiny hint that purification has not entirely disappeared.*

*More tellingly, the whole account of the feeding of the five thousand in a desolate place raises the question of ritual handwashing.* There could scarcely be enough water in this location, if there was any, for most in this huge crowd to prepare to eat by washing their hands.[30] Of course, we know from Mark 7:1–23 and parallel that Jesus and his followers did not observe this Pharisaic halakah. A reader familiar

---

28. Rudolf Bultmann notes, "Vv. 33–35 look back on the Baptist's activity as a completed and past event" (*The Gospel of John: A Commentary*, trans. G. R. Beasley-Murray, ed. R. W. N. Hoare and J. K. Riches [Oxford: Blackwell; Philadelphia: Westminster, 1971], 264n5).

29. Rodney A. Whitacre, *John*, IVPNTC (Downers Grove, IL: InterVarsity, 1999), 159.

30. Nor could the crowd be separated into clean and unclean in any other way. See further Wilson C. K. Poon, "Superabundant Table Fellowship in the Kingdom: The Feeding of the Five Thousand and the Meal Motif in Luke," *ExpTim* 114 (2003): 224–30, esp. 228–29.

only with John, however, might well wonder why Jesus chose such a location to work this miracle that would only generate the handwashing problem that it did. A primary answer, to be sure, is that meeting physical needs was far more important in his hierarchy of values. But this is not one of the questions the Fourth Evangelist is highlighting. Redactional emphases include the parallels with God providing manna in the wilderness (see esp. Exod. 16:31–35; Num. 11:6–9), suggesting that Jesus is the Deuteronomic prophet or new Moses who was predicted to be a kind of messianic figure (Deut. 18:15–18).[31] Most of the chapter continues the Fourth Gospel's strong christological emphasis, even in the section on eating Christ's flesh and drinking his blood.[32] The debate over whether this contains eucharistic allusions is a fascinating and significant one, but it does not directly bear on our topic of purification.[33] John does, nevertheless, seem concerned to emphasize Jesus as the new Passover; he alone remarks that Passovertide was near, even though Jesus was not at the festival at precisely this moment.[34]

As is well known, the feeding of the five thousand is the one miracle found in all four Gospels. Careful comparison of the four has suggested that John's version may actually be the oldest.[35] The unique mention of the crowds trying to take Jesus by force and make him king is widely acknowledged as a probably historical detail within the Fourth Gospel, not least due to its satisfaction of the criterion of embarrassment—in essence, Jesus runs away![36] Scholars who are prepared to grant some

---

31. John Lierman, "The Moses Pattern of John's Christology," in *Challenging Perspectives on the Gospel of John*, ed. John Lierman (Tübingen: Mohr Siebeck, 2006), 210–34. This theme also fits a pre-70 context better than it does a post-70 one, given its focus on the land to be inherited. See Richard Bauckham, "Messianism according to the Gospel of John," in Lierman, *Challenging Perspectives on the Gospel of John*, 34–68.

32. See throughout Paul N. Anderson, *The Christology of the Fourth Gospel: Its Unity and Disunity in the Light of John 6*, rev. ed. (Eugene, OR: Cascade Books, 2010).

33. See esp. Jan Heilmann, "A Meal in the Background of John 6:52–58?," *JBL* 137 (2018): 481–500.

34. Furthering John's theme of Jesus as the fulfillment of the Jewish feasts (Carson, *Gospel according to John*, 269).

35. Paul W. Barnett, "The Feeding of the Multitude in Mark 6/John 6," in *Gospel Perspectives*, vol. 6, *The Miracles of Jesus*, ed. David Wenham and Craig Blomberg (Sheffield: JSOT Press, 1986; repr., Eugene, OR: Wipf & Stock, 2003), 327–59.

36. Paul N. Anderson, *The Fourth Gospel and the Quest for Jesus: Modern Foundations Reconsidered* (London: T&T Clark, 2006), 162; C. H. Dodd, *Historical Tradition in the Fourth Gospel* (Cambridge: Cambridge University Press, 1963), 215.

probability to even the core of a single nature miracle typically point to feeding the five thousand.[37] At any rate, assuming that the crowds ate *something*, however it was procured, meant that they ate it without ritual handwashing. So my conclusions stand unless the entire story is sheer fiction.

The account of Jesus walking on the water in 6:16–21 is largely devoid of redactional additions or emphases, especially when compared with its parallels in Matthew and Mark. It is the one place in the chapter where there is a large body of water (the Sea of Galilee), but we must not make the mistake of automatically reading the theme of cleansing into every narrative where water appears. The passage does recall key Old Testament texts in which Yahweh strides across the sea and demonstrates his sovereign power over wind and waves (Job 9:8; Ps. 77:19). To the extent that the miraculous element of the passage seems also to involve the sudden end of the storm, enabling the boat to reach land very quickly once the wind and the rain has abetted, we certainly see Jesus producing order out of chaos,[38] akin to the concept of cleansing. But the less we argue for the presence of our theme in places where it may simply just not be there, the less we open ourselves and our hypothesis to the criticism of overkill.

The primary takeaway from both parts of John 6 and from both miracles is that ceremonial cleansing simply doesn't come into play. With the feeding of the five thousand, the most scrupulous among the Jews would have insisted on ritual handwashing, but nothing of the sort is mentioned, nor would it have been possible. With the walking on the water, at most there are intimations of the re-creation of wholeness in the natural world, but nothing at all ceremonial. John the Baptist, especially in the Synoptics, might have insisted on more asceticism in one or both contexts: fast, when insufficient bread and fish are available, and keep rowing until you overcome the storm and arrive at land. In the Fourth Gospel, he might have at least testified to his inability to

---

37. Meier, *Marginal Jew*, 2:959–67.
38. Dorothy Lee speaks of Jesus establishing his sovereignty over the powers of the sea, both natural and supernatural (*Flesh and Glory: Symbolism, Gender, and Theology in the Gospel of John* [New York: Crossroad, 2002], 83).

deal with the problems miraculously as the Coming One could. But this Coming One has now arrived, and he has come eating and drinking, and providing food and respite for his followers.[39]

## Living Water at the Feast of Tabernacles (John 7)

We come next to Jesus at the Feast of Tabernacles (John 7:2). As in the sequence of events in 2:1–11, family members present Jesus with a problem, he acts as if he is not going to do what they want because "his hour" has still not yet come, yet in his own time and way he then does what was requested. In this instance, the request involves going to the festival. When he finally goes, it is half over (v. 14). Commentators frequently observe that it is as if he simply begins speaking where he left off at the end of chapter 5.[40] He continues to amaze the crowds with his teachings, which he insists are not his own but are supplied by the one who sent him. He alludes to earlier plots to kill him, which confuses those who weren't present on (or remembering) that earlier occasion. He picks up the debate about working on the Sabbath, and the rest of the chapter describes the polarization that his teaching causes among his listeners, which ranges from calling him demon-possessed to believing that he is the Messiah.

The climax of Jesus's time in Jerusalem on this occasion comes not at the end of the account but a little beyond its midpoint. In verses 37–39, on the last and greatest day of the festival (v. 37), which would have been the eighth day,[41] Jesus cries out loudly, "Let anyone who is thirsty come to me and drink. Whoever believes in me, as Scripture has said, rivers of living water will flow from within them." Or at least that is how most commentators, including recent New Testament scholars, have taken it. A translation of verses 37b–38 that results in clearer

---

39. See Poon, "Superabundant Table Fellowship in the Kingdom," 226.
40. Herman Ridderbos notes that "a reference back to earlier dialogues is no proof of displacement of materials originally belonging together. It rather suggests the modus operandi that characterizes the Evangelist (cf., e.g., 8:14ff. with 5:31ff.; 9:5 with 8:12, etc.)" (*The Gospel according to John: A Theological Commentary*, trans. John Vriend [Grand Rapids: Eerdmans, 1997], 262).
41. George R. Beasley-Murray, *John*, 2nd ed., WBC (Nashville: Nelson, 1999), 114.

parallelism and that better fits John's high Christology appears in the NIV margin. It reads, "*And let anyone drink who believes in me. As Scripture has said, 'Out of him will flow rivers of living water.'*" The problem with the traditional rendering (as in the NIV text) is that it makes believers the direct source of bestowing the Spirit on others, although this can be alleviated by seeing them merely as the conduit for passing on what they receive (the Spirit) from Jesus. The second reading (as in the NIV margin), often called the christological reading, is probably to be preferred.[42] Maarten Menken concurs, and believes that this helps him identify the Old Testament sources of the "quotation" as Psalm 77:16 and 77:20, with the modifier "living" before "water" coming from Zechariah 14:8.[43]

Either way, the motif of "living water" has reappeared and most likely should be interpreted as before, in terms of the Spirit. What is interesting is that, even with John the Baptist apparently out of the picture, Jesus still speaks in the future tense: "rivers of living water will flow" (v. 38). The Fourth Evangelist confirms this, as he explains, "By this he meant the Spirit, whom those who believed in him were later to receive. Up to that time the Spirit had not been given, since Jesus had not yet been glorified" (v. 39). Clearly, John understands that the disciples' experience of the Spirit remains only partial, compared to what they will enjoy after Jesus's death and resurrection. Brian Johnson observes that verse 39 functions somewhat like other Johannine "after-the-fact" explanations of previously puz-

---

42. Following the NIV margin rather than the NIV. Cf. also the CEB and see Craig S. Keener, *The Gospel of John: A Commentary*, 2 vols. (Peabody, MA: Hendrickson, 2003), 1:728–29; F. F. Bruce, *The Gospel of John: Introduction, Exposition, and Notes* (Grand Rapids: Eerdmans; London: Pickering & Inglis, 1983), 181–82; J. B. Lightfoot, *The Gospel of St. John: A Newly Discovered Commentary*, ed. Ben Witherington III and Todd D. Still, assisted by Jeanette N. Hagen (Downers Grove, IL: IVP Academic, 2015), 164–65.

43. Maarten J. J. Menken, "The Origin of the Old Testament Quotation in John 7:38," *NovT* 38 (1996): 160–75. On the other hand, Joel Marcus thinks that the key text for the Feast of Tabernacles' water-drawing procession (Isa 12:3: "With joy you will draw water *from the wells of salvation* [*mimmaʿayenê hayəšûʿâ*]") was read or interpreted as "from the belly of Jesus" (*mimmēʿê yēšûʿa*) ("Rivers of Living Water from Jesus' Belly [John 7:38]," *JBL* 117 [1998]: 328–30). For a full survey of suggestions, with a very complex proposal of a combination of numerous texts as his own solution, see Germain Bienaimé, "Promesse au croyant et citation christologique en Jean 7,37–39," *ETL* 95 (2019): 1–38.

zling statements by Jesus, which argues for the authenticity of verses 37–38.[44]

Commentators have regularly noted how appropriate Jesus's claims are at the end of the Feast of Tabernacles. Daily, priests have processed from the pool of Siloam, the largest ritual immersion pool just south of the temple precincts, with flagons of water, shouting the Isaianic text, "With joy you will draw water from the wells of salvation" (Isa. 12:3). *As at Bethesda in chapter 5, Jesus takes advantage of the occasion when people are thinking about ritual purity in the context of a large* mikveh *to point them away from the existing practices, even the most joyful ones, to himself as the ultimate fulfillment of their truest meaning.*[45] Again, his claims divide the bystanders.

Of course, the Spirit is a major theme for John's Gospel, but the careful distinction between what was currently available and what would come later would not as likely have been invented after Christians believed that they always had access to the fullness of God's Spirit. Just as in 2:22 John preserves the distinction between what was understood only after the resurrection from the previous events, here likewise he is concerned not to mingle pre-Easter and post-Easter traditions or interpretations.[46] Moreover, as dramatic as 7:37–39 is, one could remove this paragraph from the narrative and it would still flow smoothly. The transition "on hearing his words" (v. 40) could apply to what Jesus has said already at the festival, though it would be a little more awkward, since the Jewish authorities would have just spoken (vv. 35–36). Most of the chapter is about the division over who Jesus is and the unbelief of the Jewish leaders. After eighteen previous references to *hydōr* ("water") in chapters 1–6, no other mention of any kind of water appears in chapter 7. After twenty-six previous references to *zōē* ("life"),

---

44. Brian D. Johnson, "Jewish Feasts and Questions of Historicity in John 5–12," in Anderson, Just, and Thatcher, *John, Jesus, and History*, 2:127. For other arguments, see Rainer Riesner, *Messias Jesus: Seine Geschichte, seine Botschaft und ihre Überlieferung* (Giessen: Brunnen, 2019), 284–86.

45. For detailed accounts of the ceremony, see Beasley-Murray, *John*, 113–14; Moloney, *Gospel of John*, 234–35. See also Lorenzo Camarero, "Dos ejemplos de formulación cristológica derásica: El enviado de Dios y la fuente de agua viva (Jn 7,28–29.37–39)," *EstBíb* 65 (2007): 85–114.

46. See Beasley-Murray, *John*, 115.

eleven of them in chapter 6 alone, not one appears in chapter 7. After twelve uses of *zaō* ("live") in previous chapters, none beside the single participle "living" appears here. The word for "river" (*potamos*) is a *hapax legomenon* in John. In other words, the topic of rivers of living water occurs only here in the Fourth Gospel, and the idea of living water occurs in chapter 7 only in verses 37–39. It is not likely, then, that someone added these verses to an already existing narrative in an intrusive fashion. But if one were looking for a historical core to the passage, and a claim that could cause the kind of division within the audience that is described here, these three verses would fit the bill well.[47]

There is also a progression in Jesus's teaching that parallels what we see in his teaching on purity. As Joseph Greene has shown, the theme of the temple in John's Gospel moves from its forerunner, the tabernacle (1:14), to another precursor with Jacob's ladder (1:51), to the literal temple itself (2:21), to it no longer being needed (4:21), to Jesus's fulfillment of the eschatological temple that provides the Spirit's living water (7:37–39).[48] Additionally, Dale Allison thinks that the image of a new Jerusalem with its fountain of living water provides key background to unite the references in 4:10–14, 6:35, and 7:37–39.[49]

So, too, the spiritual cleansing that God's very Spirit will provide does not instantly displace all concern for ritual purity. But Jesus makes no attempt to somehow build on the water-drawing ceremony and recraft it or create his own corresponding ritual. He imitates or duplicates nothing the way he imitated and at least partially duplicated John's baptism. He does not use items associated with the existing ritual the way he did with the stone jars in Cana. He is not even perceived as a rival cleanser, as he was with John, or as supplying better water than the priests do, as when he improved on the wine that was normally

---

47. For a much more elaborate though not incompatible tradition-critical theory, see Harold W. Attridge, "Thematic Development and Source Elaboration in John 7:1–36," *CBQ* 42 (1980): 160–70. Despite the title, Attridge discusses all of chapter 7 (and some of chaps. 5 and 6 as well).

48. Joseph R. Greene, "Integrating Interpretations of John 7:37–39 into the Temple Theme: The Spirit as Efflux from the New Temple," *Neot* 47 (2013): 333–53.

49. Dale C. Allison Jr., "The Living Water (John 4:10–14, 6:35c, 7:37–39)," *SVTQ* 30 (1986): 143–57.

served last. Indeed, there is no explicit comparison at all, as with the two kinds of birth in Jesus's dialogue with Nicodemus or the two kinds of water in his conversation with the Samaritan woman at the well. Without knowing about the tradition of the water-drawing ceremony at the Feast of Tabernacles, readers would never suspect that Jesus's "living water" contrasted with any other water used on that occasion. That is not to question the background or deny that Jesus is using the ritual as a springboard for his own claims, but merely to point out that *issues of ritual purity are receding further into the background.*

## Light of the World (John 8–9)

It is all but certain that the story of the woman caught in adultery (7:53–8:11) was not a part of John's original Gospel.[50] So we move immediately to 8:12 and at once encounter the second remarkable claim Jesus makes at this Feast of Tabernacles. It, too, dovetails perfectly with key customs: the daily temple services with a giant lampstand or candelabra set up to illuminate the area. On the final day, the day we have already reached in John's narrative (7:37), there was a service of darkness instead. How appropriate it is for Jesus to again indicate that he was fulfilling a key element of the Feast of Tabernacles by declaring himself to be the light of the world. The claim also makes one recall Jesus labeling his disciples the light of the world in the Synoptic tradition (Matt. 5:14), no doubt as a reflection of his own light.

But just like after Jesus spoke about rivers of living water (John 7:38), here in chapter 8 the narrative drops the topic introduced by his claim. Because the Pharisees there challenge his claim to testify about himself, the discussion turns again to the dominant Johannine theme of witness, a theme that permeates dialogue up through verse 20. Verses 21–30 include characteristic themes of John, including the contrast of "from below" with "from above" (parallel to "of this world" and "not of this world"), the theme of judgment, the lifting up of Jesus as

---

50. See esp. Jennifer Knust and Tommy Wasserman, *To Cast the First Stone: The Transmission of a Gospel Story* (Princeton: Princeton University Press, 2019).

the Son of man, and his imitation of the Father. The claim to be the light of the world stands apart from its context as much as his claim to provide rivers of living water. If only one verse were allowed to be authentic from all of chapter 8, verse 12 would stand a good chance of being that verse, and the one around which the rest of the account was constructed.[51]

Verses 31–59 describe further antagonism with the religious leadership. Verse 30 reported the encouraging news that many listening to Jesus believed in him. Now he replies that if they remain in him, they are his disciples and they will know God's liberating truth (vv. 31–32). Instead of continuing to believe him, however, they retort that they have never been enslaved (v. 33). Jesus's counterclaims and his audience's response simply escalate hostilities until, by the end of the chapter, they try to stone him; but he escapes and goes into hiding. Apparently, they were *not* prepared to "remain" in him, and the subsequent dialogue exposed their true colors.[52] It is also possible that one of the verbs in the conversation without a clearly identifiable subject, the third-person plural "they answered" (v. 33), indicates a narrowing or even a shift of conversation partners,[53] but if so, it is not obvious. At any rate, everyone who is still in spiritual slavery is unlikely to be ritually clean, though some may be. But Jesus is clear that their real problem is sin, for which they need to repent and receive forgiveness. The chapter builds to the most astounding claim Jesus makes anywhere for himself, that before Abraham was, "I am" (probably echoing Exod. 3:14).[54] High Christology dominates, so naturally this part of the chapter is most historically suspect.

---

51. Verses 12–20 divide into three segments: 12, 13–19, 20, each flowing from the preceding section(s).

52. For the major approaches to the disconnect between one group of people having believed in Jesus and the polemic that ensues, see Debbie Hunn, "Who Are 'They' in John 8:33?," *CBQ* 66 (2004): 387–99.

53. Hunn ("Who Are 'They' in John 8:33?") observes numerous unannounced partial changes of audience throughout chapters 7–8, concluding that the "they" of verse 33 (indicated in the Greek only by the third-person plural suffix on the verb "answered") switches, at least in part, to the Jewish authorities who had *not* believed in Jesus.

54. This accounts for the otherwise "bad grammar" in "Before Abraham was, I am" (v. 58). The Greek for "I am" (*egō eimi*) could also reflect dependence on passages like Isaiah 41:4, "I, the LORD—with the first of them and with the last—*I am he*" (italics added), and 43:10. See

John 9 begins with the loosest of connections to what has come before. "As he went along" (*kai paragōn*) in verse 1 discloses almost nothing about when and where this occurs. Sending a man to wash in the pool of Siloam (v. 7) indicates that Jesus is most probably still in Jerusalem. *The repetition of the claim to be the light of the world (v. 5) makes one first assume that it is the same festival time as chapters 7–8.* Chronologically, however, the next key holiday in Jerusalem was the Feast of Dedication (Hanukkah), which will be mentioned in 10:22 in language that could imply that some of the preceding narrative occurred at that festival as well (see below, 281–82). The only natural place to imagine an interval of time passing prior to between 10:21 and 10:22 is here between 8:58 and 9:1, as we will see.[55] To this day, Hanukkah is also called the Festival of Lights (cf. already in Josephus, *Ant.* 12.325); even before Jesus's day, it was referred to as "the Festival of Tabernacles of the month of Kislev" (2 Macc. 1:9), which was usually in December.[56] It could actually be easier to imagine Jesus repeating his claim to be the world's light at a second festival with similar significance rather than just later at the same one, especially since none of his other "I am" claims are repeated in the same venue, nor do any of them as naturally fit two separate Jewish holy days.

The story that dominates John 9 is Jesus's healing of a man who had been blind from birth. It is one of two two-stage miracles in the Gospels (cf. Mark 8:22–25), and it is one of three in which Jesus uses his spittle as part of the process (cf. Mark 7:33; 8:23). *This time it is the major* mikveh *south of the temple precincts that is involved.*[57] Jesus does not, though, heal this man right by the pool as he did the

---

further Catrin H. Williams, *I Am He: The Interpretation of 'Anî Hû' in Jewish and Christian Literature* (Tübingen: Mohr Siebeck, 1999).

55. Ben Witherington thinks that the change goes all the way back to 8:12. Because Hanukkah was the Festival of Lights, a saying from Jesus about being the light of the world would fit well there too (*John's Wisdom: A Commentary on the Fourth Gospel* [Louisville: Westminster John Knox, 1995], 173). See also J. C. Poirier, "Hanukkah in the Narrative Chronology of the Fourth Gospel," *NTS* 54 (2008): 465–78.

56. Beasley-Murray, *John*, 173.

57. Urban C. von Wahlde, "The Pool of Siloam: The Importance of the New Discoveries for our Understanding of Ritual Immersion in Late Second Temple Judaism and the Gospel of John," in Anderson, Just, and Thatcher, *John, Jesus, and History*, 2:155–73; Elaine A. Phillips, "The Pools of Siloam: Biblical and Post-Biblical Traces," *TynBul* 70 (2019): 41–54.

crippled man by Bethesda in 5:1–9. Rather, he commands him to go and wash himself in the pool of Siloam. The verb for "wash" (*niptō*) appears twice in verse 7 and again twice in verse 11 and once in verse 15. It also appears eight times in connection with the footwashing ceremony in chapter 13 but nowhere else in this Gospel and only in four other New Testament texts. It is a particularly appropriate verb for anything having to do with cleansing. If the man immersed himself as he was thoroughly washing his eyes, he could have become ritually pure and physically whole at the same time.[58] Other uses of mud with spittle in ancient Judaism may even suggest that the imagery denotes new creation.[59]

As we have become accustomed to seeing in John, the comparatively short account of the miracle leads to a much longer denouement afterward. Exactly as in chapter 5, John withholds the information that the healing occurred on a Sabbath until well into his report (here, v. 14). The controversy over the man's identity and the demand to find out who healed him this way have already taken place (vv. 8–13). The debates that consume the rest of the chapter move in different directions from the question of the healing itself and the cleansing it accomplished. They center on the identity of Jesus. Can he be from God if he breaks the Sabbath? Can he not be from God if he works such unprecedented healings? The previously blind man has no formal religious education but grasps basic realities better than many of those far better trained.

Verse 22 contains the famous reference to the expulsion of Jesus's followers from the synagogue that spawned J. Louis Martyn's theory of a two-level reading of John and the lack of historicity of large portions of its narrative, which represented realities in the Johannine community at the time of writing rather than in Jesus's life and times.[60] Although this theory has dominated scholarly opinion for a half-century, there

---

58. See Edward W. Klink III, *John*, ZECNT (Grand Rapids: Zondervan, 2016), 439–40; Bruce Grigsby, "Washing in the Pool of Siloam: A Thematic Anticipation of the Johannine Cross," *NovT* 27 (1985): 227–35; Jacobus Kok, "The Healing of the Blind Man in John," *JECH* 2 (2012): 36–62.

59. Daniel Frayer-Griggs, "Spittle, Clay, and Creation in John 9:6 and Some Dead Sea Scrolls," *JBL* 132 (2013): 659–70.

60. J. Louis Martyn, *History and Theology in the Fourth Gospel*, 3rd ed. (Louisville: Westminster John Knox, 2003 [orig. 1968]).

are now signs that some are recognizing its weaknesses.⁶¹ Among other issues, *it is easier to defend expulsion as a genuine but limited state of affairs in Jerusalem synagogues during Jesus's lifetime than as a more widespread reality at the end of the first century extending as far as Ephesus.*⁶² Nevertheless, as we have seen before, if one wants to consign large portions of a chapter to redaction, there still are key verses that clamor for being called historical. In John 9, it is verses 13–34 that contain more of John's recurring themes than do verses 1–12. A plausible tradition-critical dissection of the chapter along conventional twentieth-century lines of scholarship would find more historical information in the first twelve verses than in the rest of the chapter.⁶³ Jesus heals blind people in the Synoptics too, including in two stages, as we just noted. Unique to John is the use of the pool to wash off the mud he has made, but as we have seen (see above, 203, 206), *we are learning more and more about how large and important Siloam was, including for purification, so this much rings true.* There is no reason an invented story had to include the pool or a reason for the man to use it, since the method of healing, even though not unprecedented, certainly cuts against the grain of Jesus's practices elsewhere. If there is a historical core to the account at all, it is in the part about the man washing in Siloam.⁶⁴

Like Jesus's claims about offering "living water," his twofold insistence that he is the "light of the world" does not explicitly tie in with anything in John's narrative per se. Only if one knows about the services of light and darkness does the comparison and contrast emerge. The blind man's healing, on the other hand, unlike the healing of the crippled man lying by the pool of Bethesda, does involve the very medium that was normally used for ceremonial cleansing: the

---

61. Tobias Hägerland, "John's Gospel: A Two-Level Drama?," *JSNT* 25 (2003): 309–22; Edward W. Klink, "Expulsion from the Synagogue? Rethinking a Johannine Anachronism," *TynBul* 59 (2008): 99–118; Jonathan Bernier, *Aposynagōgos and the Historical Jesus in John: Rethinking the Historicity of the Johannine Expulsion Passages* (Leiden: Brill, 2013).

62. Carson, *Gospel according to John*, 369–72.

63. Matthias Rein, *Die Heilung des Blindgeborenen (Joh 9): Tradition und Redaktion* (Tübingen: Mohr Siebeck, 1995).

64. Meier, *Marginal Jew*, 2:694–98; Raymond E. Brown, *The Gospel according to John: Introduction, Translation, and Notes*, 2 vols., AB (Garden City, NY: Doubleday, 1966–70), 1:379.

pool of Siloam. Does this break the pattern of the passages in chapters 5–10 thus far being more remotely connected with ritual healing than those in chapters 1–4? Not necessarily. After all, uninformed readers will no more know that Siloam was a *mikveh* than that the Feast of Tabernacles involved rituals of water and light. Nor will they learn that fact from the Fourth Gospel. In fact, this Gospel directs their attention elsewhere when it introduces the name of the pool, by saying that "Siloam" "means 'Sent'" (9:7). The verb is *hermēneuetai*, more formally rendered, "is being interpreted" (cf. KJV, ASV). The Hebrew (or Aramaic) for both "Siloam" and "Sent" use the same three main consonants, transliterated as *š*, *l*, and *ḥ*. The two words may not actually be related etymologically, but the narrator is interpreting Jesus's command to go and wash in this specific pool as involving a play on words.[65] Jesus as both the heavenly man sent by his Father and the one who sends out his followers on missions is a recurring motif in the Fourth Gospel. So the story directs attention away from the fact that Siloam was a pool for ritual cleansing.

The other distinctive feature of this account is Jesus's use of a "mudpack" that he made and put on the man's eyes (v. 6). Mud with spittle was believed in some contexts to have curative powers,[66] and Jesus used spittle in two Synoptic healing accounts as well (Mark 7:33; 8:23). But a mudpack had to be washed off eventually, and what better a place to do so than in the largest nearby pool? Jesus may well have envisaged the man understanding that he was both ritually clean and physically healed after he bathed his eyes in the pool's water.[67] After all, as with all the passages we are examining in John 1–19, these are pre-Easter days, and Jesus would have understood at least the written law of Moses to

---

65. Cf. later rabbinic paronomasia on "Siloam," relating it to Shiloh. See Karlheinz Müller, "John 9,7 und das jüdische Verständnis des Šiloh-Spruches," *BZ* 13 (1969): 251–56.

66. C. K. Barrett, *The Gospel according to St. John: An Introduction with Commentary and Notes on the Greek Text*, 2nd ed. (London: SPCK; Philadelphia: Westminster, 1978), 358, with documentation.

67. Scholars have frequently noted the parallels between this story and that of Naaman, the leper commanded to wash in the Jordan River for cleansing (2 Kings 5). See, e.g., Antony Perrot, "'Il fit de la boue avec sa salive' (Jn 9,6): Nouvelle perspective sur un rituel énigmatique," *RB* 126 (2019): 254–63. Much less likely is his likening the mud to be washed off to the ritual described in Num. 5:11–31, the test for the suspected adulteress.

still be in effect. But as John tells the story, the focus is christological: Jesus is the sent and sending one.

At the same time, the *šalîaḥ* motif is common to John and the Synoptics and often is viewed as an authentic part of the Synoptic tradition when it appears there, precisely because prophets and other messengers from God can be sent.[68] One is not compelled to see some form of divine Christology here. And compared to a half-dozen or more other titles for Jesus in the Fourth Gospel, *šalîaḥ* does not rise above the level of a motif to a full-fledged theme.[69] It could well be authentic by almost the identical logic that I am arguing Jesus as a purifier is.[70]

John 9:35 is the other place where one could imagine an interval of time between segments of Jesus's teaching. One would assume that the investigation begun in verse 13 would occur promptly after the healing. But if Jesus left Jerusalem immediately after the end of the Feast of Tabernacles, he could have already begun his return journey to Galilee by this time. If not, the *second* summoning of the previously blind man probably occurred after Jesus left town. It is also hardly unknown for people to continue unresolved debates after an interval of time during which they were incommunicado. All these possibilities support the likelihood that Jesus's discussions with the man he healed and the Pharisees who were accusing him took place *the next time* Jesus was in Jerusalem, for the Feast of Dedication (10:22). It is to that discussion that we now must turn.

## The Good Shepherd at Hanukkah (John 10:1–39)

The main reason for suggesting that all of 10:1–39 (and arguably some of what precedes it) took place at Hanukkah is the way *the theme of*

---

68. Peder Borgen, "Observations on God's Agent and Agency in John 5–9: Tradition, Exposition and Glimpses into History," in Anderson, Just, and Thatcher, *John, Jesus, and History*, 3:423–38; A. E. Harvey, "Christ as Agent," in *The Glory of Christ in the New Testament: Studies in Christology in Memory of George Bradford Caird*, ed. L. D. Hurst and N. T. Wright (Oxford: Clarendon, 1987; repr., Eugene, OR: Wipf & Stock, 2006), 239–50.

69. More thematic are Jesus as life, light, glory, Son (of God), truth, Messiah-King, and Son of man. See Blomberg, *New Testament Theology*, 588–605.

70. Darrell L. Bock, in a discussion period after my presentation of an outline of this study at the Bible Institute of South Africa, Cape Town, July 2019.

*Jesus as shepherd unites much of the chapter.* Judaism understood the Seleucid rulers at the time of the Maccabean revolt to have been evil shepherds, just like those predicted in Ezekiel 34.[71] Their overthrow led to the hope that the new Hasmonean rulers would produce the Messiah, who would rule over an independent Israel. The celebration of this liberation at the Feast of Dedication formed a perfect occasion for Jesus to claim to be the good shepherd.[72]

Nevertheless, 10:22 lends itself to be taken most naturally as narrating a change of time and scene. We are even told, for the first time, that "it was winter," perhaps to distinguish which celebration of dedication John is describing.[73] The NIV may foreclose on interpretive options a little with its "then came," given that there is a significant textual question here. Many good manuscripts have *de* ("but," "now," "and") rather than *tote* ("then"), some include both, and some omit both. *Egeneto* can mean "came," "became," or just "was."[74] The KJV reads merely, "And it was at Jerusalem the feast of the dedication," which could easily suggest that what preceded verse 22 also occurred at that same feast. The NAB reads, "The Feast of the Dedication was then taking place in Jerusalem," while the RSV states matter-of-factly, "It was the Feast of the Dedication at Jerusalem." These kinds of translations leave the door open for Jesus's teaching earlier in the chapter to have occurred during this year's Hanukkah as well.[75]

It is harder to envision any significant interval of time between 9:41 and 10:1, and 10:1–2 introduces the metaphors of Jesus as both the gate

---

71. For a full list and discussion of relevant Old Testament and other Jewish background literature, see Johannes Beutler, "Der alttestamentlich-jüdische Hintergrund der Hirtenrede in Johannes 10," in *The Shepherd Discourse of John 10 and Its Context: Studies by Members of the Johannine Writings Seminar*, ed. Johannes Beutler and Robert T. Fortna (Cambridge: Cambridge University Press, 1981), 18–32.

72. For extensive detail, see Étienne Nodet, "La Dédicace, les Maccabées et le Messie," *RB* 93 (1986): 321–75. For details of the early celebration of the festival more generally, see Eyal Regev, "Hanukkah and the Temple of the Maccabees: Ritual and Ideology from Judas Maccabeus to Simon," *JSQ* 15 (2008): 87–114; James C. VanderKam, "Hanukkah: Its Timing and Significance According to 1 and 2 Maccabees," *JSP* 1 (1987): 23–40.

73. Hans Förster, "Zur Bedeutung von Ἐγκαίνια in Joh 10,22," *RB* 123 (2016): 400–417. Common suggestions that John was just describing the harsh conditions, or that "winter," like "night," suggested evil times, seem less likely.

74. See BDAG, s.v. *ginomai*.

75. Borchert, *John 1–11*, 337; Gary M. Burge, *Jesus and the Jewish Festivals* (Grand Rapids: Zondervan, 2012), 94–96.

for the sheep and the good shepherd himself (cf. v. 11). Careful readers have regularly observed the close link between 9:35–41 and 10:1–10, even if the repetition of "Pharisees" in 10:1 in the NIV is an interpretation to clarify to whom the plural "you" is addressed. That is why I suggested that there may be earlier places in chapter 9 for John to have envisioned a switch from the setting at the Feast of Tabernacles to one at Hanukkah. If none of these options seems probable, then we have another example of Jesus's conversation from one trip to Jerusalem carrying over to his next time there. But different from what we have seen previously, it is the *second* of these two occasions that is most fitting for the metaphor employed here: "good shepherd." If it has been the Feast of Dedication throughout all of 10:1–39, the introduction of this theme is more understandable.[76]

It also seems significant that Jesus speaks in verse 36 about "the one whom the Father set apart as his very own." "Set apart" comes from the main New Testament word for "sanctify" (*hagiazō*). The Feast of Dedication was first about celebrating the resanctifying or repurifying of the temple after the Syrians were evicted from its precincts back in 164 BC.

Neither Jesus nor John makes anything of the reference; verses 34–39 focus on Jesus as the Son of God and on his unity with his Father, challenging enough claims to provoke the crowd to another attempted (even if unsuccessful) stoning.[77] Claiming to be pure like the temple was purified might have been idiosyncratic, and even audacious, but it would not have seemed so nearly as blasphemous as a direct affirmation of deity.[78] Margaret Daly-Denton observes that at the time of Jewish independence from Antiochus Epiphanes, "the sanctuary's ritual purity was restored after its desecration during a period of apostasy on the part of Jerusalem's priestly elite and their retainers." Again, "*Enkainia*,

---

76. Margaret Daly-Denton, *John: An Earth Bible Commentary; Supposing Him to Be the Gardener* (London: Bloomsbury T&T Clark, 2017), 142.

77. Brian C. Dennert thinks that traditions of miracles at Hanukkah may also lie behind Jesus's emphasis on his works, including his miraculous signs here ("Hanukkah and the Testimony of Jesus' Works [John 10:22–39]," *JBL* 132 [2013]: 431–51).

78. On the nuancing of Jesus's claim, see J. C. O'Neill, "'Making Himself Equal with God' (John 5.17–18): The Alleged Challenge to Jewish Monotheism in the Fourth Gospel," *IBS* 17 (1995): 50–61.

meaning renewal (Gk. *kainos*, renewed, renovated, made new), surely carries a subliminal message in a strand of the early Jesus movement where God is believed to be dwelling on earth in Jesus, making all things new (Rev. 21:3–5)."[79] If some of Jesus's critics viewed this as blasphemy, perhaps they were already overly sensitized to be alert for it during the festival established to celebrate purification after desecration.[80]

The parallels between Jesus's imagery and the festival setting do not require as much extra knowledge this time as they did in chapters 7–9. *The Fourth Evangelist even chooses the name for the festival (Dedication) that links with the historical event of the reconsecration of the temple at the time of the Maccabees.* Because of the widespread use of the Maccabean literature, more people even outside of Judaism would have known something of the story than those who would have known about as-of-yet unwritten traditions concerning Jewish practices at the Feast of Tabernacles. Still, there are gaps one would have had to fill in. This is not the occasion Jesus uses to refer to himself as God's temple, while the title that Jesus does employ calls attention not to the temple's rededication but to the hoped-for messianic shepherds who would arise at that time. As it turned out, none of them was the Messiah, so the people had to wait and keep looking for another. Jesus's own role in dedicating himself remains significant, but it would have almost certainly been a spiritual rather than a (merely?) ritual dedication.[81] The connections with ritual purity are closer here than in the rest of John 5–11 but still not quite as close as they were in chapters 1–4.

## No Sign and a Sign (John 10:40–11:45)

John 10:40–42 is a Janus passage—looking both backward and forward. On the one hand, it harks back to "the early days" (*to prōton* ["at the

---

79. Daly-Denton, *John*, 142–43.

80. For this possible linkage, see James C. VanderKam, "John 10 and the Feast of the Dedication," in *Of Scribes and Scrolls: Studies on the Hebrew Bible, Intertestamental Judaism, and Christian Origins*, ed. Harold W. Attridge, John J. Collins, and Thomas H. Tobin (Lanham, MD: University Press of America, 1990), 203–14.

81. "At Dedication, Jesus takes the central liturgical element of the feast (the consecration of the Temple) and applies it to himself (10.36)" (Mark W. G. Stibbe, *John's Gospel* [London: Routledge, 1994; repr., Eugene, OR: Wipf & Stock, 2001], 74).

first"]) of Jesus's ministry. Jesus has retreated "across the Jordan to the place where John had been baptizing," presumably what 1:28 called "Bethany on the other side of the Jordan." It creates an inclusio, framing and uniting the narrative portion of chapters 1–10 (i.e., not including the prologue in 1:1–18).[82] On the other hand, it forms the introduction to the account of Lazarus's resurrection (11:1–44).[83] Especially when we read that Jesus stayed where he was for two days after he heard the news of Lazarus's illness (11:6), we realize that the distances between locations, which at least some of the original readers would have known, had something to do with Jesus's timing. As we have observed, the raising of Lazarus is the seventh, final, most dramatic, and climactic sign of those that punctuate chapters 2–11 (above, 212, 262).[84] The passion narrative for the Fourth Gospel starts no earlier than chapter 12; we have also noted that many would see the second major section of the body of the narrative not beginning until chapter 13 (above, 262).

John 10:40–42 raises several probably unanswerable questions. Did a return to the site of Jesus's early encounters with John the Baptist lead him to one last period of baptizing those who flocked his way? Was this in fact why "many people came to him" (v. 41a)? Why do the people compare Jesus with John one last time? The possibility of one final season of baptism cannot be excluded, but if part of Jesus's withdrawal from Jerusalem was to "lie low" because of the growing hostility he was receiving from some of the religious leaders there (10:39), would he have deliberately restarted the kind of ministry that had once drawn large crowds—first to John and later to him? The reference to where John had baptized can be adequately explained simply by the Fourth Evangelist's desire to identify the location to which Jesus retreated.

---

82. Carson, *Gospel according to John*, 400–401; Andrew T. Lincoln, *The Gospel according to Saint John*, BNTC (London: Continuum; Peabody, MA: Hendrickson, 2005), 312–13.

83. Bernhard Lang, "A Baptismal Raising of Lazarus: A New Interpretation of John 11," *NovT* 58 (2016): 311. While Lang is correct to see these verses introducing chapter 11, his reading of the account as an allegory about baptism seems far-fetched. Bultmann (*Gospel of John*, 393) sees 10:40–11:54 as a discrete unit, concentrating on Jesus's "decision for death."

84. "It is climactic for John especially as the decisive event that causes the Sanhedrin to pass its resolution to arrest and kill Jesus" (Alexander J. Burke Jr., *The Raising of Lazarus and the Passion of Jesus in John 11 and 12: A Study of John's Literary Structure and His Narrative Theology* [Lewiston, NY: Mellen, 2003], 55).

The mere fact that many people came to him need not mean that he was publicly teaching large crowds; it could simply refer to a steady stream of individuals or groups proceeding more quietly to learn from him, without causing another sensation.

What is the point of the people remarking that John never worked a sign—a miracle intended to point people to belief? Ernst Bammel has shown that, especially prior to AD 70, miracles were expected confirmatory signs of divinely accredited prophets in at least some Second Temple Jewish circles.[85] Others, like some in Jesus's company here, found the more biblical criterion of complete truthfulness in prediction compelling (v. 41b; cf. Deut. 18:21–22). The Johannine emphasis lies clearly on the fact that, by whatever logic, "in that place many believed in Jesus" (v. 42). There need be nothing in this short passage about ritual or moral purity, unless one includes truth-telling in prophecy as part of moral holiness. If there were underlying rituals of purification, they are clearly not in the Johannine focus. They would most likely be historical, cutting against the grain as they would have been, but there is simply not enough evidence to postulate their presence. We can at least conclude that the denigration of John for working no miracles is not likely to have been invented.[86]

The account of Lazarus's death and resurrection contains nothing explicitly related to purification either. *Such a dramatic miracle, however, involving the binding and loosing of a corpse, cannot help but raise purity-related questions.* Those who prepared Lazarus's body for burial clearly would have incurred ritual uncleanness, though that was simply a common reality in ancient life and nothing to create any stigma. The emphasis on the four-day period since his entombment (v. 17), which in turn explains the foul stench that Martha fears (v. 39), does seem to increase the emphasis on impurity.[87] Obviously,

---

85. Ernst Bammel, "John Did No Miracles: John 10:41," in *Miracles: Cambridge Studies in Their Philosophy and History*, ed. C. F. D. Moule (London: Mowbray; New York: Morehouse-Barlow, 1965), 197–202.

86. Rudolf Schnackenburg, *The Gospel according to St. John*, trans. Cecily Hastings et al., 3 vols. (London: Burns & Oates; New York: Seabury, 1980–82), 2:315; Barrett, *Gospel according to Saint John*, 387.

87. "According to the Mishnah, after three days a corpse may have decayed so badly that it can no longer be identified with certainty (*m. Yebamot* 16.3). The opening of the tomb would

Lazarus's resurrection brings him the best possible kind of restoration to purity, short of his final eternal glorification.[88] We could easily imagine him, almost instinctively, wanting immersion in water in a *mikveh* somewhere as quickly as possible, after his smelly ordeal, for both ritual and physical cleanliness. But John's text utters not a word about these topics. Theologically, the Fourth Gospel is interested in people believing that Jesus is the resurrection and the life and that such belief can obtain eternal life for any who exercise it (v. 25). Jesus as the Son of God is likewise a recurring focus of the text (vv. 4, 27; cf. already in 10:36).

Believing in Jesus ties the little and the big portions of this passage together. After his stay across the Jordan, "many believed in Jesus" (10:42). Naturally, many who saw Jesus raise Lazarus likewise "believed in him" (11:45). But those who wish to remain in unbelief can usually find reasons to do so, and the situation is no different here. Some of the onlookers report to the authorities what Jesus has done (v. 46), who in turn "called a meeting of the Sanhedrin" (v. 47). The power brokers in Israel benefited from the status quo, and they rightly recognized that too much of a public disturbance could bring Rome's wrath down on all of them (v. 48). With all the irony an unintended double meaning can muster, Caiaphas, the high priest, decides that "it is better . . . that one man die for the people than that the whole nation perish" (v. 50).[89] So the plot to take Jesus's life begins to reach a fever pitch. Jesus withdraws even further, to the village of Ephraim, and apparently engages in no public ministry at all there, to avoid drawing any attention to himself (v. 54). He cannot remain hidden indefinitely, however, because soon it will be his responsibility as a law-abiding Jew to attend the Passover festival in Jerusalem. This brings us to the last short passage we must scrutinize in this chapter.

---

be an offense not just to the people outside the tomb but also to the body within. Defenseless bodies are placed in tombs or sealed in coffins to protect them from postmortem abuse and the indignity of being seen. What cannot be seen cannot bring shame. Jesus subverts cultural expectations" (Jo-Ann A. Brant, *John*, Paideia [Grand Rapids: Baker Academic, 2011], 176).

88. Cf. Whitacre, *John*, 291.

89. Caiaphas himself most likely intended to say only that the restoration of Israel required the execution of Jesus (Moloney, *Gospel of John*, 344).

## Will He Come or Won't He? (John 11:55–57)

Ceremonial cleansing is mentioned one last time in the Book of Signs (John 11:55). The narrator certainly presumes some knowledge of Jewish law and tradition here. Attendees at the Passover festival needed to ritually immerse themselves to become pure, in order to enter the temple precincts and participate in the sacrifices and services there. *Specifically, the tradition developed that they should appear a week ahead of the start of the celebrations.*[90] Those who arrived in Jerusalem at that time began looking for Jesus (v. 56a). Fresh from learning of the Sanhedrin's plotting, the reader naturally associates this question with the danger Jesus would face if he came at all. Would he dare risk his life by putting in an appearance? Might he skip the festivities, and his obligation to participate in them, altogether (v. 56b)?

What is typically lost sight of in this line of reflection is *why* the Passover pilgrims would be asking these questions already a week ahead of the start of the feast. The answer must be that *Jesus had a reputation not only for attending the annual festivals in the liturgical calendar but also of coming on time for the proper ritual purification.*[91] *Here is one of the clearest indications that Jesus still practiced the purity laws, even if his explicit teaching has increasingly focused on the much more crucial observance of spiritual or moral purity and God's empowerment to bring it about.* Expecting that Jesus will attend, even if belatedly as with the earlier Feast of Tabernacles (cf. 7:14), the leaders take extra measures to be ready to arrest him (v. 57). The sequel to this narrative must await our next chapter, however, as we have reached the end of the period of Jesus's ministry in which ritual purity still figures in his agenda, even if in a muted way and less obviously than in his heyday of public baptisms.

---

90. The need for purification is laid down in Num. 9:6–14. Josephus tells us that pilgrims came about a week early for Passover (J.W. 6.290) and that it was for purification (J.W. 1.229) (Bruce, *Gospel of John*, 253). See von Wahlde, *Gospel and Letters of John*, 2:520.

91. Marianne Meye Thompson, nevertheless, thinks that Jesus doesn't appear when expected because he has no need of purification (*John: A Commentary*, NTL [Louisville: Westminster John Knox, 2015], 258).

## Conclusion

By the pool of Bethesda, Jesus shows himself to be a far more powerful cleansing and healing agent than the water, despite its use to turn the pool into a *mikveh* and as a location believed to produce more magical healings. The Fourth Evangelist, on the other hand, is more taken with the controversy that the incident generates because Jesus heals on a Sabbath. There is no possibility for ritual or any other kind of handwashing as Jesus multiplies the loaves and fishes in the wilderness to feed the five thousand, but that is of no concern to him. More importantly, he offers himself as the bread of life, which metaphorically satisfies people's hunger and thirst, the thirst being either a strange extension of a metaphor or a reminder of water and its purifying powers embedded deeply in the accounts of Jesus's public ministry.

In conjunction with the water-drawing rituals of the Feast of Tabernacles, Jesus offers rivers of living water related to the coming ministry of the Holy Spirit. He also identifies himself as the light of the world on the same day of that festival that a service of darkness was celebrated. He repeats the identification later, perhaps still at the Feast of Tabernacles or perhaps at the later Feast of Dedication, which was known as a small replica of Tabernacles. Powerfully illustrating that claim, he sends a man blind from birth to wash off the mudpack that Jesus put on his eyes, by immersing himself in another *mikveh*—the pool of Siloam. Again, it is not the cleansing but rather a Sabbath controversy that the Fourth Evangelist elaborates in detail. At the Feast of Dedication, Jesus identifies himself as the dedicated, sanctified one, even as the holiday commemorated the repurification of the temple in the days of the Maccabees. The resurrection of Lazarus involves an astonishing event that restores physical health and makes possible ritual purity again. This section of John ends with the Passover pilgrims questioning one another about whether Jesus will come at the time people arrived for their ritual purification. Jesus comes, but just a little later, apparently bypassing the expected process.

*Never are these references to purification John's major redactional emphases; always they appear in a place that contains greater claims to authenticity than other parts, at least by purely historical standards.* Even apart from Johannine redaction, the overall emphasis of the final form of the Gospel shows Jesus more concerned with physical healing and spiritual wholeness than with ritual purity. But the Mosaic law remains in force at least until his death and resurrection, and he has never disobeyed it thus far. Additional Pharisaic traditions are another matter, especially if they stand in the way of what he understands to be God's true will. Chapters 5–11, then, are not as immersed in purity issues, especially ritual purity issues, as chapters 1–4 are. But the issues do continue to appear, even as Jesus seems to be preparing his followers for the transition to the Spirit's ministry, in which spiritual cleansing will transform the Old Testament purity requirements. Will this trajectory of gradually moving away from a preoccupation with matters of literal, physical purification toward an emphasis on spiritual cleansing continue, as we proceed through the last ten chapters of the Fourth Gospel? Will there be a third discrete phase in Jesus's relationship with purity laws? Our next chapter addresses these questions.

# 9

# Ritual Purity Fades Away in John 12–21

The final week of Jesus's earthly life has begun. From here to the end of the Gospel of John appear the sizable majority of parallels to the Synoptics. All the canonical Gospel writers agree in giving the passion of Jesus a disproportionate amount of attention. The crucifixion, paradoxically, has become the most important event of Jesus's earthly life. Narrative time slows way down, nowhere in the Gospels more so than in this section of John. A week will be spread out over eight chapters (John 12–19). If ever the Fourth Evangelist presents historical information, it is here. The "new look on John" concurs that even several uniquely Johannine items are most likely accurate—for example, the Jews no longer having the right to execute their own criminals (18:31); Jesus's additional hearing before Annas, former high priest and father-in-law of Caiphas, the current high priest (18:13–14, 19–24); and the identification of Gabbatha, the stone pavement where Pilate sat on the judge's seat (19:13).[1]

---

1. James H. Charlesworth, *Jesus as Mirrored in John: The Genius in the New Testament* (London: Bloomsbury T&T Clark, 2019), 134, 138, 152. Cf. John A. T. Robinson, *The Priority of John*, ed. J. F. Coakley (London: SCM, 1985; Oak Park, IL: Meyer-Stone, 1987), 145–46, 267–68; Paul N. Anderson, *The Fourth Gospel and the Quest for Jesus: Modern Foundations Reconsidered* (London: T&T Clark, 2006), 84n49, 169. Donald Senior, casting his net more

The second half of this Gospel also concentrates more and more on John's key themes. John 12:44–50 reads like a digest of a number of those themes, in Jesus's final public summary of his message, as the Fourth Gospel has encapsulated it. Chapters 14–16 review and elaborate even more of them in his Upper Room Discourse with his disciples. Chapter 17 arranges many of them into what has come to be known as his "high priestly prayer." What role does purity play in these chapters? In chapters 12–13, it remains reasonably central; then it all but vanishes. When it does appear in chapters 14–21, it is clearly not a central emphasis. In each instance, a case can be made, nevertheless, that it is historically true to what happened. What Jesus will make clear is that the Spirit is soon to be poured out on his followers; in chapter 20, we will see the fulfillment of Jesus's repeated predictions of the Spirit's imminent arrival. Leading up to this event that marks the shift in the ages of God's working with humanity,[2] less and less about ritual cleansing appears, even in the background. When it does, it will each time emerge that Jesus is interested in spiritual sanctification instead.

## Preparation for Burial (John 12:1–11)

Jesus has not come to the temple or its immediate environs for the prescribed immersion in water one week before the Passover (see above, 288). Nor does the Fourth Gospel (or any other Gospel) ever hint that he purified himself on any other day leading up to the feast. What Mary of Bethany offers him, nevertheless, can be viewed as a kind of purification ceremony.[3] "Six days before the Passover" (v. 1a) could be taken as equivalent to about a week; as so often elsewhere John is more precise in his chronology than the Synoptics are. Mark and Matthew have inserted their account of this incident into their narration of events immediately

---

widely to include events leading up to the passion narrative, adds several other items ("History and Theology in the Johannine Presentation of the Causes for the Death of Jesus: John 11:45–53 as Convergence Point," in *John, Jesus, and History*, ed. Paul N. Anderson, Felix Just, and Tom Thatcher, 3 vols. (Atlanta: Society of Biblical Literature, 2007–16), 3:43–58.

2. See Craig L. Blomberg, *A New Testament Theology* (Waco: Baylor University Press, 2018), 623–37, and the literature there cited.

3. B. F. Westcott calls it "symbolic of consecration to a divine work" (*The Gospel according to St. John* [London: John Murray, 1881], 177).

leading up to Thursday night and the Passover meal, no doubt for topical or thematic reasons.[4] Luke's account of a very different woman at a very different time and place in Jesus's ministry anointing him is almost certainly a separate event altogether.[5] The only really unusual feature that the two stories have in common is that the jar containing the perfume was made of alabaster (Mark 14:3 par.; Luke 7:37). Once one learns that this was recommended as the best container for perfume (Pliny, *Nat. hist.* 13.3.19), however, the strangeness disappears. The differences between John's story and the one in Matthew and Mark, on the other hand, are comparatively minor and can be explained without having to postulate two different "anointings" during the last week of Jesus's life.[6]

Jesus returns to the home of his friends Lazarus, Mary, and Martha (vv. 1b–3). On the heels of the spectacular miracle of chapter 11, it seems odd to be told again that Lazarus was the one "whom Jesus had raised from the dead," unless the narrator simply wants to stress the amazing event even more. It may also foreshadow the notice that not just Jesus's but also Lazarus's life was in danger (12:10). The woman who lavishes her perfume on Jesus in Mark's and Matthew's accounts remains unnamed; here we are told it was Mary. The respective roles of the two sisters are consistent, interestingly, with what we learn of them in Luke 10:38–42, suggesting a form of multiple attestation of concepts in otherwise independent narratives.[7]

Marianne Meye Thompson stresses that this is not an "anointing" scene, strictly speaking. "Here Mary rubs or smears (*ēleipsen*) Jesus's feet with perfume; she does not anoint (*echrisen*) his head with

---

4. For more detail, see William L. Lane, *The Gospel according to Mark: The English Text with Introduction, Exposition, and Notes*, NICNT (Grand Rapids: Eerdmans, 1974; London: Marshall, Morgan & Scott, 1975), 491–92.

5. The critical consensus differs, but an ever-growing minority voice agrees. See the evenhanded discussion and conclusions in Craig S. Keener, *The Gospel of John: A Commentary*, 2 vols. (Peabody, MA: Hendrickson, 2003), 2:859–61.

6. They may, however, be literarily independent of each other and perhaps even reflect the influence of social memory. See Holly E. Hearon, "The Story of 'the Woman Who Anointed Jesus' as Social Memory: A Methodological Proposal for the Study of Tradition as Memory," in *Memory, Tradition, and Text: Uses of the Past in Early Christianity*, ed. Alan Kirk and Tom Thatcher (Atlanta: Society of Biblical Literature, 2005), 99–118. Hearon, however, accounts for Luke's differences the same way.

7. The lack of any verbal parallelism makes theories of John's use of Luke (or vice versa) highly speculative.

oil as one would do for a king."⁸ *Prophets, priests, and kings were anointed before or at the onset of their official service. Corpses were not anointed but rather scented with spices to temporarily mask the smell of their putrefaction. Jesus interprets Mary's lavish devotion as preparation for the day of his burial (v. 7). John views Jesus as a king, especially in his passion narrative,*⁹ *so he may see it as an ironic kind of anointing as well, but this goes beyond the historical Jesus's understanding here.* The view suggested recently that the anointing preserves portions of a funeral banquet for Lazarus, disclosing a ritual of death and mourning continued in the Johannine community, seems much less likely.¹⁰

One certainly can view Mary's action as a kind of ceremonial or symbolic cleansing, proleptically applied to Jesus's body. This is even more the case if Matthew and Mark's account of the jar of perfume being poured over his *head* is accurate. The amount of ointment could easily have flowed down to his feet, or Mary could have applied it to both or several parts of his body to simulate something closer to immersion.¹¹ It is also intriguing that John describes the nard as *pistikē*, which most likely means "pure" in verse 3.¹² In any case, what John describes is the most realistic scene, since those who reclined at table had their feet extended away from the table on the cushions on which they stretched out. The feet, then, would have been the most accessible part of the body to anyone approaching the banqueters from behind. In fact, J. F. Coakley has shown that John's account preserves numerous indications of historical priority, including at this point the somewhat scandalous perfuming of Jesus's feet.¹³ Esther Miquel argues for the authenticity of the core of the passage common to all versions based

---

8. Marianne Meye Thompson, *John: A Commentary*, NTL (Louisville: Westminster John Knox, 2015), 260.

9. See Blomberg, *New Testament Theology*, 597–600, and the literature there cited.

10. Maria Estela Aldave Medrano, "La resurrección de Lázaro y la unción en Betanía (Jn 11,1–12,11) a la luz del ritual de duelo de la antigüedad," *EstBíb* 76 (2018): 221–43.

11. See D. A. Carson, *The Gospel according to John*, PNTC (Leicester: Apollos; Grand Rapids: Eerdmans, 1991), 426–27.

12. Herman Ridderbos, *The Gospel according to John: A Theological Commentary*, trans. John Vriend (Grand Rapids: Eerdmans, 1997), 414n108.

13. J. F. Coakley, "The Anointing at Bethany and the Priority of John," *JBL* 107 (1988): 241–56. See also Edward W. Klink III, *John*, ZECNT (Grand Rapids: Zondervan, 2016), 526.

on both the criteria of embarrassment and of contextual plausibility (in the Passover setting).[14]

John's own emphases continue to lie elsewhere. Clearly, he stresses again the number of people who were coming to faith in Jesus, still influenced by the reports of Lazarus's resurrection (vv. 9–11). He also identifies the prime objector to Mary's behavior as Judas Iscariot, noting that his complaint was disingenuous. He did not really care about the poor, but only about how much he could pilfer from the group's moneybag. These details are unique to John's account, whereas Jesus's reply to the objection mostly matches what the Synoptics contain. Mary and Judas, in fact, may have been the first to fully believe that Jesus really was going to die rather than lead a rebellion against the Romans, but they reacted in diametrically opposite ways.[15]

Might John see the pouring of the perfume over Jesus as a substitute ritual purification, since he did not appear in Jerusalem in time for the prescribed one? If so, we would need more than the juxtaposition of the two passages (11:55–57; 12:1–11) to know this, since putting them back to back could also be intended to heighten the *contrast* between the two. On this view, Jesus didn't get the proper purification, and then he got a very improper one. At any rate, in viewing Mary's actions as preparation for his burial, it would seem that Jesus is moving away from thinking about purity. They will not always have him (v. 8) because he is about to die, and perfuming a dead body does not purify it. It merely covers over the decay for a short while.[16] It does, however, show Mary's great affection and loyalty.

The events of "Palm Sunday," perhaps spanning the rest of the chapter (and it is only John who introduces us to the palm branches [12:13]), temporarily delay the road to the cross and Jesus's death, while highlighting the kingship of Jesus, in which John *is* interested.

14. Esther Miquel, "Historicidad en los relatos evangélicos de las unciones de Jesús: Semejanzas entre la praxis de Jesús y la de algunos grupos filosóficos contraculturales de la época helenístico-romana," *EstBíb* 62 (2004): 3–26.
15. Frank Stagg, "Matthew," in *The Broadman Bible Commentary*, ed. Clifton J. Allen, vol. 8 (Nashville: Broadman, 1969), 231.
16. On the role of olfaction in the passage, with one scent masking another, see Dominika A. Kurek-Chomycz, "The Fragrance of Her Perfume: The Significance of Sense Imagery in John's Account of the Anointing in Bethany," *NovT* 52 (2010): 334–54.

But the delay proves quite temporary, and soon Jesus is predicting his death again (vv. 20–36). Whatever the precise context of this pericope and the next ones (vv. 37–43, 44–50),[17] we soon arrive at Passover itself, although exactly when John envisions this Passover beginning is a matter of considerable debate.

### Footwashing (John 13:1–17)

"It was just before the Passover Festival" (John 13:1a). This introduction sounds so innocuous and straightforward. Who would have imagined how much controversy this verse, along with others tied into it in various ways, could spawn? The NIV, NET, and CJB use the word "just" to convey the nearness of the celebration, though no separate Greek word modifies *pro* ("before"). But we already knew that it was no more than six days before the Passover (12:1), so a word in a translation that suggests we are closer still seems appropriate. The more significant but stranger part of 13:1 is what follows: "Jesus knew that the hour had come for him to leave this world and go to the Father. Having loved his own who were in the world, he loved them to the end." After John's several references to Jesus's hour not yet having come (2:4; 7:30; 8:20), at last it has arrived. Jesus's leaving the world and returning to his Father clearly refer to his death. Apparently, that is what the next sentence means as well: during his lifetime he exhibited love for his followers in all manner of ways; now he does not shirk from the hardest part of his ministry but determines to see it through to the end.[18] The Greek, however, is one long, cumbersome sentence, as reflected, for example, in the NASB: "Now before the Feast of the Passover, Jesus, knowing that His hour had come that He would depart from this world to the Father, having loved His own who were in the world, He loved them to the end." One prepositional phrase and two participial clauses precede

---

17. Verses 44–50 in particular may be more an epitome of Jesus's teaching phrased in the Fourth Evangelist's own terminology. See, e.g., Leon Morris, *The Gospel according to John*, rev. ed., NICNT (Grand Rapids: Eerdmans, 1995), 539.

18. George R. Beasley-Murray nicely ties this full extent of Jesus's love into all the various reasons given in the Gospel for the arrival of Jesus's "hour" (*John*, 2nd ed., WBC [Nashville: Nelson, 1999], 232–33).

the main clause, which is withheld until the very end of the sentence. Even in Greek this would be extraordinary for the opening sentence of a paragraph or single unit of thought in an otherwise reasonably straightforward biographical narrative. But it would make sense as a short paragraph in itself, introducing not just the very next events but a longer stretch of text (cf. NIV, NJB, REB). In other words, Jesus's love will not be demonstrated merely in the upcoming footwashing (vv. 2–17) but in everything that will culminate in his death.[19]

All this proves significant as we try to determine what meal John refers to in verse 2. If verse 1 merely introduces the footwashing, then the dinner in verse 2 presumably also precedes the Passover. But if verse 1 forms a headline over all of chapters 13–19, then what happened "just before" the Passover was Jesus's decision to see things through. We cannot assume, then, that the meal in verse 2 is separate from the Passover meal that marks the start of the celebration that Thursday night. How do we decide? Several more texts come into play in chapters 18–19, but we will deal with those when we come to them. After all, the original audiences of the Fourth Gospel, hearing it read, have only what has been narrated thus far on which to base a decision, along with whatever they already knew of the main contours of the gospel story.

The next independent clause is more contorted than the last one. Again the NASB well represents it in English: "During supper, the devil having already put into the heart of Judas Iscariot, the son of Simon, to betray Him, Jesus, knowing that the Father had given all things into His hands, and that He had come forth from God and was going back to God, got up from supper, and laid aside His garments; and taking a towel, He girded Himself" (vv. 2–4; italics omitted). The backbone of this sentence is that Jesus got up, laid aside, and girded. John is introducing the footwashing scene that proceeds immediately. Subordinate to this is the observation that the evening meal had come (*deipnou ginomenou*). *Deipnon* can be translated as "supper" or "dinner," but these two English words refer to the different sizes and times

---

19. Ridderbos, *Gospel according to John*, 452; William K. Grossouw, "A Note on John XIII 1–3," *NovT* 8 (1966): 124–31.

of meals and vary regionally. In Greek, though, the *deipnon* is the main meal of the day, in the evening. In appropriate contexts, it can even be translated as "banquet."[20] The Greek participial clause utilizes a genitive absolute with the verb *ginomai*, typically meaning something more akin to "become" than just to "be." Significant external evidence appears for the aorist form *genomenou* rather than the internally more probable present tense.[21] The aorist is the easier reading, so not as likely to be original, but it is probably also the earliest commentary on what John meant. We could readily render it, "when the evening meal came." *But which evening meal is that? There is only one in the context, and it has just been mentioned (in v. 1): the kickoff meal of the Passover celebration.*[22]

For any in the audience who already knew from Synoptic-like tradition that Jesus predicted Judas's betrayal at this very meal, *the fact that John precedes the account of the footwashing with this ominous notice of Judas's decision (v. 2) will further reinforce the suspicion that it is the Passover festival that has now begun.* Verses 21–30 will confirm this suspicion in considerable detail. Why tell us now already? The notice certainly gives greater poignancy to the fact that Jesus washes all his disciples' feet, including those of the man who that very night will betray him (18:1–5).[23]

The footwashing "ceremony" proceeds apace (vv. 5–15). At a meal already laden with symbolism going back to the time of the exodus, one should hardly be surprised that Jesus adds more. The Synoptics, of course, narrate Jesus's words about the bread and the cup, which have become immortalized in the celebration of the Lord's Supper by almost all Christian denominations and groups. Just as John provided

---

20. See BDAG, s.v. *deipnon*.

21. Morris, *Gospel according to John*, 546n10, although he thinks that the aorist form means that the footwashing took place after the meal, while acknowledging that it wouldn't have to imply this.

22. Ridderbos, *Gospel according to John*, 455; Karl T. Kleinknecht, "Johannes 13, die Synoptiker und die 'Methode' der johanneischen Evangelienüberlieferung," *ZTK* 82 (1985): 370–71; Gary M. Burge, *John*, NIVAC (Grand Rapids: Zondervan, 2000), 365–67.

23. J. Ramsey Michaels adds that the sense of Judas's role being predetermined (or at least already decided) is also heightened (*The Gospel of John*, NICNT [Grand Rapids: Eerdmans, 2010], 723–24).

more information about what happened immediately surrounding Jesus's baptism than the Synoptics did, yet without ever mentioning the baptism itself, so too John gives far more information about the details of this last supper (chaps. 13–17), yet without ever including what have come to be known as the "words of institution" of the Lord's Supper.

As we noted in discussing the ministry of John the Baptist (see 235–36), these phenomena have led numerous scholars to speak of an antisacramental, or at least nonsacramental, tendency on the part of the Fourth Gospel. Others have demurred, with some finding John even more sacramental, but in an incarnational sense in which John's Jesus sacralizes all human life by becoming human himself.[24] This, however, utilizes a broader definition of "sacramental," so the two views may not be as contradictory as they might at first seem. It would seem strange, nevertheless, if John saw the literal washing of fellow believers' feet as a liturgical act that should be incorporated into the regular worship of God's people.[25] Even Jesus's own baptismal ministry has faded from view, and an appeal to John 6:51–59 as referring to the Lord's Supper founders on at least two counts: (1) no one in Jesus's original audience could have understood it that way, since the Bread of Life Discourse substantially preceded Jesus's final week and Passover celebration; (2) it would require a sacramental regeneration view (i.e., requiring the Eucharist for salvation [see 6:53]), which would contradict John's dominant perspective of salvation by faith.[26]

None of this implies, however, that the footwashing scene was not charged with profound and powerful symbolism. Jesus uses language common to other ritual immersions for both washing (*niptō* [vv. 5, 6, 8, 10, 12]) and cleanliness (*katharos* [v. 10]). Churches that still practice literal footwashing can similarly provide their congregants with a very meaningful ritual. But those that do not have such a practice

---

24. See R. Wade Paschal, "Sacramental Symbolism and Physical Imagery in the Gospel of John," *TynBul* 32 (1981): 151–76.

25. Cornelis Bennema shows a pattern in John that focuses more on faithful expression than on exact replication ("Mimesis in John 13: Cloning or Creative Articulation?," *NovT* 56 [2014]: 261–74).

26. Faith in the Johannine literature must lead to abiding in love and keeping God's commandments, but never to the enactment of a specific ritual or ceremony on which salvation depends. See further Blomberg, *New Testament Theology*, 644–48, and the literature there cited.

aren't thereby deficient in some way. What, then, is Jesus doing in John 13? *At the very least, he is playing the part of the most menial of servants in a world where footwashing involved the removal of far more than just dirt.* Whether barefoot or wearing sandals, those who walked out of doors, especially in towns and cities, regularly had to step in or be splattered by garbage and sewage, including animal and human refuse, especially when a trough in the middle (or by the sides) of various streets or roads functioned as a drainage ditch. It was not only a filthy responsibility to clean someone else's feet; it was highly degrading in a culture of honor and shame. One of the marks of status was that people could rely on others to clean their feet for them. Even those without high status could expect at least not to have to clean anyone else's feet unless their social rank was the lowest in a specific gathering. For Jesus, the master and Lord, to wash his disciples' feet was not only disgusting but also dishonoring. John Christopher Thomas has studied the background literature extensively and finds no comparable account of such inversion of roles anywhere.[27] J. Ramsey Michaels calls Jesus's behavior "as remarkable for its role reversal as Mary's was for its extravagance."[28] Little wonder that Peter at first recoils from the thought! We are also reminded of Mary's wiping Jesus's feet with perfume earlier in the week (12:3),[29] though at that meal all the participants probably had already had their feet washed.

The detail given in verse 5 at first seems surprising in an otherwise brief narrative, but it is there probably just to indicate how Jesus was able to wash and then dry each person's feet one at a time. By taking off his outer garment, he kept it clean and freed up his arms and legs for his activity. By wrapping the towel around him, he kept both hands free for the washing.[30] In a setting without running water, all water needed to be used sparingly. This water would have best been

---

27. "This account of a superior voluntarily washing the feet of an inferior is without parallel in antiquity" (John Christopher Thomas, *Footwashing in John 13 and the Johannine Community* [Sheffield: JSOT Press, 1991], 187).

28. Michaels, *Gospel of John*, 725.

29. Jey J. Kanagaraj, *John*, NCCS (Eugene, OR: Cascade Books, 2013), 136.

30. Keener, *Gospel of John*, 2:908.

conserved by pouring small amounts of it over a person's feet from one container and catching the runoff in the basin below for use with the next person.[31]

Peter apparently is not the first disciple Jesus approaches with the basin and water (cf. v. 5 with v. 6). Has no one else objected? Why does Peter speak up? Given that this chapter goes on to record Jesus's prediction of Peter's denial (vv. 31–38), it is easy then to turn back and imagine that Peter is having second thoughts already about his association with this would-be Messiah, who is doing everything in the wrong way, or so he may have thought.[32] The prediction of the denial, we should add, is another link with the Synoptic Passover meal. If it weren't for the ambiguity in the relationship between verses 1–2, *everything else in chapter 13*—the footwashing, the prediction of Judas's betrayal, and the prediction of Peter's denial, including the influence of the latter two over the footwashing—*points to this being the same meal as depicted in Matthew, Mark, and Luke*. If one then asks where the footwashing would fit into the Synoptic narrative, the natural answer would be as a preparatory purification ritual prior to the meal itself. This is where it makes a difference whether we understand *deipnou ginomenou* as "while the meal was in progress" or "when they were ready for the meal to begin," though it is not impossible to imagine Jesus washing the feet of the Twelve even as things were getting underway.

Jesus's first recorded response to Peter's objection is that Peter does not yet understand what is happening (v. 7). Do we even today? After Peter emphatically insists that Jesus will never (*ou mē . . . eis ton aiōna*; colloquially, "no way into eternity") wash his feet (v. 8a), Jesus replies that unless he does wash Peter, Peter has no part with him (v. 8b). Ever impulsive, Peter now swings the pendulum to the opposite end of the spectrum and begs for considerably more of his body to be washed (v. 9)! If he remembers Jesus's baptizing ministry as one of either immersion or affusion, he may be thinking of something similar here.[33]

---

31. Morris, *Gospel according to John*, 547n19.
32. Peter's protest and Jesus's rebuke are remarkably like Mark 8:32–33, and both passages relate to Peter's inability to grasp the need for Jesus's death. See Beasley-Murray, *John*, 233.
33. Beasley-Murray (*John*, 234–35) documents the frequency of a baptismal interpretation in the early church.

But Jesus tells him that one whole-body ritual bath is enough (v. 10a). Just as people who have bathed before leaving their home to visit a neighbor normally need only to have their feet washed upon arrival, so in the spiritual realm one initial full cleansing (from the verb *louō*) is enough. After that, only partial "toppings up" are required.[34] Specifically, per the comprehensive study by Bincy Mathew, *louō* "stands for the disciples' reception of Jesus' revelatory and cleansing words and works," while *niptō* "explicates Jesus' perfect love as manifested in the footwashing, which symbolically prefigures his death on the cross."[35]

We do not need to settle the debate about whether Jesus himself has baptism in mind here, though it is certainly understandable how he might. The point is that he refocuses attention away from anything that might be considered a rebaptism, either literally or metaphorically. *Ceremonial purification certainly lurks in the background of the conversation's imagery, but Jesus is trying to point Peter in a different direction. By returning to the fact that one of the disciples is not at all clean (vv. 10b–11), he moves away from the features of the literal washing to concentrate on the spiritual realities that they are intended to symbolize.*[36] There is no attack on baptism as in the partial parallel in Papyrus Oxyrhynchus 840, which may reflect the perspective of the Naassene Gnostic sect. At most, the footwashing may have communicated a form of priestly ordination or commissioning that Jesus conferred on his disciples.[37]

34. Michaels, *Gospel of John*, 732. Klink (*John*, 581) explains, "Peter is already completely clean. Footwashing symbolizes subsequent consecration to a particular task, service to God, as his disciples." See also René Kieffer, "L'arrière-fond juif du lavement des pieds," *RB* 105 (1998): 546–55.

35. Bincy Mathew, *The Johannine Footwashing as the Sign of Perfect Love: An Exegetical Study of John 13:1–20* (Tübingen: Mohr Siebeck, 2018), 418.

36. Andrew T. Lincoln speaks of how the passage fits both "ritual purification" and "ordinary life" (*The Gospel according to Saint John*, BNTC [London: Continuum; Peabody, MA: Hendrickson, 2005], 370). Carson (*Gospel according to John*, 458) calls the footwashing "symbolic of spiritual cleansing" and "a standard of humble service." Even Francis J. Moloney, as a Catholic, explains that the author "is not concerned with the rite"; rather, "to 'have part with Jesus' through washing means to be part of the self-giving love that will bring Jesus' life to an end (cf. v. 1), symbolically anticipated by the footwashing (v. 8)" (*The Gospel of John*, SP [Collegeville, MN: Liturgical Press, 1998], 375).

37. For both of these last two points, see David Tripp, "Meanings of the Foot-Washing: John 13 and Oxyrhynchus Papyrus 840," *ExpTim* 103 (1992): 237–39.

Verses 12–15 now spell things out. After asking rhetorically if his disciples now understand (v. 12)—but how could they?—he answers his own question. *Verses 13–15 intertwine two main points that have given rise to two different interpretations, one that focuses on the disciples imitating Jesus in acts of lowly service for others, and one that highlights Jesus's nature as Suffering Servant on the eve of his execution.* Tradition critics have tried to dissect the passage to recover one or the other of these rationales in its "pure" form,[38] but it is not at all clear why the two must be seen as in tension with each other. *Understanding accurately who Jesus is and what he does should lead to proper imitation of that which his disciples are able to implement.* Of course, they cannot die for the sins of the world, but they can die to self and put others and their needs above their own, with no act of service too menial to be undertaken.[39]

Verses 16–17 could be a pair of loosely associated sayings, but they are better kept with the footwashing as Jesus's conclusion to his reflections on its meaning. The proverbial saying "no servant is greater than his master" (v. 16) was used in a variety of contexts in the ancient world; John's Jesus himself uses it differently elsewhere (15:20). Here the point is that if even the master, Jesus, so demeaned himself as to wash his followers' feet, those followers cannot excuse themselves from similarly degrading ministry because they are somehow better than or above Jesus. Instead, Jesus promises them a blessing for imitating his model (v. 17).[40] Verses 18–20 may go syntactically more with verses 12–17, but conceptually they now focus entirely on Judas's coming betrayal, so they need not detain us here.

Washing, cleansing, purity, ritual, and symbolism, along with commands to repeat and imitate all this behavior, feature prominently in the footwashing. It will be the last such episode in John's Gospel. It is harder here than in most parts of the Fourth Gospel to separate tradition from redaction, core historical events from possible theological overlay,

---

38. See esp. Fernando F. Segovia, "John 13 1–20, the Footwashing in the Johannine Tradition," *ZNW* 73 (1982): 31–51.

39. Indeed, Herold Weiss thinks that the disciples are thus being called to possible martyrdom along with Jesus ("Foot Washing in the Johannine Community," *NovT* 21 [1979]: 298–325).

40. "In short, to understand *and* to do service exemplified by Jesus is to experience the goodness of God, even more, the grace of God" (Klink, *John*, 586).

although we do see reference to Jesus's hour, coming from and going to God, the depth of his love, and his sovereign authority. Of course, in the rest of chapter 13, on the betrayal and denial, one can compare parallel accounts in the Synoptics and observe Johannine omissions and additions. Even then, they do not lead to as many distinctives as elsewhere. These disciples' behavior was sufficiently ignominious that the narratives are unlikely to have been invented. Jesus's washing of his disciples' feet was likewise too awkward and even embarrassing to have been made up.[41] As long as the laws of ceremonial cleanliness were still in force, Jesus's behavior was thoroughly understandable, even if utterly unexpected. But his concern was to give them a powerful object lesson that they could apply in the ethical realm well after issues of ritual purity were moot.[42]

An elaborate and almost complete chiasm appears in verses 1–15 (see fig. 1).[43] Whatever we make of the second reference to the betrayal destroying the otherwise perfect symmetry,[44] *labeling verse 8b as the climactic center seems justified.* It is a conditional sentence with *ean mē* in the protasis (the "if" or "unless" clause) as a requirement for salvation, just like John 3:3–5. If there is a historical core to the passage in 13:1–17 around which everything else has been built, it would be verse 8b: "Unless I wash you, you have no part with me." Even the metaphorical use of water appears in both texts. But tradition-critical dissection may be unnecessary.[45] And the emphasis on keeping Christ's

---

41. Stanley E. Porter, *John, His Gospel, and Jesus: In Pursuit of the Johannine Voice* (Grand Rapids: Eerdmans, 2015), 87.

42. See esp. Jaime Clark-Soles, "Of Footwashing and History," in Anderson, Just, and Thatcher, *John, Jesus, and History*, 2:255–69. She concludes that "the Johannine Jesus, who is a Jewish Jesus, far from abolishing purity acts that draw social boundaries, might be seen to enact and transform them" (268). My only caveat is that this was not a religious ritual being transformed but an ordinary social act of hospitality. See esp. Arland J. Hultgren, "The Johannine Footwashing (13.1–11) as Symbol of Eschatological Hospitality," *NTS* 28 (1982): 539–46. On the theological trajectory moving away from the cultic, see esp. James D. G. Dunn, "The Washing of the Disciples' Feet in John 13 1–20," *ZNW* 61 (1970): 247–52.

43. For the core of this chiasm, see Michal Wojciechowski, "La source de Jean 13.1–20," *NTS* 34 (1988): 135–41.

44. Such disruptions in an otherwise sufficiently clear pattern could also call attention to themselves. This would be appropriate in light of a potentially chiastic structure of the entire chapter centered on Judas's treachery as depicted in verses 16–20, 21–30, according to Mary L. Coloe, "Welcome into the Household of God: The Foot Washing in John 13," *CBQ* 66 (2004): 400–415.

45. John W. Pryor, *John, Evangelist of the Covenant People: The Narrative and Themes of the Fourth Gospel* (London: Darton, Longman & Todd; Downers Grove, IL: InterVarsity, 1992), 60.

**Fig. 1. Chiasm in John 13:1–15**

love (v. 1)
  Judas's coming betrayal (v. 2)
    Jesus's awareness of his role (v. 3)
      getting up from the meal (v. 4a)
        taking off his garment (v. 4b)
          beginning the footwashing (v. 5)
            Simon Peter's protest and correction (vv. 6–8a)
              must be cleaned to be in Jesus (v. 8b)
            Simon Peter's protest and correction (vv. 9–10)
  Judas's coming betrayal (v. 11)
          finishing the footwashing (v. 12a)
        putting on his garment (v. 12b)
      returning to the meal (v. 12c)
    Jesus's awareness of his role (vv. 13–14)
love by example (v. 15)*

\* No actual word for "love" appears here, but see the exegesis that takes it in precisely that fashion by Jan van der Watt, "The Meaning of Jesus Washing the Feet of His Disciples (John 13)," *Neot* 51 (2017): 25-39. For a similar and complementary chiasm in verses 4–11, see Frédéric Manns, "Le lavement des pieds: Essai sur la structure et la signification de Jean 13," *RSR* 55 (1981): 149-69, esp. 153-54.

commandments in all of chapters 13–17 is just one way in which John, even though he narrates many different aspects of Jesus's last night on earth, agrees with the Synoptics that this is no mere final supper but a covenant meal.[46] In terms of genre, Eve-Marie Becker refers to John 13 as "exemplary history" as over against the "institutional history" of the Synoptic accounts of the night of the Last Supper.[47] But again the two complement rather than contradict each other.

## Pruning the Vine's Branches (John 15:2)

The next section of John's Gospel spans chapters 14–16, presenting Jesus's Farewell Discourse. There is only one direct reference to purity or cleansing in all three chapters, and it seems to appear in passing in

---

46. Cf. Seung-In Song, "Seeing the Johannine Last Meal as a Covenant Meal (John 13 and Exodus 24)," *Bib* 100 (2019): 282–92.

47. Eve-Marie Becker, "John 13 as Counter-Memory: How the Fourth Gospel Revises Early Christian Historiography," in *The Gospel of John as Genre Mosaic*, ed. Kasper Bro Larsen (Göttingen: Vandenhoeck & Ruprecht, 2015), 269–81.

15:2. One might imagine that its treatment would be equally brief. But things are not quite this simple. One part of this unexpected complexity involves the meaning of the metaphor in this context; another has to do with its location. We will begin with the second of these issues.

The structure and composition of these three chapters has been almost endlessly debated.[48] Jesus circles back around through several key topics: going to the Father, sending the Holy Spirit, abiding in the vine, manifesting love and keeping Christ's commandments, experiencing the hatred and hostility of the world, and grief turning to joy. Questions from the disciples punctuate his address, but his replies vary in how directly they answer those questions. On top of that, 14:31 sounds like Jesus's closing words ("Come now; let us leave"). Yet 15:1 immediately continues his discourse, and no mention is made of anyone's departure until 18:1. The most popular critical theory has been to divide chapters 14–16 into at least two separate messages (chaps. 14 and 15–16) and postulate some process by which the two were brought together in either John's redaction or the traditions he inherited.[49]

Several studies, nevertheless, have more recently called this hypothesis into serious question. George Parsenios argues that chapters 15–16 follow the existing literary and rhetorical form of a "delayed exit," to emphasize Jesus's teaching here.[50] Stylistic and structural features further unite all three chapters,[51] while it is even possible to outline them according to the conventional subdivisions of Greco-Roman rhetoric.[52] *Perhaps the best proposal for identifying the structure of John 14–16 is again to see a chiasmus.* Wayne Brouwer has surveyed previous attempts

---

48. Compare and contrast John Painter, "The Farewell Discourse and the History of Johannine Christianity," *NTS* 27 (1981): 525–43; Udo Schnelle, "Die Abschiedsreden im Johannesevangelium," *ZNW* 80 (1989): 64–79; Christian Dietzfelbinger, *Der Abschied des Kommenden: Eine Auslegung der johanneischen Abschiedsreden* (Tübingen: Mohr Siebeck, 1997).

49. Fernando F. Segovia, *The Farewell of the Word: The Johannine Call to Abide* (Minneapolis: Fortress, 1991).

50. George L. Parsenios, *Departure and Consolation: The Johannine Farewell Discourses in Light of Greco-Roman Literature* (Leiden: Brill, 2005), 49–76.

51. L. Scott Kellum, *The Unity of the Farewell Discourse: The Literary Integrity of John 13.31–16.33* (London: T&T Clark, 2004).

52. John C. Stube, *A Graeco-Roman Rhetorical Reading of the Farewell Discourse* (London: T&T Clark, 2006).

and offers a reasonably persuasive model himself,[53] though it may be a bit too ambitious. Elsewhere I have made the following observations on the most compelling parts of a potentially chiastic structure and will summarize them here.

To begin with, 14:1 and 16:33 create a nice inclusio around the discourse. Disciples should not be troubled; Christ will provide the peace despite the "trouble" that the world will bring. Second, 14:2–31 introduces several themes that 16:5–33 will recapitulate. In 14:5, disciples ask where Jesus is going, but not in 16:5, when it would be more appropriate. Chapter 14:14 and 16:23–24 both deal with asking the Father for things in Jesus's name. The ministry of the Paraclete as over against the world appears in both 14:16–18 and 16:8–11. And Jesus's prediction that in a little while the disciples will not see him but then again in a little while longer they will see him recurs in 14:19–20 and 16:16–19. Third, in between these two large framing sections, 15:1–17 and 15:18–16:4 contrast the love Jesus has for his disciples with the hatred the world will have for them. Fourth, one could also divide 15:1–17 into two discrete sections: verses 1–8, on those who remain in Jesus, followed by verses 9–17, on the greatness of self-sacrificial love. Fifth, one could then see 15:1–8 and 15:18–16:4 as contrasting those who are attached to Jesus with those who are not, with the climactic center of the entire discourse coming in 15:9–17, on Christ's and the disciples' love.[54] Most commentators would agree that this is the theological heart of the discourse whether or not they see any inverse parallelism framing it, so it should cause little controversy to declare part or all of 15:1–17 as the center and climax of Jesus's teaching here.[55]

*All this places the metaphor of the vine and the branches*[56] *at a very strategic location in the discourse, introducing or immediately*

---

53. Wayne Brouwer, *The Literary Development of John 13–17: A Chiastic Reading* (Atlanta: Society of Biblical Literature, 2000).

54. Craig L. Blomberg, *The Historical Reliability of John's Gospel: Issues and Commentary* (Downers Grove, IL: IVP Academic, 2001), 19.

55. See Ridderbos, *Gospel according to John*, 522, who expands his scope to the entire New Testament. See also Fernando F. Segovia, *Love Relationships in the Johannine Tradition: Agapē/Agapan in 1 John and the Fourth Gospel* (Chico, CA: Scholars Press, 1982).

56. Or, if we follow Chrys C. Caragounis, "the vineyard and the vine" ("Vine, Vineyard, Israel, and Jesus," *SEÅ* 65 [2000]: 201–14).

*leading up to Jesus's teaching on love.* It is only by remaining in him that they can produce the desired fruit (vv. 4–8), fruit that produces and is motivated by love (vv. 16–17). Here the classic tension between divine sovereignty and human responsibility appears in its starkest form. Disciples did not choose Jesus; he chose them. But they must remain in him lest they be cut off, thrown out, and burned (vv. 2a, 6). The Johannine literature will resolve this tension, at least to a degree, by denying that those who completely leave Jesus were ever true disciples at all (1 John 2:19).[57] Here, though, Jesus is not solving theological conundrums; rather, he is issuing firm but loving commands.

It is not just unbelievers, though, who face pain or hardship. "Every branch that does bear fruit he prunes so that it will be even more fruitful" (v. 2b). Plants of various kinds require periodic pruning, in which excess or extraneous growth is trimmed off, so that water, sap, nutrients, and whatever else may be needed to bear good fruit is channeled in the directions most likely to produce it and not diverted to keeping alive unproductive or non-fruit-bearing parts of the plant.[58] The process involves the destruction of the parts of least value for the sake of the growth of the whole. When applied to the disciples in this context, the meaning is obvious: *they are not exempt from hardship or hostility, but God uses these difficulties to strengthen his true followers.*

The verb usually translated as "prune" in verse 2 (*kathairō*) most commonly means "clean" or "cleanse."[59] We have already seen it and its cognates in contexts of purification, including ritual purification. One recalls the logic of Jesus's teaching about the footwashing in chapter 13. Once one has bathed and is fully cleansed, washing one's feet is all that is needed. Once one is securely attached to the vine, one needs only periodic pruning.[60] In Greek, Jesus's teaching creates a nice play on words

---

57. For complete detail, see D. A. Carson, *Divine Sovereignty and Human Responsibility: Biblical Perspectives in Tension* (London: Marshall, Morgan & Scott; Atlanta: John Knox, 1979; repr., Eugene, OR: Wipf & Stock, 2002), 125–98.

58. "Everything is removed from the branch that tends to divert the vital power from the production of fruit" (Westcott, *Gospel according to St. John*, 217).

59. BDAG, s.v. *kathairō*.

60. Keener, *Gospel of John*, 2:996. Michaels (*Gospel of John*, 803) observes that it is now even clearer that they are clean not because of baptism but because of the word—the preached message of Jesus.

as well. The completely unproductive branch is cut off (from *airō*); the productive one must be trimmed back (from *kathairō*).[61] In fact, there is extended alliteration with the words for "branch" (*klēma*) and "fruit" (*karpon*) also starting with a *kappa* and producing a "k" sound.[62]

It is easy to forget that a vine and its branches form a collective metaphor. The word picture is not primarily about individual or personal connection with Jesus but about communal holiness and corporate solidarity. Musa Kunene unpacks this concept in detail and points out that "in the pruning image is embedded every care that the Father gives to his new covenant people including forgiveness, cleansing, assuring, blessing, sanctification, and the joy of answered prayer."[63] Pruning is not to be viewed as punitive; indeed, it is not pruning that hurts the branches in the long term. "The word of God replaces Jewish rituals of cleansing so that the new people of God are cleansed by no other means than by Jesus and his word."[64]

Occasionally, interpreters have tried to make Jesus's words here mean something quite different. Because *airō* can also mean "lift up," some have tried to avert the threat of judgment in this context by suggesting that Jesus means that the fruitless, drooping part of the vine will be lifted up, off the ground, for special attention. As in some horticulture, this could mean propping up the part that seems to be dying, perhaps on a trellis, and giving it extra care and nutrition so that it can again bear fruit.[65] This interpretation founders, nevertheless, on verse 6, where the fruitless branch is picked up only to be discarded and destroyed. More importantly, it is precisely because the verbs were normally not used in an agricultural context that we should guard against making the metaphor mean more than Jesus explicitly teaches. As Edward Klink

---

61. To reproduce the wordplay in English, we might say "clears away" and "clears clean," or "cuts off" and "cuts clean" (Beasley-Murray, *John*, 268, note a).

62. Jo-Ann A. Brant, *John*, Paideia (Grand Rapids: Baker Academic, 2011), 217.

63. Musa Victor Mdabuleni Kunene, *Communal Holiness in the Gospel of John: The Vine Metaphor as a Test Case with Lessons from African Hospitality and Trinitarian Theology* (Carlisle: Langham, 2012), 95.

64. Kunene, *Communal Holiness in the Gospel of John*, 96.

65. J. Carl Laney, "Abiding Is Believing: The Analogy of the Vine in John 15:1–6," *BSac* 146 (1989): 56–66; Bruce Wilkinson with David Kopp, *Secrets of the Vine: Breaking through to Abundance* (Sisters, OR: Multnomah Books, 2001).

explains, "The true subject matter here is not the work of a farmer . . . but the work of *the* Farmer."⁶⁶ Moreover, while *airō* can mean "lift up" in a positive sense, more commonly that which is lifted up is taken away, carried off, or removed.⁶⁷ Every major English translation renders this verb in verse 2 as "cuts off," "cuts away," "takes away," or "removes," as do the vast majority of scholars and commentators.

The links with purity, on the other hand, should not be lost. The NASB, NET, NIV, and NRSV all have notes pointing out that "prunes" could have been translated with words such as "cleans," "cleanses," "cuts back," or "trims." Indeed, these would have been far more common translations in any other context. Does this mean that Jesus is advocating some sort of ritual purity here? No, of course not; he is simply using an analogy or metaphor. In fact, the extended nature of the metaphor makes it the closest thing in John to a full-fledged parable.⁶⁸ It may well hark back also to Isaiah's famous allegory of the vine, complete with its threatened judgment (Isa. 5:1–7), or to Ezekiel 15, with its extended metaphorical use of pruning.⁶⁹ The point is that in the context of Passover, with concepts like purity and purification central, it is only natural for Jesus to use this imagery as a springboard to what he wants to inculcate in his followers: *God the Father will purify or further cleanse those who bear the fruit of sacrificial love so that they can produce still more fruit.*⁷⁰ *The spiritual (ethical or moral) arena is the one that ultimately matters.* And Jesus reminds his disciples of this at a very strategic point in his message.

Why are there no additional references in John 14–16 to the purity that has been so recurring a motif buried deep in the history of the

---

66. Klink, *John*, 651.
67. BDAG, s.v. *airō*.
68. It also contains numerous echoes of several Synoptic parables. See P. R. Choi, "I Am the Vine: An Investigation of the Relations between John 15:1–6 and Some Parables of the Synoptic Gospels," *BR* 45 (2000): 51–75.
69. Thompson, *John*, 324.
70. That fruit is in no way limited to any one aspect of the Christian life. Furthermore, "God takes care that the believer can never give himself over to rest; he continually demands something new from him, and continually gives him new strength" (Rudolf Bultmann, *The Gospel of John: A Commentary*, trans. G. R. Beasley-Murray, ed. R. W. N. Hoare and J. K. Riches [Oxford: Blackwell; Philadelphia: Westminster, 1971], 533).

tradition and probably even in the life of the historical Jesus? It is always more difficult to answer a question about why something isn't in a passage or section of Scripture than one about why something is. *What is in the Farewell Discourse—indeed, what is most unique to it of all its major themes—is the role of the Holy Spirit as Paraclete.*[71] Most of what Jesus says about the Spirit in these chapters has to do with what will happen in the future, although 14:17 explains that he already "lives with you." Soon, however, "he will be in you."[72] John has already repeatedly highlighted the role of the Spirit as the ultimate purifier; indeed, we are so used to hearing "the Holy Spirit" as a name that we forget that the adjective "holy" is itself closely tied in with purity. If he comes to dwell within believers, that can only help to increase their holiness.

## Sanctification by the Truth (John 17:17–19)

The high priestly prayer, with which this portion of Jesus's time with his disciples concludes, falls into three parts of unequal size. First Jesus prays for himself (17:1–5), then for his followers (vv. 6–19), and finally for those who will become followers through their testimony (vv. 20–25). The longest section is clearly the second, middle section; the heart of Jesus's prayer is for the protection of the disciples amid a hostile world. Jesus explicitly specifies that he is asking not that the disciples be taken out of the world but that they be safeguarded in its midst (v. 15). Just as Christ neither belongs to nor is characterized by the world of fallen humanity, neither are those who abide in him (v. 16). When many, then and now, might imagine that they would need a certain monastic or at least separatist existence to maintain their distinctives, Jesus prays for them not to be so separate that they fail to rub shoulders with the world enough to have a positive effect on it (v. 18).[73]

---

71. For elaboration, see Klink, *John*, 631–35.

72. Less probable is the textual variant that reads "he is in you." But the decision is difficult; witness the {C} rating given in the fifth edition of the United Bible Societies' *Greek New Testament*.

73. "The community can only undertake its task if it remains what it is: separated off from the world, with its existence grounded purely in the revelation of God in Jesus" (Bultmann,

At this point, Jesus implores his heavenly Father to "sanctify them by the truth." Johannes Beutler sees a reference back to verse 11 here, with its prayer for protection and unity, as introducing the concept of holiness, which Jesus now elaborates.[74] In addition, to further specify what the truth is, he declares, "Your word is truth." God's word here does not refer to Scripture, as it would come so often to mean in post–New Testament times. In verse 14 it is something Jesus has given to the disciples; in verse 6 it is what they have kept. Presumably, it is the overall message of God's will as Jesus has disclosed it, which in other contexts we learn is the fulfillment of Scripture in the person of Jesus and his teaching (esp. 5:39, 45–46).[75] The prepositional phrase *en alētheia* can be translated not only as "by the truth" (NIV, CSB; cf. NKJV, NLT: "by your truth") but also as "in the truth" (so most Eng. versions), "through thy truth" (KJV), or "in accordance with the truth" (NIV mg.). In any event, God's revealed teaching provides a key means or sphere for the disciples' further sanctification.[76]

The root of the verb translated in most English versions as "sanctify" is *hagiazō*. Its core meaning is "set something apart," although, as we have just seen, in this context it is a moral rather than spatial separation that is in view.[77] The NET employs "set them apart," while the CJB expands it to "set them apart for holiness." The CEB and the NLT both use "make them holy." The NAB and the NJB, perhaps reflecting the concept of a commission for vocation or service, both use "consecrate." The language is well suited to ritual purity and may have originated

---

*Gospel of John*, 510). But this holiness, for Jesus, "is nothing other than the fulfilment of this his being for the world" and completing his sacrifice, which is what we, too, imitate when we are holy (511). Cf. Beasley-Murray, *John*, 300.

74. Johannes Beutler, *A Commentary on the Gospel of John*, trans. Michael Tait (Grand Rapids: Eerdmans, 2017 [Ger. orig. 2013]), 436.

75. Bruce G. Schuchard, *Scripture within Scripture: The Interrelationship of Form and Function in the Explicit Old Testament Citations in the Gospel of John* (Atlanta: Scholars Press, 1992), 155–56. Cf. Adele Reinhartz, "'And the Word Was God': John's Christology and Jesus's Discourse in a Jewish Context," in *Reading the Gospel of John's Christology as Jewish Messianism: Royal, Prophetic, and Divine Messiahs*, ed. Benjamin E. Reynolds and Gabriele Boccaccini (Leiden: Brill, 2018), 89.

76. Murray J. Harris, *John*, EGGNT (Nashville: B&H Academic, 2015), 290.

77. "John's idea of holiness is not, however, physical separation from the world as much as it is separation from the world's values; like Jesus, the disciples were 'sent into the world' (17:18; cf. 20:21)" (Keener, *Gospel of John*, 2:1060–61).

in precisely such a context.⁷⁸ *But in this portion of his prayer, it is clearly preparation for further spiritual service that Jesus has in mind. Once again, language and imagery from a ceremonial or ritual setting is applied in an ethical or moral realm.*

Verse 18 proceeds to spell out the service Jesus intends in this context: "As you sent me into the world, I have sent them into the world." Jesus's words in verse 9 have puzzled many. There he announced that he was praying not for the world in general but for those the Father had given him (from the world). Now, though, we understand his rationale. It is not that he never prays for the world, but that on this occasion he is setting apart and dedicating his followers for mission to the world.⁷⁹ If a good case can be made for the authenticity of Jesus as the "sent one" (see above, 97), then a comparable case should be possible for the disciples in turn to be sent ones. They are related not in every way to Jesus as he was to the Father, but in significant ways—a balance that Christianity has always struggled to get right and that Judaism never (or perhaps almost never) claimed, even while it contained all the building blocks for a divine Messiah (recall above, 175–76, 217–20). The double similarity and double dissimilarity criterion nicely applies here.

In verse 19, Jesus concludes the portion of his prayer focusing on his disciples with his own commitment: "For them I sanctify myself, that they too may be truly sanctified." As in verse 17, the verb, here used twice, is *hagiazō*. Verse 17 used the aorist imperative of entreaty (*hagiason*), the default tense and mood for a straightforward request.⁸⁰ Verse 19 translates Jesus's present indicative verb as progressive, "I am sanctifying," no doubt to denote the unfolding action of him going to the cross—his personal consecration to his own imminent mission. That he is sanctifying himself *hyper autōn* could mean simply "for them" (NAB, NIV, NLT, CSB), but a majority of the major English translations recognize the potential here for a reference to vicarious

---

78. It was used at least in sacrificial contexts (Deut. 15:19, 21). See Beasley-Murray, *John*, 301.
79. Kanagaraj, *John*, 168.
80. "The aorist tense (perfective aspect) presents the verbal action in its entirety without reference to its internal make up. This can effectively be used to communicate specific commands" (Joseph D. Fantin, *The Greek Imperative Mood in the New Testament: A Cognitive and Communicative Approach* [New York: Peter Lang, 2010], 98).

or substitutionary atonement with *hyper* and read "for their sake(s)" (KJV, NASB, NRSV, ESV, NJB) or "on their behalf" (CJB, NET, CEB).[81] Then appears a periphrastic construction with the present subjunctive of purpose with the copula followed by a perfect passive participle (*ōsin . . . hēgiasmenoi*), which woodenly translated would yield, "in order that they might be . . . having been sanctified." The construction reflects stative verbal aspect, that they might be in a state of sanctification that involves a "complex condition or state of affairs in existence."[82] In this context, part of that complexity is that although they have already been purified, they now must be dedicated for service.[83]

To the extent that time recedes in importance in such a construction, the point would simply be that it is the most heavily "marked" of all possible verbal constructions and thus the most emphatic. *Christ is going to the cross not to accomplish something for himself but emphatically for all his followers. And "sanctification" must be read here not through a Pauline lens of growing in the faith (an interpretation that may not even do justice to Paul)*[84] *but as a solemn dedication to and preparation for a mission.*[85] Interestingly, the expression modifying the believers' sanctification in verse 17 is articular ("in the truth"), while in verse 19 it is anarthrous ("in truth"). The lack of the article here could suggest the adverbial equivalent "truly" (NIV, NET), although most English translations still say "in [by, by means of] [the] truth." Given the difficulty of determining consistent patterns of the use and nonuse of the article in short prepositional phrases of this nature, we probably should not press the difference. In verse 17, God's word is simply "truth" (without the article), immediately after "the truth" has been used. The important points are that "truth" here denotes God's revealed will, and it fits to preserve that meaning throughout

---

81. Carson (*Gospel according to John*, 567) calls the language "evocative of atonement passages elsewhere."

82. Stanley E. Porter, *Idioms of the Greek New Testament* (Sheffield: Sheffield Academic, 1992), 24.

83. Thompson, *John*, 355; cf. Klink, *John*, 721.

84. See esp. David Peterson, *Possessed by God: A New Testament Theology of Sanctification and Holiness* (Grand Rapids: Eerdmans, 1995; repr., Leicester: Apollos; Downers Grove, IL: InterVarsity, 2000).

85. Michaels, *Gospel of John*, 872–73.

the passage.[86] In any event, nothing changes the conclusion from verse 17 that Jesus has substituted a spiritual meaning for a ceremonial one with a concept ("sanctify"/"sanctification") that lends itself to both possibilities.[87]

## Purity Concerns That Don't Apply to Jesus (John 18:28)

One of the most common claims of the "new look on John" or of the participants in the Society of Biblical Literature's "John, Jesus, and History" seminar is that John contradicts the Synoptics on the date of the crucifixion and that John's chronology should be preferred.[88] Of course, the apparent differences in dating have been observed throughout church history, and a variety of solutions have been proposed.[89] But it has only been fairly recently that critical scholarship has almost unanimously agreed that the apparent contradiction is real *and* has widely supported the view that John's date is the correct one.

We have already seen how 13:1–2 enters the conversation. If verse 2 does not depict the Passover meal, then John has Jesus and the Twelve celebrating at least one day earlier than the Synoptics do. It is easy to understand how 18:28 seems to clinch matters for many readers: "Then the Jewish leaders took Jesus from Caiaphas to the palace of the Roman

---

86. F. F. Bruce observes that here being sanctified "involves their consecration for the task now entrusted to them; it involves further their inward purification and endowment with all the spiritual resources necessary for carrying out that task. This purification and endowment are the work of the Spirit, but here Jesus declares the instrument of that work to be 'the truth'—the truth embodied in the Father's 'word' which Jesus had given to the disciples as he himself had received it from the Father (verses 8, 14). The very message which they are to proclaim in his name will exercise its sanctifying effect on them: that message is the continuation of his message, just as their mission in the world is the extension of his mission" (*The Gospel of John: Introduction, Exposition, and Notes* [Grand Rapids: Eerdmans; London: Pickering & Inglis, 1983], 334).

87. D. F. Tolmie, *Jesus' Farewell to the Disciples: John 13:1–17:26 in Narratological Perspective* (Leiden: Brill, 1995), 415.

88. Robinson, *Priority of John*, 147–51; Anderson, *Fourth Gospel and the Quest for Jesus*, 170–71; Charlesworth, *Jesus as Mirrored in John*, 144.

89. The two major alternatives to harmonization and flat-out contradiction are that Jesus (like some other Jews, most notably the Essenes) followed a different calendar in celebrating the festival, or that Jesus, knowing that he was going to be arrested and crucified, simply celebrated the Passover with his disciples one day early. See further I. Howard Marshall, *Last Supper and Lord's Supper* (Exeter: Paternoster; Grand Rapids: Eerdmans, 1980; repr., Vancouver: Regent College Publishing, 2006), 71–75.

governor. By now it was early morning, and to avoid ceremonial uncleanness they did not enter the palace, because they wanted to be able to eat the Passover." Had there not been earlier reasons for thinking that chapters 13–17 reflected a portion of the evening Passover meal with which the weeklong festival began, one would naturally assume that the Fourth Evangelist was talking about the initial Passover meal here.

This is also where the issue of ritual purity reenters the discussion. Jews considered a new day to begin every twenty-four hours at sunset. The kickoff meal of the Passover feast was celebrated after dark, so it would have been considered part of the same day in which Jesus was brought before Pilate early the next morning. Serious violations of purity laws cost someone a week of ritual uncleanness (mentioned fourteen times in Lev. 13–15). Minor infractions meant that a person was unclean only until the end of the day on which the impurity incurred (mentioned twenty-three times in Lev. 11 and 15 alone).[90] Nothing in the written Torah forbade a Jew from entering a Gentile's residence. But more scrupulous observance of the oral law did lead some to stay outside because of the fear that at some point the home would have incurred corpse uncleanness and would never have been properly purified.[91] Others point to the idolatrous images and their artistic representations that adorned the buildings, especially of the more well-to-do Gentiles.[92] Violation of this tradition, without any encounter with things that defile, might well have led only to the daylong penalty.[93] That day would have ended at nightfall, making the individuals able to eat the evening Passover meal, if it still lay ahead. If the penalty for incurring uncleanness were in fact weeklong defilement, then it is strange to think of eating the Passover as referring solely to the one

---

90. Carson, *Gospel according to John*, 589.

91. Lincoln, *Gospel according to Saint John*, 460, citing m. Ohal. 18:7. See also John Christopher Thomas, "The Fourth Gospel and Rabbinic Judaism," ZNW 82 (1991): 180.

92. Brant, *John*, 242. For still other possibilities, see Urban C. von Wahlde, *The Gospel and Letters of John*, 3 vols., ECC (Grand Rapids: Eerdmans, 2010), 2:767.

93. E. W. Hengstenberg, *Commentary on the Gospel of St. John*, 2 vols. (Edinburgh: T&T Clark, 1865 [Ger. orig. 1861]), 2:369; Hermann L. Strack and Paul Billerbeck, *Kommentar zum Neuen Testament aus Talmud und Midrasch*, vol. 2, *Das Evangelium nach Markus, Lukas und Johannes und die Apostelgeschichte* (Munich: Beck, 1924), 838–39; Andreas J. Köstenberger, *John*, BECNT (Grand Rapids: Baker Academic, 2004), 146.

evening meal. It would more naturally refer to the entire festival, with its many meals. Either way, the expression *phagein to pascha* ("to eat the Passover") puzzles and perplexes.

A different solution seems more probable. The second-most important meal of the Passover festival was the lunchtime *ḥagigah* on what we would think of as the day after the opening night banquet (in this case, Friday noontime after Thursday evening). There is extended instruction concerning it in Moed, the later mishnaic order on festivals.[94] Even if the religious leaders believed that they were unclean only until the end of that day, they still would have been unclean at noon. That situation could readily explain their unwillingness to enter the Praetorium, where Pilate presided.

It used to be objected that eating "the Passover" could refer only to participating in the opening evening banquet, but "Passover" had become synonymous with the entire weeklong Feast of Unleavened Bread (see esp. Luke 22:1), and there were celebratory meals throughout.[95] Now the objection usually is couched as follows: Granted that one could use the expression to refer to participation in the entire holiday, there still is no evidence that it could ever refer merely to what was left of the holiday after it had already begun.[96] However, "eating the Passover" need not be that situation-specific. It may still refer to the entire week, with the leaders' most immediate concern being the very next set of festivities they were supposed to attend.[97] A contemporary analogy may help. A person might announce being engaged in certain spiritual disciplines in order to "really experience the spirit of Lent this year." If this announcement was made some year on Shrove Tuesday, a listener might assume that this person was thinking particularly of how they would worship on Ash Wednesday at the beginning of the Lenten season the next day. Undoubtedly, this person would rub their forehead with ashes, attend a special service, and perhaps fast as well.

---

94. It forms the very last section of Moed, which is the second of six major divisions of the Mishnah.
95. The feast of "Unleavened Bread" referred to the weeklong festival. Passover is here equated with it.
96. Morris, *Gospel according to John*, 778–79.
97. Carson, *Gospel according to John*, 590.

But if someone three weeks into Lent said exactly the same thing, one would understand them to be talking about the rest of the period up to Easter. But one would also assume that the person had been practicing these disciplines from Ash Wednesday onward, not that they somehow were redefining Lent to mean only the period starting from the third week.

Other passages in John's passion narrative come into play here as well. In 19:14, we read, "It was the day of Preparation of the Passover; it was about noon. 'Here is your king,' Pilate said to the Jews." How much clearer could John be? The Passover week can't have begun, can it? The Greek clause at the beginning of the verse is simply *ēn de paraskeuē tou pascha*—"Now it was the preparation of the Passover"—with no units of time specified. "Noon" in the next clause is, more formally, "the sixth hour," counting from sunup, which occurred on average at 6:00 a.m. This is supposed to put the matter beyond doubt. Jesus, the Lamb of God, is crucified at the time when the lambs for the Passover meal that evening were being slaughtered. And everyone knows the Fourth Gospel stresses Jesus as the Lamb of God.[98]

But wait, does it really? John the Baptist twice in the opening chapter of the Gospel points out Jesus as the "lamb" (*amnos*) of God (1:29, 36), but that is the extent of any references to lambs of any kind in the entire Gospel. The imagery of sheep permeates John 10; however, these are not sheep to be sacrificed but rather the flock of the good shepherd. A word for "lamb" will reappear twenty-nine times in Revelation, another book traditionally ascribed to John, with Jesus as that lamb in all but one instance (Rev. 13:11). But the word there is a different one altogether than in the Fourth Gospel: the sacrificial lamb (*amnos*) has become, in Revelation, a warrior ram (*arnion*).[99]

---

98. For a clear, even if vitriolic, example, see Maurice Casey, *Is John's Gospel True?* (London: Routledge, 1996), 18–25. But see also Raymond E. Brown, *The Gospel according to John: Introduction, Translation, and Notes*, 2 vols., AB (Garden City, NY: Doubleday, 1966–70), 2:555–56, 846, 895–96; C. K. Barrett, *The Gospel according to St. John: An Introduction with Commentary and Notes on the Greek Text*, 2nd ed. (London: SPCK; Philadelphia: Westminster, 1978), 48–51.

99. See, e.g., Ian Boxall, *The Revelation of Saint John*, BNTC (London: Continuum; Peabody, MA: Hendrickson, 2006), 119.

As for the sixth hour, the later rabbinic traditions, to which John supposedly alludes, disagree on the time of the sacrifices; some put them at 3:00 p.m. ("the ninth hour" [Mark 15:33–34 pars.]). For that matter, John isn't even claiming that Jesus was crucified at noon; this was the time when Pilate presented Jesus to the people as a mock king. To top it all off, there is not one word in the actual text of John 19 about the sacrificial lambs.[100] Would John's primarily Gentile audience even know about the timing of the slaughter of the Passover lambs that may or may not have even been part of the tradition yet in the first century? Little wonder that a handful of scholars are beginning to recognize how weak the case is for the common interpretation of 19:14 that commentators have for too long merely repeated without investigating it for themselves.[101]

We still have the expression "Preparation of the Passover" to deal with. Fortunately, it will recur only seventeen verses later. In 19:31, we read, *paraskeuē ēn* ("it was Preparation"), but as the verse unfolds, it is preparation for the Sabbath that John is describing. In verse 42, "the Jewish day of Preparation" unambiguously refers to the day before the Sabbath. To this day, what we would call Friday is *paraskeuē* in Greek, because it was Preparation Day for the Sabbath (Saturday). The expression "Preparation of the Passover" is thus best taken as shorthand for "Preparation for the Sabbath in Passover week" (cf. Did. 8.1; Mart. Pol. 7.1).[102] There is, then, no internal contradiction within John 19, nor any between John 19 and 13:1 or 18:28. Notice how Mark 15:42a makes this explicit: "It was Preparation Day (that is, the day before the Sabbath)." The same is true in Matthew 27:62, Luke 23:54, and John 19:42, and there are no other uses of *paraskeuē* in the New Testament. Herman Ridderbos observes, conversely, that there are no known uses of the term elsewhere by itself that refer to the day before the start of Passover.[103] *In*

---

100. Ridderbos, *Gospel according to John*, 456–57.
101. See esp. Stephan Witetschek, "The Hour of the Lamb? Some Remarks on John 19:14 and the Hour of Jesus's Condemnation and/or Crucifixion," in Anderson, Just, and Thatcher, *John, Jesus, and History*, 3:95–107, esp. 99–103.
102. Cullen I. K. Story, "The Bearing of Old Testament Terminology on the Johannine Chronology of the Final Passover of Jesus," *NovT* 31 (1989): 318.
103. Ridderbos, *Gospel according to John*, 456.

sum, then, there is no contradiction between John and the Synoptics and no preferable or more accurate chronology to adopt in the Fourth Gospel.[104]

The *"new look on John" is right about one thing here, though: John is more historically accurate than has usually been assumed by the scholarship that saw even his passion narrative as overlaid with too much distinctive theology for historical information to be salvaged.* It is simply that this historical information reinforces and supplements what we can already glean from the Synoptics, which is typically deemed bedrock historical Jesus material here.[105] That John specifies the detail about the Jewish leaders wanting to avoid ritual uncleanness takes us back to the earliest stages of the tradition and a time when ritual impurity was still important.[106] Pilate is familiar enough with their scruples that he accommodates them by coming outside each time he talks to them.

What few scholars comment on is that this very accommodation does not extend to Jesus. Jesus is brought inside the Praetorium for questioning. This seems to be more than simply an accused man not being given the same deference as his accusers. This is one argument from silence that is significant. If Jesus and his accusers were equally scrupulous about ritual purity, and since he is not being accused of breaking any of the purity laws, there would be no reason for Pilate not to meet with all of them in his courtyard. Jesus could easily have been taken to one corner of it for separate questioning. *It is more likely that both the Jewish leaders and Pilate recognized that even if Jesus obeyed the Mosaic purity laws, he had no interest in this added proscription by some of the religious leaders. Only they were worried about ritual defilement here.*[107]

104. For a full, recent discussion of all these texts from the perspective outlined here, see Brant Pitre, *Jesus and the Last Supper* (Grand Rapids: Eerdmans, 2015), 352–60.

105. See, classically, Joachim Jeremias, *The Eucharistic Words of Jesus*, trans. Norman Perrin (London: SCM; New York: Scribner, 1966).

106. Gerald L. Borchert, *John 12–21*, NAC (Nashville: Broadman & Holman, 2002), 238. Borchert notes the special category of impurity that must have been involved. See also Thomas Kazen, *Issues of Impurity in Early Judaism* (Winona Lake, IN: Eisenbrauns, 2010), 103–4.

107. See further Klink, *John*, 760, including on the irony of leaders preoccupied with ritual purity but willing to commit enormous moral sin in executing the innocent.

## Blood and Water from Jesus's Side (John 19:34)

We have already glanced at several verses in John 19 in the discussion of 18:28. Chapter 19:38–41 contains a true "anointing" for burial of Jesus's corpse by Joseph of Arimathea and Nicodemus. A mixture of myrrh and aloes weighing seventy-five pounds truly did reflect an anointing fit for a king,[108] whatever we make of Mary's action in 12:1–8. But, as we saw there, little about surrounding a corpse with spices could be considered purification. At best, it retarded the spread of the odor of the decaying body, while culturally it bestowed an honor on the individual that at least his family and friends who know about it could appreciate.[109] Whatever Mary's original intention with her flask of pure nard may have been, the fact that she used it up on Jesus while he was alive meant that it could not also function as a literal anointing substance for his corpse. So these two Jewish leaders filled the void. But we learn nothing new about purification.

Verse 34 of chapter 19, on the other hand, has intrigued readers through the ages with its possible relevance for our topic. Precisely because it was the "Preparation Day" *for the Sabbath* (v. 31), the religious leaders did not want the crucified persons or their corpses defiling the land by remaining on their instruments of execution in public over that holy day. Romans knew Jewish scruples on this topic, and there is documented precedent for their accommodating this type of request.[110] Because crucified victims died of asphyxiation rather than blood loss, they might remain alive for two or three days before expiring. Breaking the victim's legs could certainly speed up the process, even while inflicting intense pain and increasing the agony. Intending to do this to Jesus, as they did to the two men crucified with him, the soldiers found that he already appeared to be dead (vv. 32–33). Probably to make sure, one of them "pierced Jesus' side with a spear, bringing a sudden flow of blood and water" (v. 34).

---

108. Ben Witherington III, *John's Wisdom: A Commentary on the Fourth Gospel* (Louisville: Westminster John Knox, 1995), 312.
109. See further Eckhard J. Schnabel, *Jesus in Jerusalem: The Last Days* (Grand Rapids: Eerdmans, 2018), 153–56.
110. Schnabel, *Jesus in Jerusalem*, 341, citing Josephus, *J.W.* 4.317; Philo, *Flaccus* 83.

Because of the widespread appearance of both blood and water in symbolic contexts throughout Scripture, including elsewhere in the Gospels and especially in John, commentators have regularly wondered if symbolism was intended here too. Modern science, of course, will teach us that piercing the pericardial sac next to the heart within the first few hours after a person's death will lead to an outflow of both blood and a watery substance.[111] Given the frequency of warfare and execution involving swords in the ancient Roman Empire, armies undoubtedly knew this basic principle simply from observation, even if they could not have explained it with the precision that medical experts today can. Such a sword thrust could indeed demonstrate that the victim was dead, and it could allow the bodies to be taken down and buried (or disposed of in whatever way was chosen).[112]

Closely related is the view that sees John including the flow of blood and water to demonstrate Jesus's full and genuine humanity, against all docetic views, including those of emerging Gnosticism, which might have been infiltrating the Johannine community near the end of the first century.[113] Some would take the added step of correlating John 19:34 with 1 John 5:6, most likely written by the same author, which refers to Jesus as "the one who came by water and blood—Jesus Christ. He did not come by water only, but by water and blood."[114] This verse is similarly enigmatic, but there is at least a plurality, if not even a majority, of scholars who would relate it to the Gnostic (or at least proto-Gnostic) belief that the man Jesus had the Christ Spirit descend on him at his baptism but leave again before his expiry, because that which is completely divine cannot become fully human.[115] To be human is to

---

111. John Wilkinson, "The Incident of the Blood and Water in John 19.34," *SJT* 28 (1975): 149–72.

112. Bruce, *Gospel of John*, 375; Beasley-Murray, *John*, 354.

113. Borchert, *John 12–21*, 277. With or without antidocetism, we have here the climax of John's recurring presentation of Jesus's humanity (C. H. Talbert, *Reading John: A Literary and Theological Commentary on the Fourth Gospel and the Johannine Epistles*, rev. ed., RNT [Macon, GA: Smyth & Helwys, 2005], 253).

114. Kanagaraj, *John*, 190; Craig R. Koester, *Symbolism in the Fourth Gospel: Meaning, Mystery, Community*, 2nd ed. (Minneapolis: Fortress, 2003), 200.

115. E.g., Colin G. Kruse, *The Letters of John*, PNTC (Leicester: Apollos; Grand Rapids: Eerdmans, 2000), 178; cf. Constantine R. Campbell, *1, 2, and 3 John*, SGBC (Grand Rapids: Zondervan, 2017), 156–58.

have a genuinely material body, which in Gnostic thought made one inherently evil. Jesus had to have only "seemed" (from Gk. *dokeō*) to be human (hence the term "docetism"). Yet there may be enough of a gap in time between the writing of John's Gospel and the writing of the Epistles of John for new false teachings to have developed or arrived in between,[116] so it is hard to know how much stock we should place in this explanation.

A highly symbolic explanation that has proved popular with commentators and expositors down through the centuries, especially in strongly liturgical or sacramental settings, is that the water that flowed from Jesus's wounded side represented baptism while the blood stood for the Eucharist. Because John has already taught about the purifying features of the waters of baptism and of the blood of Jesus's death, symbolized in the Synoptics in the drinking of the cup at the Lord's Supper, perhaps he highlights the flow of water and blood here to remind readers of the importance of these two sacraments.[117] One does not have to infer from this interpretation sacramental regeneration (recall above, 246, 299), but that is a natural corollary that many think must follow. If one is unconvinced from the rest of the Gospel (or, indeed, from the New Testament as a whole) that either baptism or the Eucharist is a prerequisite for salvation, then one is often disinclined to follow this line of interpretation. Blood by itself, moreover, is never elsewhere in Scripture equated with the Eucharist, but only when found in tandem with bread—and possibly flesh, depending on one's interpretation of John 6:51–59 (recall above, 269).

On the other hand, the idea of some symbolism in the water and blood in 19:34 seems likely, given that Jesus has just died and given that his real humanity and real death could have readily been certified with no specific mention of what poured out of the wound in his side. Immediately after verse 34, the Fourth Evangelist refers to a solemn witness to the truth of the event, perhaps referring to the Beloved Disciple: "The man who saw

---

116. See esp. the reconstruction of the sequence and timing of the Johannine literature postulated by Raymond E. Brown, *The Community of the Beloved Disciple: The Life, Loves, and Hates of an Individual Church in New Testament Times* (Mahwah, NJ: Paulist Press, 1999).

117. Bultmann, *Gospel of John*, 678; Moloney, *Gospel of John*, 505–6.

it has given testimony, and his testimony is true. He knows that he tells the truth, and he testifies so that you also may believe" (v. 35). Verse 36 adds that both not having Jesus's bones broken and his being pierced fulfill Scripture (v. 36), which itself was a powerful testimony to its truth.[118] But the flow of water and blood is not said to fulfill Scripture, so presumably the emphasis on eyewitness testimony is directed particularly to that portion of Jesus's death.

What, then, is the most probable meaning of the water and blood in this context? C. H. Dodd, C. K. Barrett, Rudolf Schnackenburg, and G. R. Beasley-Murray all speak of *the blood as a sign of Jesus's saving death and the water representing the Spirit and eternal life, with the two symbols intimately connected.*[119] John Paul Heil elaborates: "Water, a symbol of the Spirit, comes out of the pierced side of Jesus together with blood, a symbol of his Life-giving death. By following and flowing together with the blood, the water lends to the blood its natural cleansing and quenching qualities. That blood and water together come out of the Jesus lifted up and exalted in crucifixion brings to a climax all of the narrative's previous indications of both the salvific cleansing and quenching effects of the death of Jesus."[120] More succinctly, as Marianne Meye Thompson observes, the flow of water and blood "signals the purificatory and life-giving power of Jesus' death."[121] Finally, Tricia Gates Brown notes that in 7:37-38 rivers of living water flow from Christ's "belly" (*koilia*), which is not far removed from the concept of water flowing out from his "side" (*pleura*) here.[122]

The actual event is most likely historical because of the realism of the desire for the land not to be desecrated and the nature of the outflow of

---

118. The use of Ps. 34:20 is a classic example of typology, employing a psalm believed to be Davidic. Zechariah 12:10 appears in a more overtly apocalyptic and even messianic context, with God declaring himself to be the one whom "they pierced."

119. C. H. Dodd, *Historical Tradition in the Fourth Gospel* (Cambridge: Cambridge University Press, 1963), 428; Barrett, *Gospel according to Saint John*, 557; Rudolf Schnackenburg, *The Gospel according to St. John*, trans. Cecily Hastings et al., 3 vols. (London: Burns & Oates; New York: Seabury, 1980-82), 3:294; Beasley-Murray, *John*, 358.

120. John P. Heil, *Blood and Water: The Death and Resurrection of Jesus in John 18-21* (Washington, DC: Catholic Biblical Association of America, 1995), 106.

121. Thompson, *John*, 404.

122. Tricia Gates Brown, *Spirit in the Writings of John: Johannine Pneumatology in Social-Scientific Perspective* (London: T&T Clark, 2003), 161.

liquid.[123] The earliest interpretation would have been in the context of purification.[124] Everything else follows as the tradition grows and the Fourth Evangelist compiles his final narrative. As one moves into the second and third centuries, even a link with various disciples' martyrdoms makes sense to the Christians of that time.[125] That which fits best the previous teaching of the historical Jesus is the application to the realm of spiritual-purification imagery from the world of ritual purity.

### Resurrection: The Ultimate Purification (John 20–21)

If the reawakening of Lazarus to life in this world is a form of purification, the resurrection to eternal life with a transformed body is the ultimate in making a person pure again. As one might expect, there is both continuity and discontinuity in appearance with what Jesus previously looked like. As also in the Synoptics (Matt. 28:17; Luke 24:15–16, 31), the resurrection appearances in John all have a moment of nonrecognition, followed by one of recognition, which naturally follows from the body's transformation. In John 20:15, Mary Magdalene mistakes Jesus for a gardener; in verse 16, she recognizes him after he tenderly addresses her. In the two appearances to his disciples behind locked doors, it takes them seeing his hands and side for them to be sure it is he (vv. 19–20, 26–27). In 21:4–6, the disciples in the boat converse with Jesus on the shore briefly without recognition, but then in verse 7, the Beloved Disciple and Peter both recognize who he is.[126]

The common question about whether scars reflect a glorified state probably should be answered negatively. Although only Luke narrates the ascension (Luke 24:50–53; Acts 1:9–11), the Fourth Gospel likewise makes it clear that Jesus's resurrection appearances represent an

---

123. Von Wahlde, *Gospel and Letters of John*, 2:818.
124. Rodney A. Whitacre, *John*, IVPNTC (Downers Grove, IL: InterVarsity, 1999), 466.
125. Frederick C. Klawiter, "'Living Water' and Sanguinary Witness: John 19:34 and Martyrs of the Second and Early Third Century," *JTS* 66 (2015): 553–73.
126. At the same time, the early hour, combined with the distance from shore, could be enough to explain the lack of immediate recognition. Obeying the command of someone they didn't yet recognize could reflect the belief that people on shore could sometimes see fish in shallow waters sooner than those coming in from further out on the lake. See Morris, *Gospel according to John*, 762.

intermediate phase between restoration to physical life and exaltation—reinstatement next to the Father in heaven (20:17). The scars may have been a necessary sign to convince Jesus's disciples that it was really he, but they need not last throughout eternity.[127] Of course, those who argue either that resurrections simply can't happen or that the historian must bracket them from consideration will dismiss this whole discussion as merely "theological" or, worse still, as "apologetics." Those open to the possibility of this kind of miracle, who recognize that sufficiently strong testimony should in principle be allowed to authenticate it, will find these questions more important (recall above, 15–16).

In John 20:21–22, the resurrected Jesus commissions his disciples, sending them into the world, breathes on them, and tells them to receive the Holy Spirit. Many mysteries surround these two short verses, most of them theological. One of the most common claims in a previous generation was that this is the Johannine equivalent of Pentecost (Acts 2), radically transformed.[128] A particular irony of this theory is that it interprets John in light of Acts, though there is no known literary relationship between them. Critical scholarship normally stresses staying within a given document being studied or at least within the background literature that can be assumed to have been known and utilized. But in order to concoct a major contradiction, it is willing to violate its own rules. So if using Acts can be legitimate in interpreting John, at least with respect to the coming of the Spirit, we might hazard a guess that *John 20:21–22 is more akin to the initial coming of the Holy Spirit into believers' lives, while Pentecost represents the filling or full empowerment of the Spirit.*[129] If we limit ourselves to interpreting John in the light of John, this becomes the fulfillment of the various

---

127. See Witherington, *John's Wisdom*, 342.
128. Barnabas Lindars inverts this, believing that the original was more like John's account than like Acts (*The Gospel of John*, NCB [London: Oliphants, 1972; Grand Rapids: Eerdmans, 1981], 612).
129. Bruce, *Gospel of John*, 397n18; Thomas R. Hatina, "John 20,22 in Its Eschatological Context: Promise or Fulfillment?," *Bib* 74 (1993): 196–219; Joost van Rossum, "The 'Johannine Pentecost': John 20:22 in Modern Exegesis and in Orthodox Theology," *SVTQ* 35 (1991): 149–67, showing considerable patristic support for this interpretation. Note also Cornelis Bennema, who provides some nuancing of this approach, in "The Giving of the Spirit in John's Gospel—A New Proposal?," *EvQ* 74 (2002): 195–213.

prophecies by John the Baptist and Jesus of the coming of the Spirit. Baptism in water is now supplemented by baptism in the Spirit (recall 1:33), with the latter taking precedence as more important.[130]

One final detail may well have absolutely nothing to do with the question of purification, but it remains intriguing. When Peter heard the Beloved Disciple exclaim, "It is the Lord!" (21:7), "he wrapped his outer garment around him (for he had taken it off) and jumped into the water." As we have seen repeatedly before, here is a verse with a surprising amount of detail in an otherwise sparse narrative, and we wonder what the Fourth Evangelist is communicating. The most common assumption is that Peter's excitement at realizing that it was Jesus caused him to try to hurry and get to the shore faster than had he stayed in the boat.[131] But would that have been a realistic goal? Would he be able to outswim the boat? And if that was his objective, why take the time to put his outer garment on? Nakedness may have been shameful in Judaism, but if *gymnos* here indicates wearing only his undergarment,[132] there would have been nothing shameful about that in a group of fishermen, whom Jesus must have seen similarly dressed many times before.

Of course, one possibility is that Peter was simply confused and acted impulsively, whether everything he did made sense. There is certainly precedent for this in the Gospels, but can we do any better? Verses 10–11 are odder than they might seem to those for whom the story has been domesticated by centuries of overfamiliarity. Apparently, by the time Peter arrives at the shore, Jesus, instead of giving him a welcome, simply sends him back to the boat to bring him some of the fish they had caught. But Jesus has already been cooking some fish on a charcoal fire (v. 9). Is it merely coincidence that the only other time the word for "charcoal fire" (*anthrakia*) appears in the New Testament is when Peter denies Jesus, and it is only *in this Gospel* (John 18:18)? And something is weird about the breakfast scene until they are done eating. Although the text says that they all knew that it was the Lord, the fact that John even

---

130. See Lindars, *Gospel of John*, 611; Witherington, *John's Wisdom*, 340.
131. Of many possible examples, see Beasley-Murray, *John*, 400. He notes and rejects the alternative views that Peter stayed in the water to help either the boat or the net of fish to the shore.
132. BDAG, s.v. *gymnos*.

mentions "None of the disciples dared ask him, 'Who are you?'" (v. 12) means that there still was some lingering doubt. Were they all subdued until Peter was recommissioned? The dramatic similarity between the miracle and the one surrounding Peter's original call (Luke 5:1–11) suggests some interfluentiality (recalling Paul Anderson's term [see above, 202]) between the Johannine and Lukan traditions without any direct dependence. If one is open to the possibility of miracles, multiple attestation thus supports the historicity of at least a core of the event.[133] There is no need to resort to the old hypothesis of Luke retrojecting a post-Easter version of John's account to a pre-Easter setting.[134]

We do not need to settle any of these questions to reopen the question about Peter's jumping off the boat and into the lake. Given the motif of water and purity that we have uncovered this far, is it not possible that it appears here in some form as well? John Stube remarks,

> The fact that Peter puts his clothes on before jumping into the water reveals the profound shame in his life. . . . The shame of the denials has caused a deep loss of innocence in Peter as a disciple. He therefore throws himself upon the mercy of Jesus in v. 7. Here he not only throws himself *towards* Jesus but *into* the water. This act should remind the reader of 13.9, where Peter invites Jesus to wash not only his feet but his whole body. This request of Peter in 13.9 should warn us against attributing the shame in Peter's life solely to the denials in John 18. There is clearly a root of toxic shame in Peter's life even before his rejection of Jesus in the courtyard of Annas.[135]

Even if this overly psychologizes a little, one wonders if there is a kernel of truth here. Larry George does not attempt as detailed a reconstruction but does suggest that, in light of Peter's denial of Jesus, he is exhibiting some kind of guilt.[136]

---

133. Precisely because, literarily, the accounts appear to be independent of each other (Brown, *Gospel according to John*, 2:1090–91).

134. In fact, a better case can be made that the Johannine account shows more signs of primitivity. See Graham H. Twelftree, *Jesus the Miracle Worker: A Historical and Theological Study* (Downers Grove, IL: InterVarsity, 1999), 324–35; René Latourelle, *The Miracles of Jesus and the Theology of Miracles*, trans. Matthew J. O'Connell (New York: Paulist Press, 1988), 161–65.

135. Stube, *Greco-Roman Rhetorical Reading of the Farewell Discourse*, 211 (italics original).

136. Larry Darnell George, *Reading the Tapestry: A Literary-Rhetorical Analysis of the Johannine Resurrection Narrative (John 20–21)* (New York: Peter Lang, 2000), 124.

Over thirty years ago, D. H. Gee insisted that Peter jumped into the lake to avoid encountering Jesus. The reason he was called on to bring Jesus some fish was that he was still in the water behind the boat, where the net would have been. This explains why there is no conversation between Jesus and Peter earlier, why Peter "went up" (to the shore) into the boat (from *anabainō* [NIV: "climbed back"]), and why the gathering on shore seems so awkward until Jesus takes the initiative to reinstate Peter. Gee likens the scene to Peter following Jesus at a distance at the denial, not able to avoid the scene but trying to remain in the background and failing to do so.[137] Theories about chapter 21 as a literary appendix come into play here too,[138] if one wants to employ narrative criticism the most skillfully. If Peter was this guilt-ridden, why would he have remained in the room where John 20 says that Jesus already appeared twice before? Even if we assume a different tradition-critical origin for chapter 21, how did the final redactor believe the chapters hung together? Maybe we should put a more positive spin on Peter's jumping into the lake. Just as he apparently does not want to appear too casually before his master in only his undergarment, he may want to purify himself in the lake, as if it were a *mikveh*. The Sea of Galilee certainly did function as a giant immersion pool of living water. *Peter could have been purifying himself in order to appear before Jesus in a cleansed state. But Jesus still has to ask him to reaffirm his love three times before he can be properly reinstated (vv. 15–17). Ethical or moral purity is what counts, not ritual purity in this setting.*

## Conclusion

There is no simple, linear trajectory through John's Gospel of diminishing interest in ritual purity and growing interest in moral purity. Still, like points on a scattergram, there does appear to be a general movement in these two directions, at least at the earliest or most authentic

---

137. D. H. Gee, "Why Did Peter Spring into the Sea? (John 21:7)," *JTS* 40 (1989): 481–89.

138. A generation ago, almost no one defended the original unity of chapters 1–20 and 21, whereas today many are prepared to do so. At least, 21:14 is aware that this is the third resurrection appearance in the Fourth Gospel.

levels of the tradition.[139] Mary's "anointing" in John 12:1–11 is not really a purification at all, but it does illustrate her lavish love. The footwashing in 13:1–17 can be viewed as a ceremony, but it is not likely that Jesus intended his followers to repeat it as a ritual, akin to baptism or the Lord's Supper. Rather, it served as a powerful and extended metaphor for Christ's own lowly service culminating in the crucifixion, which his followers were to imitate as far as they were called on. The Farewell Discourse predicts the Spirit beginning to fulfill his prophesied mission, performing the cleansing actions that water had previously symbolized. At the theological heart and near the center of that discourse is the cleansing activity performed on fruit-bearing branches—disciples who remained connected to and energized by Jesus, the vine (15:2). Here we are entirely in the metaphorical and spiritual realm.

In his high-priestly prayer, Jesus prays for his followers' sanctification or consecration to their mission, just as he prays the same for himself (17:17, 19). Again we have language and concepts from a background of ritual purity applied wholly in the moral or ethical realm. Concern for the Jewish leaders' scruples about not defiling themselves ritually in 18:28 stands out conspicuously from Jesus's own behavior and treatment, where apparently ritual purity is not an issue. The outflow of water and blood from Jesus's side after the soldier's spear thrust (19:34) may symbolize the life-giving nature of his death, but in any event, there is nothing ceremonial here. Jesus's resurrection is an amazing example of purification, but it doesn't really fall into any of our traditional categories. The last mention of water in John's Gospel may have absolutely nothing to do with purity issues, but it is at least intriguing to ask whether Peter's jumping into the lake could have involved some form of self-purification in his mind (21:7). If so, John's Jesus pays no attention to it, and focuses on recommissioning Peter based on his acknowledgment of his love for the Lord.

---

139. See Mira Stare, "Die Reinheitsthematik im Johannesevangelium," *SNTSU* 40 (2015): 79–95. For Stare, it is the Johannine Jesus who calls the role of cultic purification into question and brings a new understanding of being pure related to the power of Jesus's word. I agree but suggest that this aspect of the Johannine Jesus lies embedded in the earliest layers of the tradition.

It is easy to take these and earlier passages and imagine that Jesus is being portrayed simply as a supersessionist or replacement theologian. Craig Keener, however, captures the finer nuances that are needed:

> In the final analysis, it was Christ's death that would bring the true, spiritual cleansing (19:34), and this would be administered by the Spirit who would reveal the glorified Christ (7:37–39; 16:12–15). While this would not always rule out the usefulness of other Jewish purification ceremonies (9:7 . . .), they could henceforth derive their meaning only from an encounter and continuing relationship of fellowship with him through the Spirit. Nothing associated with purity among the opponents of the Johannine community was adequate to sustain its own holiness; for this, the Spirit of purification was necessary, and the Spirit of purification was available only to those who were followers of Jesus, who alone was qualified to bestow the Spirit (1:32–34; 3:31–35).[140]

Our three chapters on the Fourth Gospel highlight the role of purity concerns within it. Never rising to the level of a theme that is discussed in scholarship on the top dozen or so topics John wants to highlight theologically, purity is nevertheless a recurring motif. In every instance, a case can be made, of varying strengths admittedly, that even if one dissects the passage at hand tradition-critically, the part dealing with purity remains in the oldest layer. In every instance, other topics, which represent Johannine favorites, come more to the fore, and yet moving from ritual to moral purity occurs often enough that we cannot dismiss it as a simple figment of our imagination. Were one to compose a full-orbed study of the historical Jesus according to the designs of the fourth quest, Jesus and purity should merit at least one full chapter.[141] Inasmuch as the topic rarely gets anything like this much treatment in traditional works of Jesus research, the strategies of the fourth quest have definitely borne some fruit.

---

140. Craig S. Keener, *The Spirit in the Gospels and Acts: Divine Purity and Power* (Peabody, MA: Hendrickson, 1997), 162.

141. Wai-Yee Ng captures many of the points that probably would be expanded: "rebirth, purification, joy, satisfaction analogous to the quenching of thirst, heavenly worship, eternal life" (*Water Symbolism in John: An Eschatological Interpretation* [New York: Peter Lang, 2001], 150).

But what of the Synoptic Gospels? The last step in my proposed methodology (see above, xix) is to compare my findings from the Fourth Gospel with the best historically attested material from Matthew, Mark, and Luke. Will doing so shed any new light on our topic? Will it at least suggest that it was more prominent in the ministry of the historical Jesus than has typically been acknowledged? Our final main chapter must now turn to this topic.

# 10

# Purity and the Historical Jesus of the Synoptics

For much of church history, it was taken for granted that Jesus abolished the laws of ritual purity. Little more needed to be said on the topic. Today the subject is hotly contested, with numerous, nuanced positions across a scholarly spectrum. A survey of scholarship on the most probably historical portions of the Synoptic Gospels, along with brief looks at the major passages involved in synthesizing Jesus's position, will disclose the complexity of the topic. The perspective that emerges is not inconsistent with what we have seen in the Gospel of John, although it is John who discloses that it may have been much more prominent a concern during Jesus's life than one might imagine from reading only Matthew, Mark, and Luke. John also hints at a progression or trajectory of Jesus moving away from issues of ritual purity, precisely because the Fourth Gospel is more chronological overall than the Synoptics are, thus giving us insights we would not discern from the first three Gospels by themselves.

### Current Scholarship on Purity in the New Testament

Early in church history, various influential patristic writers developed the threefold division of the law into moral, civil, and ceremonial (or ritual) categories. For them, only the moral laws carried over into the New Testament era relatively unchanged. Issues of ritual purity clearly fell into the ceremonial category, with which Christians needed not concern themselves. A longer volume than the present one could profitably rehearse the exceptional occasions when certain Christian groups, sometimes sectarian or cultic, tried to reinstate purity practices, but these need not detain us here. The vast majority of believers over the centuries have not worried about immersing themselves in ceremonial baths after touching (or simply getting too close to) a dead body, brushing up against people with certain kinds of diseases, or having seminal emissions or menstruating (Lev. 12–15). They might wash their hands or other body parts for reasons of hygiene, but not because they were consciously thinking that God had commanded them to do so.

In places and times in which the Christian church overtly or covertly engaged in anti-Semitism, it became easy to denigrate laws of ceremonial purity as simply the outmoded restrictions of an era that was more concerned with external than internal realities. During the first and second quests for the historical Jesus, the view that Jesus did away with the law overall proved common enough.[1] That he abolished the ritual law, and especially the purity laws, was almost taken for granted, with very little written on the topic compared to the other aspects of Jesus's ministry. Less than a decade after the fall of the Third Reich and the end of World War II, German Lutheran New Testament scholar Ernst Käsemann spoke for many when he declared that Jesus denied "that impurity from external sources can penetrate into man's essential being," and that a person who made such a claim "is striking at the presuppositions of the whole classical conception of *cultus* with its sacrificial system." Moreover, a Jewish man speaking like this "has cut himself off from the community of Judaism."[2]

---

1. Particularly under the influence of Origen and Chrysostom. See further Peter J. Tomson, "Purity Laws Viewed by Church Fathers and Jesus," in *Purity and Holiness: The Heritage of Leviticus*, ed. M. J. H. M. Poorthuis and J. Schwartz (Leiden: Brill, 2000), 73–91.

2. Ernst Käsemann, "The Problem of the Historical Jesus," in *Essays on New Testament Themes*, trans. W. J. Montague (London: SCM; Naperville, IL: Allenson, 1964 [Ger. orig. 1954]), 39. Almost as sweeping in his rejection of the laws of holiness is Marcus J. Borg, *Meeting Jesus*

As we have seen, much of the third quest has distanced itself from such sweeping claims. But have they gone far enough? James Dunn, for example, concluded his study of Jesus and purity with three points: (1) Jesus was remembered as speaking on purity of heart as more important than ritual purity; (2) some thought that he took ritual purity to apply to Israel no longer; (3) he did not want to make observance of the purity laws a criterion of covenant loyalty.[3] At the other end of the spectrum, a Jewish scholar, Amy-Jill Levine, believes that Jesus was a fully observant Jew and followed various halakah, that much of what seems to suggest otherwise in the Synoptics has been misinterpreted, and that what must be interpreted as a rejection of the law is not authentic.[4]

Thomas Kazen has investigated the topic of Jesus and purity as much as any contemporary scholar and occupies some middle ground that would more or less represent the perspectives of the majority of those today who have studied this topic in detail. Kazen does not see Jesus as ever breaking the Mosaic law or as looking ahead to a time when it would be superseded, even in ritual details. Nevertheless, because his message centered on the inbreaking of God's kingly reign with its dynamic power, the law and especially ritual laws like those of purity simply were not as prioritized. In comparison, Jesus's attitude almost seemed like one of indifference to those principles.[5] And this was especially true with respect to the oral law.

Kazen questions how useful the distinction between moral and ritual purity is, since anything commanded by God is ultimately a moral issue. Jonathan Klawans, by way of contrast, finds that it still has heuristic value, and he stresses that *Jesus can be placed on a spectrum of Jewish*

---

*Again for the First Time: The Historical Jesus and the Heart of Contemporary Faith* (San Francisco: HarperSanFrancisco, 1994), 53–58.

3. James D. G. Dunn, *Jesus Remembered*, Christianity in the Making 1 (Grand Rapids: Eerdmans, 2003), 576–77.

4. See throughout Amy-Jill Levine, *The Misunderstood Jew: The Church and the Scandal of the Jewish Jesus* (New York: HarperOne, 2008).

5. "What was perceived by some as indifference may be seen as a paradoxical acceptance of the impurity concept, in which the power of the kingdom was understood as stronger than the threats associated with impurity, thus relativizing the need for conventional purification" (Thomas Kazen, *Jesus and Purity* Halakhah: *Was Jesus Indifferent to Impurity?* [Stockholm: Almqvist & Wiksell, 2002; repr., Winona Lake, IN: Eisenbrauns, 2010], 339).

*positions with respect to moral and ritual purity or defilement so that he does not have to be seen as breaking from Judaism.* Specifically, Klawans observes Philo treating the two kinds of purity analogically, Qumran as virtually identifying them or treating them identically, the earliest two centuries of rabbis as sharply separating or compartmentalizing them, and Jesus as prioritizing the moral over the ritual.[6]

There are other significant contemporary debates on purity in first-century Judaism. One of the main functions of Israelite purifying rituals was to prepare individuals for coming into the presence of a holy God, especially when they entered the tabernacle and, later, the temple, where God was believed to be very specially present. The rest of daily life was not affected nearly as much. Paula Fredriksen and Cecilia Wassén have continued to stress this,[7] but more and more scholars are acknowledging the likelihood of a much more pervasive influence of the felt need for purity in late Second Temple Judaism. Archaeologists continue to be astonished by how many remains of stepped pools of the kind that were used as *mikvaot* they are uncovering throughout the land of Israel, along with the stone water jars that were believed to maintain their purity better than those made of other materials.[8] Allowance has to be made for the possibility of other uses of both kinds of artifacts; Boaz Zissu and David Amit categorize the *mikvaot* into domestic baths, public baths, baths near synagogues, ritual baths with agricultural installations, ritual baths for use by pilgrims, and ritual baths near graves.[9] Yet even this categorization confirms the general trend suggesting that public immersion in water believed to be ritually

6. Jonathan Klawans, "The Impurity of Immorality in Ancient Judaism," *JJS* 48 (1997): 1–16.
7. Paula Fredriksen, *Jesus of Nazareth: King of the Jews* (New York: Knopf, 1999), 197–207; Cecilia Wassén, "The Jewishness of Jesus and Ritual Impurity," *SIDA* 27 (2016): 11–36.
8. Stuart S. Miller, *At the Intersection of Texts and Material Finds: Stepped Pools, Stone Vessels, and Ritual Purity among the Jews of Roman Galilee* (Göttingen: Vandenhoeck & Ruprecht, 2015), 182. See also the book-length study by Roland Deines, *Jüdische Steingefässe und pharisäische Frömmigkeit: Ein archäologisch-historischer Beitrag zum Verständnis von Joh 2.6 und der jüdischen Reinheitshalacha zur Zeit Jesu* (Tübingen: J. C. B. Mohr, 1993). More briefly, see Jürgen K. Zangenberg, "Pure Stone: Archaeological Evidence for Jewish Purity Practices in Late Second Temple Judaism (Miqwa'ot and Stone Vessels)," in *Purity and the Forming of Religious Traditions in the Ancient Mediterranean World and Ancient Judaism*, ed. Christian Frevel and Christophe Nihan (Leiden: Brill, 2013), 537–72.
9. Boaz Zissu and David Amit, "Common Judaism, Common Purity, and the Second Temple Period Judean *Miqwa'ot* (Ritual Immersion Baths)," in *Common Judaism: Explorations in*

pure occurred widely throughout Israel. Morton Jensen thus believes that all of Israel in Jesus's day "displayed certain peculiar markers of 'religious motivation' or even 'religious intensification' in terms of increasing halakic strictness and purity practices in what could be termed a purity wave."[10]

This trend has to be balanced by a second one, however. Jacob Neusner, perhaps the most prolific biblical scholar of all time, having authored or edited over nine hundred academic books, repeatedly insisted that the first-century Pharisees' agenda was to extend the levels of purity that priests were required to maintain to all the people, especially during meals.[11] At this point, most other scholars have demurred, to one degree or another, noting that a variety of motives could explain the increased emphasis on purity. Eyal Regev, for example, highlights the development of "nonpriestly purity" at Qumran. Precisely because they found the temple priests too corrupt overall but did not have a separate temple at which to officiate, they counted on a better obedience to God's law than that of any other group in Israel to bring about God's favor. So they had to establish a level of ritual purity equal to the requirements for priests even among those who had different occupations.[12]

*A fair consensus of scholars, therefore, concurs that interest in ritual purity extended well into "common Judaism" and was not merely the preoccupation of one or more of the leadership sects.*[13] Here Fredriksen correctly remarks that "the things most foreign to modern Western religiousness about ancient Judaism—the sacrifices and their attendant purity regulations—struck ancient observers as one of the few normal

---

*Second-Temple Judaism*, ed. Wayne O. McCready and Adele Reinhartz (Minneapolis: Fortress, 2008), 47–62.

10. Morton H. Jensen, "Purity and Politics in Herod Antipas's Galilee: The Case for Religious Motivation," *JSHJ* 11 (2013): 8.

11. Jacob Neusner, "Mr. Sanders' Pharisees and Mine," *SJT* 44 (1991): 73–95. See also Neusner, *The Idea of Purity in Ancient Judaism* (Leiden: Brill, 1973). For Sanders's views, see E. P. Sanders, *Jewish Law from Jesus to the Mishnah: Five Studies* (London: SCM; Harrisburg, PA: Trinity Press International, 1990), 183–353.

12. Eyal Regev, "Pure Individualism: The Idea of Non-Priestly Purity in Ancient Judaism," *JSJ* 31 (2000): 176–202.

13. Susan Haber, "Common Judaism, Common Synagogue? Purity, Holiness, and Sacred Space at the Turn of the Common Era," in McCready and Reinhartz, *Common Judaism*, 63–77.

things Jews did."[14] The Greco-Roman world puzzled over uniquely Jewish concerns for circumcision, Sabbath-keeping, and dietary laws, but the concept of appearing before one's god in a state of ritual purity was far more widespread and better understood. Ironically, it is exactly because it is not well grasped in the modern Western world that we struggle with understanding Jesus's relationship to it. One principle, however, is sufficiently straightforward: the impure could make the pure impure, but the pure could not rub off their purity onto the impure. Haggai 2:11–13 gives the classic biblical illustration of this concept.[15]

A study of Second Temple Jewish literature before the time of Jesus demonstrates a multiplicity of perspectives; cutting through them all, nevertheless, is a growing emphasis on the contamination that impurity can cause.[16] Martin Lockshin demonstrates the same thing for the early rabbinic literature: holiness is just not "contagious" the way defilement is.[17] While we must recognize that ritual impurity itself was in no way sinful, it lent itself to being stigmatized, reapplied to areas of moral impurity, and used as a tool for distinguishing in-groups and out-groups of individuals, especially when people were in a prolonged or repeated state of impurity that others believed they could have avoided or were experiencing as divine punishment. Kazen has made a good case for the emotion of disgust playing a key role in the development of what was deemed ritually impure—dead bodies, disease, bodily emissions, certain foods—which could easily be extended to disgusting and immoral behavior such as adultery, murder, and numerous other forms of evil.[18] Jamal-Dominique

---

14. Fredriksen, *Jesus of Nazareth*, 52.

15. See Tom Holmén, "A Contagious Purity: Jesus' Inverse Strategy for Eschatological Cleanliness," in *Jesus Research: An International Perspective; The First Princeton-Prague Symposium on Jesus Research, Prague 2005*, ed. James H. Charlesworth with Petr Pokorný (Grand Rapids: Eerdmans, 2009), 199–229. See also Holmén, "Jesus and the Purity Paradigm," in *Handbook for the Study of the Historical Jesus*, ed. Tom Holmén and Stanley E. Porter, 4 vols. (Leiden: Brill, 2011), 3:2709–44.

16. Craig L. Blomberg, *Contagious Holiness: Jesus' Meals with Sinners* (Downers Grove, IL: InterVarsity, 2005), 65–96.

17. Martin I. Lockshin, "Is Holiness Contagious?," in *Purity, Holiness, and Identity in Judaism and Christianity: Essays in Memory of Susan Haber*, ed. Carl S. Ehrlich, Anders Runesson, and Eileen Schuller (Tübingen: Mohr Siebeck, 2013), 261–62.

18. Thomas Kazen, *Impurity and Purification in Early Judaism and the Jesus Tradition* (Atlanta: SBL Press, 2021), 105–35.

Hopkins summarizes the role of purity in the milieu of the Gospels under four headings: (1) it "is related to a physical bodily state"; (2) "it relates to a person's behavior or disposition"; (3) "it holds social implications for a person's social status"; (4) "it determines a person's state of consecration relative to a holy God."[19]

## Purity and the Synoptic Jesus

In this world of pervasive passion for purity, Jesus of Nazareth begins his public ministry. Thomas Kazen is again a representative and generally balanced source for summarizing what we see in the Synoptic Gospels. He wants particularly to look for details that don't obviously fit any major theological motivation on the part of the evangelists, and he analyzes Markan and Q material in most detail, following the standard conviction that they form our oldest written sources. Kazen sums up his findings with seven points, at least five of which we can readily affirm. First, as we have already noted, purity practices in Jesus's day were widespread throughout all of Israel. Second, purity was therefore not entirely or even primarily observed just to enter the temple in an appropriate state for meeting God. Third, the extended use of water rituals was evolving during this period and depended on the concept of graded impurity. In other words, more severe defilement required more extensive waiting and washing. Fourth, despite some claims to the contrary, it was an issue for Jews that they not be defiled by impure food. Fifth, some of the most rabbinic characteristics of Jesus's teachings are later additions to the Jesus tradition. Sixth, accusing the Pharisees of setting aside God's law and favoring human tradition is also the product of later Christian editing. Seventh, Jesus's views on purity were thus less "halakic" and more in the mold of the Hebrew prophets.[20] We will see that there are reasons for questioning the fifth and sixth of these conclusions and at least moderating them, but the

---

19. Jamal-Dominique Hopkins, "Levitical Purification in the New Testament Gospels," in *"What Does the Scripture Say?" Studies in the Function of Scripture in Early Judaism and Christianity*, ed. Craig A. Evans and H. Daniel Zacharias, 2 vols. (London: T&T Clark, 2012), 1:180.

20. Thomas Kazen, "A Perhaps Less Halakic Jesus and Purity: On Prophetic Criticism, Halakic Innovation, and Rabbinic Anachronism," *JSHJ* 14 (2016): 120–36.

others serve as a good summary of what we can learn from the study of the Synoptics and their milieu.

## *John the Baptist*

Although we are interested primarily in Jesus, in the Synoptics, just as in the Fourth Gospel, he emerges as an adult in the context of the ministry of John the Baptist. As we saw in dealing with the Baptist in the Fourth Gospel, there are numerous facets of his ministry that the evangelists present. In the Synoptics, he appears more clearly as a prophet and forerunner to the Messiah and as an Elijah-figure, especially in his dress and diet (Mark 1:6).[21] But *any call to participate in a ritual of immersion in water in the context of late Second Temple Judaism is bound to have a purifying dimension to it.*[22] That there is never a hint of anyone whom John baptized being rebaptized, except for the mysterious "disciples" in Acts 19:1–7, suggests that in this respect John's ministry was more than preparatory and that his baptism, based on people's repentance for sins (Mark 1:4 pars.), was once for all time as a sign of the inbreaking kingdom. That the men Paul encountered in Acts 19 had never heard there was a Holy Spirit almost guarantees that they were not Jewish and that, even if they had been immersed by someone related to John's ministry, they had not understood his fundamental message about one coming who would baptize with the Spirit (Mark 1:8 pars.). That *they* were baptized again is thus no real exception to the trend.[23]

If we bracket out all the most well-known roles for John the Baptist in the Synoptics, we are once again left with a character who was a purifier. Less so than in the Fourth Gospel, there may be little need to bracket those roles in Synoptic research, but still John the purifier

---

21. Carl R. Kazmierski, *John the Baptist: Prophet and Evangelist* (Collegeville, MN: Liturgical Press, 1996), 115–17.

22. Hannah K. Harrington, "Purification in the Fourth Gospel in Light of Qumran," in *John, Qumran, and the Dead Sea Scrolls: Sixty Years of Discovery and Debate*, ed. Mary L. Coloe and Tom Thatcher (Atlanta: Society of Biblical Literature, 2011), 117–38.

23. See esp. James D. G. Dunn, *Baptism in the Holy Spirit: A Re-examination of the New Testament Teaching on the Gift of the Spirit in Relation to Pentecostalism Today* (London: SCM; Philadelphia: Westminster, 1970), 83–89. See also Eckhard J. Schnabel, *Acts*, ZECNT (Grand Rapids: Zondervan, 2012), 187–88.

emerges. Intriguingly, this appears even more clearly in the writings of Josephus, who depicted John's calling Israel to righteousness and purity symbolized by ritual bathing. Among other things, Josephus wrote that John taught that people must not use baptism "to gain pardon for whatever sins they committed, but as a consecration of the body implying that the soul was already thoroughly cleansed by right behavior" (*Ant.* 18.5.2). The Greek preposition *eis* ("for") in Mark 1:4 can also be translated as "directed toward" or "with reference to," and it is probably one of these looser senses in which baptism is "for" the forgiveness of sins.[24] Bruce Chilton determines that the claim that John "acted as a purifier on the basis of ritual bathing is the most certain—as well as the most obvious—feature of his public activity."[25] Eyal Regev admits that there is what he labels a consensus on this point, even though he offers a dissenting perspective. But he wants to stress the diversity of meanings of washings in ancient Judaism and early Christianity, reserving the term "purification" for a smaller group of ritual immersions that were repeated in order to deal with the recurrent sin that people commit or the repeated uncleanness that they incur.[26]

## *Cleansing Leprous Persons*

One of the most defiling diseases afflicting the ancient Middle East was what typically gets translated in English as "leprosy." Commentators are largely agreed that this refers to a broader collection of ailments of the skin than Hansen's disease, which is what "leprosy" typically refers to today. The one episode narrated in all three Synoptic Gospels

---

24. See esp. Murray J. Harris, *Prepositions and Theology in the Greek New Testament* (Grand Rapids: Zondervan, 2012), 227. Alternately, we may take "of repentance" as a subjective genitive ("baptism produced by repentance"), with the repentance, rather than the baptism, leading to the forgiveness of sins. Thus, "without repentance, baptism effectuates nothing" (A. B. Caneday, "Baptism in the Stone-Campbell Restoration Movement," in *Believer's Baptism: Sign of the New Covenant in Christ*, ed. Thomas R. Schreiner and Shawn D. Wright [Nashville: B&H, 2006], 306).

25. Bruce Chilton, "John the Purifier," in *Jesus in Context: Temple, Purity, and Restoration*, ed. Bruce Chilton and Craig A. Evans (Leiden: Brill, 1997), 220.

26. Eyal Regev, "Washing, Repentance, and Atonement in Early Christian Baptism and Qumranic Purification Liturgies," *JJMJS* 3 (2016): 33–60.

of Jesus healing a leprous person proves particularly telling (Mark 1:40–45 pars.). The verb that appears in Mark 1:40 and 1:41 for the healing is *katharizō*, the standard Greek verb used to indicate ritual cleansing or purification. The Egerton Gospel (Papyrus Egerton 2) has a version of this story that may be literarily independent of the Synoptic form, thus providing multiple attestation.[27] Craig Keener notes that no early Christian of whom we know invented sayings of Jesus in which he explicitly purified various foods (on Mark 7:19b, see below, 366–67). So there doesn't seem to have been good reason for them to invent accounts of Jesus explicitly touching unclean people. At least the core of the account is thus most likely authentic.[28]

Amy-Jill Levine engages in sustained invective against Christian feminists who stress Jesus's uniqueness in touching this diseased man as over against conventional Judaism, believing that their primary motive is simply to denigrate Judaism. She stresses that there were plenty of normal activities of life that made a person ceremonially unclean, even touching a corpse to prepare it for burial. Impurity must be distinguished from sin. There is no stigma in touching leprous people, especially if one is compassionately ministering to them in some fashion, and there is certainly no law, not even in the oral tradition, against touching them. One simply purified oneself afterward.[29] But all this somewhat misses the point here. Jesus will show elsewhere (in the very next passage in Matthew's sequence of events [see Matt. 8:5–13 par.]) that he can merely speak a word of healing, even from a distance, and a diseased person can be cured. That he bypasses this route in favor of directly touching the man (Mark 1:41 pars.) means that he has deliberately chosen to highlight how the skin disease does not defile him. Rather, Jesus cleanses the "leprosy" of the diseased man. He is now both ritually clean and physically healed (v. 42).

Jesus then issues a pair of somewhat cryptic commands. He tells the newly healed individual, "Go, show yourself to the priest and offer the

---

27. Robert L. Webb, "Jesus Heals a Leper: Mark 1.40–45 and Egerton Gospel 35–47," *JSHJ* 4 (2006): 177–202.
28. Craig S. Keener, *The Historical Jesus of the Gospels* (Grand Rapids: Eerdmans, 2009), 220.
29. Levine, *Misunderstood Jew*, 173–77.

sacrifices that Moses commanded for your cleansing, as a testimony to them" (v. 44). This was the prescribed Levitical practice for ending the period of uncleanness, with the priest being the final arbiter of the presence or absence of the defiling skin disease (Lev. 14:1–32). But why "as a testimony to them"? Many scholars simply assume without further discussion that this was to demonstrate that even though Jesus had the unusual power to heal instantaneously, he still obeyed the Mosaic legislation and endorsed the role of the priests and the temple sacrifice in the healed man's purification.[30] Why would this even be in question, though, unless some of Jesus's teaching or behavior thus far made some people at least wonder if he was fully compliant with the Torah? *A better option is that the testimony is to the reality of the miracle.*[31] The "leprous" man has been suddenly healed, which is not the typical situation with a person recovering from a skin disease. Skepticism is not a new phenomenon in our age; people in Jesus's world would have wondered if the man really was healed (or if he really had been sick, or if he really were the same person at all [cf. John 9:8–9]). The testimony would almost certainly have had to refer to Jesus as the healer as well.

There is a third possibility that is at the very least intriguing. The Greek phrase *eis martyrion autois* ("as a testimony to them") occurs twice elsewhere in Mark. In 6:11, most translations render the phrase "as a testimony against them." The dative pronoun could be either a dative of advantage ("to" or "for") or a dative of disadvantage ("against"). Here, when Jesus is sending out the Twelve, telling them to shake the dust off their feet at those towns that do not receive them, it is clearly a warning of impending judgment, so "against" fits best.[32] In 13:9, Jesus is predicting a coming day when the disciples will be arraigned before local councils and flogged in synagogues. He explains, "On account of me you will stand before governors and kings as witnesses *to them*"

---

30. E.g., Cecilia Wassén and Tobias Hägerland, *Jesus the Apocalyptic Prophet*, trans. Cian J. Power (London: Bloomsbury T&T Clark, 2021 [Swed. orig. 2016]), 163; Joel Marcus, *Mark 1–8*, AB (New York: Doubleday, 2000), 210.

31. Friedrich Avemarie, "Jesus and Halakhic Purity," in *The New Testament and Rabbinic Literature*, ed. Reimund Bieringer et al. (Leiden: Brill, 2010), 258–59.

32. Mark L. Strauss, *Mark*, ZECNT (Grand Rapids: Zondervan, 2014), 253; Adela Yarbro Collins, *Mark: A Commentary*, ed. Harold W. Attridge, Hermeneia (Minneapolis: Fortress, 2007), 301–2.

(italics added). Most translations take this as a dative of advantage, so that Jesus is promising that they will be able to share their faith and talk about him before the highest leaders in the land. The KJV, nevertheless, translated this verse also with a dative of disadvantage—"as a testimony against them"—because it is in a context of hostility.[33] Might a dative of disadvantage fit in 1:44 also? Edwin Broadhead thinks so, pointing to other datives of disadvantage in Mark (though without the precise construction found here), the immediate context with its provisional clash between Jesus and the religious authorities, and the overall plot in which that clash grows steadily until the time of his crucifixion.[34] Because that hostility has not yet been established, it may be that the second of our three options remains best in 1:44, but it is certainly important to stress that *the main point here is not necessarily a reminder that Jesus still kept the Mosaic law*.

In Luke 17:11–19, Jesus cures ten leprous persons, without touching them, and even then they are cured only after they exercise enough faith to leave without having been healed to seek out the priest who can confirm their cure that happens en route (v. 14). This passage shows several signs of authenticity.[35] But there is no reference to their appearing before a priest as a testimony to or against anyone. These previously leprous men are simply to go to him, without Luke specifying why, and as they go, they are cleansed. Apparently, only one of the men was also spiritually saved, and he was a Samaritan (vv. 15–19). His testimony, had Luke said anything about it, could easily have been "against" the Jewish men who never returned to thank Jesus.[36] In any

33. Strauss (*Mark*, 575) notes that the *autois* ("to them") could be negative but thinks it more likely to be positive. So also Robert H. Stein, *Mark*, BECNT (Grand Rapids: Baker Academic, 2008), 600.

34. Edwin K. Broadhead, "Mark 1,44: The Witness of the Leper," ZNW 83 (1992): 257–65. Note also R. T. France, who seems to favor it without clearly taking a stand (*The Gospel of Mark: A Commentary on the Greek Text*, NIGTC [Carlisle: Paternoster; Grand Rapids: Eerdmans, 2002], 120).

35. Stanley E. Porter, "Luke 17.11–19 and the Criteria for Authenticity Revisited," JSHJ 1 (2003): 201–24.

36. David E. Garland observes that "the text radically subverts the significance of the temple's rituals and sacrifices when offering praise to God and thanks to Jesus not only suffice for making the required offerings (Lev 14:1–32) but surpass it" (*Luke*, ZECNT [Grand Rapids: Zondervan, 2011], 691).

event, it is difficult to understand why so many commentators take it for granted that all the evangelists are trying to portray in these texts is Jesus's obedience to the law or if that is even their main point at all.

Myrick Shinall has recently put forward a vigorous defense of the view that the leprous individuals that Jesus encountered were *not* socially ostracized very much. He does not deny that they had become unclean, but he disputes that this would have led to considerable stigma and separation from others. His arguments vary from arguments from silence, to arguments that partially support his claims, to those that probably misinterpret the evidence altogether. He correctly recognizes that the evidence from Josephus, the Dead Sea Scrolls, and the early mishnaic literature all presents problems: Josephus could skew matters, Qumran contained some extreme legislation, and the early rabbis held a mixed bag of viewpoints. Leprous persons might still be allowed in smaller unwalled villages or to sit in a separate location in the synagogue. Contamination occurred not by proximity but only by touch.[37] Because the Gospels do not describe any obstacles to these diseased persons approaching Jesus, Shinall believes that we should assume that they freely mingled in society. After all, Simon the leper (Mark 14:3 par.) even hosted Jesus and his disciples in his home in Bethany.[38] As with Levine, Shinall is convinced that the main motivation for "reading in" social stigma to the Gospel accounts is to make Jesus look good at the rest of Judaism's expense.[39]

In reality, many commentators have no anti-Semitic bias; in conservative circles, they can even be somewhat uncritically pro-Israel. The Gospels give so little information in their brief healing accounts that we simply don't know what obstacles or abuse anyone who approached Jesus for healing had to confront. Simon the leper (Mark 14:3 par.) was almost certainly a man who was now healthy[40] but retained the epithet (at least in the Jesus tradition), probably in part because Simon

---

37. Myrick C. Shinall Jr., "The Social Condition of Lepers in the Gospels," *JBL* 137 (2018): 924.
38. Shinall, "Social Condition of Lepers," 929.
39. Shinall, "Social Condition of Lepers," 932–34.
40. James R. Edwards, *The Gospel according to Mark*, PNTC (Grand Rapids: Eerdmans; Leicester: Apollos, 2002), 412–13; Stein, *Mark*, 633; Eckhard J. Schnabel, *Mark: An Introduction and Commentary*, TNTC (Downers Grove, IL: IVP Academic, 2017), 344.

was the single most common Jewish man's name,⁴¹ and it was a way to distinguish him from other Simons. It is interesting that Cecilia Wassén likewise wants to guard against anti-Semitic exaggeration of the differences between Jesus and other Jews, but she does so not by denying *social* stigma, which she readily concedes, but by overly limiting the contexts in which people would have been considered *ritually* unclean (despite Mark's distinctive use of "cleansing" rather than just "healing").⁴² Perhaps both those who overestimate and those who underestimate the differences between Jesus and conventional Judaism are trying too hard to deny the others' position and criticize them for hidden motives, so that they all wind up somewhat misinterpreting the evidence in the process.

Elizabeth Shively quite recently has insisted that Jesus in Mark's Gospel "conveys an idea of purity that elevates not only what is internal but also what is external; not only the heart, but also the body."⁴³ Whether it is healing from disease, restoring those who have suffered with disabilities, or exorcising individuals with impure spirits, Jesus is foreshadowing the resurrection from the dead. "Thus, Jesus' activities address the problem of human mortality in the light of the nearness of God's reign, which signals the unmitigated presence of God with his people, and they anticipate Jesus' resurrection from the dead, which pioneers the purification of the body at the turn of the ages."⁴⁴ Shively stresses that she is dealing not with the historical Jesus but only with Mark's portrait of him.⁴⁵ But given the famous absence of any actual resurrection appearance in Mark's original narrative, foreshadowing the resurrection would not appear to be a major Markan theme. To the extent that she has made her case, it would seem better to attribute

---

41. Richard Bauckham, *Jesus and the Eyewitnesses: The Gospels as Eyewitness Testimony* (Grand Rapids: Eerdmans, 2006), 70.

42. Cecilia Wassén, "Jesus' Table Fellowship with 'Toll Collectors and Sinners': Questioning the Alleged Purity Implications," *JSHJ* 14 (2016): 157. Contrast Jodi Magness, "'They Shall See the Glory of the Lord' (Isa 35:2): Eschatological Perfection and Purity at Qumran and in Jesus' Movement," *JSHJ* 14 (2016): 115; János Bolyki, *Jesu Tischgemeinschaften* (Tübingen: Mohr Siebeck, 1998), 229.

43. Elizabeth E. Shively, "Purification of the Body and the Reign of God in the Gospel of Mark," *JTS* 71 (2020): 63.

44. Shively, "Purification of the Body," 63.

45. Shively, "Purification of the Body," 68.

the theme to a pre-Markan stage of the tradition and perhaps even to Jesus himself.

*In short, while Jesus's radical newness can be exaggerated, his ability and willingness to heal and cleanse leprous persons who came to him remained remarkable.* But there were only two incidents that the Synoptists chose to narrate with any detail. Matthew 10:8 and 11:5 and their Lukan parallels generalize and refer to both Jesus and the disciples cleansing those with leprosy, but these passages do not indicate on how large a scale this took place. *We have no way of knowing to what extent this practice occupied his time in his ministry or whether it was particularly related to a certain period, location, or other set of circumstances. It was, however, one form by which Jesus provided purity for certain people.*

### *Tax Collectors and "Sinners"*

Early in Mark's Gospel, Jesus interacts with another paradigmatic group of individuals often dubbed either unclean or outcast or both, whom Mark labels "tax collectors and sinners" (Mark 2:15 pars.). Readers not taken aback by this combination of one very specific profession with a more general slur may well be products of the domestication of and overfamiliarity with Scripture in certain circles. Tax collectors, or perhaps more properly toll collectors, often were Jews within Israel who were working as middlemen for Rome because of the profits they could accrue. Often this arose because they charged more than they needed to turn over to their Roman supervisors and kept the excess for themselves.[46] We should not be surprised that in a couple of instances "tax collectors and prostitutes" are paired, because toll collectors also sometimes functioned as pimps and/or located prostitutes for clients, particularly Roman soldiers.[47] Not every toll collector was

---

46. For the most thorough study, see Fritz Herrenbrück, *Jesus und die Zöllner: Historische und neutestamentliche-exegetische Versuchungen* (Tübingen: J. C. B. Mohr, 1990). See also John R. Donahue, "Tax Collectors and Sinners: An Attempt at Identification," *CBQ* 33 (1971): 39–61.

47. Kathleen E. Corley, *Private Women, Public Meals: Social Conflict and Women in the Synoptic Tradition* (Peabody, MA: Hendrickson, 1993), 152–58.

automatically unclean by virtue of his job, but any of them could readily come into contact with those who were unclean due to certain bodily discharges, especially when they left their toll "booths" to engage in door-to-door collections. Morally, they could easily have been viewed as traitors by their fellow Jews and ostracized for that reason alone.

Ever since E. P. Sanders's influential *Jesus and Judaism*, the view has become increasingly widespread that "sinners" does not just mean the ʿam-hāʾāreṣ ("people of the land") or ordinary folk who did not have Pharisaic zeal for the oral law, as was often previously thought.[48] Rather, they are the notoriously immoral or wicked.[49] Sanders has received some pushback, and his view may need some modification,[50] but overall he has convinced a sizable majority of scholars. If "tax collectors" were viewed as one example within this category of "sinners," the pairing of the terms is even more understandable.

In the little parable of the children in the marketplace (Matt. 11:16–19 par.), part of how Jesus views others' opinions of himself as different from John the Baptist is that they call him "a friend of tax collectors and sinners" (v. 19). Again in Luke 15:1, as part of the introduction to the parables of the lost sheep, coin, and son (vv. 3–32), we read, "Now the tax collectors and sinners were all gathering around to hear Jesus." By the time we have finished the three parables, we recognize that the lost sheep, lost coin, and lost son all correspond to these denigrated individuals. In the famous church-discipline passage (Matt. 18:15–20), Jesus talks about treating those who remain unrepentant, after repeated confrontation by others in the church, "as you would a pagan or a tax collector" (v. 17). Presumably, the two were somehow equivalent in Jesus's mind. And in the parable of the Pharisee and tax collector (Luke 18:9–14), the shock value comes from the latter going home justified rather than the former.

---

48. So esp. Joachim Jeremias, *Jerusalem in the Time of Jesus: An Investigation into Economic and Social Conditions during the New Testament Period*, trans. F. H. Cave and C. H. Cave (London: SCM; Philadelphia: Fortress, 1969 [Ger. orig. 1962]), 26–67, 259. Intriguingly, over thirty years earlier he held a view closer to what Sanders would much later articulate. See Jeremias, "Zöllner und Sünder," *ZNW* 30 (1931): 193–200.

49. E. P. Sanders, *Jesus and Judaism* (London: SCM; Philadelphia: Fortress, 1985), 174–210.

50. Bruce Chilton, "E. P. Sanders and the Question of Jesus and Purity," in Chilton and Evans, *Jesus in Context*, 221–30.

I have dealt with several of these passages in my writing on parables as well as in *Contagious Holiness: Jesus' Meals with Sinners*.[51] Cecilia Wassén takes me to task for confusing ritual impurity with moral turpitude: "So Craig Blomberg, for example, confidently exclaims: 'In banqueting with Levi, Jesus has shown himself unwilling to follow his culture's traditions about not associating with the ritually impure and the morally wicked.' In my view, this kind of reasoning is based on general misconceptions about impurity since contracting ritual impurity was neither unlawful nor always undesirable."[52] I am at a loss to determine what in the quoted words suggests either confidence or an exclamation; her language would seem just to be rhetorical denigration. Maybe she thought that I was equating "the ritually impure" with "the morally wicked," which I was not. Unfortunately, Granville Sharp's rule does not work nearly as well in English as it does in Greek, so my repetition of the definite article ("the") before "ritually impure" and "morally wicked" doesn't as obviously point out as it would have in Greek that I was separating the two categories. Wassén, additionally, seems to be either ignoring or unaware of the extent to which "tax collectors and sinners" involved themselves in activities that did ritually defile them or associated with those who did and were perceived, at least by many, as therefore having defiled themselves as well.[53] Entering their homes and/or eating with those who worshiped idols, handled corpses (as military people often did), and so on could either have actually defiled the tax collector or made others envision him as defiled.

British scholar James Crossley likewise berates me for my views in my article on Jesus's table fellowship with sinners, particularly for my treatment of the unnamed woman who anoints Jesus in Luke 7:36–50.[54] Crossley's comments come in a section in which he is unrelentingly critical of the wealthy in Jesus's world. He deduces that this woman's

---

51. Craig L. Blomberg, *Interpreting the Parables*, 2nd ed. (Downers Grove, IL: IVP Academic, 2012), 262–67, 340–47; Blomberg, *Contagious Holiness*, 149–51.
52. Wassén, "Jesus' Table Fellowship with 'Toll Collectors and Sinners,'" 139.
53. See esp. Corley, *Private Women, Public Meals*, 89–93. At the end of this section, Corley speaks straightforwardly of "Jesus' habit of eating with the ritually impure" (93).
54. James G. Crossley, *Jesus and the Chaos of History: Redirecting the Life of the Historical Jesus* (Oxford: Oxford University Press, 2015), 96–97.

willingness to break an entire jar of costly perfume shows that she is wealthy; if she is a prostitute, she must be a "high-brow" one, deserving of no sympathy whatever. If she is included among those whom Jesus treats in an unexpectedly positive fashion, then this contradicts Crossley's apparent desire to label all the wealthy as seriously corrupt.[55] Perhaps he interpreted my use of the term "riff-raff" to mean only those who are poor, whereas American usage, at least, can include those who are particularly rough, immoral, and/or socially undesirable or disreputable from any socioeconomic bracket.[56] I basically agree with Crossley's analysis of this woman, which makes it all the more ironic how vigorously he disputes me. And he must not have read (or remembered) my section on the account of Zacchaeus (Luke 19:1–10), who very much qualifies as riff-raff.[57] Zacchaeus may not be among the "down and out" who so often appear under this heading in the Synoptics (or as *merely* "outcast," another term I used to which Crossley objected), but he certainly comprises part of the "up and out"!

Speaking of Zacchaeus, we should not move on from tax collectors before commenting on this "chief" tax collector (and seemingly chief sinner). The approach that tries to vindicate Zacchaeus by taking the present tenses in Luke 19:8 as customary or iterative[58] makes little sense in its immediate context. It is, of course, possible that his reputation as a "sinner" (v. 7) is undeserved. Yet, if Sanders is correct that "the sinners" were the notoriously wicked, it would be hard to think of Zaccheus being labeled a "sinner." If his financial dealings were exemplary apart from collecting the heavily levied Roman tax, he would have cut against the grain of the average tax collector and been admired by many. It is true that the NIV's "here and now" in verse 8 predisposes the reader to a more aoristic or punctiliar use of the present tense. Nothing in the Greek *requires* it. But the "today" in verse 9 is most certainly in the

---

55. Crossley, *Jesus and the Chaos of History*, 98–133.
56. Craig L. Blomberg, "The Authenticity and Significance of Jesus' Table Fellowship with Sinners," in *Key Events in the Life of the Historical Jesus: A Collaborative Exploration of Context and Coherence*, ed. Darrell L. Bock and Robert L. Webb (Tübingen: Mohr Siebeck, 2009; Grand Rapids: Eerdmans, 2010), 215–50, esp. 232–34; Blomberg, "Jesus, Sinners and Table Fellowship," *BBR* 19 (2009): 60, 62.
57. Blomberg, *Contagious Holiness*, 151–57.
58. Esp. A. C. Mitchell, "Zacchaeus Revisited: Luke 19,8 as a Defense," *Bib* 71 (1990): 153–76.

Greek (*sēmeron*). If Zacchaeus had always been acting so uprightly, there would have been little need for his implied repentance that leads Jesus to announce that very day as the time of his salvation.[59]

As with leprous people, then, one certainly can exaggerate the difference between Jesus's attitudes and actions and those of the "average" Jewish person. But to avoid one kind of exaggeration, we don't have to exaggerate in the opposite direction and overly play down the frequent *potential* uncleanness and the *probably* outright sinfulness of many tax collectors in Jesus's day. *Jesus was linked with other notorious sinners, yet his attitude still stood out from the crowd. At the same time, we are given only two full-fledged episodes—those with Levi and with Zacchaeus—that describe Jesus's conversation with them at all.* All other mentions are generalizations (Matt. 11:19 par.; Luke 15:1) that don't enable us to determine if Jesus's fraternizing, which was viewed with disapproval by others, was something that occurred weekly, monthly, or annually with a handful or with dozens of "tax collectors and sinners."

### *Exorcisms*

It is striking how often the Synoptic Gospels refer to demon-possessed individuals as those with one or more "unclean" or "impure" (from *akathartos*) spirits (once in Mark, thirteen times in Matthew, six times in Luke). Yet, after a bit of reflection, it would seem natural to refer to the demonic realm as not merely evil but also defiling. Here is "contagious unholiness" doing its worst to damage people.[60] We do not need to enter into the debate over what actually was happening in exorcisms any more than in miracles of healing; as we saw earlier, there is widespread scholarly acknowledgment that Jesus enabled men and women to be whole again through what was at the very least *perceived* to be the channeling of God's power into a person to cure them of illness or to cast out their demons (above, 75, 117).

---

59. See I. Howard Marshall, *The Gospel of Luke: A Commentary on the Greek Text*, NIGTC (Grand Rapids: Eerdmans, 1978), 697–98.
60. See further Kazen, *Jesus and Purity* Halakhah, 300–313.

The most detailed account in Mark, or for that matter in any of the Gospels, is the exorcism of the man in the region of what various manuscripts alternately identify as Gerasa, Gadara, or Gergesa (Mark 5:1–20). The parallels in Matthew and Luke both noticeably abbreviate the episode. Uncharacteristically for the Synoptics, Mark goes into great detail about the unclean and foreboding location where the man lives, describing him in frightening and grotesque terms.[61] After specifically identifying him as "a man with an impure spirit" (v. 2), the first thing Mark tells us is that he "came from the tombs" to meet Jesus. A graveyard is, of course, unclean, as it is a place with many underground corpses. But the man didn't just come from the "cemetery"; he *lived* there (v. 3a), so he was continually impure. As with other demon-possessed individuals, then and now, he had superhuman strength and could not be bound (vv. 3b–4).[62] Mark goes into minute detail about his inability to be subdued, even with chains, even over time, even when both hands and feet had been restrained. Even the strongest person in his area could not control him. Verse 5 then restates the point about his continual presence among the rotting dead, along with his self-harm.[63] "Crying out" employs a Greek verb (*krazō*) that simply refers to speaking or shouting at a loud volume, but in context it certainly suggests some kind of anguish. The next verb confirms that supposition, as he repeatedly "cut himself with stones." The verb here is not just the potentially neutral *koptō*, but the more negative *katakoptō*. Depending on how sharp the edges of the stones were, it can be translated as either "cut" or "bruise."[64]

The frantic activity continues as he runs to Jesus from a distance and falls down before him (v. 6). While forms of *proskyneō* in the Gospels often refer to worship, they don't always, and the term itself essentially

---

61. See Matthew Thiessen, *Jesus and the Forces of Death: The Gospels' Portrayal of Ritual Impurity within First-Century Judaism* (Grand Rapids: Baker Academic, 2021), 143–44.

62. "This is a place no one would want to go for any reason. Contrary to all reason and expectation, however, Jesus goes there. He penetrates both the ritual wall of uncleanness and the formidable reputation of the [demon-possessed man]. For once, however, the explosive terror of the [man] does not prevail" (Edwards, *Gospel according to Mark*, 155–56).

63. See Darrell Bock, *Mark*, NCBC (Cambridge: Cambridge University Press, 2016), 187–89. Bock calls him "the living dead, left with no life" (189).

64. BDAG, s.v. *katakoptō*.

means to prostrate oneself before someone or something.⁶⁵ Although the KJV and the RSV translated the verb here as "worshiped," most English versions have opted for expressions like "bowed down," "bowed low," "knelt," or "fell on his knees." Given someone prone to extremes, "fell on his face" might be more realistic.⁶⁶ Translators probably have been influenced by the assumption that because the man identified Jesus as "Son of the Most High God" (v. 7), in the midst of his terror he was also expressing some kind of reverence or at least acknowledging that he was in the presence of a more powerful being. Yet a growing consensus of contemporary commentators observes that knowing a person's name was often viewed as crucial in spiritual warfare in an attempt to gain mastery over an opponent. The demonized individual is not trying to submit to Jesus but rather to ward him off, to cast him out, as it were.⁶⁷ Instead, Jesus "returns the favor" and proceeds to exorcise the afflicted man (vv. 8–13). By inquiring into the demon's name (v. 9), he shows that he can best the man in this spiritual contest. Even though that name is "Legion," reflecting the number of demons inside the man,⁶⁸ they cowered in Jesus's presence and "begged Jesus again and again" not to entirely banish them (v. 10). The combination of the imperfect tense verb (*parekalei*) with the adverbial accusative *polla* ("many times") in this context creates the picture of ongoing, repeated action.⁶⁹

The impurity in this scene is heightened even more as we learn that "a large herd of pigs was feeding on the nearby hillside" (v. 11). Swine were, of course, about the most unclean animal that Jews could imagine. Because it is not yet the time of the consummation of the kingdom

---

65. Moisés Silva, ed., *New International Dictionary of New Testament Theology and Exegesis*, 5 vols., 2nd ed. (Grand Rapids: Zondervan, 2014), 4:150.

66. Cf. NAB: "He ran up and prostrated himself before him."

67. Graham H. Twelftree, *Jesus the Exorcist: A Contribution to the Study of the Historical Jesus* (Tübingen: J. C. B. Mohr; Peabody, MA: Hendrickson, 1993; repr., Eugene, OR: Wipf & Stock, 2010), 64; Schnabel, *Mark*, 58; Ben Witherington III, *The Gospel of Mark: A Socio-Rhetorical Commentary* (Grand Rapids: Eerdmans, 2001), 90.

68. We do not have to solve the puzzle here about whether Mark is alluding to a Roman legion in an empire-critical episode.

69. It is harder to justify labeling it as an inceptive imperfect, however. See Rodney J. Decker, *Mark 1–8: A Handbook on the Greek Text* (Waco: Baylor University Press, 2014), 24–25, 121.

but merely its inauguration, evil is only partly vanquished, and Jesus agrees to the demons' request that they be sent into the pigs, whom they immediately proceed to destroy (vv. 12–13). Instead of glorying in the healing of one very troubled man, the pig farmers and others who hear about Jesus's actions rue the destruction of their livelihood and beg Jesus to leave their area (vv. 14–17). Even if raising pigs by itself didn't necessarily make one unclean, these farmers, be they Jew or Gentile, no doubt assumed that Jesus entirely disapproved of their practice. Much more frightening conflict could have ensued, so they want to distance themselves from him. Jesus obliges but insists that the healed man stay behind and continue to spread the word about what happened to him among his own people in that region (vv. 18–20).[70]

*It is difficult to exaggerate the amount of unclean defilement present in this account.* While exorcisms are a key indicator of the arrival of God's kingdom (Matt. 12:28; Luke 11:20), they go further and "effect the entry of the diseased and disabled" into the kingdom.[71] As Jodi Magness phrases it, Jesus's "exorcisms and healings as well as his emphasis on moral or ethical behavior are rooted in biblical concerns with the maintenance of holiness, since all creatures entering God's presence must be absolutely perfect."[72] This contrasts with Kazen's view that Jesus had become less concerned with purity matters because he was focusing more on the moral or ethical realm.[73] Matthew Thiessen has devoted a substantial portion of his monograph *Jesus and the Forces of Death* to demonstrating that *Jesus's exorcisms show his continued concern with all areas affected by ritual impurity*. Theissen's conclusions merit quotation at length:

> Ritual impurity remained of fundamental importance for the Gospel writers, but they were convinced that God had introduced something

---

70. The contrast with the injunction in 1:44 to silence is striking, but this man probably is a Gentile who will spread the gospel to Gentiles, where the mistaken messianic expectation of a purely military or royal Messiah is not present as it was in Judaism. See France, *Gospel of Mark*, 232–33.
71. Magness, "'They Shall See the Glory of the Lord' (Isa 35:2)," 99.
72. Magness, "'They Shall See the Glory of the Lord' (Isa 35:2)," 101.
73. Kazen, *Jesus and Purity* Halakhah, 261.

*new* into the world to deal with the sources of these impurities: Jesus. By inserting a new, mobile, and powerfully contagious force of holiness into the world in the person of Jesus, Israel's God has signaled the very coming of the kingdom—a kingdom of holiness and life that throughout the mission of Jesus overwhelms the forces and sources of impurity and death, be they pneumatic, ritual, or moral. Throughout his narrative of Jesus's life, Mark repeatedly depicts Jesus overcoming impurity after impurity. This dramatic story culminates in Jesus facing off with death itself in his crucifixion, taking ritual impurity into his very own body, only once again and with finality to come out victorious when Israel's God raises him from the dead.[74]

Although Mark does not have the Q-saying that links exorcisms to the arrival of the kingdom (Matt. 12:28; Luke 11:20), he appears to depict the same truth in narrative form. The other exorcism accounts in Mark may be much briefer (1:23–28; 7:24–30; 9:17–27), but they share several of the same characteristics of the narrative just surveyed.[75]

### *Genital Discharge*

The story of Jesus's encounter with a woman having a seemingly incurable intermittent flow of blood beyond her normal menstrual cycle (Mark 5:24b–34; see esp. vv. 25–26) contains several unique features. Jesus does not take the initiative in touching her; she reaches out and touches his cloak (v. 27). She believes that even this minor contact that she initiates will be enough to heal her (v. 28). When she does touch him, her current bleeding stops immediately, and she senses something different in her body that convinces her she is cured (v. 29). Jesus, too, senses that "power had gone out from him" (v. 30) and looks around to try to determine who, out of the large crowd pressing in on him (v. 24b), had triggered this exodus of healing power. After a brief interchange with his disciples, who protest the futility of the exercise, the woman falls at his feet and tells him it was she (vv. 31–33). He announces that it

---

74. Thiessen, *Jesus and the Forces of Death*, 179.
75. See esp. Twelftree, *Jesus the Exorcist*; Twelftree, *Jesus the Miracle Worker: A Historical and Theological Study* (Downers Grove, IL: InterVarsity, 1999), both *ad loc.*

was her faith in him, not the seemingly superstitious touch, that healed her. By adding "Go in peace and be freed from your suffering," he suggests that the healing from this malady will be long-lasting (v. 34).[76]

*Genital discharges form another key category of ritual impurity in ancient Israelite law.* Craig Evans uses this account in Mark, the story of the sinful woman deemed to be a prostitute in Luke (7:36–50), and the episode about the disabled individuals who have to be carried into the temple (Acts 3:2) as three examples of unclean people coming into contact with clean ones in contexts where defilement would normally be feared. He stresses that popular Christianity typically misses the implications for purity in texts like these when it emphasizes merely Jesus's compassion.[77] Yet this is also what Cecilia Wassén appears to do in her much more scholarly study. She observes that two conflicting trends exist in the late Second Temple period with respect to genital discharge. One requires the ceremonially defiled person to quarantine and then undergo a washing ritual; the other does not impose a time of isolation. She believes that the former reflects a utopian desire, while the latter represents actual practice.[78] But she does not give any supporting evidence from her primary sources here (the texts of Qumran or Josephus) to justify this. Numerous cultures in the history of the world have practiced a variety of forms of shunning, so it is certainly not that the stricter approach is difficult to envision. She does argue from the fact that the woman in Mark 5 appears "mingling in a crowd, without explaining or defending her presence" that it must have been a matter of comparative indifference for the people there.[79] The more lenient Jewish view also understood it to be acceptable for an unclean menstruant to appear in public if she merely washed her hands. Touching someone else

---

76. Strauss (*Mark*, 232) adds, "The traditional Hebrew farewell, 'Go in peace'. . . here means more than just 'good-bye.' It is an affirmation of not only the woman's healing, but also her restoration to wholeness (*šālôm*) in the community of God."

77. Craig A. Evans, "Who Touched Me? Jesus and the Ritually Impure," in Chilton and Evans, *Jesus in Context*, 353–76.

78. Cecilia Wassén, "Jesus and the Hemorrhaging Woman (Mark 5:24–34): Insights from Purity Laws from the Dead Sea Scrolls," in *Scripture in Transition: Essays on Septuagint, Hebrew Bible, and Dead Sea Scrolls in Honour of Raija Sollamo*, ed. Anssi Voitila and Jutta Jokiranta (Leiden: Brill, 2008), 659.

79. Wassén, "Jesus and the Hemorrhaging Woman (Mark 5:24–34)," 659.

with her hands would then not transmit her impurity to anyone else. In other words, completely opposite to Matthew Theissen, Wassén argues that Mark was not very much interested in matters of ritual purity, so we should not read in concerns here that are not explicitly present.

Once again, we encounter viewpoints that each assume more than is explicitly stated. Almost no one points out that there must have been periods of time when the woman was free from genital discharge—a constant twelve-year-loss of blood would have killed her long ago! Nothing in the text enables us to determine how often she was impure. If she was well known in Capernaum (as she must have been, given its small size), if she had been observing times of quarantine when she was unclean, if she had been ritually cleansing herself after periods of better health, and if she was known in the community to be doing this, people would simply assume that she was clean if they saw her in public. Alternately, we could imagine that she was experiencing one of her more distressing periods yet was desperate enough to seek out Jesus publicly. No one else need have known that, so why must we assume that she would have explained her presence, which would only have made things much more awkward if not even dangerous for her? It is important here to stress that we don't actually know *any* of this, any more than Wassén knows any of her postulated scenario. It is frustrating not to have received more information in Mark's text, but that was not his purpose. As with John's Gospel, we have to distinguish what the evangelists' various readers might have been expected to understand or infer, what a more exclusively Jewish pre-Gospel tradition might have communicated to its audience, and what the historical Jesus himself intended. The further back we go, the likelier it is that there are issues of ritual impurity present, with Jesus demonstrating God's power to cleanse people from that impurity. This is very similar to the position Marla Selvidge takes in seeing vestiges of strict practices concerning ritual impurity underlying the text, whereas Jesus came to do away with the entire category of impurity.[80]

80. Marla J. Selvidge, "Mark 5:25–34 and Leviticus 15:19–20: A Reaction to Restrictive Purity Regulations," *JBL* 103 (1984): 619–23. See also Selvidge, *Woman, Cult, Miracle Recital: A*

Susan Haber takes an intermediate position on what she deems to be a feminist spectrum between perceiving Jesus as strongly critiquing ritual purity and as viewing ritual purity as irrelevant.[81] After a careful study of the historical background and a close exegesis of the text, Haber decides that it is the woman's health, not her ritual purity, that forms Mark's main interest. Still, the issue of purity can't be ignored because it was an integral part of her condition. Haber determines that in both this account and in the healing of the leprous person, "Mark presents Jesus as operating within the framework of the purity legislation. Both individuals have conditions that induce a severe form of impurity, both are made well through physical contact with Jesus that is miraculous, and both are subsequently advised to undergo the appropriate purification rituals which are technical in nature."[82] Yet the main point in each case is Jesus's power to restore people to physical health. "Taken together, they demonstrate a consistency in the Markan Jesus' attitude towards the purity laws applicable to the ill and infirm, a stance that is particularly convincing for the very reason that it is incidental to both narratives."[83] We might add, to the extent that it is incidental, it is also likely to be historical.

Recent studies have taken the passage about the diseased woman in slightly different directions. Louise Gosbell analyzes it from the perspective of disability studies and the implications of her condition in the ancient Mediterranean world. She acknowledges that the woman's impurity affected her situation in this passage but argues that the social and familial consequences need more attention, especially the disabling nature of her probable infertility.[84] Mi Young Sydney Park calls attention to the woman having suffered a lot (v. 26) by her shedding of blood, and her severe affliction (vv. 29, 34), which links with Jesus's crucifixion.

---

*Redactional Critical Investigation on Mark 5:24–34* (Lewisburg, PA: Bucknell University Press; London: Associated University Presses, 1990), 86–91.

81. Susan Haber, "A Woman's Touch: Feminist Encounters with the Hemorrhaging Woman in Mark 5.24–34," *JSNT* 26 (2003): 171.

82. Haber, "A Woman's Touch," 191.

83. Haber, "A Woman's Touch," 191.

84. Louise Gosbell, "The Woman with the Flow of Blood (Mark 5:25–34) and Disability in the Ancient World," *JGAR* 2 (2018): 22–43.

Sandwiched between the two parts of the account of the resurrection of Jairus's daughter (5:21–24a, 35–43), the account of the hemorrhaging woman is tied in all the more closely to a narrative about death, followed by resurrection. Park concludes that these passages demonstrate how faith in Jesus can bring freedom from sin, death, and all forms of impurity.[85] Candida Moss, finally, observes that the bodies of both the woman and Jesus are "porous"—they "leak" apart from the control or intention of the individual. By ancient Greco-Roman standards, this made Jesus also appear sickly, weak, and perhaps feminine. But Jesus subverts this dominant view because he leaks positive power that heals the woman and hints at his true identity.[86] While each of these studies proves helpful, none of them subtracts from Haber's conclusions noted above. *Ritual impurity and purification are not major issues either in this passage in particular or for Mark in general, but they appear just enough to suggest that they may have been much more significant at the level of the historical Jesus.*

### *Death and Resurrection*

Having just noted the intercalation between the account of the cure of the hemorrhaging woman and the story of the resurrection of Jairus's daughter, we should pause just long enough to remind ourselves that *Jesus's overcoming the powers of death in this fashion certainly involves purifying the most ritually impure entity of all: the corpse.* Once again, we see Jesus initiating a defiling touch as he takes the hand of the dead girl to lift her up (5:41). Once again, too, there is no hint of this defiling Jesus; rather, he is purifying the young woman by raising her back to life.[87] The other resurrection account found among the Synoptics, the raising of the son of the widow of Nain (Luke 7:11–17), also contains a significant touch. Here Jesus touches the bier, or coffin, in which the young man has already been placed (v. 14). It appears to

---

85. Mi Young Sydney Park, "Inerrancy and Blood: Women and Christology in Leviticus 12 and 15, and Mark 5:21–43," *Presb* 45 (2019): 83–95.
86. Candida R. Moss, "The Man with the Flow of Power: Porous Bodies in Mark 5:25–34," *JBL* 129 (2010): 507–19.
87. Thiessen, *Jesus and the Forces of Death*, 178.

have been an open casket, because the boy was able to sit up (v. 15). Jesus's touching it may have indicated to the pallbearers to stop. Touching a container carrying a corpse probably would have been viewed by many as a way to incur uncleanness even without touching the body itself.[88] Once more, however, Jesus is not defiled, but he purifies and brings back to life the one who had died.

The original ending of Mark,[89] nevertheless, does not narrate an actual resurrection appearance. It is not that Mark does not believe that Jesus was raised; he has preserved Jesus's multiple resurrection predictions (Mark 8:31 pars.; 9:31 pars.; 10:34 pars.), and he has just recorded the reminder that the disciples should go to Galilee where they would meet the resurrected Jesus (16:7). But Mark's is much more a theology of the cross than of the resurrection.[90] To the extent that the resurrection of Jairus's daughter cuts a little against that grain, it is even more likely historical, at least if one is open to the concept of resurrection at all. And before one forecloses on that question, one needs to examine the sophisticated defenses of the resurrection of Jesus that have emerged in recent years,[91] along with Craig Keener's thoroughly documented catalogues of miraculous contemporary resurrections (though not yet resurrections to eternal life as in the case of Jesus).[92]

*We have now seen examples in Mark of the three major forms of ritual impurity: skin disease, genital discharge, and corpse uncleanness. While not a major issue for Mark at the redactional level or for his*

---

88. Rabbinic literature spoke of defilement by overshadowing, by coming too close to that which was impure in a variety of settings. See esp. b. Naz. 54a–b.

89. That is, the last sentences of Mark 16:1–8. For a plausible account of the origin of the longer ending of Mark (vv. 9–20), see James A. Kelhoffer, *Miracle and Mission: The Authentication of Missionaries and Their Message in the Longer Ending of Mark* (Tübingen: Mohr Siebeck, 2000).

90. See esp. David E. Garland, *A Theology of Mark's Gospel: Good News about Jesus the Messiah, the Son of God* (Grand Rapids: Zondervan, 2015), 472–506.

91. See esp. N. T. Wright, *The Resurrection of the Son of God*, Christian Origins and the Question of God 3 (London: SPCK; Minneapolis: Fortress, 2003); Michael R. Licona, *The Resurrection of Jesus: A New Historiographical Approach* (Downers Grove, IL: IVP Academic; Nottingham: Apollos, 2010).

92. Craig S. Keener, *Miracles: The Credibility of the New Testament Accounts*, 2 vols. (Grand Rapids: Baker Academic, 2011), 1:536–79; Keener, *Miracles Today: The Supernatural Work of God in the Modern World* (Grand Rapids: Baker Academic, 2021), 137–74. See also Keener, "'The Dead Are Raised' (Matthew 11:5//Luke 7:22): Resuscitation Accounts in the Gospels and Eyewitness Testimony," *BBR* 25 (2015): 55–79.

*predominantly Gentile Christian audience*,[93] *it would have been more significant for the historical Jesus within Israel.* Seth Ehorn's brief survey of the same material concurs. Somewhat like Thiessen, Ehorn concludes that Jesus as he is depicted here "is not indifferent or casual with regard to ritual impurity, but rather is consistently opposed to it."[94] But *he opposes it not by attacking those who contract it; instead, he removes its cause and restores the afflicted by providing them purity and wholeness.*

### Ritual Handwashing and Dietary Laws

For a majority of scholars, the passage in Mark that has the most direct bearing on the question of ritual purity is 7:1–23. What begins as a question from certain Pharisees to Jesus as to why his disciples ate with unwashed hands ends with Jesus seeming to abolish all food laws (v. 19b). Several exegetical cruxes occupy the exegete's attention here. What is the relationship between the two topics? It is clear that it is the Pharisees who are objecting to the nonobservance of an oral law ("the tradition of the elders" [v. 3]), so how can Mark say that "all the Jews" practice this ritual handwashing? It is clear, too, that Jesus's two-part rebuke in verses 6–8 and 9–13 focuses on examples involving oral laws ("merely human rules" [v. 7]; "human traditions" [v. 8]; "your own traditions" [v. 9]; "your tradition that you have handed down" [v. 13]), so should verses 14–15 be understood within this same context? Or is Jesus making a more sweeping claim when he says, "Nothing outside a person can defile them by going into them" (v. 15)? Is he now challenging the written law of Moses as well? Most controversial of all, how are we to interpret verse 19b, after Jesus leaves the crowd and speaks to his disciples privately? Did Jesus really abolish the Jewish dietary laws from that moment onward?

---

93. Even on the earliest of the standard options for dating Mark, in the very early 60s, he would have been addressing a church in Rome that was at least somewhat more Gentile than Jewish, even though it may have had a sizable minority of Jewish believers. See Craig L. Blomberg, *Jesus and the Gospels: An Introduction and Survey*, 3rd ed. (Nashville: B&H Academic; London: Inter-Varsity, 2022), 194–98.

94. Seth M. Ehorn, "Jesus and Ritual Impurity in Mark's Gospel," in *For Us, but Not to Us: Essays on Creation, Covenant, and Context in Honor of John H. Walton*, ed. Adam E. Miglio et al. (Eugene, OR: Pickwick, 2020), 231.

A fair cross-section of scholarship would assert that Jesus's primary focus in verses 1–5 is to deny the importance of the additional halakic tradition that has grown up around impurity in the context of meals.[95] Mark's assertion that "all the Jews" practice ceremonial handwashing before eating can easily be rhetorical hyperbole. Yet especially when we recall how pervasive the stone water jars seem to have been, it is not hard to imagine this one feature of Pharisaic tradition gaining widespread currency, particularly as the importance of purity before prayer was growing in popularity and prayers before meals were standard.[96] Verses 6–8 have often been labeled as redactional, either because they seem inappropriately harsh toward the Pharisees and scribes or because the human rules to which Isaiah 29:13 refer are quite different ones.[97] The first of these charges is bound up with the larger issue of supposed anti-Semitism in the Gospels; a short reply is that nothing is ever attributed to Jesus the Jew that is any harsher than the strong condemnations of the faithless in Israel by the prophets whose words were canonized in the Hebrew Scriptures.[98] The second charge misses the fact that Jesus is just using an analogy. The human rules may be quite different ones in Jesus's day, but they are still "merely human rules," and he perceives that his critics are, like the Israelites in Isaiah's day, merely giving lip service to worship and obedience.

The practice of corban has nothing to do with ritual purity but is another example of oral law actually impeding obedience to the written law (vv. 9–13). One can imagine a larger group of bystanders overhearing Jesus's conversation with the scribes and Pharisees. Now he calls them in closer (v. 14a). Whether the religious leaders left at this point, having just been insulted, cannot be determined, though it is easy enough to envision them doing so. The point that Jesus wants

---

95. Thomas Kazen, *Issues of Impurity in Early Judaism* (Winona Lake, IN: Eisenbrauns, 2010), 135.

96. John C. Poirier, "Purity beyond the Temple in the Second Temple Era," *JBL* 122 (2003): 256.

97. Thomas R. Hatina, "Did Jesus Quote Isaiah 29:13 against the Pharisees?," *BBR* 16 (2006): 79–94.

98. On which, see esp. Craig A. Evans and Donald A. Hagner, eds., *Anti-Semitism and Early Christianity: Issues of Polemic and Faith* (Minneapolis: Fortress, 1993).

to make in the hearing of all who remain, going back to the topic of ritual purity that started this exchange, comes in verses 14–15: "Listen to me, everyone, and understand this. Nothing outside a person can defile them by going into them. Rather, it is what comes out of a person that defiles them." How widely was Jesus applying this principle? Bruce Chilton thinks that the ministry of John the Baptist made the general populace of Israel clean overall. Jesus could assume that the ordinary person was ritually pure until their actions showed their need for further purification. So they scarcely needed ritual handwashing before each meal.[99] There is no difficulty attributing this principle to the historical Jesus, but is that all Jesus meant?

Roger Booth speaks for a number of scholars when he takes this as a typical Semitic "not *a* but *b*" construction that really means "*b* much more than *a*."[100] Of course, unclean food could make an Israelite unclean, but that topic has not been on the table. Jesus's primary thought here is what he will elaborate on in verses 20–23: it is immoral behavior, all of which emanates from impure thinking, that is the most important kind of defilement to avoid. Then again, if one takes the context of ritual handwashing to be determinative, Jesus's words could be intended more absolutely. Taking for granted that one is eating kosher food, that food cannot defile people even if they don't purify themselves by washing their hands first.[101] Sarah Whittle compares Mark 7:1–23 with the Letter of Aristeas and observes that it has some similar moral/ritual distinctions that are likened to internal/external distinctions without abolishing the ritual or the external, which is in fact given to facilitate the moral or the internal. But she finds Mark's Jesus more absolute, even with a few gray areas.[102] We may have to

---

99. Bruce Chilton, "A Generative Exegesis of Mark 7:1–23," in Chilton and Evans, *Jesus in Context*, 316.

100. Roger P. Booth, *Jesus and the Laws of Purity: Tradition History and Legal History in Mark 7* (Sheffield: JSOT Press, 1986), 219. Yair Furstenberg believes that verses 14–15 can be preserved as authentic but still viewed as part of an intra-Jewish halakic debate ("Defilement Penetrating the Body: A New Understanding of Contamination in Mark 7.15," *NTS* 54 [2008]: 176–200).

101. Eric Ottenheijm, "Impurity between Intention and Deed: Purity Disputes in First Century Judaism and in the New Testament," in Poorthuis and Schwartz, *Purity and Holiness*, 146–47.

102. Sarah Whittle, "The Letter of Aristeas and Mark 7:1–23," in *Reading Mark in Context: Jesus and Second Temple Judaism*, ed. Ben C. Blackwell, John K. Goodrich, and Jason Matson (Grand Rapids: Zondervan, 2018), 108–15.

settle the interpretation of verse 19 before we can determine how far verses 14–15 apply. After all, verses 18–19 are purported to be Jesus's explanation to the disciples of his earlier "parable" (v. 17), which they didn't understand either.

Verse 18 basically repeats verse 15a, asserting that nothing going into a person from the outside can defile them. Jesus then continues with verse 19. A hopelessly literal rendering of it might read, "for it does not go into of him into the heart but into the belly, and into the latrine it goes out, cleansing all foods." John Fischer adopts a perspective that at first glance, in English translation, appears promising. What if this is not a declaration by Jesus that *he* was cleansing all foods, but a statement that the process of bodily elimination cleanses or purges all food?[103] This may sound fine in English, but it is almost impossible in the Greek. If either the "belly" or the "latrine" was the entity that purged all food, the participle "cleansing" (*katharizōn*) would need to be in the accusative case to agree with the accusative forms of "belly" (*koilian*) or "latrine" (*aphedrōna*). If it modified "belly," it would also have to be feminine. But *katharizōn* is a *masculine* form, and it is not accusative but *nominative*. It must refer to a nominative subject. The last such subject is all the way back in verse 18: "the thing from the outside" (*to exōthen*). Yet this expression is neuter and not masculine. So now we must go back to the "he" (Jesus) who is the built-in subject of the verb "says" (*legei*) at the beginning of verse 18. There is no grammatical way around the fact that it was Jesus who cleansed all foods.[104]

Must this, though, mean the same thing as "declared all foods clean"? Maurice Casey argues that verse 15 applies solely to the original question about handwashing. Kosher food eaten with unwashed hands does not defile; it is the urine and the feces (what comes out of a person) that defile them. This is how he believes Matthew understood matters, because Matthew 15:20 ends the conversation by saying explicitly that what is eaten with unwashed hands does not defile. And here he thinks

---

103. John Fischer, "Messianic Congregations Should Exist and Should Be Very Jewish," in *How Jewish Is Christianity? Two Views on the Messianic Movement*, ed. Louis Goldberg (Grand Rapids: Zondervan, 2003), 133.

104. Decker, *Mark 1–8*, 192.

that Matthew has preserved Jesus's original intent, even though usually Matthew is editing Mark.[105] Of course, as disgusting as human waste is to most people, it was not, strictly speaking, ritually defiled or defiling in and of itself. And Casey goes on to assume that Mark then added the moral/ritual contrast of verses 20–23 as an interpretation more relevant for Gentiles that was not based on Jesus's teaching.[106]

André LaCocque believes that since the disciples refer in verse 17 to Jesus's enigmatic saying of verse 15 as a parable, we have greater flexibility in its interpretation. It need not be a sweeping absolute that abolishes the Mosaic dietary laws.[107] He recognizes that Jesus is suggesting purity rather than impurity as contagious, and he believes that Jesus did not set aside the purity codes but simply made it possible for people to be cleansed from all their impurities.[108] This is somewhat analogous to the approach that Thiessen took with the role of Jesus's exorcisms (see above, 352–54). Keener adopts a similar perspective and adds that the "parable" is not likely to have been invented, precisely because of all of its ambiguity and the controversy it caused even in its earliest context.[109] Especially because Matthew's special tradition (i.e., material unique to his Gospel) is recognized as sometimes preserving authentic material, we ought to consider Matthew 5:17 as an interpretive key here.[110] *As with the rest of the law, Jesus insists that he came not to abolish the dietary laws but to fulfill them, which in this case involves considerable transformation.*[111] Paraphrasing David deSilva, we might say that Jesus shows a striking willingness to cross boundaries and associate with those who at least some people would have deemed unclean. He fulfills the command to be holy as God is holy (Lev. 19:1) by bringing wholeness to people

---

105. Maurice Casey, *Jesus: Evidence and Argument or Mythicist Myths?* (London: Bloomsbury T&T Clark, 2014), 146–47.
106. Casey, *Jesus*, 146.
107. André LaCocque, *Jesus the Central Jew: His Times and His People* (Atlanta: SBL Press, 2015), 107.
108. LaCocque, *Jesus the Central Jew*, 119.
109. Keener, *Historical Jesus of the Gospels*, 221.
110. Craig L. Blomberg, *A New Testament Theology* (Waco: Baylor University Press, 2018), 70–71.
111. Ben F. Meyer, *The Aims of Jesus* (London: SCM, 1979; San Jose: Pickwick, 2002), 148.

across those boundaries. In short, Jesus remaps "purity and pollution along ethical lines."[112]

We still need to deal with Mark 7:19b. There are a few who understand this half-verse ("In saying this, Jesus declared all foods clean") as implying that Jesus, at the very moment he was talking to the crowds, made an announcement that all food was now "kosher," or at least that in his explanation to the disciples afterward in verses 18–19 he was making that breathtaking announcement.[113] Why, then, does Peter, possibly a decade later, have to receive the vision of animals of all kinds, clean and unclean, with God telling him to kill and eat them (Acts 10:9–16)? Why does he need that experience to overcome his reluctance in going with the Gentile messengers from Cornelius's house to preach the gospel to that centurion and his family and friends (10:19–20, 34–35)? One could reply that Peter was always a bit slow to understand new developments in God's plans and in Jesus's ministry, but all the evidence from the rest of the New Testament suggests that it was a slow, fitful process by which the entire first generation of Jesus's followers finally came to the conviction that "all food is clean, but it is wrong for a person to eat anything that causes someone else to stumble" (Rom. 14:20), or that "food does not bring us near to God; we are no worse if we do not eat, and no better if we do" (1 Cor. 8:8).[114]

The most obvious answer is that we must understand Mark 7:19b as a parenthetical comment by Mark reflecting the general Christian understanding at the time he wrote his Gospel. As we have seen, "cleansing all foods" cannot grammatically be part of Jesus's words, despite the KJV rendering of verse 19 as "because it entereth not into his heart, but into the belly, and goeth out into the draught, purging all meats." The CJB, CSB, ESV, NAB, NASB, NET, NIV, NJB, NLT, NRSV, and RSV all use parentheses to set off verse 19b from the rest of the sentence. Most of them then add a "thus" or "by/in saying this,"

---

112. David A. deSilva, "Clean and Unclean," in *Dictionary of Jesus and the Gospels*, ed. Joel B. Green, Jeannine K. Brown, and Nicholas Perrin, 2nd ed. (Downers Grove, IL: IVP Academic, 2013), 146.

113. So, apparently, Rainer Riesner, *Messias Jesus: Seine Geschichte, seine Botschaft und ihre Überlieferung* (Giessen: Brunnen, 2019), 180.

114. See France, *Gospel of Mark*, 277–79.

interpreting the participle as one of result. Even the NKJV and the CEB, which do not use parentheses, nevertheless insert a "thus." Like Jesus's full-fledged narrative parables, there was an opaque dimension to verses 14–15, in part repeated in verses 18–19a. Jesus lived as a Torah-obedient Jew because his was still the age of the law. But in fulfilling the law, he established some principles that would lead his followers to interpret the significance of his teaching as changing the way they obeyed certain parts of the law. *Mark is affirming that the Christian community by the time of the writing of his Gospel had come to believe that part of the significance of Jesus's teaching here in Mark 7 meant that in the age of the new covenant, a kosher table was now optional.*[115] *Declaring all foods clean was a key prerequisite for Jesus's Jewish followers to understand that God was likewise declaring all people clean.*

This allows verses 20–23 to be understood as essentially authentic.[116] The immorality that originates in human hearts is what defiles people, not what they eat. But this is the fulfillment of Judaism, not its denigration or supersession. The kind of exegesis to which Amy-Jill Levine, Cecilia Wassén, and Tobias Hägerland object (see above, 342–43, 346, 349) is only partially being affirmed here. As Christian Stettler explains, "It is correct to say that Jesus did away with the purity Torah—but not to put an end to Judaism. Rather he wanted to bring God's will for Israel and the world, the binding revelation of which was in the Torah, to its realization, and bring to Israel the complete purity of God's people in the last days."[117] Nevertheless, it took the first disciples' numerous encounters with less than fully observant Jewish and Samaritan groups in the early church's evangelistic ministry (esp. in Acts 8–9), Peter's vision of unclean animals from heaven and the response of Cornelius and his companions (Acts 10), the preaching in Syrian Antioch to full-fledged Gentiles rather than simply to God-fearers (Acts 11:20), and the apostolic council in Acts 15:1–29 to

---

115. Bock, *Mark*, 225.
116. Christian Stettler, "Purity of Heart in Jesus' Teaching: Mark 7:14–23 par. as an Expression of Jesus' *Basileia* Ethics," *JTS* 55 (2004): 500.
117. Stettler, "Purity of Heart in Jesus' Teaching," 501.

work this all out. Even then, there were steps taken backward as well as forward (see esp. Acts 21:17–36).

## *Other Texts*

The journey of the seventy(-two) disciples in Luke 10:1–20 includes obeying Jesus's command to stay with people who promote peace, "eating and drinking whatever they give you" (v. 7). The command is repeated in verse 8: "When you enter a town and are welcomed, eat what is offered to you." This can hardly be an injunction against the disciples being picky eaters if there are certain dishes they don't enjoy! To the extent that this mission includes Gentiles or even foreshadows the Gentile mission,[118] Jesus's point could well be not to be concerned about unclean food, or at least not to be worried about associating, even at table, with those who ate it.[119] If this seemed too shocking, he could have been interpreted as giving special instructions for a unique occasion rather than establishing an ongoing principle.

One chapter later, in Luke 11:37–41, Jesus rebukes a Pharisee who invites him to dinner and is taken aback when he notices that Jesus does not wash before the meal. Generalizing to a larger group, Jesus replies, "Now then, you Pharisees clean the outside of the cup and dish, but inside you are full of greed and wickedness. You foolish people! Did not the one who made the outside make the inside also? But now as for what is inside you—be generous to the poor, and everything will be clean for you." Verse 41a is difficult to translate; its sequence of words yields "however the things inside give alms" (*plēn ta enonta dote eleēmosynēn*). Which one of the two accusatives in the double-accusative construction is the direct object and which is the predicate object? In other words, should we translate it along the lines of "as for the things inside, give alms" or "give the things inside as alms"? Either way, what would the statement mean? The NRSV, ESV, and NASB all offer readings like the second of these but give the

---

118. Marshall, *Gospel of Luke*, 415; Garland, *Luke*, 425.
119. David L. Matson, "'Eating and Drinking Whatever They Provide' (Luke 10:5–7): Luke's Household Mission of the Seventy(-Two) in Light of the Philip Esler / E. P. Sanders Debate," *PRS* 42 (2015): 371–89.

reader no help as to what the meaning might be. Alternately, *ta enonta* could be an adverbial accusative of manner, and we could translate "give alms inwardly" in the sense of "give from your heart" (NET) or "give from what is within" (CSB). Best of all may be an adverbial accusative of respect, as with the NIV: "as for what is inside you—be generous to the poor."[120] On any of these translations, nevertheless, what follows is that "everything is/will be clean for you." Once again Jesus is cryptic, but he seems at least to be hinting at a coming change in the laws of ritual purity.[121] On the other hand, this passage also lends itself to an interpretation in which only the oral law is challenged, whereas Mark 7:1–23 still seems to be more sweeping in what it envisions.[122]

Matthew 23:25–26, however, does appear to be less sweeping. It resembles the Luke 11 passage in part, but it appears in an entirely different setting and probably represents an independent tradition.[123] Jesus reproves the scribes and Pharisees he is addressing: "You clean the outside of the cup and dish, but inside they are full of greed and self-indulgence. Blind Pharisee! First clean the inside of the cup and dish, and then the outside also will be clean." Here nothing suggests that *everything* is clean, but simply that these religious authorities need to reverse their priorities. Inward purity produces outward cleanliness. Jesus begins with a classic mixed metaphor, since cups and dishes don't contain greed and self-indulgence, although the people who use them may. But using this kind of example allows Jesus not to have to accuse his listeners of greed and self-indulgence; they can infer that for themselves. There is enough already in Matthew 23 that is directly offensive. More importantly, though, it suggests that there may be a more general principle about inside and outside that could apply beyond the specific example at hand.[124]

---

120. Marshall, *Luke*, 495; Garland, *Luke*, 494.
121. R. T. France, *The Gospel of Matthew*, NICNT (Grand Rapids: Eerdmans, 2007), 875; Matthias Konradt, *The Gospel according to Matthew: A Commentary*, trans. M. Eugene Boring (Waco: Baylor University Press, 2020), 348.
122. Tomson, "Purity Laws Viewed by Church Fathers and Jesus," 90.
123. Darrell L. Bock, *Luke*, 2 vols., BECNT (Grand Rapids: Baker, 1994–96), 2:1106–8.
124. Grant R. Osborne, *Matthew*, ZECNT (Grand Rapids: Zondervan, 2010), 852–53.

## Conclusion

Focusing just on the scholarship that *has* investigated ritual purity and the historical Jesus could make it look like it is a major topic in contemporary research. This would be misleading. Most third- and fourth-quest research barely touches on it. There is, however, noticeably more than during any previous period of study. Not surprisingly, as often when scholarship tries to fill in its gaps, some have gone overboard in the opposite direction, arguing that purity was a major issue for Jesus, even if the tradition and the evangelists later played it down. Instead of seeing Jesus as abolishing the ritual law, including laws of ritual purity, they see him as preserving them, even if placing his emphases at times elsewhere. We should take our cue from Matthew 5:17. Jesus did not come to abolish any of the law, but neither did he automatically preserve any of it unchanged. He came to fulfill it, and that requires taking each portion or theme within the Torah and running it through a filter of what Jesus did and said about it. By focusing mostly on Mark and on passages that stand a good chance of being authentic, at least at their core, we have maximized our chances of determining what the historical and not just the canonical Jesus did and spoke.

Quite a few researchers have picked up on the term "contagious" to describe either the purity or the holiness (or both) that Jesus offered. Especially when it was observed that the Hebrew Bible and Second Temple Judaism viewed impurity and/or wickedness as more contagious, this difference is striking. The study by Christian Grappe of Jesus and impurity strikingly matches my findings. The English-language abstract prefacing it states:

> Jesus' attitude toward impurity and his relative indifference concerning the ritual law are to be understood in the context of the dynamics of the coming Kingdom and of the manifestation of the Holy Spirit. Wherever the radical newness of the imminent Kingdom comes to light, one can see a new understanding of space and human responsibility. Holiness invades the secular sphere and opens up space, which brings about a

radical change in the attitude toward impurity. In turn, this gracious occupation of space by holiness results in high ethical standards.[125]

Or, as Richard Beck phrases it more succinctly, "What is striking about the gospel accounts is how Jesus reverses negativity dominance. Jesus is, to coin a term, *positivity dominant*. Contact with Jesus purifies."[126] But Beck also observes how counterintuitive this is for all religious groups, not least Christianity.

---

125. Christian Grappe, "Jésus et l'impureté," *RHPR* 84 (2004): 393.
126. Richard Beck, *Unclean: Meditations on Purity, Hospitality and Mortality* (Cambridge: Lutterworth, 2012), 30.

# Conclusion

Each chapter of this book has concluded with a reasonably detailed summary, so I will not simply repeat all that information here. I will give a much briefer precis, and then turn to key implications of my findings. Those implications will be divided between consequences for the academy and ramifications for the church. Suggestions are programmatic and by no means comprehensive. Hopefully, they will stimulate further reflection on how both institutions can improve in the areas on which this study impinges.

## Summary of Key Results

Albert Schweitzer's overview of the quest for the historical Jesus at the end of the nineteenth century proved, and still proves, to be an invaluable resource. Given the forms of research at his disposal, it was a monumental achievement. At the same time, the selection and arrangement of works summarized and critiqued clearly served to commend thoroughgoing eschatology as the key lens with which to understand Jesus of Nazareth. The remarkably widespread agreement across the scholarly spectra today that we should speak instead of inaugurated eschatology, of the already-but-not-yet kingdom, inevitably means that Schweitzer and those he critiques need to be evaluated slightly differently. Jesus's teaching was more than an interim ethic for the very short period of time before the eschaton. There are also more elements of the social gospel in Jesus's agenda than Schweitzer acknowledged, even as there are more elements in Jesus's agenda than what old liberalism recognized.

The period of "no quest" was only a diminution of Jesus research, and then largely limited to Germany. What grew up to replace it, to a significant degree, was form criticism, with its numerous hypotheses about the nature of the oral tradition between the life of Jesus and the composition of the Gospels. Two world wars also had a noticeable effect on the slowing of scholarship, especially in Germany, while the Third Reich spawned the greatest cluster of searches for an Aryan Jesus. Rudolf Bultmann's work towered over everyone else's during these decades; whatever criticisms his version of form criticism merited, his allegiance to the Confessing Church and rejection of Nazism shone brightly during those dark days. In the 1950s, several of his former students began the "new quest" of the historical Jesus. Their epistemology broke from Bultmann more than their portraits of Jesus did, because they recognized the need for Christian faith to be based on at least a skeleton of historical facts about him. But residues of the atomism of form criticism and the anti-Semitism of the previous decades could still be detected here and there.

The third quest planted the historical Jesus squarely within an early first-century milieu in Israel. It addressed larger issues of Jesus's aims and goals. It studied his deeds as much as his teachings. It recognized the interconnectedness of all the elements of his life and the need to synthesize its findings into a consistent and plausible whole. It branched out into interdisciplinary research, particularly sociological analysis of the relevant cultures and events of Jesus's day, to help interpret him better. The third quest refined and supplemented the criteria of authenticity that had begun to develop with Bultmann and his students. More and more Synoptic material, especially that which was multiply attested, turned out to show good promise of being authentic. Yet, as in the previous quests, at least since Friedrich Schleiermacher, very little of the Gospel of John was ever deemed useful in reconstructing the historical Jesus. By the turn of the millennium, nevertheless, a significant percentage of the guild was viewing him as an eschatological prophet, a herald of the kingdom, who at least implicitly made a variety of messianic claims.

The 1990s also turned out to be the heyday of a throwback quest. Although Robert Funk would declare almost everyone who significantly disagreed with him to be a "pretend quester," it was his Jesus Seminar that, at least in its overall findings, acted as if classic form criticism, anti-Semitism, and the earliest period of the new quest had never been supplanted or even modified. Its cochairs, Marcus Borg and John Dominic Crossan, leading Jesus scholars in their own right, replaced the apocalyptic Jesus with a sapiential one. Its historical findings were about as pessimistic as Bultmann's had been in his most skeptical years. Because the Jesus Seminar and its leaders courted media attention to an unprecedented extent among biblical scholars, public awareness of their perspective outstripped the percentage of the guild that they actually represented.

The 2000s have seen a wide diversity of perspectives so far. It is always hardest for historians to write about the period nearest to their own, because they have the greatest wealth of information about it and the least amount of time to determine which developments will have the greatest staying power and the most lasting effects. Some of the research of the last twenty years has used third-quest methodology; a much smaller amount has propagated Funk and company. Significant studies have authenticated even more of the Synoptic material than was heretofore thought possible. New criteria have been proposed and critiqued; perhaps the most promising is the double similarity and double dissimilarity criterion, also known as the criterion of historical plausibility. Despite occasional claims to the contrary, three approaches to the oral tradition begun in the twentieth century have continued to show the overall probability of a more conservative transmission than was thought to be the case in the halcyon years of form criticism. The guarded tradition hypothesis showed how much of the narratives of Jesus's life could have been memorized. Informal, controlled tradition highlighted a certain flexibility in the retelling of epic material but within clearly fixed limits. Social memory, finally, pointed out checks and balances involved in the traditioning process, which would have fostered reasonably careful preservation of accurate historical information throughout the first thirty to forty years of oral tradition.

Most historical Jesus research throughout the last sixty years has functioned as if the "new look on John" had never emerged. This new look is a movement, nevertheless, that showed how, despite all the ways in which the Fourth Gospel stands out noticeably from its three canonical peers, a growing number of its details actually hold out hope for being historically trustworthy, at times even more so than some of their Synoptic counterparts. The "new look" was given its biggest boost by the formation of the "John, Jesus, and History" seminar in the Society of Biblical Literature, which has been providing for the past twenty years much of the crucial scholarship in this arena. Various factors explain the noticeably different style and contents of the Fourth Gospel, but the best criteria of authenticity can nevertheless help to validate a surprising amount of Johannine material. Paul Anderson's historical Jesus book best demonstrates how far researchers have come.

It is appropriate, as a result, to speak of a newly emerging fourth quest of the historical Jesus. To the extent that it continues, with new studies building on what has already appeared, it will be an area of scholarship that gives John's Gospel parity with the Synoptics as a potential "database" for historical information about Jesus of Nazareth. One of several possible ways of going further with the fourth quest is what the second half of this book has undertaken. A particularly useful criterion of authenticity involves identifying passages or portions of passages that cut against the grain of the redaction or most emphasized theology of a given Gospel writer. If one brackets both the changes to one's sources that recur the most frequently and the overall themes that simply prove the most pervasive, what remains stands a higher chance of being historical. If one can discern patterns of contents or consistent emphases among these remaining details, then they may well represent key motifs in the life of the historical Jesus.

Applying this approach to John's Gospel yields one candidate for such a motif fairly quickly: purity, especially ritual purity. Unique to the Fourth Gospel is the extent to which Jesus is embedded in the ministry of John the Baptist at the outset of his public career. In fact, it is only in John where we read that Jesus himself baptized, adopting a classic purification rite. A large cluster of purity concepts appears in John 1–4, which is

# Conclusion

largely devoted to Jesus's public career before the so-called great Galilean ministry that dominates the first half of the Synoptics narratives. In addition to John's baptism appear the transformation into wine of water used in purity rituals, an attempt to purify the temple, discussion with Nicodemus about the purifying nature of spiritual rebirth, and the offer of the purifying water of salvation to the Samaritan woman at the well.

The second main chronological section of John (chaps. 5–11) initiates a change on this front. Whereas chapters 1–4 show Jesus imitating John the Baptist and paralleling his ministry, chapters 5–11 correspond to the period in the Synoptics in which Jesus is caricatured more as a "party lover" than an ascetic (Matt. 11:18–19 // Luke 7:33–34). Particularly after John the Baptist is imprisoned and then executed, Jesus appears to go his own way. There are still plenty of references to purity, but Jesus is increasingly setting the stage for moving beyond *ritual* purity concerns even as he continues to fulfill them. The water motif is still prevalent, but it is Jesus rather than other conduits who provides cleansing and wholeness. He bypasses the pool of Bethesda, requires no handwashing in the wilderness, claims to fulfill the water-drawing ritual of Sukkoth, improves on the cleansing power of Siloam, brings to completion the full meaning of the repurification of the temple, and overcomes the ultimate impurity of the grave with the resurrection of Lazarus.

Chapters 12–21 begin with a couple of important rituals related to purification but then almost entirely abandon the topic. The traces that remain are more about spiritual sanctification than about ritual cleansing. The transformation to the new age, with its Spirit-filled purification, is nearly complete. Still, the brief references that do appear occur in highly strategic places: Passover and the preparation for Jesus's death, including footwashing; the theological center of a possibly chiastically arranged Farewell Discourse, with its focus on pruning/cleansing; at the heart of a prayer with remarkable parallels to all but one of the petitions of the Synoptic Lord's Prayer, with Jesus's and the believers' further dedication to God; soon after Jesus dies, with the cleansing outflow of water and blood; and accompanying his resurrection, with Peter's puzzling immersion.

How does the motif of the historical Jesus and purity in John correspond to what we find on the topic in the Synoptics? Few Jesus books since the rise of modern scholarship have treated the issue very much; those limiting their scope to the Synoptics have done so even less. Those that have discussed the topic have often focused almost solely on Mark 7:1–23 and the controversy over ritual handwashing that leads to Jesus seemingly declaring all foods clean. A closer look sees that the Synoptics treat Jesus coming into contact with people with all the other major forms of ritual impurity that can afflict human beings: leprous skin, genital discharge, and physical death. By extension to the unseen realm, Jesus exorcises impure spirits and raises people from the dead. Throughout most of the quests (or the various phases of the ongoing quest), the main conclusion has been that Jesus simply anticipated the imminent supersession of the laws of ritual purity as part of the end of the ritual or ceremonial law more generally. A more careful look at the Synoptic tradition suggests that he fulfills these laws instead, but the upshot remains that one need not literally follow them.

By allowing the Gospel of John to be mined for historical nuggets, one can learn that Jesus developed this position gradually throughout his ministry, not all at once on the day of his baptism by John. There is no progression or development in the Synoptics here, only in the Fourth Gospel. In John, we better appreciate how much Jesus was like John before he started to go his separate way. Because we have a more consistently chronological arrangement of material, we can trace the progression of Jesus's enactment of his views on the relationship between ritual and moral purity, between ceremonial and spiritual cleansing. Because we have a largely different collection of events to illustrate these points, we realize that purity and purification were bigger concerns for Jesus during his lifetime than we would probably guess if we had only the Synoptics. We have not discovered some contradictory or revolutionary insights that might call into question the whole enterprise of questing for Jesus, but we have identified a topic to which we probably should have been devoting much more attention for some time. We also gain insights into Jesus's nuancing of that topic that we wouldn't have noticed otherwise. Perhaps most importantly, the principle of "contagious holiness" may be extended from Jesus's table fellowship with sinners to every other area of interpersonal purity.

## Contemporary Implications

### For Research

There are doubtless additional, recurring motifs that a careful analysis of the core material in John's Gospel—what is left after one brackets the sections that unpack his favorite theological emphases—will disclose. As we noted above (see 281, 281n70), Darrell Bock has suggested the šalîaḥ motif as one such example: Jesus as the "Sent One." Other christological titles or categories may lend themselves to this approach as well. I suspect that Paul Anderson's interest in a strong affirmation of women surrounding Jesus and a nonsacramental, noninstitutional ecclesiology would do so too. On a larger scale, scholars should test Anderson's distinctive criteria of authenticity and/or use their own to see if other small or large parts of the Fourth Gospel could be authenticated. Those with considerable years of expertise in the Johannine literature should consider producing their own syntheses of historical Jesus material, giving John and the Synoptics parity in their undertaking, and see what their findings yield.

The elephant in the room remains John's high Christology. It is time to recall what existing research has already accomplished: showing bits of equally high Christology in the Synoptics and reminding us of how much in John still was cryptic to his followers, not least because it was couched in metaphor. Research into the flexibility of Jewish monotheism allows for considerably higher Christology than is still widely recognized. Did the Jewish Jesus of history take another step beyond that, if the Johannine portrait is to be believed? There is no denying that this would be the case. But was it really a step that would have put him outside the pale of the Judaism of his day? That has not actually been demonstrated.

There still remains John's distinctive style and vocabulary. Here I repeat what I have said before. These literary features, no doubt, *are* due largely to the author of the Fourth Gospel, but the style and vocabulary do not determine the accuracy of the contents. Anyone familiar with translating one language into another knows the variety of ways one can faithfully render someone else's words. Anyone familiar with the metrical (and rhyming) psalms in the history of English hymnody knows that their style and vocabulary are dramatically different from other more formally equivalent *English* translations. But few would deny that the contents represent the gist and sometimes much more than the gist of each psalm. Did Jesus ever speak the words "I am the good shepherd" (John 10:11)? He might have. The Lukan parable of the lost sheep likens God to a shepherd (Luke 15:3–7), and Luke summarizes Jesus's message as "the Son of man came to seek and to save the lost" (Luke 19:10). Both passages are frequently accepted as authentic, at which point the historical Jesus is implicitly claiming to be God's agent as shepherd to recover the lost. Even if Jesus never spoke the closest Aramaic equivalent to "I am the good shepherd," John would not have been out of line in attributing that claim to him.

This book, however, is making a much more modest claim with respect to the Fourth Gospel. It is focusing primarily on the issue of purity. Had John wanted to sum it up with an "I am" saying, he could have attributed to Jesus the words "I am the purifier of the impure" or "I am the cleanser of the unclean." Throughout his ministry, he made the impure pure, the unclean clean—first ritually, then morally as well. As time went by, his focus became more and more on the spiritual or ethical dimension of purity as he came to fulfill all forms of purity laws. When he touched those who were ritually unclean (or when they touched him), he did not become defiled; they, rather, were made whole. When he mingled with those who were morally unclean, in many instances his interaction led to their becoming his followers. When he raised people from the dead, and when God raised *him* from the dead, he overcame the ultimate impurity and made it possible for his followers to do so as well. All of these themes merit more extensive study.

### *For Christian Living*

What would happen if Jesus's followers today took seriously on a widespread scale their abilities and responsibilities to be conduits for purifying the impure? What if Christians became known not for being the most tolerant of all people, for that would mean tolerating even egregious sin—child abuse, rape, human trafficking, gang killings and other forms of mass slaughter, and so on—but rather for being the most loving of all people, especially for the victims of those horrible sins. What if on an interpersonal level, even as they sought to bring perpetrators to justice, they did so without any hint of vindictiveness, because they knew that they were the recipients of a loving God's forgiveness of all their own injustices? What if the thoughtfulness and kindness of everyone who bore Jesus's name became legendary on social media, in political campaigns, in every sector of the public arena? What if the Christian response to the so-called aggressive atheists of our world was to present more persuasive and better-thought-out arguments given calmly and even happily in reply? What if God's people thought about what kinds of words and actions were most likely to bring others to human flourishing? What if they cared at least as much about the physical wherewithal of those already born as many do about the unborn? What if Christians were known for having the most fulfilling sexual lives, either by being monogamously, heterosexually married or happily celibate? What if Christians committed themselves to draw on the power of the Spirit in order to live such congenial and appealing lives that it was more likely that their attractive character would rub off on others around them than that they would be corrupted by the evil in the world? What if they commended every good thing that remains in a fallen world, thanks to general revelation or natural theology, more than denouncing every evil?

Similar examples could be multiplied. The good news is that significant numbers of Christians in various times and places around the world throughout church history have done precisely these things, even if not necessarily all at the same time. It is possible for it to happen again. It also takes encouragement, accountability, and unity—within and among churches, parachurch ministries, and smaller, more informal networks of Christians. Of course, Christians are all still deeply fallen and flawed human beings, dependent solely on God's grace for every good thing in life. But enough sanctification is possible for there to be substantial healing in many of these areas. Plus, modeling genuine repentance and forgiveness can be as powerful a model as never needing to repent or to forgive. More goes on every day in countless groups of Christians around the world that never makes any news and certainly not secular news. Traveling widely around the world and getting to know believers in many diverse locations from many different walks of life is one of the best ways of getting a glimpse of just how much redemptive purification is already taking place. And much like the famous half-empty, half-full cup, what one looks for and concentrates on can make a huge difference.

In short, then, Jesus is a purifier. He calls his followers to transmit purity—wholeness and human flourishing—to others. Genuine transformation cannot come through coercion but can come only through a magnetic winsomeness of life and a consistency of character, even when it leads to various forms of suffering. If we have to choose, holiness must always trump happiness, but holiness can also produce great happiness. If we trace the trajectory of the texts we have studied in John, we see that contagious holiness is symbolized in baptism, is joyfully celebrated at weddings, banishes religious and institutional corruption, produces and stems from new birth, prioritizes the outcast, heals the sick, substitutes for superstitious and counterfeit imitations, satisfies and nourishes, refreshes like water for thirst, provides guidance like light in the darkness, shepherds those needing good leaders, brings life out of death, prepares and honors those about to die, displays love in menial service to others, stays connected to the Vine but allows hardship to prune it to bear even more fruit, sets people apart by God's word, fulfills all demands for ritual equivalents, is perfected in live-giving death, receives the Spirit, and prepares for coming resurrection life with the risen Jesus.

With results like these, it is difficult to agree with those who say that the quest for the historical Jesus has played itself out. With results like these, it is misguided at best and dangerous at worst to argue against all questing. The quest for the historical Jesus should continue unabated, and it is the fourth quest or phase that currently holds out the most hope of substantial progress.

# Index of Authors

Aarde, Andries van. *See* van Aarde, Andries
Adinolfi, Federico, 203n84, 255
Ådna, Jostein, 150n64
Alexander, Loveday, 139n14
Allen, David M., 20n71
Allison, Dale C., Jr., 19, 83n52, 84–89, 95n95, 102, 150–52, 159, 161, 208, 274
Althaus, Paul, 35n5, 48n49
Amit, David, 336
Amos, Roger, 261
An, Hannah S., 252n105
Anderson, Paul, 200–203, 204n87, 208, 212n134, 220, 226–27, 242n67, 269n32, 269n36, 291n1, 376, 379
Appold, Mark, 203
Arterbury, Andrew, 2n5
Askwith, E. H., 63n105, 187
Aslan, Reza, 141
Atkins, J. D., 267n26
Attridge, Harold W., 213n138, 274n47
Aulén, Gustav, 60, 61n93
Avemarie, Friedrich, 343n31

Baasland, Ernst, 48nn50–51
Bailey, Kenneth E., 51n62, 146, 168, 173
Baird, J. Arthur, 167n118
Baird, William, 4n11, 4n13, 30
Bammel, Ernst, 286n85
Barbour, R. S., 38n18, 58n83
Barclay, William, 166n115
Barnett, Paul, 259n1, 269n35
Barrett, C. K., 280n66, 286n86, 318n98, 324
Bartholomä, Philipp, 209–10, 211n131
Barton, Stephen, 188n30
Bauckham, Richard, 26n88, 167n117, 170n128, 172, 188–90, 191n38, 192–93, 194n51, 200, 204n95, 215n144, 218, 237n46, 244n74, 247n86, 269n31, 346n41
Baur, Ferdinand Christian, 4–5, 29
Bayer, Hans F., 175n145
Beasley-Murray, George, 194n51, 243n68, 250n96, 251n101, 271n41, 273nn45–46, 277n56, 296n18, 301nn32–33, 309n61, 312n73, 313n78, 322n112, 324, 327n131
Beck, James R., 137n8
Beck, Richard, 371
Becker, Eve-Marie, 180n2, 305
Bell, Donald L., 40n24
Belle, Gilbert van. *See* van Belle, Gilbert
Belleville, Linda L., 246n80
Benedict XVI (pope). *See* Ratzinger, Joseph
Bennema, Cornelis, 235n39, 236n45, 299n25, 326n129
Bernier, Jonathan, 158n94, 185n17, 203n80, 279n61
Beutler, Johannes, 205n108, 282n71, 312n74
Bienaimé, Germain, 272n43
Bilde, Per, 2n3, 20n70
Billerbeck, Paul, 316n93
Birch, Jonathan C. P., 2n4
Bird, Michael F., 94n93, 168n121, 170n128
Blanton, Ward, 13, 14n48
Blass, F., 105n2
Blomberg, Craig L., 37n16, 48n48, 49n54, 50n58, 58n82, 71n6, 93n86, 100n114, 106n3, 123n67, 124n74, 124n77, 125n78, 129n93, 136n1, 165n113, 166n114, 188n30, 189n34, 192n43, 193–200, 202n73, 211n133, 213n139, 223n1, 224n2, 225n8, 228nn16–17, 229n18, 229n20, 239n51, 252n103, 260n3, 267n27, 269n35, 281n69, 292n2, 294n9,

299n26, 307n54, 338n16, 349, 350nn56–57, 361n93, 365n110
Bock, Darrell L., 120n57, 125n80, 153–54, 155nn82–83, 157, 176n147, 196n59, 281n70, 352n63, 367n115, 369n123, 379
Bockmuehl, Markus, 96
Boer, Martinus C. de. *See* de Boer, Martinus C.
Bolyki, János, 346n42
Bond, Helen K., 180n2, 194n52
Booth, Roger P., 363
Borchert, Gerald L., 175n144, 197, 250n97, 262n9, 282n75, 320n106, 322n113
Borg, Marcus, 75, 107–8, 111–13, 121, 132–33, 138, 144, 226, 334n2, 375
Borgen, Peder, 204n88, 204n92, 215n145, 281n68
Boring, M. Eugene, 63n103
Bornkamm, Günther, 38–39, 41n27, 42n31, 55
Bourgel, Jonathan, 253n107
Bousset, Wilhelm, 12n41, 34n2, 44, 61
Boxall, Ian, 318n99
Boyarin, Daniel, 76, 102, 231n24
Boyd, Gregory A., 111n21
Brandon, S. G. F., 59, 141
Brant, Jo-Ann A., 204n94, 213n138, 254, 287n87, 309n62, 316n92
Braun, Herbert, 62
Breech, James, 107n9
Brewer, Todd, 54n67
Bridges, Linda McKinnish, 203n85
Broadhead, Edwin, 344
Brodie, Thomas, 139, 140n17
Bromiley, Geoffrey, 3n7
Brouwer, Wayne, 215n146, 306, 307n53
Brown, Dan, 128
Brown, Raymond E., 183–84, 262n7, 279n64, 318n98, 323n116, 328n133
Brown, Tricia Gates, 324

Bruce, F. F., 217, 272n42, 288n90, 315n86, 322n112, 326n129
Bruce, Patricia, 265n20
Brustein, William I., 53n65
Bryan, Steven M., 267n25
Buchanan, George, 59
Bühner, Ruben A., 218–19
Bultmann, Rudolf, 34–35, 37–38, 40, 43, 46–48, 50, 52–53, 62, 65–67, 108, 246n84, 268n28, 285n83, 310n70, 311n73, 323n117, 374–75
Burge, Gary, 205n100, 282n75, 298n22
Burke, Alexander J., Jr., 285n84
Burns, David, 13
Byrskog, Samuel, 166, 167n116, 171n131

Caba, José, 59
Calvert, D. G. A., 56n76
Camarero, Lorenzo, 273n45
Campbell, Constantine R., 322n115
Caneday, A. B., 341n24
Capps, Donald, 137n7
Caragounis, Chrys C., 307n56
Carrier, Richard, 139, 141
Carson, D. A., 182, 183nn10–12, 185n19, 189, 214n142, 245n76, 256n117, 262n8, 266n22, 279n62, 285n82, 294n11, 302n36, 308n57, 314n81, 316n90, 317n97
Carter, Warren, 90, 92, 194n51, 204n98
Case, Shirley Jackson, 43, 44n35, 62n98
Casey, Maurice, 22n75, 188–89, 195n53, 195n55, 318n98, 364, 365nn105–6
Chapple, Allan, 197n63
Charlesworth, James H., 11, 130n97, 137n3, 175n142, 175n144, 206–8, 291n1, 315n88

Childs, Hal, 140
Chilton, Bruce, 75, 83n53, 121, 128n90, 137n6, 341, 348n50, 363
Choi, P. R., 205n109, 310n68
Chubb, Thomas, 11
Clark-Soles, Jaime, 204n97, 304n42
Claussen, Carsten, 207n117, 240n56
Coakley, J. F., 186, 294
Collins, Adela Yarbro, 343n32
Coloe, Mary, 204n93, 254, 304n44
Conzelmann, Hans, 39, 41n27, 55
Cooper, Karl T., 240n58
Corley, Kathleen E., 347n47, 349n53
Cotterell, F. Peter, 245n77
Craffert, Pieter, 140
Crossan, John Dominic, 36n11, 84, 107–8, 113–19, 121, 129, 132, 134, 138, 141, 144, 147, 375
Crossley, James, 153n79, 176n151, 349–50
Culpepper, R. Alan, 194n51, 203, 205n104, 231n25, 244n75, 267n24
Cunningham, Geikie, 18

Daly-Denton, Margaret, 283, 284n79
Daniélou, Jean, 232n28
Davey, J. Ernest, 244n75
Dawes, Gregory W., 10n33
Day, Janeth Norfleete, 252n104
de Boer, Martinus C., 185n17, 188n30
Debrunner, A., 105n2
Decker, Rodney J., 353n69, 364n104
DeConick, April D., 129n95, 167n119
Deines, Roland, 336n8
de la Fuente, Alfonso, 188n30
Denaux, Adelbert, 180n2

# Index of Authors

Dennert, Brian C., 283n77
Denton, Donald L., Jr., 115n40
Derico, T. M., 146n44
Derrett, J. Duncan M., 253n106
deSilva, David A., 365, 366n112
Dibelius, Martin, 47, 50, 52
Diehl, Judith A., 90n70
Dietzfelbinger, Christian, 306n48
Dockery, David S., 252n104
Dodd, C. H., 36, 180–83, 195n55, 204n85, 220, 251n100, 269n36, 324
Donahue, John R., 347n46
Donne, Anthony Le. *See* Le Donne, Anthony
Downing, Gerald, 107n9, 109n16, 157n90
Duling, Dennis C., 41n26
Dundes, Alan, 139n15
Dungan, David L., 14n49
Dunn, James D. G., 63n102, 79n39, 145–47, 168n121, 171n131, 304n42, 335, 340n23

Easton, Burton Scott, 64
Ebeling, Gerhard, 35n4, 39
Eddy, Paul R., 169n123
Edersheim, Alfred, 18
Edwards, David L., 186n21
Edwards, James R., 345n40, 352n62
Edwards, Sarah A., 56n78
Egelkraut, Helmuth L., 259n1
Ehorn, Seth, 361
Ehrman, Bart D., 22n75, 86–87, 89, 130, 173
Elledge, Roderick, 97n105
Ellis, E. Earle, 188n30
Ellis, Peter F., 252n102
Ensor, Peter W., 205n103, 210
Eppstein, Victor, 241n60
Ern Loke, Andrew Ter. *See* Loke, Andrew Ter Ern
Eskola, Timo, 78, 79n37

Evans, Craig A., 70n4, 120n57, 128n90, 130n97, 131n102, 164n112, 241n63, 356, 362n98
Eve, Eric, 172n134
Everton, Sean F., 123n66

Fantin, Joseph D., 313n80
Farnell, F. David, 20n69
Farrar, Frederic, 18
Ferda, Tucker S., 11, 43n32
Fiorenza, Elisabeth Schüssler. *See* Schüssler Fiorenza, Elisabeth
Fischer, John, 364
Flusser, David, 76, 102
Förster, Hans, 282n73
Förster, Niclas, 249n92
Fortna, Robert T., 176n151
Foster, Paul, 172
Foster, Timothy D., 245n79
France, R. T., 344n34, 354n70, 366n114, 369n121
Frayer-Griggs, Daniel, 278n59
Fredriksen, Paula, 87–89, 243n67, 336–37
Freud, Sigmund, 136
Frey, Jörg, 188n28, 192–93, 195nn54–55, 227n14, 228n16, 236n41, 249n91, 251n101
Freyne, Sean, 92, 162n106, 228n16
Fuchs, Ernst, 39, 55
Fuente, Alfonso de la. *See* de la Fuente, Alfonso
Fuller, Reginald H., 45n38, 56n78
Funk, Robert W., 105, 107–8, 114n38, 117, 120n59, 121, 122n64, 122n66, 124–28, 129n94, 132–34, 138, 147, 375
Furstenberg, Yair, 363n100

Gadamer, Hans-Georg, 39
Garber, Zev, 75n27
Gardner-Smith, Percival, 61, 64
Garland, David E., 90n72, 344n36, 360n90, 369n120

Gathercole, Simon J., 9n30
Gee, D. H., 329
George, Larry Darnell, 328
Gerhardsson, Birger, 50–51, 166, 167n116
Gnilka, Joachim, 96, 175n144
Godzieba, A. J., 179n1
Goetz, Stewart C., 58n82
Goguel, Maurice, 62
Goodacre, Mark, 42n29
Gosbell, Louise, 358
Goulet-Cazé, Marie-Odile, 107n5
Graham, Steven A., 204n91
Grappe, Christian, 370, 371n125
Greene, Joseph, 274
Grigsby, Bruce, 278n58
Grindheim, Sigurd, 97
Grossouw, William K., 297n19
Grundmann, Walter, 54
Gullatta, Richard, 139n16
Gundry, Stanley N., 224n4

Haacker, Klaus, 52
Haber, Susan, 337n13, 358–59
Habermas, Gary R., 147n48
Hägerland, Tobias, 144n35, 162n108, 185n17, 279n61, 343n30, 367
Hagner, Donald A., 75n26, 362n98
Hahn, Ferdinand, 59
Hakola, Raimo, 185n18
Harnack, Adolf Karl Gustav von, 6, 13, 28, 43
Harrington, Hannah K., 340n22
Harris, Horton, 29
Harris, Murray J., 264n14, 312n76, 341n24
Harrisville, Roy A., 11n39, 16n58
Harvey, Anthony E., 60, 281n68
Harvey, Van A., 21n72
Hatina, Thomas R., 326n129, 362n97

# Index of Authors

Hays, Richard, 108n12, 126
Head, Peter M., 17n59, 36n8
Headlam, Arthur Cayley, 64, 187
Hearon, Holly E., 293n6
Hegel, G. W. F., 4
Heil, John Paul, 324
Heilmann, Jan, 205n102, 269n33
Hengel, Martin, 45, 110n19, 128, 149–50, 155, 157
Hengstenberg, E. W., 18n66, 249n94, 316n93
Herzog, William R., II, 92
Herrenbrück, Fritz, 347n46
Heschel, Susannah, 36n8, 54nn68–69
Higgins, Angus John Brockhurst, 65, 187
Hill, David, 63n102
Hodge, Charles, 12
Hodgson, Peter C., 5n16
Holladay, Carl R., 13n47
Holland, Henry Scott, 64, 187
Holmberg, Bengt, 162n106
Holmén, Tom, 158–60, 338n15
Holtzmann, Heinrich Julius, 8n29
Hooker, Morna D., 55n76, 58n83, 156
Hoover, Roy W., 114n38, 121n60, 121nn62–63, 122n64, 122n66, 129n94
Hopkins, Jamal-Dominique, 338–39
Horsley, Richard, 90, 92, 141, 143n29
Huebenthal, Sandra, 170n128
Hull, William E., 46n46
Hultgren, Arland J., 304n42
Hume, David, 15
Humphreys, Colin, 198n63
Hunn, Debbie, 276nn52–53
Hurtado, Larry W., 74n17, 217–18
Hylen, Susan E., 253n108

Ingolfsland, Dennis, 109n14, 115n42

Jacobs, Maretha, 69n2
Jacobson, Arland, 137n8
Jenkins, Philip, 125n80
Jensen, Morton H., 337
Jeremias, Joachim, 36, 54, 55n72, 55nn74–75, 130n96, 146, 320n105, 348n48
Jipp, Joshua W., 184n15
Jobes, Karen, 239, 245n79
Johnson, Brian D., 194n52, 205n99, 263n10, 272, 273n44
Johnson, Luke T., 20n69
Jojko, Bernadeta, 251n98
Jones, Larry Paul, 230n21
Joseph, Simon J., 143–44

Kähler, Martin, 19, 35, 46, 61, 66, 89, 127
Kanagaraj, Jey J., 249n93, 300n29, 313n79, 322n114
Käsemann, Ernst, 37, 40n23, 53, 55, 97, 334
Kasser, Rodolphe, 130n98
Kazen, Thomas, 228n16, 320n106, 335, 338–39, 351n60, 354, 362n95
Kazmierski, Carl, 234, 340n21
Keck, Leander, 96
Keener, Craig S., 15n53, 16n57, 110, 152–53, 157, 167, 168n121, 170n127, 175n143, 176n147, 204n98, 232n30, 235, 236n41, 237n47, 245n78, 272n42, 293n5, 300n30, 308n60, 312n77, 331, 342, 360, 365
Keith, Chris, 156–57, 162, 172n136
Kelber, Werner H., 167n116
Kelhoffer, James A., 360n89
Kellum, L. Scott, 306n51
Kelly, Stewart E., 15n55
Kertelge, Karl, 59
Keylock, Leslie R., 48n53
Kieffer, René, 302n34
Kierspel, Lars, 53n66
Killie, D. Andrew, 136
Kim, Sehyun, 216n148
Kim, Yung Suk, 216n149
King, J. S., 183n12

Kirk, Alan, 170
Kissinger, Warren S., 4n10, 6n19, 24n79, 28n97, 43n33, 46
Kittel, Gerhard, 54
Klausner, Joseph, 46, 54n70, 61, 62n97
Klawans, Jonathan, 335–36
Klawiter, Frederick C., 325n125
Kleinknecht, Karl T., 298n22
Klink, Edward W., III, 185n17, 234n35, 278n58, 279n61, 294n13, 303n40, 309, 310n66, 311n71, 320n107
Kloppenborg, John S., 109n14
Knight, George W., 224n4
Knight, Jonathan, 175n144
Knust, Jennifer, 275n50
Koch, Dietrich-Alex, 232n28
Koester, Craig R., 182n9, 264n17, 322n114
Kok, Jacobus, 278n58
Konradt, Matthias, 369n121
Kopp, David, 309n65
Köstenberger, Andreas J., 316n93
Krentz, Edgar, 15n54
Kruse, Colin G., 322n115
Kümmel, Werner Georg, 3n8, 29n100, 61n95, 67n114
Kunene, Musa Victor Mdabuleni, 309
Kurek-Chomycz, Dominika A., 295n16

Labahn, Michael, 55n73
LaCocque, André, 75, 365
Lane, William L., 293n4
Laney, J. Carl, 309n65
Lang, Bernhard, 285n83
Lang, Marijke H., 11n38
Lapide, Pinchas, 76, 102
Larsen, Kasper Bro, 213n138
Latourelle, René, 58n81, 59, 328n134
Lea, Thomas D., 188n30
Le Donne, Anthony, 137–38, 145, 156–57, 162, 179n1

# Index of Authors

Lee, Dorothy, 239, 240n55, 270n38
Lee, Sang-Il, 160n103
Lentzen-Deis, Fritzleo, 59
Léon-Dufour, Xavier, 66
Le Peau, Andrew T., 243n72
Lessing, Gotthold Ephraim, 2–3, 20, 25, 61
Levine, Amy-Jill, 75, 120n57, 335, 342, 345, 367
Lewis, C. S., 22n76
Licona, Michael, 157n90, 211n132, 360n91
Lierman, John, 200n67, 269n31
Lightfoot, J. B., 26, 272n42
Lincoln, Andrew T., 195n53, 217n151, 233n31, 245n79, 285n82, 302n36, 316n91
Lindars, Barnabas, 244n75, 326n128, 327n130
Ling, Tim, 204n90
Linnemann, Eta, 22n76
Litwa, M. David, 138–39
Lockshin, Martin, 338
Lohfink, Gerhard, 175n144
Loisy, Alfred, 6, 30, 77
Loke, Andrew Ter Ern, 176n146
Lonergan, Bernard J. F., 78, 120
Lord, A. B., 51, 52n63, 168
Luz, Ulrich, 76n29, 144n33

Mack, Burton L., 107–11, 117, 134, 138
Mackinnon, James, 43n33
Maddox, Randy L., 40n23
Magness, Jodi, 346n42, 354
Manns, Frédéric, 305
Manson, T. W., 49
Marcus, Joel, 236, 272n43, 343n30
Marsh, Clive, 134n108, 179n1
Marshall, I. Howard, 37n16, 38n17, 90n72, 184n16, 225n6, 229nn19–20, 315n89, 351n59, 368n118, 369n120
Martin, Ralph P., 2n2
Martyn, J. Louis, 183–85, 278n60

Marxsen, Willi, 41n27
Mathew, Bincy, 302
Mathews, Alice, 253n108
Matson, David L., 368n119
Matson, Mark A., 195n54
Matthews, Shailer, 43n34
Mburu, Elizabeth W., 205n105
McArthur, Harvey K., 65n112
McDonald, Lee Martin, 162n106, 174–75, 176n149
McDowell, Josh, 22n76
McEleney, Neil J., 59n84
McGaughy, Lane C., 108n13
McGrath, James F., 242n67
McGrew, Lydia, 192, 244n73
McHugh, John F., 232n27, 242n65
McIver, Robert K., 170n128, 172n133, 173n139
McKnight, Edgar V., 34n3
McKnight, Scot, 89, 90n71, 137n6
Meadors, Edward, 96
Mealand, David, 56n78
Medrano, Maria Estela Aldave, 294n10
Meggitt, Justin, 140
Meier, John P., 20, 23, 69n2, 88, 98–101, 103, 108n11, 126, 133–34, 158, 227, 251n99, 254n112, 260n4, 270n37, 279n64
Mendels, Doron, 171n133
Menken, Maarten, 272
Merkley, Paul, 59n85
Merz, Annette, 91, 161, 163n109, 164n110, 164n112, 193
Meyer, Ben F., 76–80, 84, 94, 99, 119, 120n57, 126, 365n111
Meyer, Marvin, 130n98
Michaelis, Johann David, 3, 25n83
Michaels, J. Ramsey, 121, 234n34, 234n38, 239n54, 263n12, 298n23, 300, 302n34, 308n60, 314n85
Millard, Alan, 49n56
Miller, Ed L., 231nn22–23

Miller, John, 137n4
Miller, Robert J., 120n57
Miller, Stuart S., 336n8
Miller, Susan, 254n19
Miquel, Esther, 294, 295n14
Mitchell, A. C., 350n58
Mitton, Leslie, 62
Modica, Joseph B., 90n71
Moessner, David P., 259n1
Moller, Hilde Brekke, 73n11, 74n18
Moloney, Francis J., 188n30, 234n35, 243n71, 249n94, 263n10, 273n45, 287n89, 302n36, 323n117
Moreno, Antonio Garcia, 188n30
Morgan, Robert, 10n34
Morris, Leon, 191–93, 233n32, 249n91, 256n117, 263n11, 296n17, 298n21, 301n31, 317n96, 325n126
Morton, Russell, 4n11
Moss, Candida, 359
Motyer, Stephen, 53n66, 185n18
Moxnes, Halvor, 13n45, 17n62, 206n111
Müller, Karlheinz, 280n65
Murphy, Catherine M., 235n39, 236
Mussner, Franz, 42n30, 59
Myles, Robert J., 127n85

Nash, Ronald H., 139n14
Neely, Brent, 254n19
Neill, Stephen, 69n1
Neufeld, Thomas Yoder, 91, 143
Neusner, Jacob, 337
Newman, Carey C., 95n95
Ng, Esther Yue L., 142n26
Ng, Wai-Yee, 230n21, 331n141
Nodet, Étienne, 176n148, 205, 206n110, 282n72
Nordsieck, Reinhard, 204n85
North, Wendy Sproston. *See* Sproston North, Wendy E.
Numada, Jonathan, 185n18

Oakman, Douglas, 141
O'Day, Gail R., 253n108
Olrik, Axel, 48, 51
O'Neill, J. C., 6n21, 7n26, 9n32, 13, 283n78
Ong, Hughson T., 172n134, 192, 202n73
Orlov, Andrei, 176n146, 218
Os, Bas van, 137n3
Osborne, Grant R., 42n29, 369n124
Osiander, Andreas, 197n61
Oswald, Roy M., 137n8
Ottenheijm, Eric, 363n101
Oudtshoorn, André van. *See* van Oudtshoorn, André
Owen, Paul L., 74n17

Paganini, Simone, 165n113
Pagola, José, 148–49, 157, 177n151
Painter, John, 182n8, 306n48
Pals, Daniel L., 18n63, 24nn81–82
Park, Mi Young Sydney, 358–59
Parsenios, George, 205n107, 210, 213n138, 306
Paschal, R. Wade, 299n24
Patterson, Stephen J., 107n9, 120n57
Paulus, Eberhard Gottlob, 3–4, 11, 24
Pentecost, J. Dwight, 224n5
Perrin, Nicholas, 48n48, 110n18
Perrin, Norman, 40, 41nn26–27
Perrot, Antony, 280n67
Pesch, Rudolf, 59
Peterson, David, 314n84
Phillips, Elaine A., 277n57
Piccirillo, Michele, 233n33
Piovanelli, Pierluigi, 74
Pitre, Brant, 320n104
Poirier, J. C., 122n65, 277n55, 362n96
Pokorny, Petr, 162n106
Poon, Wilson C. K., 268n30, 271n39
Porter, Stanley E., 46, 57n79, 160, 172n134, 176n150, 187n26, 188n29, 200n66, 202n73, 304n41, 314n82, 344n35
Powell, Mark A., 70n4, 83n53
Pressensé, Edmund de, 24
Pryor, John W., 214n141, 248n87, 266n22, 304n45
Puig i Tàrrech, Armand, 147–49, 157, 176n148
Pummer, Reinhard, 254n110

Raglan, Lord, 139n15
Rainbow, Paul A., 194n51
Ramsay, William, 22n76
Rank, Otto, 139n15
Ranke, Leopold von, 37n14
Ratzinger, Joseph, 148–49
Redman, Judith Christine Single, 167n119, 184n16
Reed, Jonathan L., 238n49
Regev, Eyal, 282n72, 337, 341
Reimarus, Hermann Samuel, 2–3, 7, 10–11, 29, 59
Rein, Matthias, 279n63
Reinhartz, Adele, 312n75
Reiser, Marius, 125n79
Renan, Ernest, 5–6, 12–13, 17, 28, 43n32, 259
Repschinski, Boris, 165n113
Reynolds, Benjamin J., 204n89
Reynolds, H. R., 214n140
Richards, E. Randolph, 197n63
Riches, John, 60
Ridderbos, Herman, 234n37, 249n90, 256n117, 271n40, 294n12, 297n19, 298n22, 307n55, 319n100, 319n103
Riesenfeld, Harald, 50, 51n59
Riesner, Rainer, 155n84, 175n145, 216, 217n150, 233n33, 238n48, 241n61, 273n44, 366n113
Rios, Cesar Motta, 253n106
Robeck, Cecil M., 164n111
Robinson, James M., 37, 40n25, 64
Robinson, J. Armitage, 63, 187
Robinson, John A. T., 65, 133, 177–79, 185–88, 195n54, 196n60, 220, 241n62, 242nn65–66, 243n70, 291n1, 315n88
Rodríguez, Rafael, 169, 171n130, 229n20
Rojas-Flores, Gonzalo, 242n65
Ronning, John, 231n24
Rossum, Joost van. *See* van Rossum, Joost
Rucio, Fernando Bernejo, 179n1
Ryan, Jordan, 69n3

Sanday, William, 63
Sanders, E. P., 49n53, 79–84, 86–87, 93, 102, 126, 133, 241n63, 337n11, 348, 350
Sandnes, Karl O., 246n82
Sasse, Markus, 266n21
Scheffler, Eben, 5n17, 12n42
Schlatter, Adolf, 45–46, 64
Schleiermacher, Friedrich, 4, 11–12, 26–28, 111, 374
Schmidt, K. L., 47
Schnabel, Eckhard J., 7n25, 321nn109–10, 340n23, 345n40, 353n67
Schnackenburg, Rudolf, 59, 286n86, 324
Schnelle, Udo, 213n137, 225n8, 306n48
Schottroff, Luise, 60, 142n25
Schröter, Jens, 144–45, 157, 171n132
Schuchard, Bruce G., 312n75
Schüssler Fiorenza, Elisabeth, 141–43
Schwartz, Barry, 171n133
Schweitzer, Albert, 1, 6–10, 13–18, 23–24, 27n94, 28n98, 29–31, 33–37, 42–46, 67, 79, 82, 84, 87–88, 94, 136, 259, 373–74
Schwemer, Anna Maria, 110n19, 128, 149–50, 155
Scott, Bernard B., 7n23, 19n67, 126n82
Scrimgeour, Andrew D., 107n10
Seal, Darlene M., 136n1

Seccombe, David, 96
Segal, Alan F., 218n154
Segovia, Fernando F., 303n38, 306n49, 307n55
Segundo, Juan Luis, 60, 101n117
Selvidge, Marla, 357
Semler, Johann Salomo, 3
Senior, Donald, 291n1
Sharp, Granville, 245, 349
Shinall, Myrick C., Jr., 120n57, 345
Shively, Elizabeth, 346
Siegert, Folker, 221n162
Silva, Moisés, 353n65
Simpson, Benjamin I., 196n59
Simpson, Thomas W., 267n26
Small, Jocelyn P., 167n117
Smith, D. Moody, 188n30, 194n51, 200n66
Snodgrass, Klyne R., 100n114, 144n33
Söding, Thomas, 149
Song, Seung-In, 230n21, 305n46
Sparks, Kenton, 26n87
Sproston North, Wendy E., 192, 212n135
Stagg, Frank, 295n15
Stahl, Neta, 75n26
Staley, Jeffrey, 231n25
Stare, Mira, 330n139
Stassen, Glen, 91
Stauffer, Ethelbert, 44
Stegemann, Wolfgang, 60, 142n25
Stein, Robert, 57–58, 95n95, 197n61, 344n33, 345n40
Stettler, Christian, 367
Stewart, Robert B., 120n57, 147n48
Stibbe, Mark W. G., 284n81
Story, Cullen I. K., 319n102
Stovell, Beth M., 183n12, 216n148
Strack, H. L., 18n64, 316n93
Strauss, David Friedrich, 5, 8, 10, 12, 14, 29, 35, 50, 58, 344n33, 356n76
Strauss, Mark L., 343n32
Strecker, Christian, 140n22

Strobel, Lee, 22n76
Stube, John C., 306n52, 328
Stuhlmacher, Peter, 21n73, 96

Talbert, C. H., 117n50, 248n89, 322n113
Talmage, James E., 18n63
Tàrrech, Armand Puig i. See Puig i Tàrrech, Armand
Tatum, W. Barnes, 33n1
Taussig, Hal, 131n101
Taylor, Joan E., 203n84, 235n39, 255
Taylor, Vincent, 49–50, 64
Thatcher, Tom, 92n81, 159n97, 214, 215n143
Thate, Michael J., 10n35
Theissen, Gerd, 90, 91n75, 145n38, 161, 163n109, 164n110, 164n112, 168n120, 193
Thielman, Frank, 20n69
Thiessen, Matthew, 352n61, 354, 355n74, 357, 359n87, 361, 365
Thiselton, Anthony C., 39n22, 50n57
Thomas, John Christopher, 300, 316n91
Thomas, Robert L., 20n69, 224n4
Thompson, Marianne Meye, 188n30, 232n29, 236, 238n50, 242n64, 243n69, 288n91, 293, 294n8, 310n69, 314n83, 324
Thompson, Robin, 264n15, 265n19
Tillich, Paul, 186
Tolmie, D. F., 315n87
Tomson, Peter J., 334n1, 369n122
Toney, Carl N., 2n2
Tovey, Derek M. H., 204n96, 213n138
Tripolitis, Antonia, 139n14
Tripp, David, 302n37
Trocmé, Etienne, 92, 143
Troeltsch, Ernst, 15, 21, 23, 31
Twelftree, Graham H., 164n112, 203n84, 255n114, 261n5, 328n134, 353n67, 355n75

van Aarde, Andries, 137n5
van Belle, Gilbert, 200n66
VanderKam, James C., 282n72, 284n80
van der Watt, Jan G., 203n79, 305
Vanhoye, Albert, 267n23
van Os, Bas. See Os, Bas van
van Oudtshoorn, André, 213n136
van Rossum, Joost, 326n129
Vansina, Jan, 168, 169n122
van Voorst, Robert E., 22n74
Vatri, Alessandro, 173n138
Vermes, Geza, 71–75, 79, 82, 87, 101–2, 111, 126
Vledder, Evert Jan, 241n63
von Wahlde, Urban C., 203n83, 216n147, 240n59, 243n67, 264n16, 265n18, 277n57, 288n90, 316n92, 325n123
Voorst, Robert E. van. See van Voorst, Robert E.
Voorwinde, Stephen, 231n25

Wahlde, Urban C. von. See von Wahlde, Urban C.
Wallace, Daniel B., 160n100
Wassén, Cecilia, 144n35, 241n63, 336, 343n30, 346, 349, 356–57, 367
Wasserman, Tommy, 275n50
Watson, Francis, 116n43
Watt, Jan G. van der. See van der Watt, Jan G.
Watts, Fraser, 137n8
Weaver, Walter P., 33n1
Webb, Robert, 153–54, 155n83, 157, 159, 160n98, 176n147, 204n93, 232n28, 342n27
Wedderburn, A. J. M., 67
Weeden, Theodore, 168n121
Weiss, Herold, 303n39
Weiss, Johannes, 7–8, 29
Wells, Paul, 16n56

Wenham, David, 56n77, 82–83, 120n57, 146n44, 155, 175n145, 188n30, 204n97, 229n18
Westcott, B. F., 26, 292n3, 308n58
Westerholm, Martin, 27
Westerholm, Stephen, 27
Wheaton, Gerry, 239
Whitacre, Rodney A., 248n88, 256n116, 268n29, 287n88, 325n124
Whittle, Sarah, 363
Wieand, David J., 264n15
Wilckens, Ulrich, 149
Wilkinson, Bruce, 309n65
Wilkinson, John, 322n111
Williams, Catrin H., 180n2, 277n54
Williams, Peter J., 231
Willis, Wendell, 36n11
Wilson, Jeffrey, 250n95
Wink, Walter, 235n39
Winter, Dagmar, 161–62
Witetschek, Stephan, 319n101
Witherington, Ben, III, 70–71, 91, 96–98, 113n34, 143n29, 246n81, 247n85, 277n55, 321n108, 326n127, 327n130, 353n67
Witkamp, L. T., 264n13
Witmer, Amanda, 75
Wojciechowski, Michal, 304n43
Wrede, William, 8–9, 14, 28, 29n99, 94
Wright, Brian J., 160
Wright, N. T., 33n1, 69, 78, 93–95, 96n97, 97–98, 103, 116, 118–19, 126, 161, 193, 360n91
Wurst, Gregor, 130n98

Yancey, Philip, 23n77
Yarbrough, Robert, 45n41
Yoder, John Howard, 91–92
Yoon, David I., 205n106

Zahn, Theodor, 18n66, 25–26, 64
Zahrnt, Heinz, 35n5, 45n39
Zangenberg, Jürgen K., 336n8
Zeitlin, Irving, 74, 75n21
Zimmermann, Ruben, 100n114, 169, 204n86, 205n101, 213n136, 239n52, 240
Zissu, Boaz, 336

# Index of Scripture and Other Ancient Writings

## Old Testament

### Genesis
2:2  206

### Exodus
3:14  276
16:31–35  269
20:8–11  266

### Leviticus
11  316
11:33  238
12–15  334
13–15  316
14:1–32  343, 344n36
15  316
19:1  365

### Numbers
5:11–31  280n67
9:6–14  288n90
11:6–9  269

### Deuteronomy
15:19  313n78
15:21  313n78
18:15–18  269
18:21–22  286
25:5–10  253n108

### 2 Kings
5  280n67

### Job
9:8  270

### Psalms
34:20  324n118
69:9  241
77:16  272
77:19  270
77:20  272
104:15  239
110  219

### Proverbs
8–9  142

### Isaiah
5:1–7  310
12:3  272n43, 273
29:13  362
35:5–6  164, 260, 260n2
40:3  233
41:4  276n54
43:10  276n54

### Ezekiel
15  310
34  282
36:25–27  234, 245

### Daniel
7:13  125
9:24–27  30
12:1–4  95

### Hosea
10:12  252

### Joel
2:23  252
3:18  239

### Amos
9:13–14  239

### Haggai
2:11–13  338

### Zechariah
10:7  239
12:10  324n118
14:8  272
14:21  243

### Malachi
3:1  243
3:1–4  243
3:3–4  243

## New Testament

### Matthew
3:2  247, 260
4:17  81, 247, 260
5:14  275
5:17  365, 370
5:17–20  98
5:21–48  91, 98
5:33–34  98
5:38–39  98
7:13–14  217
7:28–29  98
8:5–13  256, 342
9:27  138
9:35  168
10:8  347
10:23  7, 14, 259
11:5  164, 347
11:11  98
11:16–19  247, 348
11:18–19  377
11:19  348, 351
11:25–27  214
12:8  47
12:28  354–55
15:20  364
15:22  138
15:24  97
16:16–19  14, 77
16:18  159
18:3  244
18:15–20  348
18:17  348
19:1  262
19:16  216
19:23–25  216
20:1–16  92
21:43  55
23  369
23:25–26  369
24  115
27:62  319
28:17  325

### Mark
1:4  340–41
1:6  340
1:8  340
1:9–11  96

1:10 233
1:14–15 163
1:15 151
1:23–28 355
1:40 342
1:40–45 342
1:41 342
1:42 342
1:44 248, 343–44, 354n70
2:1–12 266
2:1–3:6 164
2:10 97
2:15 347
2:22 198, 239
3:6 197
3:13–19 98, 163
3:31–35 165
5:1–20 352
5:2 352
5:3 352
5:3–4 352
5:5 352
5:6 352
5:7 353
5:8–13 353
5:9 353
5:10 353
5:11 353
5:12–13 354
5:14 248
5:14–17 354
5:18–20 354
5:21–24 359
5:24 355
5:24–34 355
5:25–26 355
5:26 358
5:27 355
5:28 355
5:29 355, 358
5:30 355
5:31–33 355
5:34 356, 358
5:35–43 359
5:41 359
6:7–13 98, 168
6:8 110
6:11 343
6:14–29 190, 247
6:50 217
7 367
7:1–5 362
7:1–23 268, 361, 363, 369, 378
7:3 361
7:6–8 361–62
7:7 361

7:8 361
7:9 361
7:9–13 361–62
7:10 165
7:13 361
7:14 362
7:14–15 361, 363–64, 367
7:15 361, 364–65
7:17 364–65
7:18 364
7:18–19 364, 366–67
7:19 342, 361, 364, 366
7:20–23 363, 365, 367
7:24–30 355
7:24–8:30 182
7:33 277, 280
7:36–50 356
8:22–25 277
8:22–26 132
8:23 277, 280
8:27–30 96
8:31 360
8:32–33 301n32
8:38 97
9:17–27 355
9:31 360
9:37 97
10:1 259, 262
10:19 165
10:34 360
10:47–48 138
11:1–11 96
11:12–14 96
11:15–17 96, 241
11:15–18 27
11:18 197
12:1–10 96
12:17 47, 121
12:35–37 96
13 82
13:1–2 159
13:2 191
13:6 217
13:9 343
14:3 293, 345
14:9 191
14:58 191, 242
14:61–65 219
14:62 95
15:33–34 319
15:42 319
16:1–8 360n89
16:7 360
16:9–20 360n89

## Luke

1:26–38 219
2:22 248
3:1–9:50 259
5:1–11 328
5:39 239
7:1–10 256
7:11–17 359
7:14 359
7:15 360
7:18–23 260
7:33–34 260, 377
7:36–50 349
7:37 293
9:51 262
9:51–18:14 229
9:51–18:34 259
10:1–20 98, 168, 368
10:4 110
10:7 368
10:8 368
10:18–19 164
10:38–42 293
11 369
11:20 164, 354–55
11:37–41 368
11:41 368
12:49 97
15:1 348, 351
15:3–7 217, 380
15:3–32 348
17:11–19 344
17:14 344
17:15–19 344
18:1–8 93
18:9–14 348
19:1–10 350
19:7 350
19:8 350
19:9 350
19:10 380
20:27–33 253n108
22:1 317
23:54 319
24:15–16 325
24:31 325
24:50–53 325

## John

1 215, 230, 234, 240
1–4 257, 280, 284, 290, 377

1–6 273
1–10 285
1–11 198
1–19 280
1–20 329n138
1:1 217, 231
1:1–18 27, 219, 231, 285
1:3 231
1:6–8 231
1:14 231, 274
1:15 231, 233
1:17 231, 239, 262
1:19 233
1:19–20 232
1:19–40 232
1:19–4:42 263
1:23 233
1:27 233
1:28 233, 285
1:29 318
1:29–36 234
1:30 233
1:32–34 331
1:33 233, 245–46, 327
1:34 234
1:36 318
1:40 232
1:41 234
1:49 234
1:51 274
2 237, 244
2–4 202, 224
2–11 285
2–12 262
2:1–11 237, 271
2:1–12 237
2:4 296
2:6 237, 248
2:9 237–38
2:10 238–39
2:11 237
2:13–22 27, 240, 243
2:15–16 132
2:18 242
2:19 191, 214, 242
2:20–22 242
2:21 274
2:21–22 191
2:22 273
2:23 197
2:23–25 244
3 244, 248, 250, 250n95

3–12 241
3:1 244
3:1–9 246–47
3:1–21 209
3:3 216, 245
3:3–5 304
3:3–8 244
3:4 245–46
3:5 216, 245–46
3:6 246
3:7 246
3:8 246
3:9 246
3:12 245
3:12–15 245
3:13 214
3:14 207, 209
3:15 214, 246
3:16–21 247, 250
3:21 209, 214, 246
3:22 247, 251
3:22–23 250, 260
3:22–36 247
3:23 232, 247
3:24 190, 247, 260
3:25 247
3:26 248
3:27–30 248, 250
3:31–35 250, 331
4 250, 254–55
4:1 250
4:1–30 209
4:1–44 250
4:2 250n97, 251
4:3 247, 251
4:4–15 252
4:4–44 251
4:7–15 252
4:10–14 274
4:16–18 252
4:19–24 252
4:21 274
4:23 252
4:24 252
4:25–26 252
4:43–54 263
4:45–54 255
4:46–52 132
4:46–54 198, 258
4:53–54 256
5 263, 267, 271, 278

# Index of Scripture and Other Ancient Writings 393

5–10  258, 263, 280
5–11  259, 261, 284, 290, 377
5:1  263
5:1–9  132, 264n13, 278
5:2  264
5:3–4  265
5:6  265n20
5:7  265
5:8  265
5:9  263, 265, 265n20, 266
5:11  265n20
5:14  265n20
5:15  265n20
5:16–18  206
5:17  266
5:18  266
5:19–30  267
5:24–25  267
5:31  271n40
5:31–47  267
5:33  255
5:33–34  267
5:33–35  268n28
5:35  255, 268
5:36  255
5:39  312
5:39–40  267
5:45–46  312
6  268, 274
6:16–21  270
6:22–59  209
6:35  268, 274
6:51–59  299, 323
6:53  299
7  271, 273–74
7–8  276n53
7–9  284
7:2  271
7:14  271, 288
7:15  132
7:30  296
7:35–36  273
7:37  271, 275
7:37–38  271, 273, 324
7:37–39  271, 273–74, 331
7:38  272, 275
7:39  272
7:40  273
7:53–8:11  275
8  275–76
8–9  275

8:12  271n40, 275–76, 276n51, 277n55
8:12–20  276n51
8:12–59  209
8:13–19  276n51
8:14  271n40
8:20  275, 276n51, 296
8:21–30  275
8:25  216
8:30  276
8:31–32  276
8:31–59  276
8:33  276, 276n53
8:58  217, 276n54, 277
9  277, 279, 283
9:1  277
9:1–12  279
9:5  271n40, 277
9:6  280
9:6–7  132
9:7  266, 277–78, 280, 331
9:7–8  277
9:8–9  343
9:8–13  278
9:11  278
9:13  278, 281
9:13–34  279
9:14  263, 278
9:15  278
9:22  183, 278
9:35  281
9:35–41  283
9:41  282
10  262, 318
10:1  282–83
10:1–2  282
10:1–10  283
10:1–39  281, 283
10:11  283, 380
10:20  133
10:21  277
10:22  277, 281–82
10:25  216
10:30  187, 217
10:34–39  283
10:36  283, 284n81, 287
10:39  285
10:40  255
10:40–42  262, 284–85
10:40–11:45  284

10:40–11:54  285n83
10:41  255, 285–86
10:42  286–87
11  191, 261–63, 285n83, 293
11–12  262
11:1  262
11:1–44  285
11:1–45  212
11:2  190
11:4  287
11:6  285
11:17  286
11:18  262
11:25  287
11:27  287
11:39  286
11:45  287
11:46  287
11:47  287
11:48  287
11:50  287
11:54  287
11:54–57  262
11:55  288
11:55–57  261, 263, 288, 295
11:56  288
11:57  288
12  262–63, 285
12–13  292
12–19  291
12–20  263
12–21  199, 291, 377
12:1  262, 292, 296
12:1–3  293
12:1–6  133
12:1–8  191, 321
12:1–11  292, 295, 330
12:3  294, 300
12:7  294
12:8  295
12:9–11  295
12:10  293
12:13  295
12:20–36  296
12:37–43  296
12:44–50  292, 296
13  285, 300–301, 304–5, 308
13–17  299, 305, 316

13–19  297
13–20  262–63
13:1  296–98, 302n36, 305, 319
13:1–2  301, 315
13:1–15  304–5
13:1–17  296, 304, 330
13:2  297–98, 305, 315
13:2–4  297
13:2–17  297
13:3  305
13:4  305
13:5  299–301, 305
13:6  299, 301
13:6–8  305
13:7  301
13:8  299, 301, 302n36, 304–5
13:9  301, 328
13:9–10  305
13:10  299, 302
13:10–11  302
13:11  305
13:12  299, 303, 305
13:12–15  303
13:12–17  303
13:13–14  305
13:13–15  303
13:15  305
13:16  303
13:16–17  303
13:16–20  304n44
13:17  303
13:18–20  303
13:21–30  298, 304n44
13:31–38  301
14  306
14–16  292, 305–6, 310
14–21  292
14:1  307
14:1–31  209
14:2–31  307
14:5  214, 307
14:8  214
14:14  307
14:16–18  307
14:17  255, 311
14:19–20  307

14:22  214
14:31  306
15–16  306
15:1  306
15:1–8  307
15:1–17  307
15:2  305–6, 308, 310, 330
15:4–8  308
15:6  308–9
15:9–17  307
15:16–17  308
15:18–16:4  307
15:20  303
16:5  307
16:5–33  307
16:8–11  307
16:12–15  331
16:16–19  307
16:17–18  214
16:23–24  307
16:29–30  216
16:31–33  216
16:33  307
17  292
17:1–5  311
17:6–19  311
17:8  315n86
17:9  313
17:11  312
17:14  312, 315n86
17:15  311
17:16  311
17:17  314–15, 330
17:17–19  311
17:18  311, 312n77, 313
17:19  314, 330
17:20–25  311
18  328
18–19  297
18–20  133
18:1  306
18:1–5  298
18:13–14  291
18:18  327
18:19–24  291
18:28  315, 319, 321
18:31  291
18:36  216
19  319, 321
19:13  291
19:14  318–19
19:31  319, 321
19:32–33  321

19:34 321–22,
    330–31
19:35 324
19:36 324
19:38–41 321
19:42 319
20 133, 292, 329
20–21 325
20:11–19 210
20:11–29 209
20:15 325
20:16 325
20:17 326
20:19–20 325
20:21 312n77
20:21–22 326
20:22 255
20:26–27 325
20:28 217
21 329, 329n138
21:2 232
21:4–6 325
21:7 325, 327–28, 330
21:9 327
21:12 328
21:14 329n138
21:15–17 329
21:25 20, 212

Acts

1:9–11 325
2 326
2:38 236
3:2 356
5 356
8–9 367
9:25 164
10 367
10:9–16 366
10:19–20 366
10:34–35 366
11:20 367
15:1–29 367
15:28 165
19 340
19:1 164
19:1–7 232, 237, 340
19:3 164
19:30 164
20:25 130
21:17–36 368

Romans

14:20 366

1 Corinthians

1:12–14 250
1:14–17 249n94, 250n97
3:16–17 159
6:19 159
7 165
7:10–12 50
8:8 366

Ephesians

2:20–22 159
5 165

Philippians

2:6–11 219

Hebrews

1:3 248

1 Peter

2:4–8 159

2 Peter

1:9 248

1 John

2:19 308
5:6 322

Revelation

4–5 219
13:11 318
21:3–5 284

Old Testament Apocrypha

2 Maccabees

1:9 277

Dead Sea Scrolls

4Q521 164

Philo

*Against Flaccus*

83 321n110

Josephus

*Jewish Antiquities*

18.5.2 341
12.325 277

*Jewish War*

1.229 288n90
4.317 321n110
6.290 288n90

Rabbinic Literature

Mishnah

*Tractate Nazir*

54a–b 360n88

*Tractate Niddah*

4:1 253

*Tractate Ohalot*

18:7 316n91

*Tractate Yebamot*

16.3 286n87

Apostolic Fathers

Didache

8.1 319

Martyrdom of Polycarp

7.1 319

New Testament Apocrypha and Pseudepigrapha

Gospel of Thomas

20 121n61
65 121n61
97 121n61
98 121n61
114 129

Pseudo-Clement

*Recognitions*

1.54 232
1.60 232

Greco-Roman Literature

Pliny the Elder

*Natural History*

13.3.19 293